Data Pipelines with Apache Airflow

Data Pipelines
with Apache Airflow

BAS HARENSLAK
AND JULIAN DE RUITER

MANNING

SHELTER ISLAND

For online information and ordering of this and other Manning books, please visit
www.manning.com. The publisher offers discounts on this book when ordered in quantity.
For more information, please contact

> Special Sales Department
> Manning Publications Co.
> 20 Baldwin Road
> PO Box 761
> Shelter Island, NY 11964
> Email: orders@manning.com

Manning Publications Co.
20 Baldwin Road
PO Box 761
Shelter Island, NY 11964

Development editor:	Tricia Louvar
Technical development editor:	Arthur Zubarev
Review editor:	Aleks Dragosavljević
Production editor:	Deirdre S. Hiam
Copy editor:	Michele Mitchell
Proofreader:	Keri Hales
Technical proofreader:	Al Krinker
Typesetter:	Dennis Dalinnik
Cover designer:	Marija Tudor

ISBN: 9781617296901
Printed in the United States of America

brief contents

contents

preface

We've both been fortunate to be data engineers in interesting and challenging times. For better or worse, many companies and organizations are realizing that data plays a key role in managing and improving their operations. Recent developments in machine learning and AI have opened a slew of new opportunities to capitalize on. However, adopting data-centric processes is often difficult, as it generally requires coordinating jobs across many different heterogeneous systems and tying everything together in a nice, timely fashion for the next analysis or product deployment.

In 2014, engineers at Airbnb recognized the challenges of managing complex data workflows within the company. To address those challenges, they started developing Airflow: an open source solution that allowed them to write and schedule workflows and monitor workflow runs using the built-in web interface.

The success of the Airflow project quickly led to its adoption under the Apache Software Foundation, first as an incubator project in 2016 and later as a top-level project in 2019. As a result, many large companies now rely on Airflow for orchestrating numerous critical data processes.

Working as consultants at GoDataDriven, we've helped various clients adopt Airflow as a key component in projects involving the building of data lakes/platforms, machine learning models, and so on. In doing so, we realized that handing over these solutions can be challenging, as complex tools like Airflow can be difficult to learn overnight. For this reason, we also developed an Airflow training program at GoData-Driven, and have frequently organized and participated in meetings to share our knowledge, views, and even some open source packages. Combined, these efforts have helped us explore the intricacies of working with Airflow, which were not always easy to understand using the documentation available to us.

In this book, we aim to provide a comprehensive introduction to Airflow that covers everything from building simple workflows to developing custom components and designing/managing Airflow deployments. We intend to complement many of the excellent blogs and other online documentation by bringing several topics together in one place, using a concise and easy-to-follow format. In doing so, we hope to kickstart your adventures with Airflow by building on top of the experience we've gained through diverse challenges over the past years.

acknowledgments

This book would not have been possible without the support of many amazing people. Colleagues from GoDataDriven and personal friends supported us and provided valuable suggestions and critical insights. In addition, Manning Early Access Program (MEAP) readers posted useful comments in the online forum.

Reviewers from the development process also contributed helpful feedback: Al Krinker, Clifford Thurber, Daniel Lamblin, David Krief, Eric Platon, Felipe Ortega, Jason Rendel, Jeremy Chen, Jiri Pik, Jonathan Wood, Karthik Sirasanagandla, Kent R. Spillner, Lin Chen, Philip Best, Philip Patterson, Rambabu Posa, Richard Meinsen, Robert G. Gimbel, Roman Pavlov, Salvatore Campagna, Sebastián Palma Mardones, Thorsten Weber, Ursin Stauss, and Vlad Navitski.

At Manning, we owe special thanks to Brian Sawyer, our acquisitions editor, who helped us shape the initial book proposal and believed in us being able to see it through; Tricia Louvar, our development editor, who was very patient in answering all our questions and concerns, provided critical feedback on each of our draft chapters, and was an essential guide for us throughout this entire journey; and to the rest of the staff as well: Deirdre Hiam, our project editor; Michele Mitchell, our copyeditor; Keri Hales, our proofreader; and Al Krinker, our technical proofreader.

Bas Harenslak

I would like to thank my friends and family for their patience and support during this year-and-a-half adventure that developed from a side project into countless days, nights, and weekends. Stephanie, thank you for always putting up with me working at the computer. Miriam, Gerd, and Lotte, thank you for your patience and belief in me while writing this book. I would also like to thank the team at GoDataDriven for their support and dedication to always learn and improve, I could not have imagined being the author of a book when I started working five years ago.

Julian de Ruiter

First and foremost, I'd like to thank my wife, Anne Paulien, and my son, Dexter, for their endless patience during the many hours that I spent doing "just a little more work" on the book. This book would not have been possible without their unwavering support. In the same vein, I'd also like to thank our family and friends for their support and trust. Finally, I'd like to thank our colleagues at GoDataDriven for their advice and encouragement, from whom I've also learned an incredible amount in the past years.

about this book

Data Pipelines with Apache Airflow was written to help you implement data-oriented work-flows (or pipelines) using Airflow. The book begins with the concepts and mechanics involved in programmatically building workflows for Apache Airflow using the Python programming language. Then the book switches to more in-depth topics such as extending Airflow by building your own custom components and comprehensively testing your workflows. The final part of the book focuses on designing and managing Airflow deployments, touching on topics such as security and designing architectures for several cloud platforms.

Who should read this book

Data Pipelines with Apache Airflow is written both for scientists and engineers who are looking to develop basic workflows in Airflow, as well as engineers interested in more advanced topics such as building custom components for Airflow or managing Air-flow deployments. As Airflow workflows and components are built in Python, we do expect readers to have intermediate experience with programming in Python (i.e., have a good working knowledge of building Python functions and classes, understand-ing concepts such as *args and **kwargs, etc.). Some experience with Docker is also beneficial, as most of our code examples are run using Docker (though they can also be run locally if you wish).

How this book is organized: A road map

The book consists of four sections that cover a total of 18 chapters.

Part 1 focuses on the basics of Airflow, explaining what Airflow is and outlining its basic concepts.

- Chapter 1 discusses the concept of data workflows/pipelines and how these can be built using Apache Airflow. It also discusses the advantages and disadvantages of Airflow compared to other solutions, including in which situations you might not want to use Apache Airflow.

- Chapter 2 goes into the basic structure of pipelines in Apache Airflow (also known as DAGs), explaining the different components involved and how these fit together.

- Chapter 3 shows how you can use Airflow to schedule your pipelines to run at recurring time intervals so that you can (for example) build pipelines that incrementally load new data over time. The chapter also dives into some intricacies in Airflow's scheduling mechanism, which is often a source of confusion.

- Chapter 4 demonstrates how you can use templating mechanisms in Airflow to dynamically include variables in your pipeline definitions. This allows you to reference things such as schedule execution dates within your pipelines.

- Chapter 5 demonstrates different approaches for defining relationships between tasks in your pipelines, allowing you to build more complex pipeline structures with branches, conditional tasks, and shared variables.

Part 2 dives deeper into using more complex Airflow topics, including interfacing with external systems, building your own custom components, and designing tests for your pipelines.

- Chapter 6 shows how you can trigger workflows in other ways that don't involve fixed schedules, such as files being loaded or via an HTTP call.

- Chapter 7 demonstrates workflows using operators that orchestrate various tasks outside Airflow, allowing you to develop a flow of events through systems that are not connected.

- Chapter 8 explains how you can build custom components for Airflow that allow you to reuse functionality across pipelines or integrate with systems that are not supported by Airflow's built-in functionality.

- Chapter 9 discusses various options for testing Airflow workflows, touching on several properties of operators and how to approach these during testing.

- Chapter 10 demonstrates how you can use container-based workflows to run pipeline tasks within Docker or Kubernetes and discusses the advantages and disadvantages of these container-based approaches.

Part 3 focuses on applying Airflow in practice and touches on subjects such as best practices, running/securing Airflow, and a final demonstrative use case.

- Chapter 11 highlights several best practices to use when building pipelines, which will help you to design and implement efficient and maintainable solutions.
- Chapter 12 details several topics to account for when running Airflow in a production setting, such as architectures for scaling out, monitoring, logging, and alerting.
- Chapter 13 discusses how to secure your Airflow installation to avoid unwanted access and to minimize the impact in the case a breach occurs.
- Chapter 14 demonstrates an example Airflow project in which we periodically process rides from New York City's Yellow Cab and Citi Bikes to determine the fastest means of transportation between neighborhoods.

Part 4 explores how to run Airflow in several cloud platforms and includes topics such as designing Airflow deployments for the different clouds and how to use built-in operators to interface with different cloud services.

- Chapter 15 provides a general introduction by outlining which Airflow components are involved in (cloud) deployments, introducing the idea behind cloud-specific components built into Airflow, and weighing the options of rolling out your own cloud deployment versus using a managed solution.
- Chapter 16 focuses on Amazon's AWS cloud platform, expanding on the previous chapter by designing deployment solutions for Airflow on AWS and demonstrating how specific components can be used to leverage AWS services.
- Chapter 17 designs deployments and demonstrates cloud-specific components for Microsoft's Azure platform.
- Chapter 18 addresses deployments and cloud-specific components for Google's GCP platform.

People new to Airflow should read chapters 1 and 2 to get a good idea of what Airflow is and what it can do. Chapters 3–5 provide important information about Airflow's key functionality. The rest of the book discusses topics such as building custom components, testing, best practices, and deployments and can be read out of order, based on the reader's particular needs.

About the code

All source code in listings or text is in a `fixed-width font like this` to separate it from ordinary text. Sometimes code is also **in bold** to highlight code that has changed from previous steps in the chapter, such as when a new feature adds to an existing line of code.

In many cases, the original source code has been reformatted; we've added line breaks and reworked indentation to accommodate the available page space in the book. In rare cases, even this was not enough, and listings include line-continuation markers (➡). Additionally, comments in the source code have often been removed from the listings when the code is described in the text. Code annotations accompany many of the listings, highlighting important concepts.

References to elements in the code, scripts, or specific Airflow classes/variables/values are often in *italics* to help distinguish them from the surrounding text.

Source code for all examples and instructions to run them using Docker and Docker Compose are available in our GitHub repository (https://github.com/BasPH/data-pipelines-with-apache-airflow) and can be downloaded via the book's website (www.manning.com/books/data-pipelines-with-apache-airflow).

> **NOTE** Appendix A provides more detailed instructions on running the code examples.

All code samples have been tested with Airflow 2.0. Most examples should also run on older versions of Airflow (1.10), with small modifications. Where possible, we have included inline pointers on how to do so. To help you account for differences in import paths between Airflow 2.0 and 1.10, appendix B provides an overview of changed import paths between the two versions.

LiveBook discussion forum

Purchase of *Data Pipelines with Apache Airflow* includes free access to a private web forum run by Manning Publications where you can make comments about the book, ask technical questions, and receive help from the author and other users. To access the forum and subscribe to it, go to https://livebook.manning.com/#!/book/data-pipelines-with-apache-airflow/discussion. This page provides information on how to get on the forum once you're registered, what kind of help is available, and its rules of conduct.

Manning's commitment to our readers is to provide a venue where a meaningful dialogue between individual readers and between readers and the authors can take place. It is not a commitment to any specific amount of participation on the part of the authors, whose contribution to the forum remains voluntary (and unpaid). We suggest you try asking the authors some challenging questions lest their interest stray! The forum and the archives of previous discussions will be accessible from the publisher's website as long as the book is in print.

about the authors

BAS HARENSLAK is a data engineer at GoDataDriven, a company developing data-driven solutions located in Amsterdam, Netherlands. With a background in software engineering and computer science, he enjoys working on software and data as if they are challenging puzzles. He favors working on open source software, is a committer on the Apache Airflow project, and is co-organizer of the Amsterdam Airflow meetup.

JULIAN DE RUITER is a machine learning engineer with a background in computer and life sciences and has a PhD in computational cancer biology. As an experienced software developer, he enjoys bridging the worlds of data science and engineering by using cloud and open source software to develop production-ready machine learning solutions. In his spare time, he enjoys developing his own Python packages, contributing to open source projects, and tinkering with electronics.

about the cover illustration

The figure on the cover of *Data Pipelines with Apache Airflow* is captioned "Femme de l'Isle de Siphanto," or Woman from Island Siphanto. The illustration is taken from a collection of dress costumes from various countries by Jacques Grasset de Saint-Sauveur (1757–1810), titled *Costumes de Différents Pays*, published in France in 1797. Each illustration is finely drawn and colored by hand. The rich variety of Grasset de Saint-Sauveur's collection reminds us vividly of how culturally apart the world's towns and regions were just 200 years ago. Isolated from each other, people spoke different dialects and languages. In the streets or in the countryside, it was easy to identify where they lived and what their trade or station in life was just by their dress.

The way we dress has changed since then and the diversity by region, so rich at the time, has faded away. It is now hard to tell apart the inhabitants of different continents, let alone different towns, regions, or countries. Perhaps we have traded cultural diversity for a more varied personal life—certainly for a more varied and fast-paced technological life.

At a time when it is hard to tell one computer book from another, Manning celebrates the inventiveness and initiative of the computer business with book covers based on the rich diversity of regional life of two centuries ago, brought back to life by Grasset de Saint-Sauveur's pictures.

Part 1

Getting started

This part of the book will set the stage for your journey into building pipelines for all kinds of wonderful data processes using Apache Airflow. The first two chapters are aimed at giving you an overview of what Airflow is and what it can do for you.

First, in chapter 1, we'll explore the concepts of data pipelines and sketch the role Apache Airflow plays in helping you implement these pipelines. To set expectations, we'll also compare Airflow to several other technologies, and discuss when it might or might not be a good fit for your specific use case. Next, chapter 2 will teach you how to implement your first pipeline in Airflow. After building the pipeline, we'll also examine how to run this pipeline and monitor its progress using Airflow's web interface.

Chapters 3–5 dive deeper into key concepts of Airflow to give you a solid understanding of Airflow's underpinnings.

Chapter 3 focuses on scheduling semantics, which allow you to configure Airflow to run your pipelines at regular intervals. This lets you (for example) write pipelines that load and process data efficiently on a daily, weekly, or monthly basis. Next, in chapter 4, we'll discuss templating mechanisms in Airflow, which allow you to dynamically reference variables such as execution dates in your pipelines. Finally, in chapter 5, we'll dive into different approaches for defining task dependencies in your pipelines, which allow you to define complex task hierarchies, including conditional tasks, branches, and so on.

If you're new to Airflow, we recommend making sure you understand the main concepts described in chapters 3–5, as these are key to using it effectively.

Airflow's scheduling semantics (described in chapter 3) can be especially confusing for new users, as they can be somewhat counterintuitive when first encountered.

After finishing part 1, you should be well-equipped to write your own basic pipelines in Apache Airflow and be ready to dive into some more advanced topics in parts 2–4.

Meet Apache Airflow

This chapter covers

- Showing how data pipelines can be represented in workflows as graphs of tasks
- Understanding how Airflow fits into the ecosystem of workflow managers
- Determining if Airflow is a good fit for you

People and companies are continuously becoming more data-driven and are developing data pipelines as part of their daily business. Data volumes involved in these business processes have increased substantially over the years, from megabytes per day to gigabytes per minute. Though handling this data deluge may seem like a considerable challenge, these increasing data volumes can be managed with the appropriate tooling.

This book focuses on Apache Airflow, a batch-oriented framework for building data pipelines. Airflow's key feature is that it enables you to easily build scheduled data pipelines using a flexible Python framework, while also providing many building blocks that allow you to stitch together the many different technologies encountered in modern technological landscapes.

Airflow is best thought of as a spider in a web: it sits in the middle of your data processes and coordinates work happening across the different (distributed) systems. As such, Airflow is not a data processing tool in itself but orchestrates the different components responsible for processing your data in data pipelines.

In this chapter, we'll first give you a short introduction to data pipelines in Apache Airflow. Afterward, we'll discuss several considerations to keep in mind when evaluating whether Airflow is right for you and demonstrate how to make your first steps with Airflow.

1.1   Introducing data pipelines

Data pipelines generally consist of several tasks or actions that need to be executed to achieve the desired result. For example, say we want to build a small weather dashboard that tells us what the weather will be like in the coming week (figure 1.1). To implement this live weather dashboard, we need to perform something like the following steps:

1 Fetch weather forecast data from a weather API.
2 Clean or otherwise transform the fetched data (e.g., converting temperatures from Fahrenheit to Celsius or vice versa), so that the data suits our purpose.
3 Push the transformed data to the weather dashboard.

Figure 1.1   Overview of the weather dashboard use case, in which weather data is fetched from an external API and fed into a dynamic dashboard

As you can see, this relatively simple pipeline already consists of three different tasks that each perform part of the work. Moreover, these tasks need to be executed in a specific order, as it (for example) doesn't make sense to try transforming the data before fetching it. Similarly, we can't push any new data to the dashboard until it has undergone the required transformations. As such, we need to make sure that this implicit task order is also enforced when running this data process.

1.1.1   Data pipelines as graphs

One way to make dependencies between tasks more explicit is to draw the data pipeline as a graph. In this graph-based representation, tasks are represented as nodes in the graph, while dependencies between tasks are represented by directed edges between the task nodes. The direction of the edge indicates the direction of the dependency, with an edge pointing from task A to task B, indicating that task A needs to be completed before task B can start. Note that this type of graph is generally called a *directed graph*, due to the directions in the graph edges.

Applying this graph representation to our weather dashboard pipeline, we can see that the graph provides a relatively intuitive representation of the overall pipeline (figure 1.2). By just quickly glancing at the graph, we can see that our pipeline consists of three different tasks, each corresponding to one of the tasks outlined. Other than this, the direction of the edges clearly indicates the order in which the tasks need to be executed: we can simply follow the arrows to trace the execution.

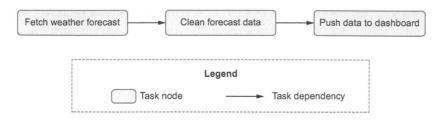

Figure 1.2   Graph representation of the data pipeline for the weather dashboard. Nodes represent tasks and directed edges represent dependencies between tasks (with an edge pointing from task A to task B, indicating that task A needs to be run before task B).

This type of graph is typically called a *directed acyclic graph* (DAG), as the graph contains *directed* edges and does not contain any loops or cycles (*acyclic*). This acyclic property is extremely important, as it prevents us from running into circular dependencies (figure 1.3) between tasks (where task A depends on task B and vice versa). These circular dependencies become problematic when trying to execute the graph, as we run into a situation where task 2 can only execute once task 3 has been completed, while task 3 can only execute once task 2 has been completed. This logical inconsistency leads to a deadlock type of situation, in which neither task 2 nor 3 can run, preventing us from executing the graph.

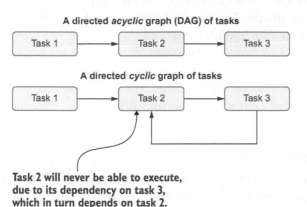

Figure 1.3   Cycles in graphs prevent task execution due to circular dependencies. In acyclic graphs (top), there is a clear path to execute the three different tasks. However, in cyclic graphs (bottom), there is no longer a clear execution path due to the interdependency between tasks 2 and 3.

Note that this representation is different from cyclic graph representations, which can contain cycles to illustrate iterative parts of algorithms (for example), as are common in many machine learning applications. However, the acyclic property of DAGs is used by Airflow (and many other workflow managers) to efficiently resolve and execute these graphs of tasks.

1.1.2   *Executing a pipeline graph*

A nice property of this DAG representation is that it provides a relatively straightforward algorithm that we can use for running the pipeline. Conceptually, this algorithm consists of the following steps:

1   For each open (= uncompleted) task in the graph, do the following:
   – For each edge pointing *toward* the task, check if the "upstream" task on the other end of the edge has been completed.
   – If all upstream tasks have been completed, add the task under consideration to a queue of tasks to be executed.
2   Execute the tasks in the execution queue, marking them completed once they finish performing their work.
3   Jump back to step 1 and repeat until all tasks in the graph have been completed.

To see how this works, let's trace through a small execution of our dashboard pipeline (figure 1.4). On our first loop through the steps of our algorithm, we see that the *clean* and *push* tasks still depend on upstream tasks that have not yet been completed. As such, the *dependencies* of these tasks have not been satisfied, so at this point they can't be added to the execution queue. However, the *fetch* task does not have any incoming edges, meaning that it does not have any unsatisfied upstream dependencies and can therefore be added to the execution queue.

After completing the *fetch* task, we can start the second loop by examining the dependencies of the *clean* and *push* tasks. Now we see that the *clean* task *can* be executed as its upstream dependency (the *fetch* task) has been completed. As such, we can add the task to the execution queue. The *push* task can't be added to the queue, as it depends on the *clean* task, which we haven't run yet.

In the third loop, after completing the *clean* task, the *push* task is finally ready for execution as its upstream dependency on the *clean* task has now been satisfied. As a result, we can add the task to the execution queue. After the *push* task has finished executing, we have no more tasks left to execute, thus finishing the execution of the overall pipeline.

1.1.3   *Pipeline graphs vs. sequential scripts*

Although the graph representation of a pipeline provides an intuitive overview of the tasks in the pipeline and their dependencies, you may find yourself wondering why we wouldn't just use a simple script to run this linear chain of three steps. To illustrate some advantages of the graph-based approach, let's jump to a slightly bigger example. In this new use case, we've been approached by the owner of an umbrella company,

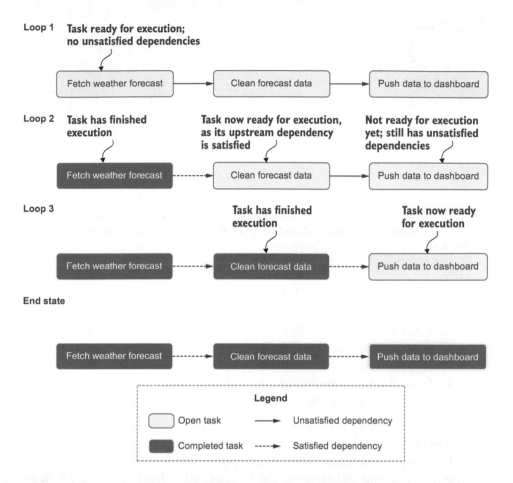

Figure 1.4 Using the DAG structure to execute tasks in the data pipeline in the correct order: depicts each task's state during each of the loops through the algorithm, demonstrating how this leads to the completed execution of the pipeline (end state)

who was inspired by our weather dashboard and would like to try to use machine learning (ML) to increase the efficiency of their operation. To do so, the company owner would like us to implement a data pipeline that creates an ML model correlating umbrella sales with weather patterns. This model can then be used to predict how much demand there will be for the company's umbrellas in the coming weeks, depending on the weather forecasts for those weeks (figure 1.5).

To build a pipeline for training the ML model, we need to implement something like the following steps:

1 Prepare the sales data by doing the following:
   – Fetching the sales data from the source system
   – Cleaning/transforming the sales data to fit requirements

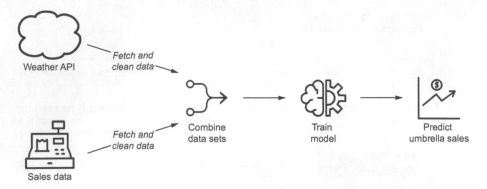

Figure 1.5   Overview of the umbrella demand use case, in which historical weather and sales data are used to train a model that predicts future sales demands depending on weather forecasts

   2 Prepare the weather data by doing the following:
- Fetching the weather forecast data from an API
- Cleaning/transforming the weather data to fit requirements

   3 Combine the sales and weather data sets to create the combined data set that can be used as input for creating a predictive ML model.

   4 Train the ML model using the combined data set.

   5 Deploy the ML model so that it can be used by the business.

This pipeline can be represented using the same graph-based representation that we used before, by drawing tasks as nodes and data dependencies between tasks as edges.

    One important difference from our previous example is that the first steps of this pipeline (fetching and clearing the weather/sales data) are in fact independent of each other, as they involve two separate data sets. This is clearly illustrated by the two separate branches in the graph representation of the pipeline (figure 1.6), which can be executed in parallel if we apply our graph execution algorithm, making better use of available resources and potentially decreasing the running time of a pipeline compared to executing the tasks sequentially.

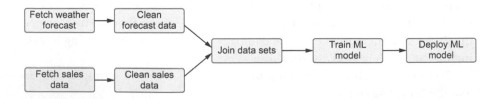

Figure 1.6   Independence between sales and weather tasks in the graph representation of the data pipeline for the umbrella demand forecast model. The two sets of fetch/cleaning tasks are independent as they involve two different data sets (the weather and sales data sets). This independence is indicated by the lack of edges between the two sets of tasks.

Another useful property of the graph-based representation is that it clearly separates pipelines into small incremental tasks rather than having one monolithic script or process that does all the work. Although having a single monolithic script may not initially seem like that much of a problem, it can introduce some inefficiencies when tasks in the pipeline fail, as we would have to rerun the entire script. In contrast, in the graph representation, we need only to rerun any failing tasks (and any downstream dependencies).

1.1.4 Running pipeline using workflow managers

Of course, the challenge of running graphs of dependent tasks is hardly a new problem in computing. Over the years, many so-called "workflow management" solutions have been developed to tackle this problem, which generally allow you to define and execute graphs of tasks as workflows or pipelines.

Some well-known workflow managers you may have heard of include those listed in table 1.1.

Table 1.1   Overview of several well-known workflow managers and their key characteristics.

Name	Originated at[a]	Workflows defined in	Written in	Scheduling	Backfilling	User interface[b]	Installation platform	Horizontally scalable
Airflow	Airbnb	Python	Python	Yes	Yes	Yes	Anywhere	Yes
Argo	Applatix	YAML	Go	Third party[c]		Yes	Kubernetes	Yes
Azkaban	LinkedIn	YAML	Java	Yes	No	Yes	Anywhere	
Conductor	Netflix	JSON	Java	No		Yes	Anywhere	Yes
Luigi	Spotify	Python	Python	No	Yes	Yes	Anywhere	Yes
Make		Custom DSL	C	No	No	No	Anywhere	No
Metaflow	Netflix	Python	Python	No		No	Anywhere	Yes
Nifi	NSA	UI	Java	Yes	No	Yes	Anywhere	Yes
Oozie		XML	Java	Yes	Yes	Yes	Hadoop	Yes

a. Some tools were originally created by (ex-)employees of a company; however, all tools are open sourced and not represented by one single company.
b. The quality and features of user interfaces vary widely.
c. https://github.com/bitphy/argo-cron.

Although each of these workflow managers has its own strengths and weaknesses, they all provide similar core functionality that allows you to define and run pipelines containing multiple tasks with dependencies.

One of the key differences between these tools is how they define their workflows. For example, tools such as Oozie use static (XML) files to define workflows, which provides legible workflows but limited flexibility. Other solutions such as Luigi and

Airflow allow you to define workflows as code, which provides greater flexibility but can be more challenging to read and test (depending on the coding skills of the person implementing the workflow).

Other key differences lie in the extent of features provided by the workflow manager. For example, tools such as Make and Luigi do not provide built-in support for scheduling workflows, meaning that you'll need an extra tool like Cron if you want to run your workflow on a recurring schedule. Other tools may provide extra functionality such as scheduling, monitoring, user-friendly web interfaces, and so on built into the platform, meaning that you don't have to stitch together multiple tools yourself to get these features.

All in all, picking the right workflow management solution for your needs will require some careful consideration of the key features of the different solutions and how they fit your requirements. In the next section, we'll dive into Airflow—the focus of this book—and explore several key features that make it particularly suited for handling data-oriented workflows or pipelines.

1.2   Introducing Airflow

In this book, we focus on Airflow, an open source solution for developing and monitoring workflows. In this section, we'll provide a helicopter view of what Airflow does, after which we'll jump into a more detailed examination of whether it is a good fit for your use case.

1.2.1   Defining pipelines flexibly in (Python) code

Similar to other workflow managers, Airflow allows you to define pipelines or workflows as DAGs of tasks. These graphs are very similar to the examples sketched in the previous section, with tasks being defined as nodes in the graph and dependencies as directed edges between the tasks.

In Airflow, you define your DAGs using Python code in DAG files, which are essentially Python scripts that describe the structure of the corresponding DAG. As such, each DAG file typically describes the set of tasks for a given DAG and the dependencies between the tasks, which are then parsed by Airflow to identify the DAG structure (figure 1.7). Other than this, DAG files typically contain some additional metadata about the DAG telling Airflow how and when it should be executed, and so on. We'll dive into this scheduling more in the next section.

One advantage of defining Airflow DAGs in Python code is that this programmatic approach provides you with a lot of flexibility for building DAGs. For example, as we will see later in this book, you can use Python code to dynamically generate optional tasks depending on certain conditions or even generate entire DAGs based on external metadata or configuration files. This flexibility gives a great deal of customization in how you build your pipelines, allowing you to fit Airflow to your needs for building arbitrarily complex pipelines.

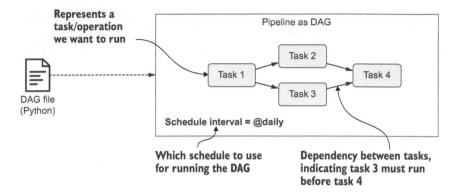

Figure 1.7 Airflow pipelines are defined as DAGs using Python code in DAG files. Each DAG file typically defines one DAG, which describes the different tasks and their dependencies. Besides this, the DAG also defines a schedule interval that determines when the DAG is executed by Airflow.

In addition to this flexibility, another advantage of Airflow's Python foundation is that tasks can execute any operation that you can implement in Python. Over time, this has led to the development of many Airflow extensions that enable you to execute tasks across a wide variety of systems, including external databases, big data technologies, and various cloud services, allowing you to build complex data pipelines bringing together data processes across many different systems.

1.2.2 Scheduling and executing pipelines

Once you've defined the structure of your pipeline(s) as DAG(s), Airflow allows you to define a schedule interval for each DAG, which determines exactly when your pipeline is run by Airflow. This way, you can tell Airflow to execute your DAG every hour, every day, every week, and so on, or even use more complicated schedule intervals based on Cron-like expressions.

To see how Airflow executes your DAGs, let's briefly look at the overall process involved in developing and running Airflow DAGs. At a high level, Airflow is organized into three main components (figure 1.8):

- *The Airflow scheduler*—Parses DAGs, checks their schedule interval, and (if the DAGs' schedule has passed) starts scheduling the DAGs' tasks for execution by passing them to the Airflow workers.
- *The Airflow workers*—Pick up tasks that are scheduled for execution and execute them. As such, the workers are responsible for actually "doing the work."
- *The Airflow webserver*—Visualizes the DAGs parsed by the scheduler and provides the main interface for users to monitor DAG runs and their results.

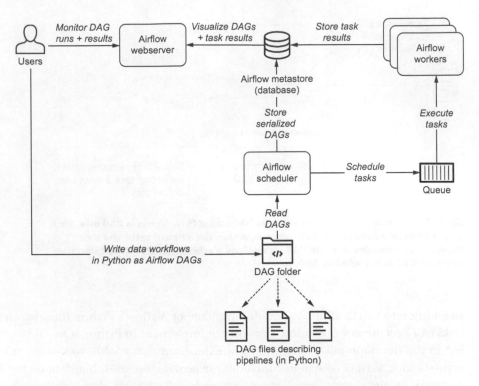

Figure 1.8 Overview of the main components involved in Airflow (e.g., the Airflow webserver, scheduler, and workers)

The heart of Airflow is arguably the scheduler, as this is where most of the magic happens that determines when and how your pipelines are executed. At a high level, the scheduler runs through the following steps (figure 1.9):

1. Once users have written their workflows as DAGs, the files containing these DAGs are read by the scheduler to extract the corresponding tasks, dependencies, and schedule interval of each DAG.

2. For each DAG, the scheduler then checks whether the schedule interval for the DAG has passed since the last time it was read. If so, the tasks in the DAG are scheduled for execution.

3. For each scheduled task, the scheduler then checks whether the dependencies (= upstream tasks) of the task have been completed. If so, the task is added to the execution queue.

4. The scheduler waits for several moments before starting a new loop by jumping back to step 1.

The astute reader might have noticed that the steps followed by the scheduler are, in fact, very similar to the algorithm introduced in section 1.1. This is not by accident, as

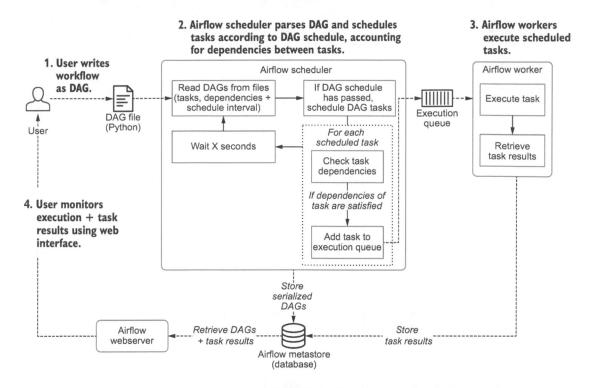

Figure 1.9   Schematic overview of the process involved in developing and executing pipelines as DAGs using Airflow

Airflow is essentially following the same steps, adding some extra logic on top to handle its scheduling logic.

Once tasks have been queued for execution, they are picked up by a pool of Airflow workers that execute tasks in parallel and track their results. These results are communicated to Airflow's metastore so that users can track the progress of tasks and view their logs using the Airflow web interface (provided by the Airflow webserver).

1.2.3   *Monitoring and handling failures*

In addition to scheduling and executing DAGs, Airflow also provides an extensive web interface that can be used for viewing DAGs and monitoring the results of DAG runs. After you log in (figure 1.10), the main page provides an extensive overview of the different DAGs with summary views of their recent results (figure 1.11).

For example, the graph view of an individual DAG provides a clear overview of the DAG's tasks and dependencies (figure 1.12), similar to the schematic overviews we've been drawing in this chapter. This view is particularly useful for viewing the structure of a DAG (providing detailed insight into dependencies between tasks), and for viewing the results of individual DAG runs.

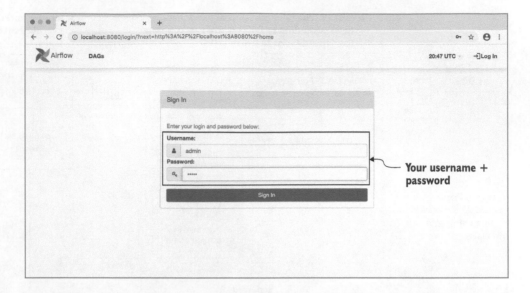

Figure 1.10   The login page for the Airflow web interface. In the code examples accompanying this book, a default user "admin" is provided with the password "admin."

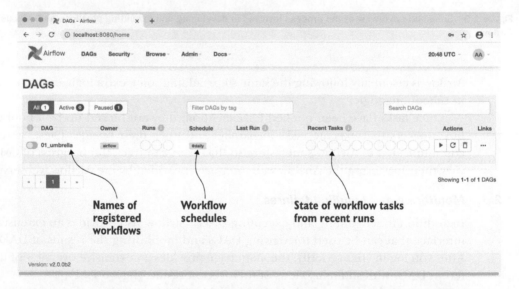

Figure 1.11   The main page of Airflow's web interface, showing an overview of the available DAGs and their recent results

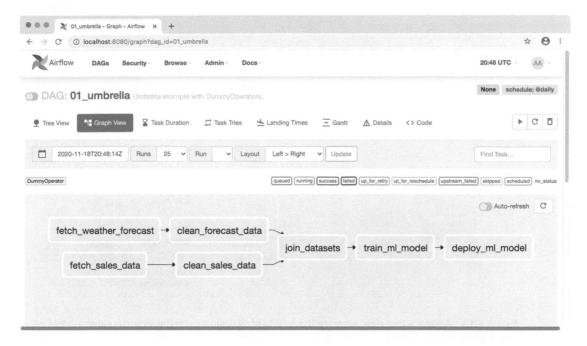

Figure 1.12 The graph view in Airflow's web interface, showing an overview of the tasks in an individual DAG and the dependencies between these tasks

Besides this graph view, Airflow also provides a detailed tree view that shows all running and historical runs for the corresponding DAG (figure 1.13). This is arguably the most powerful view provided by the web interface, as it gives you a quick overview of how a DAG has performed over time and allows you to dig into failing tasks to see what went wrong.

By default, Airflow can handle failures in tasks by retrying them a couple of times (optionally with some wait time in between), which can help tasks recover from any intermittent failures. If retries don't help, Airflow will record the task as being failed, optionally notifying you about the failure if configured to do so. Debugging task failures is pretty straightforward, as the tree view allows you to see which tasks failed and dig into their logs. The same view also enables you to clear the results of individual tasks to rerun them (together with any tasks that depend on that task), allowing you to easily rerun any tasks after you make changes to their code.

1.2.4   *Incremental loading and backfilling*

One powerful feature of Airflow's scheduling semantics is that the schedule intervals not only trigger DAGs at specific time points (similar to, for example, Cron), but also provide details about the last and (expected) next schedule intervals. This essentially

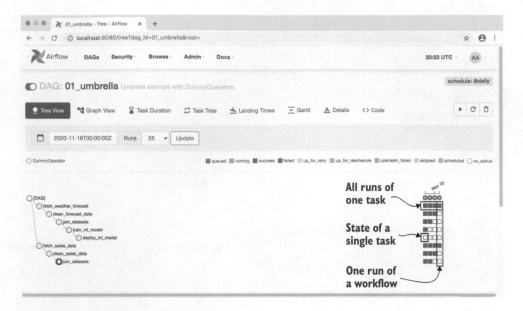

Figure 1.13   Airflow's tree view, showing the results of multiple runs of the umbrella sales model DAG (most recent + historical runs). The columns show the status of one execution of the DAG and the rows show the status of all executions of a single task. Colors (which you can see in the e-book version) indicate the result of the corresponding task. Users can also click on the task "squares" for more details about a given task instance, or to reset the state of a task so that it can be rerun by Airflow, if desired.

allows you to divide time into discrete intervals (e.g., every day, week, etc.), and run your DAG for each of these intervals.[1]

This property of Airflow's schedule intervals is invaluable for implementing efficient data pipelines, as it allows you to build incremental data pipelines. In these incremental pipelines, each DAG run processes only data for the corresponding time slot (the data's *delta*) instead of having to reprocess the entire data set every time. Especially for larger data sets, this can provide significant time and cost benefits by avoiding expensive recomputation of existing results.

Schedule intervals become even more powerful when combined with the concept of *backfilling*, which allows you to execute a new DAG for historical schedule intervals that occurred in the past. This feature allows you to easily create (or *backfill*) new data sets with historical data simply by running your DAG for these past schedule intervals. Moreover, by clearing the results of past runs, you can also use this Airflow feature to easily rerun any historical tasks if you make changes to your task code, allowing you to easily reprocess an entire data set when needed.

---

[1] If this sounds a bit abstract to you now, don't worry, as we provide more detail on these concepts later in the book.

1.3   When to use Airflow

After this brief introduction to Airflow, we hope you're sufficiently enthusiastic about getting to know Airflow and learning more about its key features. However, before going any further, we'll first explore several reasons you might want to choose to work with Airflow (as well as several reasons you might not), to ensure that Airflow is indeed the best fit for you.

1.3.1   Reasons to choose Airflow

In the past sections, we've already described several key features that make Airflow ideal for implementing batch-oriented data pipelines. In summary, these include the following:

- The ability to implement pipelines using Python code allows you to create arbitrarily complex pipelines using anything you can dream up in Python.
- The Python foundation of Airflow makes it easy to extend and add integrations with many different systems. In fact, the Airflow community has already developed a rich collection of extensions that allow Airflow to integrate with many different types of databases, cloud services, and so on.
- Rich scheduling semantics allow you to run your pipelines at regular intervals and build efficient pipelines that use incremental processing to avoid expensive recomputation of existing results.
- Features such as backfilling enable you to easily (re)process historical data, allowing you to recompute any derived data sets after making changes to your code.
- Airflow's rich web interface provides an easy view for monitoring the results of your pipeline runs and debugging any failures that may have occurred.

An additional advantage of Airflow is that it is open source, which guarantees that you can build your work on Airflow without getting stuck with any vendor lock-in. Managed Airflow solutions are also available from several companies (should you desire some technical support), giving you a lot of flexibility in how you run and manage your Airflow installation.

1.3.2   Reasons not to choose Airflow

Although Airflow has many rich features, several of Airflow's design choices may make it less suitable for certain cases. For example, some use cases that are not a good fit for Airflow include the following:

- Handling streaming pipelines, as Airflow is primarily designed to run recurring or batch-oriented tasks, rather than streaming workloads.
- Implementing highly dynamic pipelines, in which tasks are added/removed between every pipeline run. Although Airflow can implement this kind of dynamic behavior, the web interface will only show tasks that are still defined in

the most recent version of the DAG. As such, Airflow favors pipelines that do not change in structure every time they run.

- Teams with little or no (Python) programming experience, as implementing DAGs in Python can be daunting with little Python experience. In such teams, using a workflow manager with a graphical interface (such as Azure Data Factory) or a static workflow definition may make more sense.

- Similarly, Python code in DAGs can quickly become complex for larger use cases. As such, implementing and maintaining Airflow DAGs require proper engineering rigor to keep things maintainable in the long run.

Also, Airflow is primarily a workflow/pipeline management platform and does not (currently) include more extensive features such as maintaining data lineages, data versioning, and so on. Should you require these features, you'll probably need to look at combining Airflow with other specialized tools that provide those capabilities.

1.4   *The rest of this book*

By now you should (hopefully) have a good idea of what Airflow is and how its features can help you implement and run data pipelines. In the remainder of this book, we'll begin by introducing the basic components of Airflow that you need to be familiar with to start building your own data pipelines. These first few chapters should be broadly applicable and appeal to a wide audience. For these chapters, we expect you to have intermediate experience with programming in Python (~one year of experience), meaning that you should be familiar with basic concepts such as string formatting, comprehensions, args/kwargs, and so on. You should also be familiar with the basics of the Linux terminal and have a basic working knowledge of databases (including SQL) and different data formats.

After this introduction, we'll dive deeper into more advanced features of Airflow such as generating dynamic DAGs, implementing your own operators, running containerized tasks, and so on. These chapters will require some more understanding of the involved technologies, including writing your own Python classes, basic Docker concepts, file formats, and data partitioning. We expect this second part to be of special interest to the data engineers in the audience.

Finally, several chapters toward the end of the book focus on topics surrounding the deployment of Airflow, including deployment patterns, monitoring, security, and cloud architectures. We expect these chapters to be of special interest for people interested in rolling out and managing Airflow deployments, such as system administrators and DevOps engineers.

Summary

- Data pipelines can be represented as DAGs, which clearly define tasks and their dependencies. These graphs can be executed efficiently, taking advantage of any parallelism inherent in the dependency structure.

- Although many workflow managers have been developed over the years for executing graphs of tasks, Airflow has several key features that makes it uniquely suited for implementing efficient, batch-oriented data pipelines.
- Airflow consists of three core components: the webserver, the scheduler, and the worker processes, which work together to schedule tasks from your data pipelines and help you monitor their results.

Anatomy of
an Airflow DAG

2

This chapter covers

- Running Airflow on your own machine
- Writing and running your first workflow
- Examining the first view at the Airflow interface
- Handling failed tasks in Airflow

In the previous chapter, we learned why working with data and the many tools in the data landscape is not easy. In this chapter, we get started with Airflow and check out an example workflow that uses basic building blocks found in many workflows.

It helps to have some Python experience when starting with Airflow since workflows are defined in Python code. The gap in learning the basics of Airflow is not that big. Generally, getting the basic structure of an Airflow workflow up and running is easy. Let's dig into a use case of a rocket enthusiast to see how Airflow might help him.

2.1 Collecting data from numerous sources

Rockets are one of humanity's engineering marvels, and every rocket launch attracts attention all around the world. In this chapter, we cover the life of a rocket enthusiast named John who tracks and follows every single rocket launch. The news about rocket launches is found in many news sources that John keeps track of, and, ideally, John would like to have all his rocket news aggregated in a single location. John recently picked up programming and would like to have some sort of automated way to collect information of all rocket launches and eventually some sort of personal insight into the latest rocket news. To start small, John decided to first collect images of rockets.

2.1.1 Exploring the data

For the data, we make use of the Launch Library 2 (https://thespacedevs.com/llapi), an online repository of data about both historical and future rocket launches from various sources. It is a free and open API for anybody on the planet (subject to rate limits).

John is currently only interested in upcoming rocket launches. Luckily, the Launch Library provides exactly the data he is looking for (https://ll.thespacedevs.com/2.0.0/launch/upcoming). It provides data about upcoming rocket launches, together with URLs of where to find images of the respective rockets. Here's a snippet of the data this URL returns.

Listing 2.1 Example curl request and response to the Launch Library API

```
$ curl -L "https://ll.thespacedevs.com/2.0.0/launch/upcoming"
{
  ...
  "results": [
    {
      "id": "528b72ff-e47e-46a3-b7ad-23b2ffcec2f2",
      "url": "https://.../528b72ff-e47e-46a3-b7ad-23b2ffcec2f2/",
      "launch_library_id": 2103,
      "name": "Falcon 9 Block 5 | NROL-108",
      "net": "2020 12-19T14.00:00Z",
      "window_end": "2020-12-19T17:00:00Z",
      "window_start": "2020-12-19T14:00:00Z",
      "image": "https://spacelaunchnow-prod-east.nyc3.digitaloceanspaces.com/media/launch_images/falcon2520925_image_20201217060406.jpeg",
      "infographic": ".../falcon2520925_infographic_20201217162942.png",
      ...
    },
    {
      "id": "57c418cc-97ae-4d8e-b806-bb0e0345217f",
      "url": "https://.../57c418cc-97ae-4d8e-b806-bb0e0345217f/",
      "launch_library_id": null,
      "name": "Long March 8 | XJY-7 & others",
      "net": "2020-12-22T04:29:00Z",
      "window_end": "2020-12-22T05:03:00Z",
```

The response is a JSON document, as you can see by the structure.

Inspect the URL response with curl from the command line.

The square brackets indicate a list.

All values within these curly braces refer to one single rocket launch.

A URL to an image of the launching rocket

Here we see information such as rocket ID and start and end time of the rocket launch window.

```
        "window_start": "2020-12-22T04:29:00Z",
        "image": "https://.../long2520march_image_20201216110501.jpeg",
        "infographic": null,
        ...
    },
    ...
  ]
}
```

As you can see, the data is in JSON format and provides rocket launch information, and for every launch, there's information about the specific rocket, such as ID, name, and the image URL. This is exactly what John needs, and he initially draws the plan in figure 2.1 to collect the images of upcoming rocket launches (e.g., to point his screen-saver to the directory holding these images):

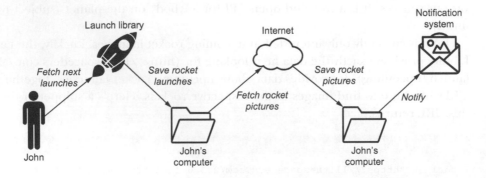

Figure 2.1   John's mental model of downloading rocket pictures

Based on the example in figure 2.1, we can see that, at the end of the day, John's goal is to have a directory filled with rocket images, such as the image in figure 2.2 of the Ariane 5 ECA rocket.

2.2   *Writing your first Airflow DAG*

John's use case is nicely scoped, so let's check out how to program his plan. It's only a few steps and, in theory, with some Bash-fu, you could work it out in a one-liner. So why would we need a system like Airflow for this job?

The nice thing about Airflow is that we can split a large job, which consists of one or more steps, into individual "tasks" that together form a DAG. Multiple tasks can be run in parallel, and tasks can run different technologies. For example, we could first run a Bash script and next run a Python script. We broke down John's mental model of his workflow into three logical tasks in Airflow in figure 2.3.

Why these three tasks, you might ask? Why not download the launches and corre-sponding pictures in one single task? Or why not split them into five tasks? After all,

**Figure 2.2 Example image
of the Ariane 5 ECA rocket**

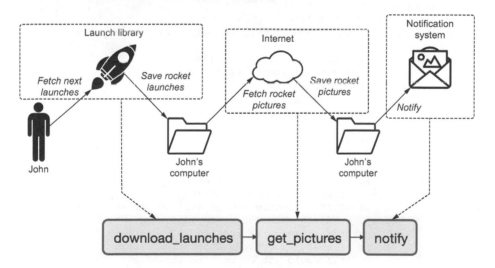

Figure 2.3 John's mental model mapped to tasks in Airflow

we have five arrows in John's plan. These are all valid questions to ask while developing a workflow, but the truth is, there's no right or wrong answer. There are several points to take into consideration, though, and throughout this book we work out many of these use cases to get a feeling for what is right and wrong. The code for this workflow is as follows.

Listing 2.2   DAG for downloading and processing rocket launch data

```python
import json
import pathlib

import airflow
import requests
import requests.exceptions as requests_exceptions
from airflow import DAG
from airflow.operators.bash import BashOperator
from airflow.operators.python import PythonOperator
```

Instantiate a DAG object; this is the starting point of any workflow.

The name of the DAG

```python
dag = DAG(
    dag_id="download_rocket_launches",
    start_date=airflow.utils.dates.days_ago(14),
    schedule_interval=None,
)
```

The date at which the DAG should first start running

At what interval the DAG should run

Apply Bash to download the URL response with curl.

```python
download_launches = BashOperator(
    task_id="download_launches",
    bash_command="curl -o /tmp/launches.json -L
      'https://ll.thespacedevs.com/2.0.0/launch/upcoming'",
    dag=dag,
)
```

The name of the task

A Python function will parse the response and download all rocket pictures.

```python
def _get_pictures():
    # Ensure directory exists
    pathlib.Path("/tmp/images").mkdir(parents=True, exist_ok=True)

    # Download all pictures in launches.json
    with open("/tmp/launches.json") as f:
        launches = json.load(f)
        image_urls = [launch["image"] for launch in launches["results"]]
        for image_url in image_urls:
            try:
                response = requests.get(image_url)
                image_filename = image_url.split("/")[-1]
                target_file = f"/tmp/images/{image_filename}"
                with open(target_file, "wb") as f:
                    f.write(response.content)
                print(f"Downloaded {image_url} to {target_file}")
            except requests_exceptions.MissingSchema:
                print(f"{image_url} appears to be an invalid URL.")
            except requests_exceptions.ConnectionError:
                print(f"Could not connect to {image_url}.")
```

```
get_pictures = PythonOperator(          Call the Python function in the
    task_id="get_pictures",             DAG with a PythonOperator.
    python_callable=_get_pictures,
    dag=dag,
)

notify = BashOperator(
    task_id="notify",
    bash_command='echo "There are now $(ls /tmp/images/ | wc -l) images."',
    dag=dag,
)
                                                Set the order of
download_launches >> get_pictures >> notify     execution of tasks.
```

Let's break down the workflow. The DAG is the starting point of any workflow. All tasks within the workflow reference this DAG object so that Airflow knows which tasks belong to which DAG.

Listing 2.3 Instantiating a DAG object

```
                      The DAG class takes two              The name of the DAG
                      required arguments.                  displayed in the Airflow
dag = DAG(                                                 user interface (UI)
    dag_id="download_rocket_launches",
    start_date=airflow.utils.dates.days_ago(14),          The datetime at which
    schedule_interval=None,                                the workflow should
)                                                          first start running
```

Note the (lowercase) dag is the name assigned to the instance of the (uppercase) DAG class. The instance name could have any name; you can name it rocket_dag or whatever_name_you_like. We will reference the variable (lowercase dag) in all operators, which tells Airflow which DAG the operator belongs to.

Also note we set schedule_interval to None. This means the DAG will not run automatically. For now, you can trigger it manually from the Airflow UI. We will get to scheduling in section 2.4.

Next, an Airflow workflow script consists of one or more operators, which perform the actual work. In listing 2.4, we apply the BashOperator to run a Bash command.

Listing 2.4 Instantiating a BashOperator to run a Bash command

```
download_launches = BashOperator(          The name of
    task_id="download_launches",           the task
    bash_command="curl -o /tmp/launches.json 'https://    The Bash command
        ll.thespacedevs.com/2.0.0/launch/upcoming'",      to execute
    dag=dag,
)          Reference to the
           DAG variable
```

Each operator performs a single unit of work, and multiple operators together form a workflow or DAG in Airflow. Operators run independently of each other, although you can define the order of execution, which we call *dependencies* in Airflow. After all,

John's workflow wouldn't be useful if you first tried downloading pictures while there is no data about the location of the pictures. To make sure the tasks run in the correct order, we can set dependencies between tasks.

Listing 2.5 Defining the order of task execution

```
download_launches >> get_pictures >> notify
```
⊣ **Arrows set the order of execution of tasks.**

In Airflow, we can use the *binary right shift operator* (i.e., *"rshift"* [>>]) to define dependencies between tasks. This ensures the get_pictures task runs only after download _launches has completed successfully, and the notify task runs only after get_pictures has completed successfully.

> **NOTE** In Python, the rshift operator (>>) is used to shift bits, which is a common operation in, for example, cryptography libraries. In Airflow, there is no use case for bit shifting, and the rshift operator was overridden to provide a readable way to define dependencies between tasks.

2.2.1 *Tasks vs. operators*

You might wonder what the difference is between tasks and operators. After all, they both execute a bit of code. In Airflow, *operators* have a single piece of responsibility: they exist to perform one single piece of work. Some operators perform generic work, such as the BashOperator (used to run a Bash script) or the PythonOperator (used to run a Python function); others have more specific use cases, such as the EmailOperator (used to send an email) or the SimpleHTTPOperator (used to call an HTTP endpoint). Either way, they perform a single piece of work.

The role of a DAG is to orchestrate the execution of a collection of operators. That includes the starting and stopping of operators, starting consecutive tasks once an operator is done, ensuring dependencies between operators are met, and so on.

In this context and throughout the Airflow documentation, we see the terms *operator* and *task* used interchangeably. From a user's perspective, they refer to the same thing, and the two often substitute each other in discussions. Operators provide the implementation of a piece of work. Airflow has a class called BaseOperator and many subclasses inheriting from the BaseOperator, such as PythonOperator, EmailOperator, and OracleOperator.

There is a difference, though. Tasks in Airflow manage the execution of an operator; they can be thought of as a small wrapper or manager around an operator that ensures the operator executes correctly. The user can focus on the work to be done by using operators, while Airflow ensures correct execution of the work via tasks (figure 2.4).

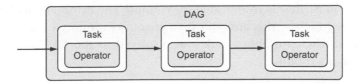

Figure 2.4   DAGs and operators are used by Airflow users. Tasks are internal components to manage operator state and display state changes (e.g., started/finished) to the user.

2.2.2   *Running arbitrary Python code*

Fetching the data for the next rocket launches was a single curl command in Bash, which is easily executed with the BashOperator. However, parsing the JSON result, selecting the image URLs from it, and downloading the respective images require a bit more effort. Although all this is still possible in a Bash one-liner, it's often easier and more readable with a few lines of Python or any other language of your choice. Since Airflow code is defined in Python, it's convenient to keep both the workflow and execution logic in the same script. For downloading the rocket pictures, we implemented listing 2.6.

Listing 2.6   Running a Python function using the `PythonOperator`

```
def _get_pictures():                        ← Python function to call          Create pictures directory
    # Ensure directory exists                                                   if it doesn't exist.
    pathlib.Path("/tmp/images").mkdir(parents=True, exist_ok=True)   ←

    # Download all pictures in launches.json          Open the result from
    with open("/tmp/launches.json") as f:       ←    the previous task.
        launches = json.load(f)
        image_urls = [launch["image"] for launch in launches["results"]]
        for image_url in image_urls:
            try:                                             Download
                response = requests.get(image_url)   ←       each image.
                image_filename = image_url.split("/")[-1]
                target_file = f"/tmp/images/{image_filename}"
                with open(target_file, "wb") as f:
                    f.write(response.content)
                print(f"Downloaded {image_url} to {target_file}")
            except requests_exceptions.MissingSchema:
                print(f"{image_url} appears to be an invalid URL.")
            except requests_exceptions.ConnectionError:
                print(f"Could not connect to {image_url}.")

get_pictures = PythonOperator(           Instantiate a PythonOperator
    task_id="get_pictures",          ←  to call the Python function.
    python_callable=_get_pictures,       Point to the Python
    dag=dag,                         ←   function to execute.
)
```

Store each image. →

Print to stdout; this will be captured in Airflow logs. →

The PythonOperator in Airflow is responsible for running any Python code. Just like the BashOperator used before, this and all other operators require a task_id. The task_id is referenced when running a task and displayed in the UI. The use of a PythonOperator is always twofold:

1 We define the operator itself (get_pictures).
2 The python_callable argument points to a callable, typically a function (*_get_pictures*).

When running the operator, the Python function is called and will execute the function. Let's break it down. The basic usage of the PythonOperator always looks like figure 2.5.

```
def _get_pictures():                         ┐
    # do work here ...                       ├─ PythonOperator callable

get_pictures = PythonOperator(
    task_id="get_pictures",
    python_callable =_get_pictures,          ├─ PythonOperator
    dag=dag
)
```

Figure 2.5   The python_callable argument in the PythonOperator points to a function to execute.

Although not required, for convenience we keep the variable name get_pictures equal to the task_id.

Listing 2.7   Ensures that the output directory exists and creates it if it doesn't

```
# Ensure directory exists
pathlib.Path("/tmp/images").mkdir(parents=True, exist_ok=True)
```

The first step in the callable is to ensure the directory in which the images will be stored exists, as shown in listing 2.7. Next, we open the result downloaded from the Launch Library API and extract the image URLs for every launch.

Listing 2.8   Extracts image URLs for every rocket launch

```
                    Open the rocket launches' JSON.
                                                      Read as a dict so we
with open("/tmp/launches.json") as f:   ←─┘          can mingle the data.
    launches = json.load(f)                      ←
    image_urls = [launch["image"] for launch in launches["results"]]   ←─┐

                    For every launch, fetch the element "image".
```

Each image URL is called to download the image and save it in /tmp/images.

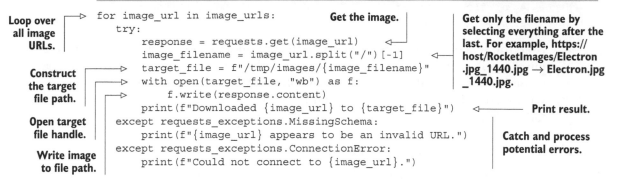

Listing 2.9 Downloads all images from the retrieved image URLs

Loop over all image URLs.

Construct the target file path.

Open target file handle.

Write image to file path.

```
for image_url in image_urls:
    try:
        response = requests.get(image_url)
        image_filename = image_url.split("/")[-1]
        target_file = f"/tmp/images/{image_filename}"
        with open(target_file, "wb") as f:
            f.write(response.content)
        print(f"Downloaded {image_url} to {target_file}")
    except requests_exceptions.MissingSchema:
        print(f"{image_url} appears to be an invalid URL.")
    except requests_exceptions.ConnectionError:
        print(f"Could not connect to {image_url}.")
```

Get the image.

Get only the filename by selecting everything after the last. For example, https://host/RocketImages/Electron.jpg_1440.jpg → Electron.jpg_1440.jpg.

Print result.

Catch and process potential errors.

2.3 Running a DAG in Airflow

Now that we have our basic rocket launch DAG, let's get it up and running and view it in the Airflow UI. The bare minimum Airflow consists of three core components: a scheduler, a webserver, and a database. In order to get Airflow up and running, you can either install Airflow in your Python environment or run a Docker container.

2.3.1 Running Airflow in a Python environment

There are several steps to installing and running Airflow as a Python package from PyPi:

```
pip install apache-airflow
```

Make sure you install `apache-airflow` and not just `airflow`. After joining the Apache Foundation in 2016, the PyPi `airflow` repository was renamed to `apache-airflow`. Since many people were still installing `airflow` instead of removing the old repository, it was kept as a dummy to provide everybody a message pointing to the correct repository.

Some operating systems come with a Python installation. Running just `pip install apache-airflow` will install Airflow in this "system" environment. When working on Python projects, it is desirable to keep each project in its own Python environment to create a reproducible set of Python packages and avoid dependency clashes. Such environments are created with tools such as these:

- pyenv: https://github.com/pyenv/pyenv
- Conda: https://docs.conda.io
- virtualenv: https://virtualenv.pypa.io

After installing Airflow, start it by initializing the metastore (a database in which all Airflow state is stored), creating a user, copying the rocket launch DAG into the DAGs directory, and starting the scheduler and webserver:

1 airflow db init
2 airflow users create --username admin --password admin --firstname Anonymous --lastname Admin --role Admin --email admin@example.org

```
3  cp download_rocket_launches.py ~/airflow/dags/
4  airflow webserver
5  airflow scheduler
```

Note the scheduler and webserver are both continuous processes that keep your terminal open, so either run in the background with `airflow webserver` and/or open a second terminal window to run the scheduler and webserver separately. After you're set up, go to http://localhost:8080 and log in with username "admin" and password "admin" to view Airflow.

2.3.2   *Running Airflow in Docker containers*

Docker containers are also popular to create isolated environments to run a reproducible set of Python packages and avoid dependency clashes. However, Docker containers create an isolated environment on the operating system level, whereas Python environments isolate only on the Python runtime level. As a result, you can create Docker containers that contain not only a set of Python packages, but also other dependencies such as database drivers or a GCC compiler. Throughout this book we will demonstrate Airflow running in Docker containers in several examples.

Running Docker containers requires a Docker Engine to be installed on your machine. You can then run Airflow in Docker with the following command.

Listing 2.10   Running Airflow in Docker

```
docker run \                          Expose on host
-ti \                                 port 8080.
-p 8080:8080 \          ◄
-v ➥ /path/to/dag/download_rocket_launches.py:/opt/airflow/dags/    Mount DAG file
      download_rocket_launches.py \                                  in container.
--entrypoint=/bin/bash \          Airflow Docker image
--name airflow \
apache/airflow:2.0.0-python3.8 \    ◄      Initialize the metastore
-c '( \                                    in the container.
airflow db init && \          ◄
Create ➥ airflow users create --username admin --password admin --firstname
a user.        Anonymous --lastname Admin --role Admin --email admin@example.org \
); \
airflow webserver & \        ◄┐  Start the webserver.
airflow scheduler \        ◄──┘
'                              Start the scheduler.
```

NOTE   If you're familiar with Docker, you would probably argue it's not desirable to run multiple processes in a single Docker container as shown in listing 2.10. The command is a single command, intended for demonstration purposes to get up and running quickly. In a production setting, you should run the Airflow webserver, scheduler, and metastore in separate containers, explained in detail in chapter 10.

It will download and run the Airflow Docker image `apache/airflow`. Once running, you can view Airflow on http://localhost:8080 and log in with username "admin" and password "admin".

2.3.3 *Inspecting the Airflow UI*

The first view of Airflow on http://localhost:8080 you will see is the login screen, shown in figure 2.6.

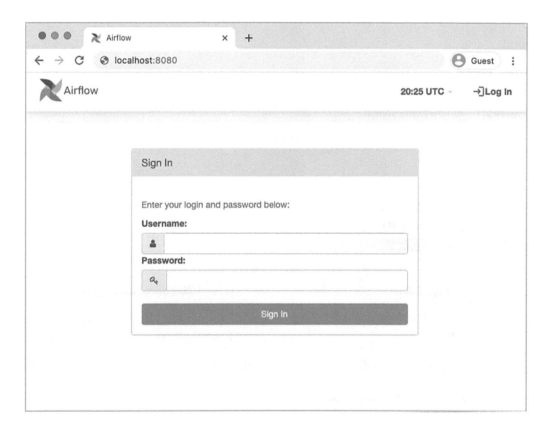

Figure 2.6 Airflow login view

After logging in, you can inspect the download_rocket_launches DAG, as shown in figure 2.7.

This is the first glimpse of Airflow you will see. Currently, the only DAG is the download_rocket_launches, which is available to Airflow in the DAGs directory. There's a lot of information on the main view, but let's inspect the download_rocket_launches DAG first. Click on the DAG name to open it and inspect the so-called graph view (figure 2.8).

Figure 2.7   Airflow home screen

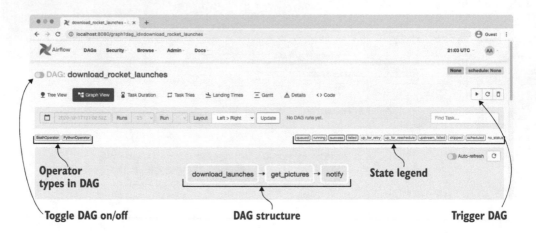

Figure 2.8   Airflow graph view

This view shows us the structure of the DAG script provided to Airflow. Once placed in the DAGs directory, Airflow will read the script and pull out the bits and pieces that together form a DAG, so it can be visualized in the UI. The graph view shows us the structure of the DAG, and how and in which order all tasks in the DAG are connected and will be run. This is one of the views you will probably use the most while developing your workflows.

The state legend shows all colors you might see when running, so let's see what happens and run the DAG. First, the DAG needs to be "on" in order to be run; toggle the button next to the DAG name for that. Next, click the Play button to run it.

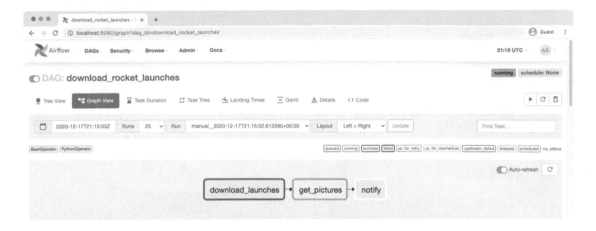

Figure 2.9   Graph view displaying a running DAG

After triggering the DAG, it will start running and you will see the current state of the workflow represented by colors (figure 2.9). Since we set dependencies between our tasks, consecutive tasks only start running once the previous tasks have been completed. Let's check the result of the *notify* task. In a real use case, you probably want to send an email or, for example, Slack notification to inform about the new images. For sake of simplicity, it now prints the number of downloaded images. Let's check the logs.

All task logs are collected in Airflow, so we can search in the UI for output or potential issues in case of failure. Click on a completed notify task, and you will see a pop-up with several options, as shown in figure 2.10.

Click on the top-center Log button to inspect the logs, as shown in figure 2.11. The logs are quite verbose by default but display the number of downloaded images in the log. Finally, we can open the /tmp/images directory and view them. When running in Docker, this directory only exists inside the Docker container and not on your host system. You must therefore first get into the Docker container:

```
docker exec -it airflow /bin/bash
```

After that you get a Bash terminal in the container and can view the images in /tmp/images, (figure 2.12).

2.4 Running at regular intervals

Rocket enthusiast John is happy now that he has a workflow up and running in Airflow, which he can trigger every now and then to collect the latest rocket pictures. He can see the status of his workflow in the Airflow UI, which is already an improvement compared to a script on the command line he was running before. But he still needs to trigger his workflow by hand periodically, which could be automated. After all, nobody likes doing repetitive tasks that computers are good at doing themselves.

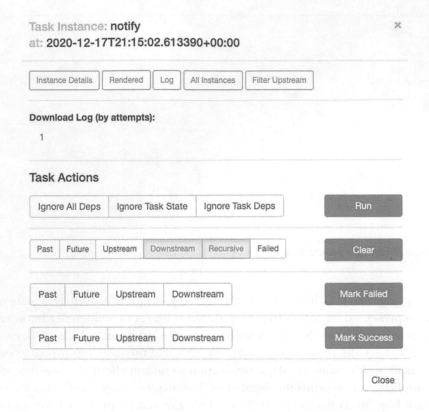

Figure 2.10   Task pop-up options

```
*** Reading local file: /opt/airflow/logs/download_rocket_launches/notify/2020-12-17T21:15:02.613390+00:00/1.log
[2020-12-17 21:15:30,917] {taskinstance.py:826} INFO - Dependencies all met for <TaskInstance: download_rocket_launches.notify 2020-12-17T2:
[2020-12-17 21:15:30,923] {taskinstance.py:826} INFO - Dependencies all met for <TaskInstance: download_rocket_launches.notify 2020-12-17T2:
[2020-12-17 21:15:30,923] {taskinstance.py:1017} INFO -
--------------------------------------------------------------------------------
[2020-12-17 21:15:30,923] {taskinstance.py:1018} INFO - Starting attempt 1 of 1
[2020-12-17 21:15:30,923] {taskinstance.py:1019} INFO -
--------------------------------------------------------------------------------
[2020-12-17 21:15:30,931] {taskinstance.py:1038} INFO - Executing <Task(BashOperator): notify> on 2020-12-17T21:15:02.613390+00:00
[2020-12-17 21:15:30,933] {standard_task_runner.py:51} INFO - Started process 1483 to run task
[2020-12-17 21:15:30,937] {standard_task_runner.py:75} INFO - Running: ['airflow', 'tasks', 'run', 'download_rocket_launches', 'notify', '2(
[2020-12-17 21:15:30,938] {standard_task_runner.py:76} INFO - Job 6: Subtask notify
[2020-12-17 21:15:30,969] {logging_mixin.py:103} INFO - Running <TaskInstance: download_rocket_launches.notify 2020-12-17T21:15:02.613390+0(
[2020-12-17 21:15:30,993] {taskinstance.py:1230} INFO - Exporting the following env vars:
AIRFLOW_CTX_DAG_OWNER=airflow
AIRFLOW_CTX_DAG_ID=download_rocket_launches
AIRFLOW_CTX_TASK_ID=notify
AIRFLOW_CTX_EXECUTION_DATE=2020-12-17T21:15:02.613390+00:00
AIRFLOW_CTX_DAG_RUN_ID=manual__2020-12-17T21:15:02.613390+00:00
[2020-12-17 21:15:30,994] {bash.py:135} INFO - Tmp dir root location:
 /tmp
[2020-12-17 21:15:30,994] {bash.py:158} INFO - Running command: echo "There are now $(ls /tmp/images/ | wc -l) images."
[2020-12-17 21:15:31,002] {bash.py:169} INFO - Output:
[2020-12-17 21:15:31,006] {bash.py:173} INFO - There are now 2 images.
[2020-12-17 21:15:31,006] {bash.py:177} INFO - Command exited with return code 0
[2020-12-17 21:15:31,021] {taskinstance.py:1135} INFO - Marking task as SUCCESS. dag_id=download_rocket_launches, task_id=notify, execution_
[2020-12-17 21:15:31,037] {taskinstance.py:1195} INFO - 0 downstream tasks scheduled from follow-on schedule check
[2020-12-17 21:15:31,070] {local_task_job.py:118} INFO - Task exited with return code 0
```

Figure 2.11   Print statement displayed in logs

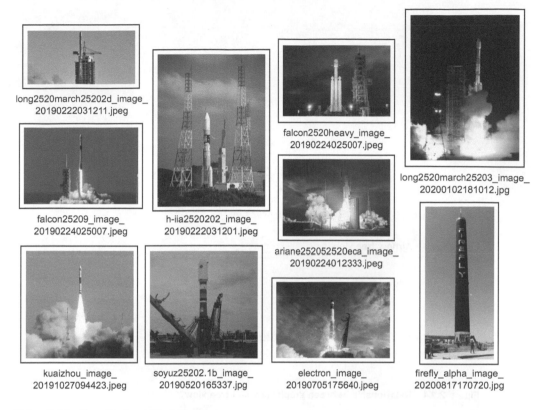

long2520march25202d_image_
20190222031211.jpeg

falcon25209_image_
20190224025007.jpeg

h-iia2520202_image_
20190222031201.jpeg

falcon2520heavy_image_
20190224025007.jpeg

ariane252052520eca_image_
20190224012333.jpeg

long2520march25203_image_
20200102181012.jpg

kuaizhou_image_
20191027094423.jpeg

soyuz25202.1b_image_
20190520165337.jpg

electron_image_
20190705175640.jpeg

firefly_alpha_image_
20200817170720.jpg

Figure 2.12 Resulting rocket pictures

In Airflow, we can schedule a DAG to run at certain intervals, for example once an hour, day, or month. This is controlled on the DAG by setting the `schedule_interval` argument.

Listing 2.11   Running a DAG once a day

```
dag = DAG(
    dag_id="download_rocket_launches",
    start_date=airflow.utils.dates.days_ago(14),
    schedule_interval="@daily",          ⊲——————  Airflow alias for 0 0
)                                                  * * * (i.e., midnight)
```

Setting the `schedule_interval` to `@daily` tells Airflow to run this workflow once a day so that John doesn't have to trigger it manually once a day. This behavior is best viewed in the tree view, as shown in figure 2.13.

The tree view is similar to the graph view but displays the graph structure as it runs over time. An overview of the status of all runs of a single workflow can be seen in figure 2.14.

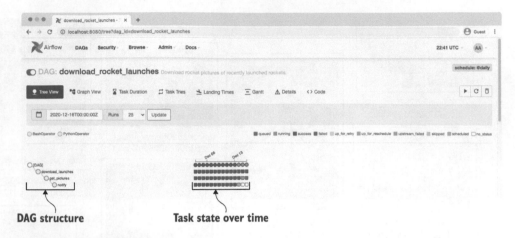

Figure 2.13   Airflow tree view

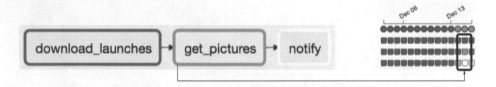

Figure 2.14   Relationship between graph view and tree view

The structure of the DAG is displayed to fit a "rows and columns" layout, specifically the status of all runs of the specific DAG, where each column represents a single run at some point in time.

When we set the schedule_interval to @daily, Airflow knew it had to run this DAG once a day. Given the start_date provided to the DAG of 14 days ago, that means the time from 14 days ago up to now can be divided into 14 equal intervals of one day. Since both the start and end date of these 14 intervals lie in the past, they will start running once we provide a schedule_interval to Airflow. The semantics of the schedule interval and various ways to configure it are covered in more detail in chapter 3.

2.5   Handling failing tasks

So far we've seen only green in the Airflow UI. But what happens if something fails? It's not uncommon for tasks to fail, which could be for a multitude of reasons (e.g., an external service is down, network connectivity issues, or a broken disk).

Say, for example, at some point we experienced a network hiccup while getting John's rocket pictures. As a consequence, the Airflow task fails, and we see the failing task in the Airflow UI. It would look figure 2.15.

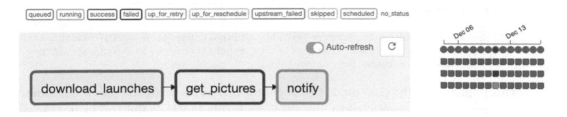

Figure 2.15 Failure displayed in graph view and tree view

The specific failed task would be displayed in red in both the graph and tree views, as a result of not being able to get the images from the internet, and therefore raise an error. The successive `notify` task would not run at all because it's dependent on the successful state of the `get_pictures` task. Such task instances are displayed in orange. By default, all previous tasks must run successfully, and any successive task of a failed task will not run.

Let's figure out the issue by inspecting the logs again. Open the logs of the `get_pictures` task (figure 2.16).

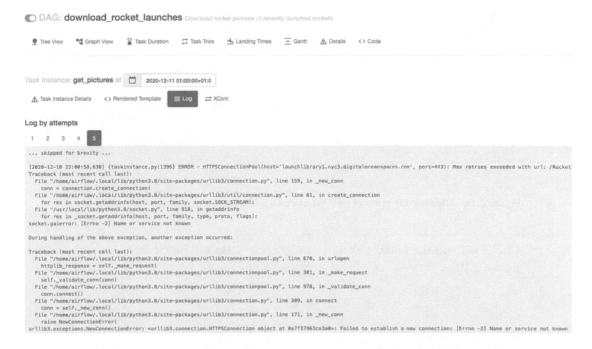

Figure 2.16 Stack trace of failed `get_pictures` task

In the stack trace, we uncover the potential cause of the issue:

```
urllib3.exceptions.NewConnectionError: <urllib3.connection.HTTPSConnection
    object at 0x7f37963ce3a0>: Failed to establish a new connection: [Errno
    -2] Name or service not known
```

This indicates urllib3 (i.e., the HTTP client for Python) is trying to establish a connection but cannot, which could hint at a firewall rule blocking the connection or no internet connectivity. Assuming we fixed the issue (e.g., plugged in the internet cable), let's restart the task.

> **NOTE** It is unnecessary to restart the entire workflow. A nice feature of Airflow is that you can restart from the point of failure and onward, without having to restart any previously succeeded tasks.

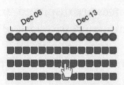

Figure 2.17   Click on a failed task for options to clear it.

Click the failed task, and then click the Clear button in the pop-up (figure 2.17). It will show you the tasks you're about to clear, meaning you will reset the state of these tasks and Airflow will rerun them, as shown in figure 2.18.

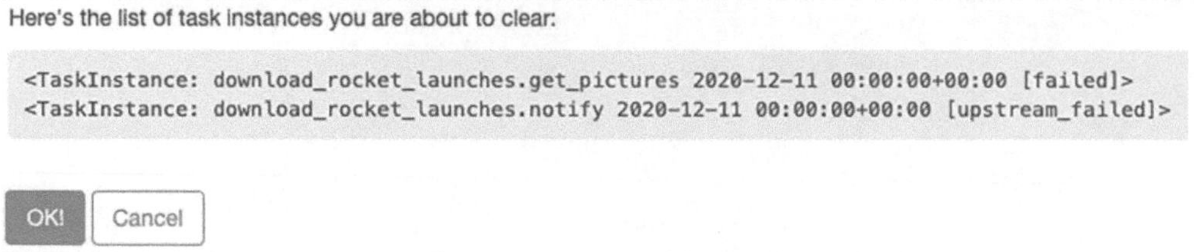

Here's the list of task instances you are about to clear:

```
<TaskInstance: download_rocket_launches.get_pictures 2020-12-11 00:00:00+00:00 [failed]>
<TaskInstance: download_rocket_launches.notify 2020-12-11 00:00:00+00:00 [upstream_failed]>
```

OK!   Cancel

Figure 2.18   Clearing the state of `get_pictures` and successive tasks

Click OK! and the failed task and its successive tasks will be cleared, as can be seen in figure 2.19.

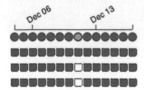

Figure 2.19   Cleared tasks displayed in graph view

Assuming the connectivity issues are resolved, the tasks will now run successfully and make the whole tree view green (figure 2.20).

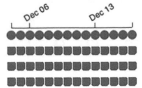

**Figure 2.20   Successfully completed
tasks after clearing failed tasks**

In any piece of software, there are many reasons for failure. In Airflow workflows, sometimes failure is accepted, sometimes it is not, and sometimes it is only in certain conditions. The criteria for dealing with failure can be configured on any level in the workflow and is covered in more detail in chapter 4.

After clearing the failed tasks, Airflow will automatically rerun these tasks. If all goes well, John will now have downloaded the rocket images resulting from the failed tasks. Note that the called URL in the `download_launches` task simply requests the next rocket launches—meaning it will return the next rocket launches at the time of calling the API. Incorporating the runtime context at which a DAG was run into your code is covered in chapter 4.

Summary

- Workflows in Airflow are represented in DAGs.
- Operators represent a single unit of work.
- Airflow contains an array of operators both for generic and specific types of work.
- The Airflow UI offers a graph view for viewing the DAG structure and tree view for viewing DAG runs over time.
- Failed tasks can be restarted anywhere in the DAG.

Scheduling in Airflow 3

This chapter covers

- Running DAGs at regular intervals
- Constructing dynamic DAGs to process data incrementally
- Loading and reprocessing past data sets using backfilling
- Applying best practices for reliable tasks

In the previous chapter, we explored Airflow's UI and showed you how to define a basic Airflow DAG and run it every day by defining a scheduled interval. In this chapter, we will dive a bit deeper into the concept of scheduling in Airflow and explore how this allows you to process data incrementally at regular intervals. First, we'll introduce a small use case focused on analyzing user events from our website and explore how we can build a DAG to analyze these events at regular intervals. Next, we'll explore ways to make this process more efficient by taking an incremental approach to analyzing our data and understanding how this ties into Airflow's concept of execution dates. Finally, we'll finish by showing how we can fill in past gaps in our data set using backfilling and discussing some important properties of proper Airflow tasks.

3.1 An example: Processing user events

To understand how Airflow's scheduling works, we'll first consider a small example. Imagine we have a service that tracks user behavior on our website and allows us to analyze which pages users (identified by an IP address) accessed. For marketing purposes, we would like to know how many different pages users access and how much time they spend during each visit. To get an idea of how this behavior changes over time, we want to calculate these statistics daily, as this allows us to compare changes across different days and larger time periods.

For practical reasons, the external tracking service does not store data for more than 30 days, so we need to store and accumulate this data ourselves, as we want to retain our history for longer periods of time. Normally, because the raw data might be quite large, it would make sense to store this data in a cloud storage service such as Amazon's S3 or Google's Cloud Storage, as they combine high durability with relatively low costs. However, for simplicity's sake, we won't worry about these things and will keep our data locally.

To simulate this example, we have created a simple (local) API that allows us to retrieve user events. For example, we can retrieve the full list of available events from the past 30 days using the following API call:

```
curl -o /tmp/events.json http://localhost:5000/events
```

This call returns a (JSON-encoded) list of user events we can analyze to calculate our user statistics.

Using this API, we can break our workflow into two separate tasks: one for fetching user events and another for calculating the statistics. The data itself can be downloaded using the BashOperator, as we saw in the previous chapter. For calculating the statistics, we can use a PythonOperator, which allows us to load the data into a Pandas DataFrame and calculate the number of events using a *groupby* and an *aggregation*. Altogether, this gives us the DAG shown in listing 3.1.

Listing 3.1   Initial (unscheduled) version of the event DAG (dags/01_unscheduled.py)

```
import datetime as dt
from pathlib import Path

import pandas as pd
from airflow import DAG
from airflow.operators.bash import BashOperator
from airflow.operators.python import PythonOperator

dag = DAG(
    dag_id="01_unscheduled",
    start_date=dt.datetime(2019, 1, 1),          ◁──┤ Define the start
    schedule_interval=None,                            date for the DAG.
)                                            ◁──┤ Specify that this is an
                                                   unscheduled DAG.
```

```
fetch_events = BashOperator(
    task_id="fetch_events",
    bash_command=(
        "mkdir -p /data && "
        "curl -o /data/events.json "          ◁──  Fetch and store the
        "https://localhost:5000/events"             events from the API.
    ),
    dag=dag,
)
```

```
def _calculate_stats(input_path, output_path):          Load the events
    """Calculates event statistics."""                  and calculate
                                                         the required
    events = pd.read_json(input_path)                    statistics.
    stats = events.groupby(["date", "user"]).size().reset_index()
    Path(output_path).parent.mkdir(exist_ok=True)
    stats.to_csv(output_path, index=False)          Make sure the
                                                     output directory
                                                     exists and write
                                                     results to CSV.

calculate_stats = PythonOperator(
    task_id="calculate_stats",
    python_callable=_calculate_stats,
    op_kwargs={
        "input_path": "/data/events.json",
        "output_path": "/data/stats.csv",
    },
    dag=dag,
)
                                         Set order of
fetch_events >> calculate_stats    ◁──┘  execution.
```

Now we have our basic DAG, but we still need to make sure it's run regularly by Air-flow. Let's get it scheduled so that we have daily updates!

3.2 *Running at regular intervals*

As we saw in chapter 2, Airflow DAGs can be run at regular intervals by defining a sched-uled interval for it using the schedule_interval argument when initializing the DAG. By default, the value of this argument is None, which means the DAG will not be sched-uled and will be run only when triggered manually from the UI or the API.

3.2.1 *Defining scheduling intervals*

In our example of ingesting user events, we would like to calculate statistics daily, so it would make sense to schedule our DAG to run once every day. As this is a common use case, Airflow provides the convenient macro @daily for defining a daily scheduled interval, which runs our DAG once every day at midnight.

> **Listing 3.2 Defining a daily schedule interval (dags/02_daily_schedule.py)**

```
dag = DAG(
    dag_id="02_daily_schedule",
    schedule_interval="@daily",                    Schedule the DAG to run
    start_date=dt.datetime(2019, 1, 1),            every day at midnight.
    ...
)                                                  Date/time to start
                                                   scheduling DAG runs
```

Airflow also needs to know when we want to start executing the DAG, specified by its start date. Based on this start date, Airflow will schedule the first execution of our DAG to run at the first schedule interval *after* the start date (start + interval). Subsequent runs will continue executing at schedule intervals following this first interval.

> **NOTE** Pay attention to the fact that Airflow starts tasks in an interval at the end of the interval. If developing a DAG on January 1, 2019 at 13:00, with a `start_date` of 01-01-2019 and `@daily` interval, this means it first starts running at midnight. At first, nothing will happen if you run the DAG on January 1 at 13:00 until midnight is reached.

For example, say we define our DAG with a start date on the first of January, as previously shown in listing 3.2. Combined with a daily scheduling interval, this will result in Airflow running our DAG at midnight on every day following the first of January (figure 3.1). Note that our first execution takes place on the second of January (the first interval following the start date) and not the first. We'll get into the reasoning behind this behavior later in this chapter (section 3.4).

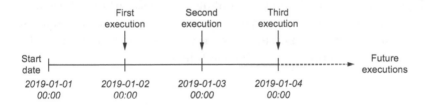

Figure 3.1 Schedule intervals for a daily scheduled DAG with a specified start date (2019-01-01). Arrows indicate the time point at which a DAG is executed. Without a specified end date, the DAG will keep being executed every day until the DAG is switched off.

Without an end date, Airflow will (in principle) keep executing our DAG on this daily schedule until the end of time. However, if we already know that our project has a fixed duration, we can tell Airflow to stop running our DAG after a certain date using the `end_date` parameter.

```
Listing 3.3   Defining an end date for the DAG (dags/03_with_end_date.py)

dag = DAG(
    dag_id="03_with_end_date",
    schedule_interval="@daily",
    start_date=dt.datetime(year=2019, month=1, day=1),
    end_date=dt.datetime(year=2019, month=1, day=5),
)
```

This will result in the full set of schedule intervals shown in figure 3.2.

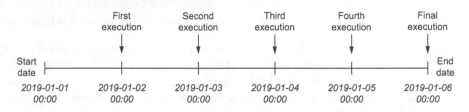

Figure 3.2   Schedule intervals for a daily scheduled DAG with specified start (2019-01-01) and end dates (2019-01-06), which prevents the DAG from executing beyond this date

3.2.2   *Cron-based intervals*

So far, all our examples have shown DAGs running at daily intervals. But what if we want to run our jobs on hourly or weekly intervals? And what about more complicated intervals in which we may want to run our DAG at 23:45 every Saturday?

To support more complicated scheduling intervals, Airflow allows us to define scheduling intervals using the same syntax as used by cron, a time-based job scheduler used by Unix-like computer operating systems such as macOS and Linux. This syntax consists of five components and is defined as follows:

```
# ┌─────────── minute (0 - 59)
# │ ┌───────── hour (0 - 23)
# │ │ ┌─────── day of the month (1 - 31)
# │ │ │ ┌───── month (1 - 12)
# │ │ │ │ ┌─── day of the week (0 - 6) (Sunday to Saturday;
# │ │ │ │ │      7 is also Sunday on some systems)
# * * * * *
```

In this definition, a cron job is executed when the time/date specification fields match the current system time/date. Asterisks (*) can be used instead of numbers to define unrestricted fields, meaning we don't care about the value of that field.

Although this cron-based representation may seem a bit convoluted, it provides us with considerable flexibility for defining time intervals. For example, we can define hourly, daily, and weekly intervals using the following cron expressions:

- `0 * * * *` = hourly (running on the hour)
- `0 0 * * *` = daily (running at midnight)
- `0 0 * * 0` = weekly (running at midnight on Sunday)

Besides this, we can also define more complicated expressions such as the following:

- `0 0 1 * *` = midnight on the first of every month
- `45 23 * * SAT` = 23:45 every Saturday

Additionally, cron expressions allow you to define collections of values using a comma (,) to define a list of values or a dash (-) to define a range of values. Using this syntax, we can build expressions that enable running jobs on multiple weekdays or multiple sets of hours during a day:

- `0 0 * * MON,WED,FRI` = run every Monday, Wednesday, Friday at midnight
- `0 0 * * MON-FRI` = run every weekday at midnight
- `0 0,12 * * *` = run every day at 00:00 and 12:00

Airflow also provides support for several macros that represent shorthand for commonly used scheduling intervals. We have already seen one of these macros (`@daily`) for defining daily intervals. An overview of the other macros supported by Airflow is shown in table 3.1.

Table 3.1 Airflow presets for frequently used scheduling intervals

Preset	Meaning
`@once`	Schedule once and only once.
`@hourly`	Run once an hour at the beginning of the hour.
`@daily`	Run once a day at midnight.
`@weekly`	Run once a week at midnight on Sunday morning.
`@monthly`	Run once a month at midnight on the first day of the month.
`@yearly`	Run once a year at midnight on January 1.

Although Cron expressions are extremely powerful, they can be difficult to work with. As such, it may be a good idea to test your expression before trying it out in Airflow. Fortunately, there are many tools[1] available online that can help you define, verify, or explain your Cron expressions in plain English. It also doesn't hurt to document the reasoning behind complicated cron expressions in your code. This may help others (including future you!) understand the expression when revisiting your code.

---

[1] https://crontab.guru translates cron expressions to human-readable language.

3.2.3 *Frequency-based intervals*

An important limitation of cron expressions is that they are unable to represent certain frequency-based schedules. For example, how would you define a cron expression that runs a DAG once every three days? It turns out that you could write an expression that runs on every first, fourth, seventh, and so on day of the month, but this approach would run into problems at the end of the month as the DAG would run consecutively on both the 31st and the first of the next month, violating the desired schedule.

This limitation of cron stems from the nature of cron expressions, as they define a pattern that is continuously matched against the current time to determine whether a job should be executed. This has the advantage of making the expressions stateless, meaning that you don't have to remember when a previous job was run to calculate the next interval. However, as you can see, this comes at the price of some expressiveness.

What if we really want to run our DAG once every three days? To support this type of frequency-based schedule, Airflow also allows you to define scheduling intervals in terms of a relative time interval. To use such a frequency-based schedule, you can pass a `timedelta` instance (from the datetime module in the standard library) as a schedule interval.

Listing 3.4   Defining a frequency-based schedule interval (dags/04_time_delta.py)

```
dag = DAG(                                              timedelta gives the ability
    dag_id="04_time_delta",                             to use frequency-based
    schedule_interval=dt.timedelta(days=3),        ◁┘  schedules.
    start_date=dt.datetime(year=2019, month=1, day=1),
    end_date=dt.datetime(year=2019, month=1, day=5),
)
```

This would result in our DAG being run every three days following the start date (on the 4th, 7th, 10th, and so on of January 2019). Of course, you can also use this approach to run your DAG every 10 minutes (using `timedelta(minutes=10)`) or every two hours (using `timedelta(hours=2)`).

3.3 *Processing data incrementally*

Although we now have our DAG running at a daily interval (assuming we stuck with the `@daily` schedule), we haven't quite achieved our goal. For one, our DAG is downloading and calculating statistics for the entire catalog of user events every day, which is hardly efficient. Moreover, this process is only downloading events for the past 30 days, which means we are not building any history for earlier dates.

3.3.1 *Fetching events incrementally*

One way to solve these issues is to change our DAG to load data incrementally, in which we only load events from the corresponding day in each schedule interval and only calculate statistics for the new events (figure 3.3).

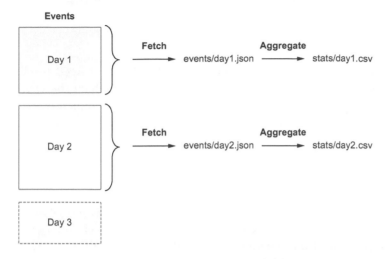

Figure 3.3 Fetching and processing data incrementally

This incremental approach is much more efficient than fetching and processing the entire data set, as it significantly reduces the amount of data that has to be processed in each schedule interval. Additionally, because we are now storing our data in separate files per day, we also have the opportunity to start building a history of files over time, way past the 30-day limit of our API.

To implement incremental processing in our workflow, we need to modify our DAG to download data for a specific day. Fortunately, we can adjust our API call to fetch events for the current date by including start and end date parameters:

```
curl -O http://localhost:5000/events?start_date=2019-01-01&end_date=2019-01-02
```

Together, these date parameters indicate the time range for which we would like to fetch events. Note that in this example `start_date` is inclusive, while `end_date` is exclusive, meaning we are effectively fetching events that occur between 2019-01-01 00:00:00 and 2019-01-01 23:59:59.

We can implement this incremental data fetching in our DAG by changing our bash command to include the two dates.

Listing 3.5 Fetching events for a specific time interval (dags/05_query_with_dates.py)

```
fetch_events = BashOperator(
    task_id="fetch_events",
    bash_command=(
        "mkdir -p /data && "
        "curl -o /data/events.json "
        "http://localhost:5000/events?"
        "start_date=2019-01-01&"
        "end_date=2019-01-02"
```

```
    ),
    dag=dag,
)
```

However, to fetch data for any other date than 2019-01-01, we need to change the command to use start and end dates that reflect the day for which the DAG is being executed. Fortunately, Airflow provides us with several extra parameters for doing so, which we'll explore in the next section.

3.3.2   *Dynamic time references using execution dates*

For many workflows involving time-based processes, it is important to know for which time interval a given task is being executed. For this reason, Airflow provides tasks with extra parameters that can be used to determine for which schedule interval a task is being executed (we'll go into more detail on these parameters in the next chapter).

The most important of these parameters is called the execution_date, which represents the date and time for which our DAG is being executed. Contrary to what the name of the parameter suggests, the execution_date is not a date but a timestamp, which reflects the start time of the schedule interval for which the DAG is being executed. The end time of the schedule interval is indicated by another parameter called the next_execution_date. Together these dates define the entire length of a task's schedule interval (figure 3.4).

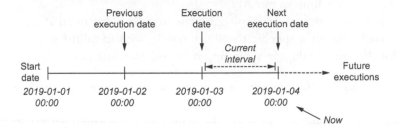

Figure 3.4   Execution dates in Airflow

Airflow also provides a previous_execution_date parameter, which describes the start of the previous schedule interval. Although we won't be using this parameter here, it can be useful for performing analyses that contrast data from the current time interval with results from the previous interval.

In Airflow, we can use these execution dates by referencing them in our operators. For example, in the BashOperator, we can use Airflow's templating functionality to include the execution dates dynamically in our Bash command. Templating is covered in detail in chapter 4.

Listing 3.6 Using templating for specifying dates (dags/06_templated_query.py)

```
fetch_events = BashOperator(
    task_id="fetch_events",
    bash_command=(
        "mkdir -p /data && "
        "curl -o /data/events.json "
        "http://localhost:5000/events?"
        "start_date={{execution_date.strftime('%Y-%m-%d')}}"
        "&end_date={{next_execution_date.strftime('%Y-%m-%d')}}"
    ),
    dag=dag,
)
```

Formatted execution_date inserted with Jinja templating

next_execution_date holds the execution date of the next interval.

In this example, the syntax `{{variable_name}}` is an example of using Airflow's Jinja-based (http://jinja.pocoo.org) templating syntax for referencing one of Airflow's specific parameters. Here, we use this syntax to reference the execution dates and format them to the expected string format using the datetime strftime method (as both execution dates are datetime objects).

Because the `execution_date` parameters are often used in this fashion to reference dates as formatted strings, Airflow also provides several shorthand parameters for common date formats. For example, the `ds` and `ds_nodash` parameters are different representations of the `execution_date`, formatted as YYYY-MM-DD and YYYYM-MDD, respectively. Similarly, `next_ds`, `next_ds_nodash`, `prev_ds`, and `prev_ds_nodash` provide shorthand notations for the next and previous execution dates, respectively.[2]

Using these shorthand notations, we can also write our incremental fetch command as follows.

Listing 3.7 Using template shorthand (dags/07_templated_query_ds.py)

```
fetch_events = BashOperator(
    task_id="fetch_events",
    bash_command=(
        "mkdir -p /data && "
        "curl -o /data/events.json "
        "http://localhost:5000/events?"
        "start_date={{ds}}&"
        "end_date={{next_ds}}"
    ),
    dag=dag,
)
```

ds provides YYYY-MM-DD formatted execution_date.

next_ds provides the same for next_execution_date.

This shorter version is quite a bit easier to read. However, for more complicated date (or datetime) formats, you will likely still need to use the more flexible strftime method.

---

[2] See https://airflow.readthedocs.io/en/stable/macros-ref.html for an overview of all available shorthand options.

3.3.3   *Partitioning your data*

Although our new `fetch_events` task now fetches events incrementally for each new schedule interval, the astute reader may have noticed that each new task is simply overwriting the result of the previous day, meaning that we are effectively not building any history.

One way to solve this problem is to simply append new events to the events.json file, which would allow us to build our history in a single JSON file. However, a drawback of this approach is that it requires any downstream processing jobs to load the entire data set, even if we are only interested in calculating statistics for a given day. Additionally, it also makes this file a single point of failure, by which we may risk losing our entire data set should this file become lost or corrupted.

An alternative approach is to divide our data set into daily batches by writing the output of the task to a file bearing the name of the corresponding execution date.

> **Listing 3.8   Writing event data to separate files per date (dags/08_templated_path.py)**

```
fetch_events = BashOperator(
    task_id="fetch_events",
    bash_command=(
        "mkdir -p /data/events && "
        "curl -o /data/events/{{ds}}.json "        ◁── Response written to
        "http://localhost:5000/events?"                 templated filename
        "start_date={{ds}}&"
        "end_date={{next_ds}}",
    dag=dag,
)
```

This would result in any data being downloaded for an execution date of 2019-01-01 being written to the file /data/events/2019-01-01.json.

This practice of dividing a data set into smaller, more manageable pieces is a common strategy in data storage and processing systems and is commonly referred to as *partitioning*, with the smaller pieces of a data set the *partitions*. The advantage of partitioning our data set by execution date becomes evident when we consider the second task in our DAG (`calculate_stats`), in which we calculate statistics for each day's worth of user events. In our previous implementation, we were loading the entire data set and calculating statistics for our entire event history, every day.

> **Listing 3.9   Previous implementation for event statistics (dags/01_scheduled.py)**

```
def _calculate_stats(input_path, output_path):
    """Calculates event statistics."""
    Path(output_path).parent.mkdir(exist_ok=True)
    events = pd.read_json(input_path)
    stats = events.groupby(["date", "user"]).size().reset_index()
    stats.to_csv(output_path, index=False)
```

```
calculate_stats = PythonOperator(
    task_id="calculate_stats",
    python_callable=_calculate_stats,
    op_kwargs={
        "input_path": "/data/events.json",
        "output_path": "/data/stats.csv",
    },
    dag=dag,
)
```

However, using our partitioned data set, we can calculate these statistics more efficiently for each separate partition by changing the input and output paths of this task to point to the partitioned event data and a partitioned output file.

Listing 3.10 Calculating statistics per execution interval (dags/08_templated_path.py)

```
def _calculate_stats(**context):        ◁─┤  Receive all context
    """Calculates event statistics."""      variables in this dict.
    input_path = context["templates_dict"]["input_path"]     ◁─┐
    output_path = context["templates_dict"]["output_path"]      │  Retrieve the
                                                                │  templated
    Path(output_path).parent.mkdir(exist_ok=True)              │  values from the
                                                                │  templates_dict
    events = pd.read_json(input_path)                          │  object.
    stats = events.groupby(["date", "user"]).size().reset_index()
    stats.to_csv(output_path, index=False)


calculate_stats = PythonOperator(
    task_id="calculate_stats",
    python_callable=_calculate_stats,
    templates_dict={                             │  Pass the values that we
        "input_path": "/data/events/{{ds}}.json",   ◁─┘  want to be templated.
        "output_path": "/data/stats/{{ds}}.csv",
    },
    dag=dag,
)
```

Although these changes may look somewhat complicated, they mostly involve boilerplate code for ensuring that our input and output paths are templated. To achieve this templating in the PythonOperator, we need to pass any arguments that should be templated using the operator's templates_dict parameter. We then can retrieve the templated values inside our function from the context object that is passed to our _calculate_stats function by Airflow.[3]

If this all went a bit too quickly, don't worry; we'll dive into the task context in more detail in the next chapter. The important point to understand here is that these

---

[3] For Airflow 1.10.x, you'll need to pass the extra argument provide_context=True to the PythonOperator; otherwise, the _calculate_stats function won't receive the context values.

changes allow us to compute our statistics incrementally, by only processing a small subset of our data each day.

3.4 *Understanding Airflow's execution dates*

Because execution dates are such an important part of Airflow, let's take a minute to make sure we fully understand how these dates are defined.

3.4.1 *Executing work in fixed-length intervals*

As we've seen, we can control when Airflow runs a DAG with three parameters: a start date, a schedule interval, and an (optional) end date. To actually start scheduling our DAG, Airflow uses these three parameters to divide time into a series of schedule intervals, starting from the given start date and optionally ending at the end date (figure 3.5).

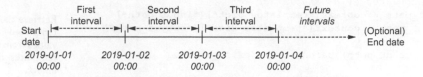

Figure 3.5   Time represented in terms of Airflow's scheduling intervals. Assumes a daily interval with a start date of 2019-01-01.

In this interval-based representation of time, a DAG is executed for a given interval as soon as the time slot of that interval has passed. For example, the first interval in figure 3.5 would be executed as soon as possible after 2019-01-01 23:59:59, because by then the last time point in the interval has passed. Similarly, the DAG would execute for the second interval shortly after 2019-01-02 23:59:59, and so on, until we reach our optional end date.

An advantage of using this interval-based approach is that it is ideal for performing the type of incremental data processing we saw in the previous sections, as we know exactly for which interval of time a task is executing for—the start and end of the corresponding interval. This is in stark contrast to, for example, a time point–based scheduling system such as cron, where we only know the current time for which our task is being executed. This means that, for example in cron, we either have to calculate or guess where our previous execution left off by assuming that the task is executing for the previous day (figure 3.6).

Understanding that Airflow's handling of time is built around schedule intervals also helps understand how execution dates are defined within Airflow. For example, say we have a DAG that follows a daily schedule interval, and then consider the corresponding interval that should process data for 2019-01-03. In Airflow, this interval will be run shortly after 2019-01-04 00:00:00, because at that point we know we will no longer

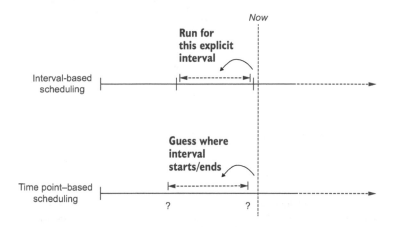

Figure 3.6 Incremental processing in interval-based scheduling windows (e.g., Airflow) versus windows derived from time point–based systems (e.g., cron). For incremental (data) processing, time is typically divided into discrete time intervals that are processed as soon as the corresponding interval has passed. Interval-based scheduling approaches (such as Airflow) explicitly schedule tasks to run for each interval while providing exact information to each task concerning the start and the end of the interval. In contrast, time point–based scheduling approaches only execute tasks at a given time, leaving it up to the task itself to determine for which incremental interval the task is executing.

be receiving any new data for 2019-01-03. Thinking back to our explanation of using execution dates in our tasks from the previous section, what do you think that the value of execution_date will be for this interval?

Many people expect that the execution date of this DAG run will be 2019-01-04, as this is the moment at which the DAG is actually run. However, if we look at the value of the execution_date variable when our tasks are executed, we will actually see an execution date of 2019-01-03. This is because Airflow defines the execution date of a DAG as the start of the corresponding interval. Conceptually, this makes sense if we consider that the execution date marks our schedule interval rather than the moment our DAG is actually executed. Unfortunately, the naming can be a bit confusing.

With Airflow execution dates being defined as the start of the corresponding schedule intervals, they can be used to derive the start and end of a specific interval (figure 3.7). For example, when executing a task, the start and end of the corresponding interval are defined by the execution_date (the start of the interval) and the next_execution date (the start of the next interval) parameters. Similarly, the previous schedule interval can be derived using the previous_execution_date and execution_date parameters.

However, one caveat to keep in mind when using the previous_execution_date and next_execution_date parameters in your tasks is that these are only defined for

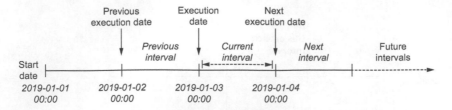

Figure 3.7   Execution dates in the context of schedule intervals. In Airflow, the execution date of a DAG is defined as the start time of the corresponding schedule interval rather than the time at which the DAG is executed (which is typically the end of the interval). As such, the value of `execution_date` points to the start of the current interval, while the `previous_execution_date` and `next_execution_date` parameters point to the start of the previous and next schedule intervals, respectively. The current interval can be derived from a combination of the `execution_date` and the `next_execution_date`, which signifies the start of the next interval and thus the end of the current one.

DAG runs following the schedule interval. As such, the values of these parameters will be undefined for any runs that are triggered manually using Airflow UI or CLI because Airflow cannot provide information about next or previous schedule intervals if you are not following a schedule interval.

3.5   *Using backfilling to fill in past gaps*

As Airflow allows us to define schedule intervals from an arbitrary start date, we can also define past intervals from a start date in the past. We can use this property to perform historical runs of our DAG for loading or analyzing past data sets—a process typically referred to as *backfilling*.

3.5.1   *Executing work back in time*

By default, Airflow will schedule and run any past schedule intervals that have not been run. As such, specifying a past start date and activating the corresponding DAG will result in all intervals that have passed before the current time being executed. This behavior is controlled by the DAG `catchup` parameter and can be disabled by setting `catchup` to false.

Listing 3.11   Disabling `catchup` to avoid running past runs (dags/09_no_catchup.py)

```
dag = DAG(
    dag_id="09_no_catchup",
    schedule_interval="@daily",
    start_date=dt.datetime(year=2019, month=1, day=1),
    end_date=dt.datetime(year=2019, month=1, day=5),
    catchup=False,
)
```

With this setting, the DAG will only be run for the most recent schedule interval rather than executing all open past intervals (figure 3.8). The default value for `catchup` can

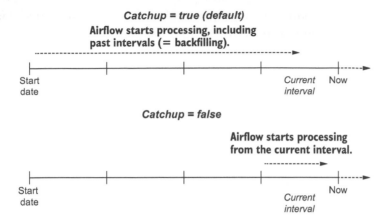

Figure 3.8 Backfilling in Airflow. By default, Airflow will run tasks for all past intervals up to the current time. This behavior can be disabled by setting the `catchup` parameter of a DAG to false, in which case Airflow will only start executing tasks from the current interval.

be controlled from the Airflow configuration file by setting a value for the `catchup_by_default` configuration setting.

Although backfilling is a powerful concept, it is limited by the availability of data in source systems. For example, in our example use case we can load past events from our API by specifying a start date up to 30 days in the past. However, as the API only provides up to 30 days of history, we cannot use backfilling to load data from earlier days.

Backfilling can also be used to reprocess data after we have made changes in our code. For example, say we make a change to our `calc_statistics` function to add a new statistic. Using backfilling, we can clear past runs of our `calc_statistics` task to reanalyze our historical data using the new code. Note that in this case we aren't limited by the 30-day limit of our data source, as we have already loaded these earlier data partitions as part of our past runs.

3.6 *Best practices for designing tasks*

Although Airflow does much of the heavy lifting when it comes to backfilling and rerunning tasks, we need to ensure our tasks fulfill certain key properties for proper results. In this section, we dive into two of the most important properties of proper Airflow tasks: atomicity and idempotency.

3.6.1 *Atomicity*

The term *atomicity* is frequently used in database systems, where an atomic transaction is considered an indivisible and irreducible series of database operations such that either all occur or nothing occurs. Similarly, in Airflow, tasks should be defined so that they either succeed and produce some proper result or fail in a manner that does not affect the state of the system (figure 3.9).

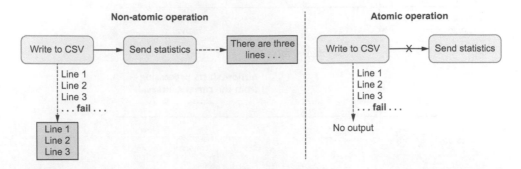

Figure 3.9   Atomicity ensures either everything or nothing completes. No half work is produced, and as a result, incorrect results are avoided down the line.

As an example, consider a simple extension to our user event DAG, in which we would like to add some functionality that sends an email of our top 10 users at the end of each run. One simple way to add this is to extend our previous function with an additional call to some function that sends an email containing our statistics.

Listing 3.12   Two jobs in one task, to break atomicity (dags/10_non_atomic_send.py)

```
def _calculate_stats(**context):
    """Calculates event statistics."""
    input_path = context["templates_dict"]["input_path"]
    output_path = context["templates_dict"]["output_path"]

    events = pd.read_json(input_path)
    stats = events.groupby(["date", "user"]).size().reset_index()
    stats.to_csv(output_path, index=False)

    email_stats(stats, email="user@example.com")    ◁────┐
```
Sending an email after writing to CSV creates two pieces of work in a single function, which breaks the atomicity of the task.

Unfortunately, a drawback of this approach is that the task is no longer atomic. Can you see why? If not, consider what happens if our `email_stats` function fails (which is bound to happen if our email server is a bit flaky). In this case, we will already have written our statistics to the output file at `output_path`, making it seem as if our task succeeded even though it ended in failure.

To implement this functionality in an atomic fashion, we could simply split the email functionality into a separate task.

Listing 3.13 Splitting into multiple tasks to improve atomicity (dags/11_atomic_send.py)

```
def _send_stats(email, **context):
    stats = pd.read_csv(context["templates_dict"]["stats_path"])
    email_stats(stats, email=email)        ◁─┐    Split off the email_stats
                                              │    statement into a separate
                                              │    task for atomicity.
send_stats = PythonOperator(
    task_id="send_stats",
    python_callable=_send_stats,
    op_kwargs={"email": "user@example.com"},
    templates_dict={"stats_path": "/data/stats/{{ds}}.csv"},
    dag=dag,
)

calculate_stats >> send_stats
```

This way, failing to send an email no longer affects the result of the `calculate_stats` task, but only fails `send_stats`, thus making both tasks atomic.

From this example, you might think that separating all operations into individual tasks is sufficient to make all our tasks atomic. However, this is not necessarily true. To understand why, think about if our event API had required us to log in before querying for events. This would generally require an extra API call to fetch some authentication token, after which we can start retrieving our events.

Following our previous reasoning of one operation = one task, we would have to split these operations into two separate tasks. However, doing so would create a strong dependency between them, as the second task (fetching the events) will fail without running the first shortly before. This strong dependency between means we are likely better off keeping both operations within a single task, allowing the task to form a single, coherent unit of work.

Most Airflow operators are already designed to be atomic, which is why many operators include options for performing tightly coupled operations such as authentication internally. However, more flexible operators such as the Python and Bash operators may require you to think carefully about your operations to make sure your tasks remain atomic.

3.6.2 Idempotency

Another important property to consider when writing Airflow tasks is idempotency. Tasks are said to be idempotent if calling the same task multiple times with the same inputs has no additional effect. This means that rerunning a task without changing the inputs should not change the overall output.

For example, consider our last implementation of the `fetch_events` task, which fetches the results for a single day and writes this to our partitioned data set.

Listing 3.14 Existing implementation for fetching events (dags/08_templated_paths.py)

```
fetch_events = BashOperator(
    task_id="fetch_events",
    bash_command=(
        "mkdir -p /data/events && "
        "curl -o /data/events/{{ds}}.json "          ← Partitioning by setting
        "http://localhost:5000/events?"                  templated filename
        "start_date={{ds}}&"
        "end_date={{next_ds}}"
    ),
    dag=dag,
)
```

Rerunning this task for a given date would result in the task fetching the same set of events as its previous execution (assuming the date is within our 30-day window), and overwriting the existing JSON file in the /data/events folder, producing the same result. As such, this implementation of the fetch events task is clearly idempotent.

To show an example of a non-idempotent task, consider using a single JSON file (/data/events.json) and simply appending events to this file. In this case, rerunning a task would result in the events simply being appended to the existing data set, thus duplicating the day's events (figure 3.10). As such, this implementation is not idempotent, as additional executions of the task change the overall result.

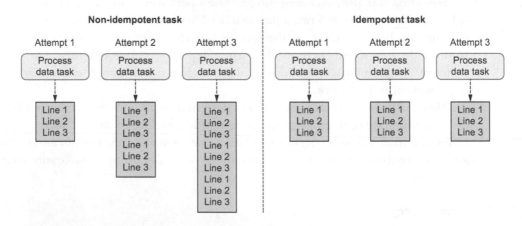

Figure 3.10 An idempotent task produces the same result, no matter how many times you run it. Idempotency ensures consistency and the ability to deal with failure.

In general, tasks that write data can be made idempotent by checking for existing results or making sure that previous results are overwritten by the task. In time-partitioned data sets, this is relatively straightforward, as we can simply overwrite the corresponding partition. Similarly, for database systems, we can use upsert operations to insert data, which allows us to overwrite existing rows that were written by previous task executions.

However, in more general applications, you should carefully consider all side effects of your task and make sure they are performed in an idempotent fashion.

Summary

- DAGs can run at regular intervals by setting the schedule interval.
- The work for an interval is started at the end of the interval.
- The schedule interval can be configured with cron and timedelta expressions.
- Data can be processed incrementally by dynamically setting variables with templating.
- The execution date refers to the start datetime of the interval, not to the actual time of execution.
- A DAG can be run back in time with backfilling.
- Idempotency ensures tasks can be rerun while producing the same output results.

Templating tasks using the Airflow context 4

This chapter covers

- Rendering variables at runtime with templating
- Variable templating with the `PythonOperator` versus other operators
- Rendering templated variables for debugging purposes
- Performing operations on external systems

In the previous chapters, we touched the surface of how DAGs and operators work together and how to schedule a workflow in Airflow. In this chapter, we look in-depth at what operators represent, what they are, how they function, and when and how they are executed. We also demonstrate how operators can be used to communicate with remote systems via hooks, which allows you to perform tasks such as loading data into a database, running a command in a remote environment, and performing workloads outside of Airflow.

4.1 Inspecting data for processing with Airflow

Throughout this chapter, we will work out several components of operators with the help of a (fictitious) stock market prediction tool that applies sentiment analysis, which we'll call StockSense. Wikipedia is one the largest public information resources on the internet. Besides the wiki pages, other items such as pageview counts are also publicly available. For the purposes of this example, we will apply the axiom that an increase in a company's pageviews shows a positive sentiment, and the company's stock is likely to increase. On the other hand, a decrease in pageviews tells us a loss in interest, and the stock price is likely to decrease.

4.1.1 Determining how to load incremental data

The Wikimedia Foundation (the organization behind Wikipedia) provides all pageviews since 2015 in machine-readable format.[1] The pageviews can be downloaded in gzip format and are aggregated per hour per page. Each hourly dump is approximately 50 MB in gzipped text files and is somewhere between 200 and 250 MB in size unzipped.

Whenever working with any sort of data, these are essential details. Any data, both small and big, can be complex, and it is important to have a technical plan of approach before building a pipeline. The solution is always dependent on what you, or other users, want to do with the data, so ask yourself and others questions such as "Do we want to process the data again at some other time in the future?"; "How do I receive the data (e.g., frequency, size, format, source type)?"; and "What are we going to build with the data?" After knowing the answers to such questions, we can address the technical details.

Let's download one single hourly dump and inspect the data by hand. In order to develop a data pipeline, we must understand how to load it in an incremental fashion and how to work the data (figure 4.1).

---

[1] https://dumps.wikimedia.org/other/pageviews. The structure and technical details of Wikipedia pageviews data is documented here: https://meta.wikimedia.org/wiki/Research:Page_view and https://wikitech.wikimedia.org/wiki/Analytics/Data_Lake/Traffic/Pageviews.

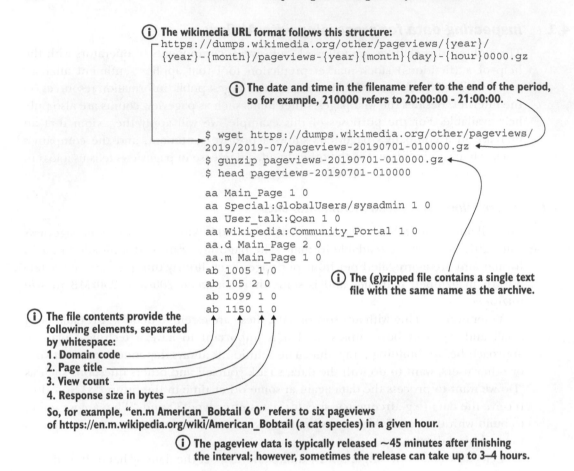

Figure 4.1   **Downloading and inspecting Wikimedia pageviews data**

We see the URLs follow a fixed pattern, which we can use when downloading the data in batch fashion (briefly touched on in chapter 3). As a thought experiment and to validate the data, let's see what the most commonly used domain codes are for July 7, 10:00–11:00 (figure 4.2).

Seeing the top results, 1061202 en and 995600 en.m, tells us the most viewed domains between July 7 10:00 and 11:00 are "en" and "en.m" (the mobile version of .en), which makes sense given English is the most used language in the world. Also, results are returned as we expect to see them, which confirms there are no unexpected characters or misalignment of columns, meaning we don't have to perform any additional processing to clean up the data. Oftentimes, cleaning and transforming data into a consistent state is a large part of the work.

```
$ wget https://dumps.wikimedia.org/other/pageviews/  2019/2019-07/pageviews-20190707-110000.gz
$ gunzip pageviews-20190707-110000.gz
$ awk -F' ' '{print $1}' pageviews-20190707-110000  | sort | uniq -c | sort -nr | head

1061202 en
995600 en.m
300753 ja.m
286381 de.m
257751 de
226334 ru
201930 ja
198182 fr.m
193331 ru.m
171510 it.m
```

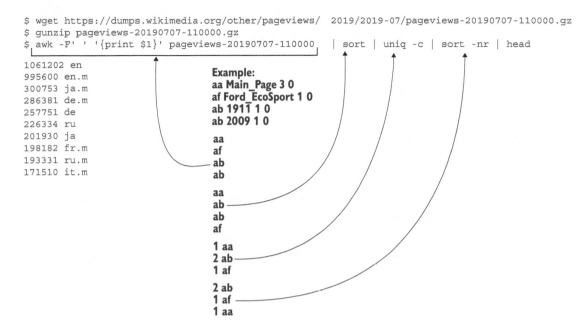

Example:
aa Main_Page 3 0
af Ford_EcoSport 1 0
ab 1911 1 0
ab 2009 1 0

aa
af
ab
ab

aa
ab
ab
af

1 aa
2 ab
1 af

2 ab
1 af
1 aa

Figure 4.2   **First simple analysis on Wikimedia pageviews data**

4.2   *Task context and Jinja templating*

Now let's put all this together and create the first version of a DAG pulling in the Wikipedia pageview counts. Let's start simple by downloading, extracting, and reading the data. We've selected five companies (Amazon, Apple, Facebook, Google, and Microsoft) to initially track and validate the hypothesis (figure 4.3).

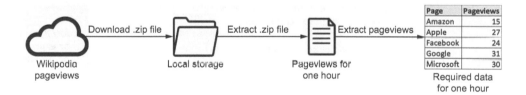

Figure 4.3   **First version of the StockSense workflow**

The first step is to download the .zip file for every interval. The URL is constructed of various date and time components:

```
https://dumps.wikimedia.org/other/pageviews/
{year}/{year}-{month}/pageviews-{year}{month}{day}-{hour}0000.gz
```

For every interval, we'll have to insert the date and time for that specific interval in the URL. In chapter 3, we briefly touched on scheduling and how to use the execution date in our code for it to execute one specific interval. Let's dive a bit deeper into how that works. There are many ways to download the pageviews; however, let's focus on the BashOperator and PythonOperator. The method to insert variables at runtime in those operators can be generalized to all other operator types.

4.2.1   *Templating operator arguments*

To start, let's download the Wikipedia pageviews using the BashOperator, which takes an argument, bash_command, to which we provide a Bash command to execute—all components of the URL where we need to insert a variable at runtime start and end with double curly braces.

Listing 4.1   Downloading Wikipedia pageviews with the BashOperator

```
import airflow.utils.dates
from airflow import DAG
from airflow.operators.bash import BashOperator

dag = DAG(
  dag_id="chapter4_stocksense_bashoperator",
  start_date=airflow.utils.dates.days_ago(3),
  schedule_interval="@hourly",
)

get_data = BashOperator(
  task_id="get_data",
  bash_command=(
    "curl -o /tmp/wikipageviews.gz "
    "https://dumps.wikimedia.org/other/pageviews/"
    "{{ execution_date.year }}/"                            ◁─── Double curly braces denote a variable inserted at runtime.
    "{{ execution_date.year }}-"
    "{{ '{:02}'.format(execution_date.month) }}/"
    "pageviews-{{ execution_date.year }}"
    "{{ '{:02}'.format(execution_date.month) }}"            ◁─┐ Any Python variable or expression can be provided.
    "{{ '{:02}'.format(execution_date.day) }}-"
    "{{ '{:02}'.format(execution_date.hour) }}0000.gz"     ◁─┘
  ),
  dag=dag,
)
```

As briefly touched on in chapter 3, the execution_date is one of the variables that is "magically" available in the runtime of a task. The double curly braces denote a Jinja-templated string. Jinja is a templating engine, which replaces variables and/or expressions in a templated string at runtime. Templating is used when you, as a programmer, don't know the value of something at the time of writing, but do know the value of something at runtime. An example is when you have a form in which you can insert your name, and the code prints the inserted name (figure 4.4).

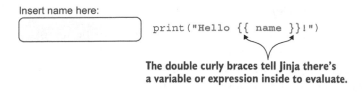

Insert name here:

```
print("Hello {{ name }}!")
```

The double curly braces tell Jinja there's a variable or expression inside to evaluate.

Figure 4.4 **Not all variables are known upfront when writing code, for example, when using interactive elements such as forms.**

The value of name is not known when programming because the user will enter their name in the form at runtime. What we do know is that the inserted value is assigned to a variable called name, and we can then provide a templated string, "Hello {{ name }}!", to render and insert the value of name at runtime.

In Airflow, you have a number of variables available at runtime from the task context. One of these variables is execution_date. Airflow uses the Pendulum (https://pendulum.eustace.io) library for datetimes, and execution_date is such a Pendulum datetime object. It is a drop-in replacement for native Python datetime, so all methods that can be applied to Python can also be applied to Pendulum. Just like you can do datetime.now().year, you get the same result with pendulum.now().year.

Listing 4.2 Pendulum behavior equal to native Python datetime

```
>>> from datetime import datetime
>>> import pendulum
>>> datetime.now().year
2020
>>> pendulum.now().year
2020
```

The Wikipedia pageviews URL requires zero-padded months, days, and hours (e.g., "07" for hour 7). Within the Jinja-templated string we therefore apply string formatting for padding:

```
{{ '{:02}'.format(execution_date.hour) }}
```

> **Which arguments are templated?**
>
> It is important to know not all operator arguments can be templates! Every operator can keep an allowlist of attributes that can be made into templates. By default, they are not, so a string {{ name }} will be interpreted as literally {{ name }} and not templated by Jinja, unless included in the list of attributes that can be templated. This list is set by the attribute template_fields on every operator. You can check these attributes in the documentation (https://airflow.apache.org/docs); go to the operator of your choice and view the template_fields item.
>
> Note the elements in template_fields are names of class attributes. Typically, the argument names provided to __init__ match the class attributes names, so everything listed in template_fields maps 1:1 to the __init__ arguments. However, technically it's possible they don't, and it should be documented as to which class attribute an argument maps.

4.2.2   *What is available for templating?*

Now that we understand which arguments of an operator can be templated, which variables do we have at our disposal for templating? We've seen execution_date used before in a number of examples, but more variables are available. With the help of the PythonOperator, we can print the full task context and inspect it.

Listing 4.3   Printing the task context

```python
import airflow.utils.dates
from airflow import DAG
from airflow.operators.python import PythonOperator

dag = DAG(
    dag_id="chapter4_print_context",
    start_date=airflow.utils.dates.days_ago(3),
    schedule_interval="@daily",
)


def _print_context(**kwargs):
    print(kwargs)


print_context = PythonOperator(
    task_id="print_context",
    python_callable=_print_context,
    dag=dag,
)
```

Running this task prints a dict of all available variables in the task context.

Listing 4.4   All context variables for the given execution date

```python
{
    'dag': <DAG: print_context>,
    'ds': '2019-07-04',
    'next_ds': '2019-07-04',
    'next_ds_nodash': '20190704',
    'prev_ds': '2019-07-03',
    'prev_ds_nodash': '20190703',
    ...
}
```

All variables are captured in **kwargs and passed to the print() function. All these variables are available at runtime. Table 4.1 provides a description of all available task context variables.

Table 4.1 All task context variables

Key	Description	Example
`conf`	Provides access to Airflow configuration	`airflow.configuration` `.AirflowConfigParser` object
`dag`	The current DAG object	DAG object
`dag_run`	The current `DagRun` object	`DagRun` object
`ds`	`execution_date` formatted as %Y-%m-%d	"2019-01-01"
`ds_nodash`	`execution_date` formatted as %Y%m%d	"20190101"
`execution_date`	The start datetime of the task's interval	`pendulum.datetime` `.DateTime` object
`inlets`	Shorthand for `task.inlets`, a feature to track input data sources for data lineage	[]
`macros`	`airflow.macros` module	`macros` module
`next_ds`	`execution_date` of the next interval (= end of current interval) formatted as %Y-%m-%d	"2019-01-02"
`next_ds_nodash`	`execution_date` of the next interval (= end of current interval) formatted as %Y%m%d	"20190102"
`next_execution_ date`	The start datetime of the task's next interval (= end of current interval)	`pendulum.datetime` `.DateTime` object
`outlets`	Shorthand for `task.outlets`, a feature to track output data sources for data lineage	[]
`params`	User-provided variables to the task context	{}
`prev_ds`	`execution_date` of the previous interval formatted as %Y-%m-%d	"2018-12-31"
`prev_ds_nodash`	`execution_date` of the previous interval formatted as %Y%m%d	"20181231"
`prev_execution_ date`	The start datetime of the task's previous interval	`pendulum.datetime` `.DateTime` object
`prev_execution_ date_success`	Start datetime of the last successfully completed run of the same task (only in past)	`pendulum.datetime` `.DateTime` object
`prev_start_date_ success`	Date and time on which the last successful run of the same task (only in past) was started	`pendulum.datetime` `.DateTime` object

Table 4.1   All task context variables *(continued)*

Key	Description	Example
`run_id`	The `DagRun`'s `run_id` (a key typically composed of a prefix + datetime)	"manual__2019-01-01T00:00:00+00:00"
`task`	The current operator	`PythonOperator` object
`task_instance`	The current `TaskInstance` object	`TaskInstance` object
`task_instance_key_str`	A unique identifier for the current `TaskInstance` (`{dag_id}__{task_id}__{ds_nodash}`)	"dag_id__task_id__20190101"
`templates_dict`	User-provided variables to the task context	{}
`test_mode`	Whether Airflow is running in test mode (configuration property)	False
`ti`	The current `TaskInstance` object, same as `task_instance`	`TaskInstance` object
`tomorrow_ds`	ds plus one day	"2019-01-02"
`tomorrow_ds_nodash`	ds_nodash plus one day	"20190102"
`ts`	execution_date formatted according to ISO8601 format	"2019-01-01T00:00:00+00:00"
`ts_nodash`	execution_date formatted as %Y%m%dT%H%M%S	"20190101T000000"
`ts_nodash_with_tz`	ts_nodash with time zone information	"20190101T000000+0000"
`var`	Helpers objects for dealing with Airflow variables	{}
`yesterday_ds`	ds minus one day	"2018-12-31"
`yesterday_ds_nodash`	ds_nodash minus one day	"20181231"

Printed using a PythonOperator run manually in a DAG with execution date 2019-01-01T00:00:00, @daily interval.

4.2.3   *Templating the PythonOperator*

The `PythonOperator` is an exception to the templating shown in section 4.2.1. With the `BashOperator` (and all other operators in Airflow), you provide a string to the `bash_command` argument (or whatever the argument is named in other operators), which is automatically templated at runtime. The `PythonOperator` is an exception to this standard, because it doesn't take arguments that can be templated with the runtime context, but instead a `python_callable` argument in which the runtime context can be applied.

Let's inspect the code downloading the Wikipedia pageviews as shown in listing 4.1 with the `BashOperator`, but now implemented with the `PythonOperator`. Functionally, this results in the same behavior.

Listing 4.5   Downloading Wikipedia pageviews with the `PythonOperator`

```
from urllib import request

import airflow
from airflow import DAG
from airflow.operators.python import PythonOperator

dag = DAG(
    dag_id="stocksense",
    start_date=airflow.utils.dates.days_ago(1),
    schedule_interval="@hourly",
)


def _get_data(execution_date):
    year, month, day, hour, *_ = execution_date.timetuple()
    url = (
        "https://dumps.wikimedia.org/other/pageviews/"
        f"{year}/{year}-{month:0>2}/"
        f"pageviews-{year}{month:0>2}{day:0>2}-{hour:0>2}0000.gz"
    )
    output_path = "/tmp/wikipageviews.gz"
    request.urlretrieve(url, output_path)


get_data = PythonOperator(
    task_id="get_data",
    python_callable=_get_data,
    dag=dag,
)
```

The Python-Operator takes a Python function, whereas the BashOperator takes a Bash command as a string to execute.

Functions are first-class citizens in Python, and we provide a *callable*[2] (a function is a callable object) to the python_callable argument of the PythonOperator. On execution, the PythonOperator executes the provided callable, which could be any function. Since it is a function, and not a string as with all other operators, the code within the function cannot be automatically templated. Instead, the task context variables can be provided and used in the given function, as shown in figure 4.5.

provide_context in the Airflow 1 and Airflow 2 PythonOperator

In Airflow 1, the task context variables must be provided explicitly by setting an argument on the PythonOperator provide_context=True, which passes all(!) task context variables to your callable:

```
PythonOperator(
    task_id="pass_context",
    python_callable=_pass_context,
```

---

[2] In Python, any object implementing __call__() is considered a callable (e.g., functions/methods).

(continued)
```
    provide_context=True,
    dag=dag,
)
```

In Airflow 2, the `PythonOperator` determines which context variables must be passed along to your callable by inferring these from the callable argument names. It is therefore not required to set `provide_context=True` anymore:

```
PythonOperator(
    task_id="pass_context",
    python_callable=_pass_context,
    dag=dag,
)
```

To remain backward compatible, the `provide_context` argument is still supported in Airflow 2; however, you can safely remove it when running on Airflow 2.

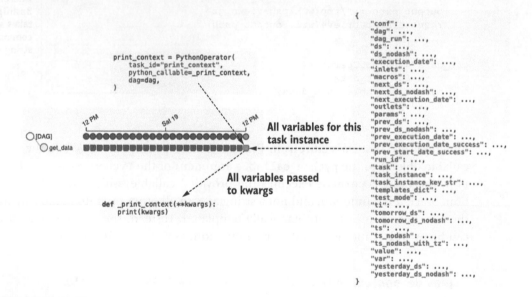

Figure 4.5   Providing task context with a `PythonOperator`

Python allows capturing keyword arguments in a function. This has various use cases, mainly for if you don't know the keyword arguments supplied upfront and to avoid having to explicitly write out all expected keyword argument names.

Listing 4.6 Keyword arguments stored in kwargs

```
def _print_context(**kwargs):
    print(kwargs)
```
← **Keyword arguments can be captured with two asterisks (**). A convention is to name the capturing argument kwargs.**

To indicate to your future self and to other readers of your Airflow code about your intentions of capturing the Airflow task context variables in the keyword arguments, a good practice is to name this argument appropriately (e.g., "context").

Listing 4.7 Renaming kwargs to context for expressing intent to store task context

```
def _print_context(**context):
    print(context)
```
← **Naming this argument context indicates we expect Airflow task context.**

```
print_context = PythonOperator(
    task_id="print_context",
    python_callable=_print_context,
    dag=dag,
)
```

The context variable is a dict of all context variables, which allows us to give our task different behavior for the interval it runs in, for example, to print the start and end datetime of the current interval:

Listing 4.8 Printing start and end date of interval

```
def _print_context(**context):
    start = context["execution_date"]
    end = context["next_execution_date"]
    print(f"Start: {start}, end: {end}")
```
← **Extract the execution_date from the context.**

```
print_context = PythonOperator(
    task_id="print_context", python_callable=_print_context, dag=dag
)

# Prints e.g.:
# Start: 2019-07-13T14:00:00+00:00, end: 2019-07-13T15:00:00+00:00
```

Now that we've seen a few basic examples, let's dissect the PythonOperator downloading the hourly Wikipedia pageviews as seen in listing 4.5 (figure 4.6).

The _get_data function called by the PythonOperator takes one argument: **context. As we've seen before, we could accept all keyword arguments in a single argument named **kwargs (the double asterisk indicates all keyword arguments, and kwargs is the actual variable's name). For indicating we expect task context variables, we could rename it to **context. There is yet another way in Python to accept keywords arguments, though.

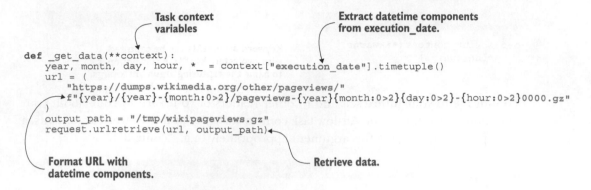

```
def _get_data(**context):
    year, month, day, hour, *_ = context["execution_date"].timetuple()
    url = (
        "https://dumps.wikimedia.org/other/pageviews/"
        f"{year}/{year}-{month:0>2}/pageviews-{year}{month:0>2}{day:0>2}-{hour:0>2}0000.gz"
    )
    output_path = "/tmp/wikipageviews.gz"
    request.urlretrieve(url, output_path)
```

Task context variables

Extract datetime components from execution_date.

Format URL with datetime components.

Retrieve data.

Figure 4.6   The `PythonOperator` takes a function instead of string arguments and thus cannot be Jinja-templated. In this called function, we extract datetime components from the `execution_date` to dynamically construct the URL.

Listing 4.9   Explicitly expecting variable `execution_date`

```
def _get_data(execution_date, **context):
    year, month, day, hour, *_ = execution_date.timetuple()
    # ...
```

This tells Python we expect to receive an argument named execution_date. It will not be captured in the context argument.

What happens under the hood is that the _get_data function is called with all context variables as keyword arguments:

Listing 4.10   All context variables are passed as keyword arguments

```
_get_data(conf=..., dag=..., dag_run=..., execution_date=..., ...)
```

Python will then check if any of the given arguments is expected in the function signature (figure 4.7).

The first argument conf is checked and not found in the signature (expected arguments) of _get_data and thus added to **context. This is repeated for dag and

```
_get_data(conf=..., dag=..., dag_run=..., execution_date=..., ...)
```

conf in the signature?   **If no, add to **context.**

```
def _get_data(execution_date, **context):
    year, month, day, hour, *_ = execution_date.timetuple()
    # ...
```

Figure 4.7   Python determines if a given keyword argument is passed to one specific argument in the function, or to the ** argument if no matching name was found.

dag_run since both arguments are not in the function's expected arguments. Next is execution_date, which we expect to receive, and thus its value is passed to the execution_date argument in _get_data() (figure 4.8).

```
_get_data(conf=..., dag=..., dag_run=..., execution_date=..., ...)
```

execution_date in the signature?
If yes, pass to argument.

```
def _get_data(execution_date, **context):
    year, month, day, hour, *_ = execution_date.timetuple()
    # ...
```

Figure 4.8   `_get_data` expects an argument named `execution_date`. No default value is set, so it will fail if not provided.

The end result with this example is that a keyword with the name execution_date is passed along to the execution_date argument and all other variables are passed along to **context since they are not explicitly expected in the function signature (figure 4.9).

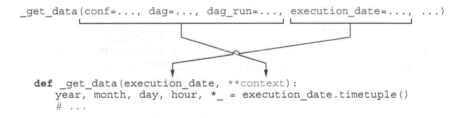

```
_get_data(conf=..., dag=..., dag_run=..., execution_date=..., ...)
```

```
def _get_data(execution_date, **context):
    year, month, day, hour, *_ = execution_date.timetuple()
    # ...
```

Figure 4.9   Any named argument can be given to `_get_data()`. `execution_date` must be provided explicitly because it's listed as an argument, all other arguments are captured by `**context`.

Now, we can directly use the execution_date variable instead of having to extract it from **context with context["execution_date"]. In addition, your code will be more self-explanatory and tools such as linters and type hinting will benefit by the explicit argument definition.

4.2.4   *Providing variables to the PythonOperator*

Now that we've seen how the task context works in operators and how Python deals with keywords arguments, imagine we want to download data from more than one data source. The _get_data() function could be duplicated and slightly altered to support a second data source. The PythonOperator, however, also supports supplying additional arguments to the callable function. For example, say we start by making the output_path configurable, so that, depending on the task, we can configure the output _path instead of having to duplicate the entire function just to change the output path (figure 4.10).

```
def _get_data(output_path, **context):
    year, month, day, hour, *_ = context["execution_date"].timetuple()
    url = (
        "https://dumps.wikimedia.org/other/pageviews/"
        f"{year}/{year}-{month:0>2}/pageviews-{year}{month:0>2}{day:0>2}-{hour:0>2}0000.gz"
    )
    request.urlretrieve(url, output_path)
```

output_path now configurable via argument

Figure 4.10   The output_path is now configurable via an argument.

The value for output_path can be provided in two ways. The first is via an argument: op_args.

Listing 4.11   Providing user-defined variables to the PythonOperator callable

```
get_data = PythonOperator(
    task_id="get_data",
    python_callable=_get_data,
    op_args=["/tmp/wikipageviews.gz"],
    dag=dag,
)
```

Provide additional variables to the callable with op_args.

On execution of the operator, each value in the list provided to op_args is passed along to the callable function (i.e., the same effect as calling the function as such directly: _get_data("/tmp/wikipageviews.gz")).

Since output_path in figure 4.10 is the first argument in the _get_data function, the value of it will be set to /tmp/wikipageviews.gz when run (we call these *non-keyword arguments*). A second approach is to use the op_kwargs argument, shown in the following listing.

Listing 4.12   Providing user-defined kwargs to callable

```
get_data = PythonOperator(
    task_id="get_data",
    python_callable=_get_data,
    op_kwargs={"output_path": "/tmp/wikipageviews.gz"},
    dag=dag,
)
```

A dict given to op_kwargs will be passed as keyword arguments to the callable.

Similar to op_args, all values in op_kwargs are passed along to the callable function, but this time as keyword arguments. The equivalent call to _get_data would be

```
_get_data(output_path="/tmp/wikipageviews.gz")
```

Note that these values can contain strings and thus can be templated. That means we could avoid extracting the datetime components inside the callable function itself and instead pass templated strings to our callable function.

Listing 4.13 Providing templated strings as input for the callable function

```
def _get_data(year, month, day, hour, output_path, **_):
    url = (
        "https://dumps.wikimedia.org/other/pageviews/"
        f"{year}/{year}-{month:0>2}/"
        f"pageviews-{year}{month:0>2}{day:0>2}-{hour:0>2}0000.gz"
    )
    request.urlretrieve(url, output_path)


get_data = PythonOperator(
    task_id="get_data",
    python_callable=_get_data,
    op_kwargs={
        "year": "{{ execution_date.year }}",          ◁────  User-defined keyword
        "month": "{{ execution_date.month }}",                arguments are templated
        "day": "{{ execution_date.day }}",                    before passing to the
        "hour": "{{ execution_date.hour }}",                  callable.
        "output_path": "/tmp/wikipageviews.gz",
    },
    dag=dag,
)
```

4.2.5 *Inspecting templated arguments*

A useful tool to debug issues with templated arguments is the Airflow UI. You can inspect the templated argument values after running a task by selecting it in either the graph or tree view and clicking the Rendered Template button (figure 4.11).

The rendered template view displays all attributes of the given operator that are render-able and their values. This view is visible per task instance. Consequently, a task must be scheduled by Airflow before being able to inspect the rendered attributes for the given task instance (i.e., you have to wait for Airflow to schedule the next task instance). During development, this can be impractical. The Airflow Command Line Interface (CLI) allows us to render templated values for any given datetime.

Listing 4.14 Rendering templated values for any given execution date

```
# airflow tasks render stocksense get_data 2019-07-19T00:00:00
# ------------------------------------------------------------
# property: templates_dict
```

```
# -----------------------------------------------------------
None

# -----------------------------------------------------------
# property: op_args
# -----------------------------------------------------------
[]

# -----------------------------------------------------------
# property: op_kwargs
# -----------------------------------------------------------
{'year': '2019', 'month': '7', 'day': '19', 'hour': '0', 'output_path':
    '/tmp/wikipageviews.gz'}
```

Task Instance: **get_data** at   📅   2020-12-19 08:00:00+01:0

⚠ Task Instance Details   ⟨ ⟩ Rendered Template   ≡ Log   ⇄ XCom

Rendered Template

templates_dict

op_args

```
1  []
```

op_kwargs

```
1  {
2      "day": "19",
3      "hour": "7",
4      "month": "12",
5      "output_path": "/tmp/wikipageviews.gz",
6      "year": "2020"
7  }
```

Figure 4.11 Inspecting the rendered template values after running a task

The CLI provides us with exactly the same information as shown in the Airflow UI, without having to run a task, which makes it easier to inspect the result. The command to render templates using the CLI is

```
airflow tasks render [dag id] [task id] [desired execution date]
```

You can enter any datetime and the Airflow CLI will render all templated attributes as if the task would run for the desired datetime. Using the CLI does not register anything in the metastore and is thus a more lightweight and flexible action.

4.3 Hooking up other systems

Now that we've worked out how templating works, let's continue the use case by processing the hourly Wikipedia pageviews. The following two operators will extract the archive and process the extracted file by scanning over it and selecting the pageview counts for the given page names. The result is then printed in the logs.

Listing 4.15 Reading pageviews for given page names

```
extract_gz = BashOperator(
    task_id="extract_gz",
    bash_command="gunzip --force /tmp/wikipageviews.gz",
    dag=dag,
)


def _fetch_pageviews(pagenames):
    result = dict.fromkeys(pagenames, 0)
    with open(f"/tmp/wikipageviews", "r") as f:
        for line in f:
            domain_code, page_title, view_counts, _ = line.split(" ")
            if domain_code == "en" and page_title in pagenames:
                result[page_title] = view_counts

    print(result)
    # Prints e.g. "{'Facebook': '778', 'Apple': '20', 'Google': '451',
     'Amazon': '9', 'Microsoft': '119'}"


fetch_pageviews = PythonOperator(
    task_id="fetch_pageviews",
    python_callable=_fetch_pageviews,
    op_kwargs={
        "pagenames": {
            "Google",
            "Amazon",
            "Apple",
            "Microsoft",
            "Facebook",
        }
    },
    dag=dag,
)
```

Annotations:
- **Open the file written in previous task.** → `with open(f"/tmp/wikipageviews", "r") as f:`
- **Extract the elements on a line.** → `domain_code, page_title, view_counts, _ = line.split(" ")`
- **Check if page_title is in given pagenames.** → `if domain_code == "en" and page_title in pagenames:`
- **Filter only domain "en."** → `if domain_code == "en" and page_title in pagenames:`

This prints, for example, {'Apple': '31', 'Microsoft': '87', 'Amazon': '7', 'Facebook': '228', 'Google': '275'}. As a first improvement, we'd like to write these counts to our own database, which allow us to query it with SQL and ask questions such as, "What is the average hourly pageview count on the Google Wikipedia page?" (figure 4.12).

We have a Postgres database to store the hourly pageviews. The table to keep the data contains three columns, shown in listing 4.16.

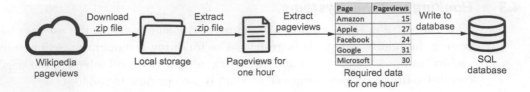

Figure 4.12   Conceptual idea of workflow. After extracting the pageviews, write the pageview counts to a SQL database.

Listing 4.16   `CREATE TABLE` statement for storing output

```
CREATE TABLE pageview_counts (
    pagename VARCHAR(50) NOT NULL,
    pageviewcount INT NOT NULL,
    datetime TIMESTAMP NOT NULL
);
```

The pagename and pageviewcount columns respectively hold the name of the Wikipedia page and the number of pageviews for that page for a given hour. The datetime column will hold the date and time for the count, which equals Airflow's execution _date for an interval. An example INSERT query would look as follows.

Listing 4.17   `INSERT` statement storing output in the pageview_counts table

```
INSERT INTO pageview_counts VALUES ('Google', 333, '2019-07-17T00:00:00');
```

This code currently prints the found pageview count, and now we want to connect the dots by writing those results to the Postgres table. The PythonOperator currently prints the results but does not write to the database, so we'll need a second task to write the results. In Airflow, there are two ways of passing data between tasks:

- By using the Airflow metastore to write and read results between tasks. This is called XCom and covered in chapter 5.
- By writing results to and from a persistent location (e.g., disk or database) between tasks.

Airflow tasks run independently of each other, possibly on different physical machines depending on your setup, and therefore cannot share objects in memory. Data between tasks must therefore be persisted elsewhere, where it resides after a task finishes and can be read by another task.

Airflow provides one mechanism out of the box called XCom, which allows storing and later reading any *picklable* object in the Airflow metastore. Pickle is Python's serialization protocol, and serialization means converting an object in memory to a format that can be stored on disk to be read again later, possibly by another process. By default, all objects built from basic Python types (e.g., string, int, dict, list) can be pickled.

Examples of non-picklable objects are database connections and file handlers. Using XComs for storing pickled objects is only suitable for smaller objects. Since Airflow's metastore (typically a MySQL or Postgres database) is finite in size and pickled objects are stored in blobs in the metastore, it's typically advised to apply XComs only for transferring small pieces of data such as a handful of strings (e.g., a list of names).

The alternative for transferring data between tasks is to keep the data outside Airflow. The number of ways to store data are limitless, but typically a file on disk is created. In the use case, we've fetched a few strings and integers, which in itself are not space-consuming. With the idea in mind that more pages might be added, and thus data size might grow in the future, we'll think ahead and persist the results on disk instead of using XComs.

In order to decide how to store the intermediate data, we must know where and how the data will be used again. Since the target database is a Postgres, we'll use the PostgresOperator to insert data. First, we must install an additional package to import the PostgresOperator class in our project:

```
pip install apache-airflow-providers-postgres
```

Airflow 2 providers packages

Since Airflow 2, most operators are installed via separate pip packages. This avoids installing dependencies you probably won't use while keeping the core Airflow package small. All additional pip packages are named

```
apache-airflow-providers-*
```

Only a few core operators remain in Airflow, such as the BashOperator and PythonOperator. Refer to the Airflow documentation to find the apache-airflow-providers package for your needs.

The PostgresOperator will run any query you provide it. Since the PostgresOperator does not support inserts from CSV data, we will first write SQL queries as our intermediate data first.

Listing 4.18 Writing INSERT statements to feed to the PostgresOperator

```
def _fetch_pageviews(pagenames, execution_date, **_):
    result = dict.fromkeys(pagenames, 0)          ◁— Initialize result for all
    with open("/tmp/wikipageviews", "r") as f:        pageviews with zero.
        for line in f:
            domain_code, page_title, view_counts, _ = line.split(" ")
            if domain_code == "en" and page_title in pagenames:
                result[page_title] = view_counts    ◁—
                                                     Store pageview
                                                     count.
    with open("/tmp/postgres_query.sql", "w") as f:
        for pagename, pageviewcount in result.items():
            f.write(
```

For each result, write SQL query.

```
                        "INSERT INTO pageview_counts VALUES ("
                        f"'{pagename}', {pageviewcount}, '{execution_date}'"
                        ");\n"
                )

fetch_pageviews = PythonOperator(
    task_id="fetch_pageviews",
    python_callable=_fetch_pageviews,
    op_kwargs={"pagenames": {"Google", "Amazon", "Apple", "Microsoft",
        "Facebook"}},
    dag=dag,
)
```

Running this task will produce a file (/tmp/postgres_query.sql) for the given interval, containing all the SQL queries to be run by the PostgresOperator. See the following example.

Listing 4.19 Multiple `INSERT` queries to feed to the `PostgresOperator`

```
INSERT INTO pageview_counts VALUES ('Facebook', 275, '2019-07-18T02:00:00+00:00');
INSERT INTO pageview_counts VALUES ('Apple', 35, '2019-07-18T02:00:00+00:00');
INSERT INTO pageview_counts VALUES ('Microsoft', 136, '2019-07-18T02:00:00+00:00');
INSERT INTO pageview_counts VALUES ('Amazon', 17, '2019-07-18T02:00:00+00:00');
INSERT INTO pageview_counts VALUES ('Google', 399, '2019-07-18T02:00:00+00:00');
```

Now that we've generated the queries, it's time to connect the last piece of the puzzle.

Listing 4.20 Calling the `PostgresOperator`

```
from airflow.providers.postgres.operators.postgres import PostgresOperator

dag = DAG(..., template_searchpath="/tmp")          ←─┤ Path to search
                                                        for sql file

write_to_postgres = PostgresOperator(
    task_id="write_to_postgres",
    postgres_conn_id="my_postgres",                 ←─ Identifier to credentials
                                                       to use for connection
    sql="postgres_query.sql",                       ←─ SQL query or path to file
    dag=dag,                                            containing SQL queries
)
```

The corresponding graph view will look like figure 4.13.

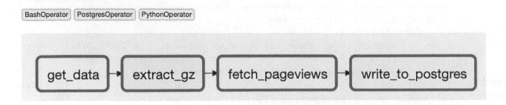

Figure 4.13 DAG fetching hourly Wikipedia pageviews and writing results to Postgres

The PostgresOperator requires filling in only two arguments to run a query against a Postgres database. Intricate operations such as setting up a connection to the database and closing it after completion are handled under the hood. The postgres_conn_id argument points to an identifier holding the credentials to the Postgres database. Airflow can manage such credentials (stored encrypted in the metastore), and operators can fetch one of the credentials when required. Without going into detail, we can add the my_postgres connection in Airflow with the help of the CLI.

Listing 4.21 Storing credentials in Airflow with the CLI

```
airflow connections add \
--conn-type postgres \
--conn-host localhost \
--conn-login postgres \
--conn-password mysecretpassword \     The connection
my_postgres                            identifier
```

The connection is then visible in the UI (it can also be created from there). Go to Admin > Connections to view all connections stored in Airflow (figure 4.14).

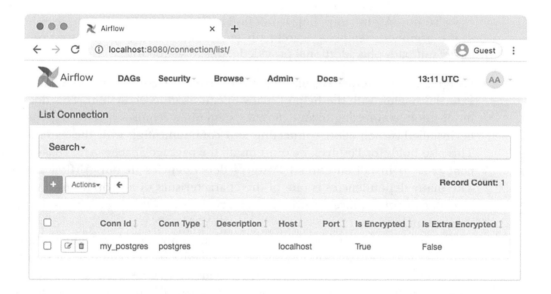

Figure 4.14   Connection listed in Airflow UI

Once a number of DAG runs have completed, the Postgres database will hold a few counts:

```
"Amazon",12,"2019-07-17 00:00:00"
"Amazon",11,"2019-07-17 01:00:00"
```

```
"Amazon",19,"2019-07-17 02:00:00"
"Amazon",13,"2019-07-17 03:00:00"
"Amazon",12,"2019-07-17 04:00:00"
"Amazon",12,"2019-07-17 05:00:00"
"Amazon",11,"2019-07-17 06:00:00"
"Amazon",14,"2019-07-17 07:00:00"
"Amazon",15,"2019-07-17 08:00:00"
"Amazon",17,"2019-07-17 09:00:00"
```

There's a number of things to point out in this last step. The DAG has an additional argument: `template_searchpath`. Besides a string `INSERT INTO ...`, the content of files can also be templated. Each operator can read and template files with specific extensions by providing the file path to the operator. In the case of the `Postgres-Operator`, the argument SQL can be templated and thus a path to a file holding a SQL query can also be provided. Any filepath ending in .sql will be read, templates in the file will be rendered, and the queries in the file will be executed by the `Postgres-Operator`. Again, refer to the documentation of the operators and check the field `template_ext`, which holds the file extensions that can be templated by the operator.

> **NOTE** Jinja requires you to provide the path to search for files that can be templated. By default, only the path of the DAG file is searched for, but since we've stored it in /tmp, Jinja won't find it. To add paths for Jinja to search, set the argument template_searchpath on the DAG and Jinja will traverse the default path plus additional provided paths to search for.

Postgres is an external system and Airflow supports connecting to a wide range of external systems with the help of many operators in its ecosystem. This does have an implication: connecting to an external system often requires specific dependencies to be installed, which allow connecting and communicating with the external system. This also holds for Postgres; we must install the package `apache-airflow-providers-postgres` to install additional Postgres dependencies in our Airflow installation. The many dependencies is one of the characteristics of any orchestration system—in order to communicate with many external systems it is inevitable to install many dependencies.

Upon execution of the `PostgresOperator`, a number of things happen (figure 4.15). The `PostgresOperator` will instantiate a so-called *hook* to communicate with Postgres. The hook deals with creating a connection, sending queries to Postgres and closing the connection afterward. The operator is merely passing through the request from the user to the hook in this situation.

> **NOTE** An operator determines what has to be done; a hook determines how to do something.

When building pipelines like these, you will only deal with operators and have no notion of any hooks, because hooks are used internally in operators.

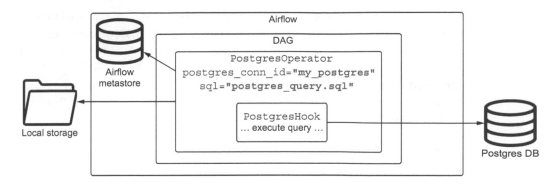

Figure 4.15 Running a SQL script against a Postgres database involves several components. Provide the correct settings to the `PostgresOperator`, and the `PostgresHook` will do the work under the hood.

After a number of DAG runs, the Postgres database will contain a few records extracted from the Wikipedia pageviews. Once an hour, Airflow now automatically downloads the new hourly pageviews data set, unzips it, extracts the desired counts, and writes these to the Postgres database. We can now ask questions such as "At which hour is each page most popular?"

Listing 4.22 SQL query asking which hour is most popular per page

```
SELECT x.pagename, x.hr AS "hour", x.average AS "average pageviews"
FROM (
 SELECT
   pagename,
   date_part('hour', datetime) AS hr,
   AVG(pageviewcount) AS average,
   ROW_NUMBER() OVER (PARTITION BY pagename ORDER BY AVG(pageviewcount) DESC)
 FROM pageview_counts
 GROUP BY pagename, hr
) AS x
WHERE row_number=1;
```

This listing gives us the most popular time to view given pages is between 16:00 and 21:00, shown in table 4.2.

Table 4.2 Query results showing which hour is most popular per page

Pagename	Hour	Average pageviews
Amazon	18	20
Apple	16	66
Facebook	16	500
Google	20	761
Microsoft	21	181

With this query, we have now completed the envisioned Wikipedia workflow, which performs a full cycle of downloading the hourly pageview data, processing the data, and writing results to a Postgres database for future analysis. Airflow is responsible for orchestrating the correct time and order of starting tasks. With the help of the task runtime context and templating, code is executed for a given interval, using the date-time values that come with that interval. If all is set up correctly, the workflow can now run until infinity.

Summary

- Some arguments of operators can be templated.
- Templating happens at runtime.
- Templating the `PythonOperator` works different from other operators; variables are passed to the provided callable.
- The result of templated arguments can be checked with `airflow tasks render`.
- Operators can communicate with other systems via hooks.
- Operators describe *what* to do; hooks determine *how* to do work.

Defining dependencies between tasks

This chapter covers

- Examining how to define task dependencies in an Airflow DAG
- Explaining how to implement joins using trigger rules
- Showing how to make tasks conditional on certain conditions
- Giving a basic idea of how trigger rules affect the execution of your tasks
- Demonstrating how to use XComs to share state between tasks
- Examining how Airflow 2's Taskflow API can help simplify Python-heavy DAGs

In previous chapters, we saw how to build a basic DAG and define simple dependencies between tasks. In this chapter, we will further explore exactly how task dependencies are defined in Airflow and how these capabilities can be used to implement more complex patterns, including conditional tasks, branches, and joins. Toward the end of the chapter, we'll also dive into XComs (which allow passing data between different tasks in a DAG run), and discuss the merits and drawbacks of using this type of approach. We'll also show how Airflow 2's new Taskflow API can help simplify DAGs that make heavy use of Python tasks and XComs.

5.1 Basic dependencies

Before going into more complex task dependency patterns such as branching and conditional tasks, let's first take a moment to examine the different patterns of task dependencies that we've encountered in the previous chapters. This includes both linear chains of tasks (tasks that are executed one after another), and fan-out/fan-in patterns (which involve one task linking to multiple downstream tasks, or vice versa). To make sure we're all on the same page, we'll briefly go into the implications of these patterns in the next few sections.

5.1.1 Linear dependencies

So far, we've mainly focused on examples of DAGs consisting of a single linear chain of tasks. For example, our rocket launch–picture fetching DAG from chapter 2 (figure 5.1) consisted of a chain of three tasks: one for downloading launch metadata, one for downloading the images, and one for notifying us when the entire process has been completed.

> **Listing 5.1 Tasks in the rocket picture–fetching DAG (chapter02/dags/listing_2_10.py)**

```
download_launches = BashOperator(...)
get_pictures = PythonOperator(...)
notify = BashOperator(...)
```

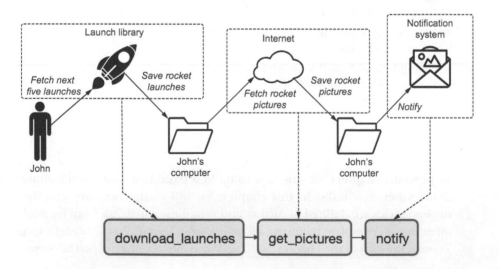

Figure 5.1   Our rocket-picture-fetching DAG from chapter 2 (originally shown in figure 2.3) consists of three tasks: downloading metadata, fetching the images, and sending a notification.

In this type of DAG, each task must be completed before going to the next, because the result of the preceding task is required as input for the next. As we have seen, Airflow allows us to indicate this type of relationship between two tasks by creating a dependency between them using the right bitshift operator.

> **Listing 5.2   Adding dependencies between the tasks (chapter02/dags/listing_2_10.py)**

```
download_launches >> get_pictures          Set task dependencies
get_pictures >> notify                     one-by-one...

download_launches >> get_pictures >> notify    ... or set multiple
                                               dependencies in one go.
```

Task dependencies effectively tell Airflow that it can only start executing a given task once its upstream dependencies have finished executing successfully. In the example, this means that get_pictures can only start executing once download_launches has run successfully. Similarly, notify can only start once the get_pictures task has been completed without error.

One advantage of explicitly specifying task dependencies is that it clearly defines the (implicit) ordering in our tasks. This enables Airflow to schedule tasks only when their dependencies have been met, which is more robust than (for example) scheduling individual tasks one after another using Cron and hoping that preceding tasks will have completed by the time the second task is started (figure 5.2). Moreover, any errors will be propagated to downstream tasks by Airflow, effectively postponing their execution. This means that in the case of a failure in the download_launches task, Airflow won't try to execute the get_pictures task for that day until the issue with download _launches has been resolved.

5.1.2   Fan-in/-out dependencies

In addition to linear chains of tasks, Airflow's task dependencies can be used to create more complex dependency structures between tasks. For an example, let's revisit our umbrella use case from chapter 1, in which we wanted to train a machine learning model to predict the demand for our umbrellas in the upcoming weeks based on the weather forecast.

As you might remember, the main purpose of the umbrella DAG was to fetch weather and sales data daily from two different sources and combine the data into a data set for training our model. As such, the DAG (figure 5.2) starts with two sets of tasks for fetching and cleaning our input data, one for the weather data (fetch_weather and clean_weather) and one for the sales data (fetch_sales and clean_sales). These tasks are followed by a task (join_datasets) that takes the resulting cleaned sales and weather data and joins them into a combined data set for training a model. Finally, this data set is used to train the model (train_model), after which the model is deployed by the final task (deploy_model).

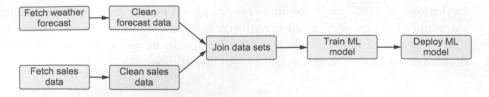

Figure 5.2   Overview of the DAG from the umbrella use case in chapter 1

Thinking about this DAG in terms of dependencies, there is a linear dependency between the `fetch_weather` and `clean_weather` tasks, as we need to fetch the data from our remote data source before we can do any cleaning of the data. However, because the fetching/cleaning of the weather data is independent of the sales data, there is no cross dependency between the weather and sales tasks. This means we can define the dependencies for the `fetch` and `clean` tasks as follows.

```
fetch_weather >> clean_weather
fetch_sales >> clean_sales
```

Upstream of the two `fetch` tasks, we also could have added a dummy `start` task representing the start of our DAG. In this case, this task is not strictly necessary, but it helps illustrate the implicit fan-out occurring at the beginning of our DAG, in which the start of the DAG kicks off both the `fetch_weather` and `fetch_sales` tasks. Such a fan-out dependency (linking one task to multiple downstream tasks) could be defined as follows.

```
from airflow.operators.dummy import DummyOperator

start = DummyOperator(task_id="start")        ◁——————  Create a dummy start task.
start >> [fetch_weather, fetch_sales]    ◁┐  Create a fan-out
                                          │  (one-to-multiple) dependency.
```

In contrast to the parallelism of the `fetch`/`clean` tasks, building the combined data set requires input from both the weather and sales branches. As such, the `join_datasets` task has a dependency on both the `clean_weather` and `clean_sales` tasks and can run only once both these upstream tasks have been completed successfully. This type of structure, where one task has a dependency on multiple upstream tasks, is often referred to as a *fan-in structure*, as it consists of multiple upstream tasks "fanning into" a single downstream task. In Airflow, fan-in dependencies can be defined as follows.

Listing 5.5   Adding a fan-in (multiple-to-one) dependency (dags/01_start.py)

```
[clean_weather, clean_sales] >> join_datasets
```

After fanning in with the `join_datasets` task, the remainder of the DAG is a linear chain of tasks for training and deploying the model.

Listing 5.6   Adding the remaining dependencies (dags/01_start.py)

```
join_datasets >> train_model >> deploy_model
```

Combined, this should give something similar to the DAG shown in figure 5.3.

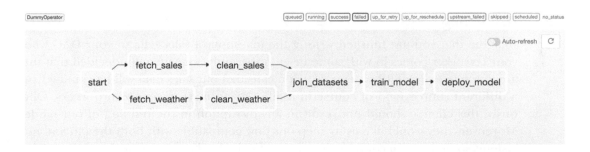

Figure 5.3   The umbrella DAG, as rendered by Airflow's graph view. This DAG performs several tasks, including fetching and cleaning sales data, combining them into a data set, and using the data set to train a machine learning model. Note that the handling of sales/weather data happens in separate branches of the DAG, as these tasks are not directly dependent on each other.

What do you think happens if we now start executing this DAG? Which tasks will start running first? Which tasks do you think will (not) be running in parallel?

As you might expect, if we run the DAG, Airflow will start by first running the `start` task (figure 5.4). After the `start` task completes, it will initiate the `fetch_sales` and `fetch_weather` tasks, which will run in parallel (assuming your Airflow is configured to have multiple workers). Completion of either of the `fetch` tasks will result in the start of the corresponding cleaning tasks (`clean_sales` or `clean_weather`). Only once both the `clean` tasks have been completed can Airflow finally start executing the `join_datasets` task. Finally, the rest of the DAG will execute linearly, with `train_model` running as soon as the `join_datasets` task has been completed and `deploy_model` running after completion of the `train_model` task.

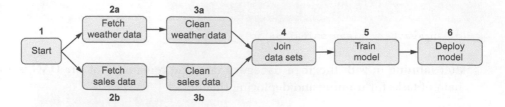

Figure 5.4   The execution order of tasks in the umbrella DAG, with numbers indicating the order in which tasks are run. Airflow starts by executing the *start* task, after which it can run the *sales/weather* `fetch` and clean tasks in parallel (as indicated by the a/b suffix). Note that this means that the weather/sales paths run independently, meaning that 3b may, for example, start executing before 2a. After completing both `clean` tasks, the rest of the DAG proceeds linearly with the execution of the `join`, `train`, and `deployment` tasks.

5.2   Branching

Imagine that you just finished writing the ingestion of sales data in your DAG when your coworker comes in with some news. Apparently, management decided that they are going to switch ERP systems, which means that our sales data will be coming from a different source (and of course in a different format) in one or two weeks. Obviously, this change should not result in any disruption in the training of our model. Moreover, they would like us to keep our flow compatible with both the old and new systems so that we can continue to use historical sales data in our future analyses. How would you go about solving this problem?

5.2.1   Branching within tasks

One approach could be to rewrite our sales ingestion tasks to check the current execution date and use that to decide between two separate code paths for ingesting and processing the sales data. For example, we could rewrite our sales cleaning task to something like this.

Listing 5.7   Branching within the cleaning task (dags/02_branch_task.py)

```
def _clean_sales(**context):
    if context["execution_date"] < ERP_CHANGE_DATE:
        _clean_sales_old(**context)
    else
        _clean_sales_new(**context)

...

clean_sales_data = PythonOperator(
    task_id="clean_sales",
    python_callable=_clean_sales,
)
```

In this example, _clean_sales_old is a function that does the cleaning for the old sales format and _clean_sales_new does the same for the new format. As long as the result of these is compatible (in terms of columns, data types, etc.), the rest of our DAG can stay unchanged and doesn't need to worry about differences between the two ERP systems.

Similarly, we could make our initial ingestion step compatible with both ERP systems by adding code paths for ingesting from both systems.

Listing 5.8 Branching within the fetch task (dags/02_branch_task.py)

```python
def _fetch_sales(**context):
    if context["execution_date"] < ERP_CHANGE_DATE:
        _fetch_sales_old(**context)
    else:
        _fetch_sales_new(**context)
    ...
```

Combined, these changes would allow our DAG to handle data from both systems in a relatively transparent fashion, as our initial fetching/cleaning tasks make sure that the sales data arrives in the same (processed) format independent of the corresponding data source.

An advantage of this approach is that it allows us to incorporate some flexibility in our DAGs without having to modify the structure of the DAG itself. However, this approach works only in cases where the branches in our code consist of similar tasks. Here, for example, we effectively have two branches in our code that both perform a fetching and cleaning operation with minimal differences. But what if loading data from the new data source requires a very different chain of tasks (figure 5.5)? In that case, we may be better off splitting our data ingestion into two separate sets of tasks.

Figure 5.5 A possible example of different sets of tasks between the two ERP systems. If there is a lot of commonality between different cases, you may be able to get away with a single set of tasks and some internal branching. However, if there are many differences between the two flows (such as shown here for the two ERP systems), you may be better off taking a different approach.

Another drawback of this approach is that it is difficult to see which code branch is being used by Airflow during a specific DAG run. For example, in figure 5.6, can you

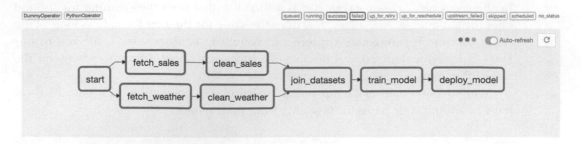

Figure 5.6 Example run for a DAG that branches between two ERP systems within the `fetch_sales` and `clean_sales` tasks. Because this branching happens within these two tasks, it is not possible to see which ERP system was used in this DAG run from this view. This means we would need to inspect our code (or possibly our logs) to identify which ERP system was used.

guess which ERP system was used for this specific DAG run? This seemingly simple question is quite difficult to answer using only this view, as the actual branching is hidden within our tasks. One way to solve this is to include better logging in our tasks, but as we will see there are also other ways to make branching more explicit in the DAG itself.

Finally, we can only encode this type of flexibility into our tasks by falling back to general Airflow operators such as the `PythonOperator`. This prevents us from leveraging functionality provided by more specialized Airflow operators, which allow us to perform more complicated work with minimal coding effort. For example, if one of our data sources happened to be a SQL database, it would save us a lot of work if we could simply use the `MysqlOperator` to execute a SQL query, as this allows us to delegate the actual execution of the query (together with authentication, etc.) to the provided operator.

Fortunately, checking for conditions within tasks is not the only way to perform branching in Airflow. In the next section, we will show how to weave branches into your DAG structure, which provides more flexibility than the task-based approach.

5.2.2 *Branching within the DAG*

Another way to support the two different ERP systems in a single DAG is to develop two distinct sets of tasks (one for each system) and allow the DAG to choose whether to execute the tasks for fetching data from either the old or new ERP system (figure 5.7).

Building the two sets of tasks is relatively straightforward: we can simply create tasks for each ERP system separately using the appropriate operators and link the respective tasks.

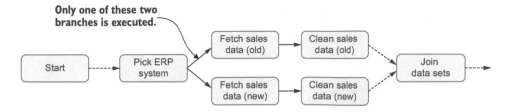

Figure 5.7 Supporting two ERP systems using branching within the DAG, implementing different sets of tasks for both systems. Airflow can choose between these two branches using a specific branching task (here, "Pick ERP system"), which tells Airflow which set of downstream tasks to execute.

Listing 5.9 Adding extra fetch/clean tasks (dags/03_branch_dag.py)

```
fetch_sales_old = PythonOperator(...)
clean_sales_old = PythonOperator(...)

fetch_sales_new = PythonOperator(...)
clean_sales_new = PythonOperator(...)

fetch_sales_old >> clean_sales_old
fetch_sales_new >> clean_sales_new
```

Now we still need to connect these tasks to the rest of our DAG and make sure that Airflow knows which it should execute when.

Fortunately, Airflow provides built-in support for choosing between sets of downstream tasks using the BranchPythonOperator. This operator is (as the name suggests) similar to the PythonOperator in the sense that it takes a Python callable as one of its main arguments.

Listing 5.10 Branching with the BranchPythonOperator (dags/03_branch_dag.py)

```
def _pick_erp_system(**context):
    ...

pick_erp_system = BranchPythonOperator(
    task_id="pick_erp_system",
    python_callable=_pick_erp_system,
)
```

However, in contrast to the PythonOperator, callables passed to the BranchPython-Operator are expected to return the ID of a downstream task as a result of their computation. The returned ID determines which of the downstream tasks will be executed after completion of the branch task. Note that you can also return a list of task IDs, in which case Airflow will execute all referenced tasks.

In this case, we can implement our choice between the two ERP systems by using the callable to return the appropriate task_id depending on the execution date of the DAG.

Listing 5.11   Adding the branching condition function (dags/03_branch_dag.py)

```
def _pick_erp_system(**context):
    if context["execution_date"] < ERP_SWITCH_DATE:
        return "fetch_sales_old"
    else:
        return "fetch_sales_new"

pick_erp_system = BranchPythonOperator(
    task_id="pick_erp_system",
    python_callable=_pick_erp_system,
)

pick_erp_system >> [fetch_sales_old, fetch_sales_new]
```

This way, Airflow will execute our set of "old" ERP tasks for execution dates occurring before the switch date while executing the new tasks after this date. Now, all that needs to be done is connect these tasks with the rest of our DAG.

To connect our branching task to the start of the DAG, we can add a dependency between our previous start task and the pick_erp_system task.

Listing 5.12   Connecting the branch to the start task (dags/03_branch_dag.py)

```
start_task >> pick_erp_system
```

Similarly, you might expect that connecting the two cleaning tasks is as simple as adding a dependency between the cleaning tasks and the join_datasets task (similar to our earlier situation where clean_sales was connected to join_datasets).

Listing 5.13   Connecting the branch to the join_datasets task (dags/03_branch_dag.py)

```
[clean_sales_old, clean_sales_new] >> join_datasets
```

However, if you do this, running the DAG would result in the join_datasets task and all its downstream tasks being skipped by Airflow. (You can try it out if you wish.)

The reason for this is that, by default, Airflow requires all tasks upstream of a given task to complete successfully before that the task itself can be executed. By connecting both of our cleaning tasks to the join_datasets task, we created a situation where this can never occur, as only one of the cleaning tasks is ever executed. As a result, the join_datasets task can never be executed and is skipped by Airflow (figure 5.8).

This behavior that defines when tasks are executed is controlled by so-called *trigger rules* in Airflow. Trigger rules can be defined for individual tasks using the trigger _rule argument, which can be passed to any operator. By default, trigger rules are set to all_success, meaning that all parents of the corresponding task need to succeed before the task can be run. This never happens when using the BranchPythonOperator, as it skips any tasks that are not chosen by the branch, which explains why the join_datasets task and all its downstream tasks were also skipped by Airflow.

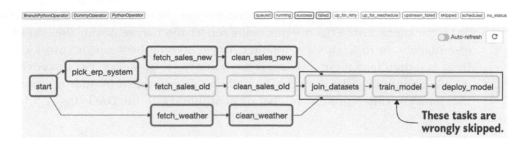

Figure 5.8 Combining branching with the wrong trigger rules will result in downstream tasks being skipped. In this example, the `fetch_sales_new` task is skipped as a result of the sales branch. This results in all tasks downstream of the `fetch_sales_new` task also being skipped, which is clearly not what we want.

To fix this situation, we can change the trigger rule of `join_datasets` so that it can still trigger if one of its upstream tasks is skipped. One way to achieve this is to change the trigger rule to `none_failed`, which specifies that a task should run as soon as all of its parents are done with executing and none have failed.

Listing 5.14   Fixing the trigger rule of the join_datasets task (dags/03_branch_dag.py)

```
join_datasets = PythonOperator(
    ...,
    trigger_rule="none_failed",
)
```

This way, `join_datasets` will start executing as soon as all of its parents have finished executing without any failures, allowing it to continue its execution after the branch (figure 5.9).

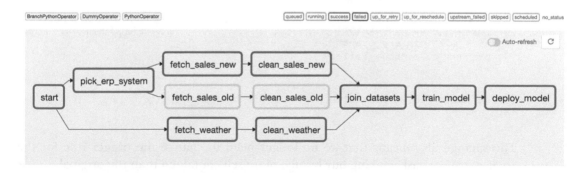

Figure 5.9   Branching in the umbrella DAG using trigger rule `none_failed` for the `join_datasets` task, which allows it (and its downstream dependencies) to still execute after the branch

One drawback of this approach is that we now have three edges going into the join_datasets task. This doesn't really reflect the nature of our flow, in which we essentially want to fetch sales/weather data (choosing between the two ERP systems first) and then feed these two data sources into join_datasets. For this reason, many people choose to make the branch condition more explicit by adding a dummy task that joins the different branches before continuing with the DAG (figure 5.10).

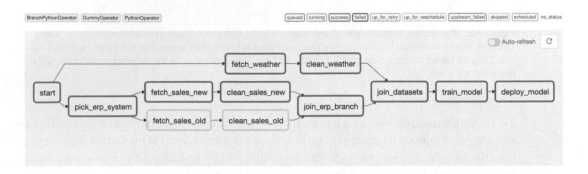

Figure 5.10   To make the branching structure more clear, you can add an extra join task after the branch, which ties the lineages of the branch together before continuing with the rest of the DAG. This extra task has the added advantage that you don't have to change any trigger rules for other tasks in the DAG, as you can set the required trigger rule on the join task. (Note that this means you no longer need to set the trigger rule for the join_datasets task.)

To add such a dummy task to our DAG, we can use the built-in DummyOperator provided by Airflow.

Listing 5.15   Adding a dummy join task for clarity (dags/04_branch_dag_join.py)

```python
from airflow.operators.dummy import DummyOperator

join_branch = DummyOperator(
    task_id="join_erp_branch",
    trigger_rule="none_failed"
)

[clean_sales_old, clean_sales_new] >> join_branch
join_branch >> join_datasets
```

This change also means that we no longer need to change the trigger rule for the join_datasets task, making our branch more self-contained than the original.

5.3 Conditional tasks

Airflow also provides you with other mechanisms for skipping specific tasks in your DAG depending on certain conditions. This allows you to make certain tasks run only if certain data sets are available, or only if your DAG is executing for the most recent execution date.

For example, in our umbrella DAG (figure 5.3), we have a task that deploys every model we train. However, consider what happens if a colleague makes some changes to the cleaning code and wants to use backfilling to apply these changes to the entire data set. In this case, backfilling the DAG would also result in deploying many old instances of our model, which we certainly aren't interested in.

5.3.1 Conditions within tasks

We can avoid this issue by changing the DAG to only deploy the model for the most recent DAG run, as this ensures we only deploy one version of our model: the one trained on the most recent data set. One way to do this is to implement the deployment using the `PythonOperator` and explicitly checking the execution date of the DAG within the deployment function.

Listing 5.16 Implementing a condition within a task (dags/05_condition_task.py)

```
def _deploy(**context):
    if context["execution_date"] == ...:
        deploy_model()

deploy = PythonOperator(
    task_id="deploy_model",
    python_callable=_deploy,
)
```

Although this implementation should have the intended effect, it has the same drawbacks as the corresponding branching implementation: it confounds the deployment logic with the condition, we can no longer use any other built-in operators than the `PythonOperator`, and tracking of task results in the Airflow UI becomes less explicit (figure 5.11).

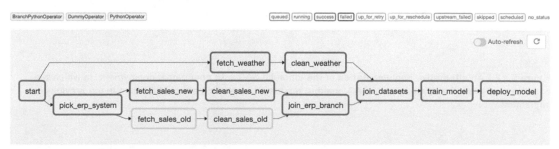

Figure 5.11 Example run for umbrella DAG with a condition inside the `deploy_model` task, which ensures that the deployment is only performed for the latest run. Because the condition is checked internally within the `deploy_model` task, we cannot discern from this view whether the model was actually deployed.

5.3.2 *Making tasks conditional*

Another way to implement conditional deployments is to make the deployment task itself conditional, meaning that it is only executed based on a predefined condition (in this case whether the DAG run is the most recent). In Airflow, you can make tasks conditional by adding a task to the DAG that tests the said condition and ensures any downstream tasks are skipped if the condition fails.

Additionally, we can make our deployment conditional by adding a task that checks if the current execution is the most recent DAG execution and adding our deployment task downstream of this task.

Listing 5.17   Building the condition into the DAG (dags/06_condition_dag.py)

```
def _latest_only(**context):
    ...


latest_only = PythonOperator(
    task_id="latest_only",
    python_callable=_latest_only,
    dag=dag,
)


latest_only >> deploy_model
```

This now means that our DAG should look something like what's shown in figure 5.12, with the `train_model` task now connected to our new task and the `deploy_model` task downstream of this new task.

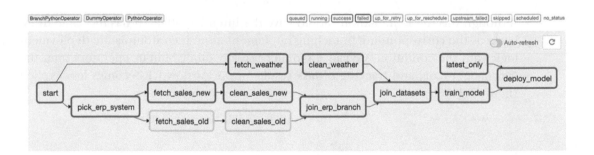

Figure 5.12   An alternative implementation of the umbrella DAG with conditional deployment, in which the condition is included as a task in the DAG, making the condition much more explicit than in our previous implementation.

Next, we need to fill in our `_latest_only` function to make sure that downstream tasks are skipped if the `execution_date` does not belong to the most recent run. To do so, we need to check our execution date and, if required, raise an `AirflowSkip-Exception` from our function, which is Airflow's way of allowing us to indicate that the condition and all its downstream tasks should be skipped, thus skipping the deployment.

This gives us something like the following implementation for our condition.

Listing 5.18   Implementing the _latest_only condition (dags/06_condition_dag.py)

```
from airflow.exceptions import AirflowSkipException                          Find the boundaries for
                                                                            our execution window.
def _latest_only(**context):
    left_window = context["dag"].following_schedule(context["execution_date"])   ◁─┘
    right_window = context["dag"].following_schedule(left_window)

    now = pendulum.now("UTC")                    ◁─┤ Check if our current time
    if not left_window < now <= right_window:         is within the window.
        raise AirflowSkipException("Not the most recent run!")
```

We can check if this does what we expect by executing our DAGs for a few dates. This should show something similar to figure 5.13, where we see that our deployment task has been skipped in all DAG runs except the latest one.

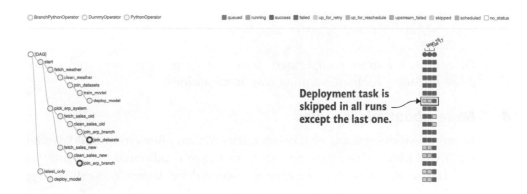

Figure 5.13   Result of our `latest_only` condition for three runs of our umbrella DAG. This tree view shows that our deployment task was only run for the most recent execution window, as the deployment task was skipped on previous executions. This shows that our condition indeed functions as expected.

How does this work? Essentially, what happens is that when our condition task (`latest _only`) raises an `AirflowSkipException`, the task is finished and assigned a skipped state. Next, Airflow looks at the trigger rules of any downstream tasks to determine if they should be triggered. In this case, we only have one downstream task (the deployment task), which uses the default trigger rule `all_success`, indicating that the task should only execute if all its upstream tasks are successful. In this case, this is not true as its parent (the condition task) has a skipped state rather than success, and therefore the deployment is skipped.

Conversely, if the condition task does not raise an `AirflowSkipException`, it completes successfully and is given a success status. As such, the deployment task gets triggered as all its parents have completed successfully, and we get our deployment.

5.3.3   *Using built-in operators*

As only running tasks for the most recent DAG run is a common use case, Airflow also provides the built-in `LatestOnlyOperator` class. This operator effectively performs the same job as our custom-built implementation based on the `PythonOperator`. Using the `LatestOnlyOperator`, we can also implement our conditional deployment like this, which saves us writing our own complex logic.

Listing 5.19   Using the built-in LatestOnlyOperator (dags/07_condition_dag_op.py)

```
from airflow.operators.latest_only import LatestOnlyOperator

latest_only = LatestOnlyOperator(
    task_id="latest_only",
    dag=dag,
)

train_model >> latest_only >> deploy_model
```

Of course, for more complicated cases, the `PythonOperator`-based route provides more flexibility for implementing custom conditions.

5.4   *More about trigger rules*

In the previous sections, we have seen how Airflow allows us to build dynamic behavior DAGs, which allows us to encode branches or conditional statements directly into our DAGs. Much of this behavior is governed by Airflow's so-called trigger rules, which determine exactly when a task is executed. We skipped over trigger rules relatively quickly in the previous sections, so now we'll explore what they represent and what you can do with them in more detail.

To understand trigger rules, we first have to examine how Airflow executes tasks within a DAG run. In essence, when Airflow is executing a DAG, it continuously checks each of your tasks to see whether it can be executed. As soon as a task is deemed ready for execution, it is picked up by the scheduler and scheduled to be executed. As a result, the task is executed as soon as Airflow has an execution slot available.

So how does Airflow determine when a task can be executed? That is where trigger rules come in.

5.4.1 What is a trigger rule?

Trigger rules are essentially the conditions that Airflow applies to tasks to determine whether they are ready to execute, as a function of their dependencies (= preceding tasks in the DAG). Airflow's default trigger rule is `all_success`, which states that all of a task's dependencies must have completed successfully before the task itself can be executed.

To see what this means, let's jump back to our initial implementation of the umbrella DAG (figure 5.4), which does not use any trigger rules other than the default `all_success` rule. If we were to start executing this DAG, Airflow would start looping over its tasks to determine which tasks can be executed (i.e., which tasks have no dependencies that have not been completed successfully).

In this case, only the `start` task satisfies this condition by not having any dependencies. As such, Airflow starts executing our DAG by first running the `start` task (figure 5.14a). Once the `start` task has been completed successfully, the `fetch_weather` and `fetch_sales` tasks become ready for execution, as their only dependency now satisfies their trigger rule (figure 5.14b). By following this pattern of execution, Airflow can continue executing the remaining tasks in the DAG until the entire DAG has been executed.

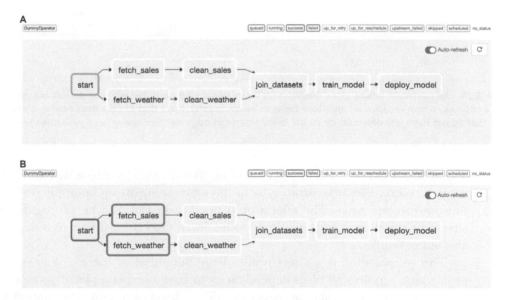

Figure 5.14 Tracing the execution of the basic umbrella DAG (figure 5.4) using the default trigger rule `all_success`. (A) Airflow initially starts executing the DAG by running the only task that has no preceding tasks that have not been completed successfully: the `start` task. **(B)** Once the `start` task has been completed with success, other tasks become ready for execution and are picked up by Airflow.

5.4.2   *The effect of failures*

Of course, this only sketches the situation for a happy flow, in which all of our tasks complete successfully. What, for example, happens if one of our tasks encounters an error during execution?

We can easily test this by simulating a failure in one of the tasks. For example, by simulating a failed `fetch_sales` task, we can see that Airflow will record the failure by assigning the `fetch_sales` the failed state rather than the success state (figure 5.15). This means that the downstream `clean_sales` task can no longer be executed, as it requires `fetch_sales` to be successful. As a result, the `clean_sales` task is assigned the state `upstream_failed`, which indicates that it cannot proceed as a result of the upstream failure.

Figure 5.15   An upstream failure stops downstream tasks from being executed with the default trigger rule `all_success`, which requires all upstream tasks to be successful. Note that Airflow does continue executing tasks that do not have any dependency on the failed task (`fetch_weather` and `clean_weather`).

This type of behavior, where the result of upstream tasks also affects downstream tasks, is often referred to as *propagation*, as in this case the upstream failure is *propagated* to the downstream tasks. The effects of skipped tasks can also be propagated downstream by the default trigger rule, resulting in all tasks downstream of a skipped task also being skipped.

This propagation is a direct result of the definition of the `all_success` trigger rule, which requires all of its dependencies to have been completed successfully. As such, if it encounters a skip or failure in a dependency, it has no other option than to fail in the same manner, thus propagating the skip or failure.

5.4.3 Other trigger rules

Airflow also supports several other trigger rules. These rules allow for different types of behavior when responding to successful, failed, or skipped tasks.

For example, let's look back at our branching pattern between the two ERP systems in section 5.2. In this case, we had to adjust the trigger rule of the task joining the branch (done by the `join_datasets` or `join_erp_branch` tasks) to avoid downstream tasks being skipped, because with the default trigger rule the skips resulting from the branch would be propagated downstream, resulting in all tasks after the branch being skipped as well. In contrast, the `none_failed` trigger rule only checks if all upstream tasks have been completed without failing. This means that it tolerates both successful and skipped tasks while still waiting for all upstream tasks to complete before continuing, making the trigger rule suitable for joining the two branches. Note that in terms of propagation this means the rule does not propagate skips. It does, however, still propagate failures, meaning that any failures in the `fetch/clean` tasks will still halt the execution of downstream tasks.

Similarly, other trigger rules can be used to handle other types of situations. For example, the trigger rule `all_done` can be used to define tasks that are executed as soon as their dependencies are finished executing, regardless of their results. This can, for example, be used to execute cleanup code (e.g., shutting down your machine or cleaning up resources) that you would like to run regardless of what happens. Another category of trigger rules includes eager rules such as `one_failed` or `one_success`, which don't wait for all upstream tasks to complete before triggering but require only one upstream task to satisfy their condition. As such, these rules can be used to signal early failure of tasks or to respond as soon as one task out of a group of tasks has been completed successfully.

Although we won't go any deeper into trigger rules here, we hope this gives you an idea of the role of trigger rules in Airflow and how they can be used to introduce more complex behavior into your DAG. For a complete overview of the trigger rules and some potential use cases, see table 5.1.

Table 5.1 An overview of the different trigger rules supported by Airflow

Trigger rule	Behavior	Example use case
`all_success` (default)	Triggers when all parent tasks have been completed successfully	The default trigger rule for a normal workflow
`all_failed`	Triggers when all parent tasks have failed (or have failed as a result of a failure in their parents)	Trigger error handling code in situations where you expected at least one success among a group of tasks
`all_done`	Triggers when all parents are done with their execution, regardless of their resulting state	Execute cleanup code that you want to execute when all tasks have finished (e.g., shutting down a machine or stopping a cluster)

Table 5.1   An overview of the different trigger rules supported by Airflow (continued)

Trigger rule	Behavior	Example use case
one_failed	Triggers as soon as at least one parent has failed; does not wait for other parent tasks to finish executing	Quickly trigger some error handling code, such as notifications or rollbacks
one_success	Triggers as soon as one parent succeeds; does not wait for other parent tasks to finish executing	Quickly trigger downstream computations/notifications as soon as one result becomes available
none_failed	Triggers if no parents have failed but have either completed successfully or been skipped	Join conditional branches in Airflow DAGs, as shown in section 5.2
none_skipped	Triggers if no parents have been skipped but have either completed successfully or failed	Trigger a task if all upstream tasks were executed, ignoring their result(s)
dummy	Triggers regardless of the state of any upstream tasks	Testing

5.5   *Sharing data between tasks*

Airflow also allows you to share small pieces of data between tasks using XComs.[1] The idea behind XComs is that they essentially allow you to exchange messages between tasks, enabling some level of shared state.

5.5.1   *Sharing data using XComs*

To see how this works, let's look back at our umbrella use case (figure 5.3). Imagine that when training our model (in the train_model task), the trained model is registered in a model registry using a randomly generated identifier. To deploy the trained model, we somehow need to pass this identifier to the deploy_model task so that it knows which version of the model it should deploy.

One way to solve this problem is to use XComs to share the model identifier between the train_model and deploy_model tasks. In this case, the train_model task is responsible for pushing the XCom value, which essentially publishes the value and makes it available for other tasks. We can publish XCom values explicitly within our task using the xcom_push method, which is available on the task instance in the Airflow context.

Listing 5.20   Pushing Xcom values explicitly using xcom_push (dags/09_xcoms.py)

```
def _train_model(**context):
    model_id = str(uuid.uuid4())
    context["task_instance"].xcom_push(key="model_id", value=model_id)
```

---

[1] XCom is an abbreviation of "cross-communication."

```
train_model = PythonOperator(
    task_id="train_model",
    python_callable=_train_model,
)
```

This call to xcom_push effectively tells Airflow to register our model_id value as an XCom value for the corresponding task (train_model) and the corresponding DAG and execution date. After running this task, you can view these published XCom values in the web interface in the "Admin > XComs" section (figure 5.16), which shows an overview of all published XCom values.

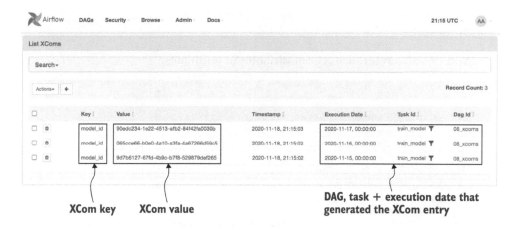

Figure 5.16 Overview of registered XCom values (under Admin > XComs in the web interface)

You can retrieve the XCom value in other tasks using the xcom_pull method, which is the inverse of xcom_push.

Listing 5.21 Retrieving XCom values using xcom_pull (dags/09_xcoms.py)

```
def _deploy_model(**context):
    model_id = context["task_instance"].xcom_pull(
        task_ids="train_model", key="model_id"
    )
    print(f"Deploying model {model_id}")

deploy_model = PythonOperator(
    task_id="deploy_model",
    python_callable=_deploy_model,
)
```

This tells Airflow to fetch the XCom value with key model_id from the train_model task, which matches the model_id we previously pushed in the train_model task. Note that xcom_pull also allows you to define the dag_id and execution date when fetching

XCom values. By default, these parameters are set to the current DAG and execution date so that xcom_pull only fetches values published by the current DAG run.[2]

We can verify this works by running the DAG, which should give us something like the following result for the deploy_model task.

```
[2020-07-29 20:23:03,581] {python.py:105} INFO - Exporting the following env
➥ vars:
AIRFLOW_CTX_DAG_ID=chapter5_09_xcoms
AIRFLOW_CTX_TASK_ID=deploy_model
AIRFLOW_CTX_EXECUTION_DATE=2020-07-28T00:00:00+00:00
AIRFLOW_CTX_DAG_RUN_ID=scheduled__2020-07-28T00:00:00+00:00
[2020-07-29 20:23:03,584] {logging_mixin.py:95} INFO - Deploying model
➥ f323fa68-8b47-4e21-a687-7a3d9b6e105c
[2020-07-29 20:23:03,584] {python.py:114} INFO - Done.
➥ Returned value was: None
```

You can also reference XCom variables in templates.

Listing 5.22   **Using XCom values in templates (dags/10_xcoms_template.py)**

```python
def _deploy_model(templates_dict, **context):
    model_id = templates_dict["model_id"]
    print(f"Deploying model {model_id}")


deploy_model = PythonOperator(
    task_id="deploy_model",
    python_callable=_deploy_model,
    templates_dict={
        "model_id": "{{task_instance.xcom_pull(
        ➥ task_ids='train_model', key='model_id')}}"
    },
)
```

Finally, some operators also provide support for automatically pushing XCom values. For example, the BashOperator has an option xcom_push, which when set to true tells the operator to push the last line written to stdout by the bash command as an XCom value. Similarly, the PythonOperator will publish any value returned from the Python callable as an XCom value. This means you can also write our example as follows.

Listing 5.23   **Using return to push XComs (dags/11_xcoms_return.py)**

```python
def _train_model(**context):
    model_id = str(uuid.uuid4())
    return model_id
```

This works by registering the XCom under the default key return_value, as we can see by looking in the Admin section (figure 5.17).

---

[2] You can specify other values to fetch values from other DAGs or other execution dates, but we would strongly recommend against this unless you have an extremely good reason to do so.

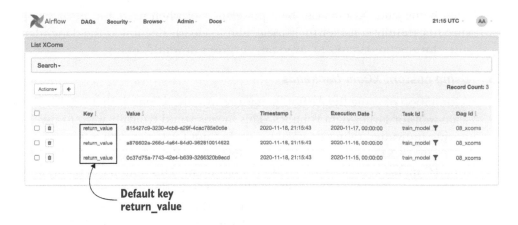

Figure 5.17 Implicit XComs from the `PythonOperator` are registered under the `return_value` key.

5.5.2 When (not) to use XComs

Although XComs may seem pretty useful for sharing state between tasks, their use also has some drawbacks. For example, one is that they add a hidden dependency between tasks, as the pulling task has an implicit dependency on the task pushing the required value. In contrast to explicit task dependencies, this dependency is not visible in the DAG and will not be taken into account when scheduling the tasks. As such, you're responsible for making sure that tasks with XCom dependencies are executed in the correct order; Airflow won't do this for you. These hidden dependencies become even more complicated when sharing XCom values between different DAGs or execution dates, which is also not a practice we would recommend following.

XComs can also be a bit of an anti-pattern when they break the atomicity of an operator. For example, we've seen people use an operator to fetch an API token in one task and then pass the token to the next task using an XCom. In this case, a drawback was that the token expired after a couple of hours, meaning that any rerun of the second task failed. A better approach may have been to combine the fetching of the token in the second task, as this way both the refreshing of the API token and performing the associated work happen in one go (thus keeping the task atomic).

Finally, a technical limitation of XComs is that any value stored by an XCom needs to support being serialized. This means that some Python types, such as lambdas or many multiprocessing related classes, generally cannot be stored in an XCom (though you probably shouldn't want to do that anyway). Additionally, the size of an XCom value may be limited by the backend used to store them. By default, XComs are stored in the Airflow metastore and are subject to the following size limits:

- *SQLite*—Stored as BLOB type, 2GB limit
- *PostgreSQL*—Stored as BYTEA type, 1 GB limit
- *MySQL*—Stored as BLOB type, 64 KB limit

That being said, XComs can be a powerful tool when used appropriately. Just make sure to carefully consider their usage and to clearly document the dependencies they introduce between tasks to avoid any surprises down the road.

5.5.3 Using custom XCom backends

A limitation of using the Airflow metastore to store XComs is that it generally does not scale well for larger data volumes. This means you'd typically want to use XComs for storing individual values or small results but not for larger data sets.

To make XComs more flexible, Airflow 2 introduces an option for specifying a custom XCom backend for your Airflow deployment. This option essentially allows you to define a custom class that Airflow will use for storing/retrieving XComs. The only requirement is that this class inherits from the BaseXCom base class and implements two static methods for serializing and deserializing values, respectively.

Listing 5.24   Skeleton for a custom XCom backend (lib/custom_xcom_backend.py)

```
from typing import Any
from airflow.models.xcom import BaseXCom

class CustomXComBackend(BaseXCom):

    @staticmethod
    def serialize_value(value: Any):
        ...

    @staticmethod
    def deserialize_value(result) -> Any:
        ...
```

In this custom backend class, the serialize method is called whenever an XCom value is pushed within an operator, whereas the deserialize method is called when XCom values are pulled from the backend. Once you have the desired backend class, you can configure Airflow to use the class with the xcom_backend parameter in the Airflow config.

Custom XCom backends greatly expand the options you have for storing XCom values. For example, if you'd like to store larger XCom values in relatively cheap and scalable cloud storage, you could implement a custom backend for cloud services such as Azure Blob storage, Amazon's S3, or Google's GCS. As Airflow 2 matures, we expect backends for common services to become more generally available, meaning you won't have to build your own backends for these services.

5.6   Chaining Python tasks with the Taskflow API

Although XComs can be used to share data between Python tasks, the API can be cumbersome to use, especially if you're chaining a large number of tasks. To solve this issue, Airflow 2 adds a new decorator-based API for defining Python tasks and their dependencies called the *Taskflow API*. Although not without its flaws, the Taskflow API can considerably simplify your code if you're primarily using `PythonOperators` and passing data between them as XComs.

5.6.1 Simplifying Python tasks with the Taskflow API

To see what the Taskflow API looks like, let's revisit our tasks for training and deploying the machine learning model. In our previous implementation, these tasks and their dependencies were defined as follows.

Listing 5.25 Defining train/deploy tasks using the regular API (dags/09_xcoms.py)

```
def _train_model(**context):
    model_id = str(uuid.uuid4())
    context["task_instance"].xcom_push(key="model_id", value=model_id)

def _deploy_model(**context):
    model_id = context["task_instance"].xcom_pull(
        task_ids="train_model", key="model_id"
    )
    print(f"Deploying model {model_id}")


with DAG(...) as dag:
    ...

    train_model = PythonOperator(
        task_id="train_model",
        python_callable=_train_model,
    )

    deploy_model = PythonOperator(
        task_id="deploy_model",
        python_callable=_deploy_model,
    )

    ...
    join_datasets >> train_model >> deploy_model
```

Defining the train/deploy functions → (marks `def _train_model` and `def _deploy_model`)

Sharing the model ID using XComs → (marks `xcom_push` and `xcom_pull` lines)

Creating the train/deploy tasks using the PythonOperator → (marks `train_model = PythonOperator(` and `deploy_model = PythonOperator(`)

Setting dependencies between the tasks → (marks `join_datasets >> train_model >> deploy_model`)

A drawback of this approach is that it first requires us to define a function (e.g., `_train_model` and `_deploy_model`), which we then need to wrap in a `PythonOperator` to create the Airflow task. Moreover, to share the model ID between the two tasks, we need to explicitly use `xcom_push` and `xcom_pull` within the functions to send/retrieve the model's ID value. Defining this data dependency is cumbersome and prone to break if we change the key of the shared value, which is referenced in two different locations.

The Taskflow API aims to simplify the definition of this type of (`PythonOperator`-based) task by making it easier to convert Python functions to tasks and making the sharing of variables via XComs between these tasks more explicit in the DAG definition. To see how this works, let's start by converting these functions to use this alternative API.

First, we can change the definition of our `train_model` task into a relatively simple Python function, decorated with the new `@task` decorator added by the Taskflow API.

Listing 5.26   Defining the train task using the Taskflow API (dags/12_taskflow.py)

```
...
from airflow.decorators import task
...

with DAG(...) as dag:
    ...
    @task
    def train_model():
        model_id = str(uuid.uuid4())
        return model_id
```

This effectively tells Airflow to wrap our `train_model` function so that we can use it to define Python tasks using the Taskflow API. Note that we are no longer explicitly pushing the model ID as an XCom, but simply returning it from the function so that the Taskflow API can take care of passing it on to the next task.

Similarly, we can define our `deploy_model` task as follows.

Listing 5.27   Defining the deploy task using the Taskflow API (dags/12_taskflow.py)

```
@task
def deploy_model(model_id):
    print(f"Deploying model {model_id}")
```

Here, the model ID is also no longer retrieved using `xcom_pull` but simply passed to our Python function as an argument. Now, the only thing left to do is to connect the two tasks, which we can do using a syntax that looks suspiciously like normal Python code.

Listing 5.28   Defining dependencies between Taskflow tasks (dags/12_taskflow.py)

```
model_id = train_model()
deploy_model(model_id)
```

This code should result in a DAG with two tasks (`train_model` and `deploy_model`) and a dependency between the two tasks (figure 5.18).

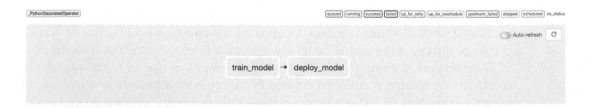

Figure 5.18   Subset of our previous DAG containing the `train/deploy` tasks, in which tasks and their dependencies are defined using the Taskflow API

Comparing the new code to our previous implementation, the Taskflow-based approach provides similar results with code that is easier to read and looks more like normal Python code. But how does it work?

In essence, when we call the decorated `train_model` function, it creates a new operator instance for the `train_model` task (shown as the `_PythonDecoratedOperator` in figure 5.18). From the return statement in the `train_model` function, Airflow recognizes that we are returning a value that will automatically be registered as an XCom returned from the task. For the `deploy_model` task, we also call the decorated function to create an operator instance, but now also pass along the `model_id` output from the `train_model` task. In doing so, we're effectively telling Airflow that the `model_id` output from `train_model` should be passed as an argument to the decorated `deploy_model` function. This way, Airflow will both realize there is a dependency between the two tasks and take care of passing the XCom values between the two tasks for us.

5.6.2   When (not) to use the Taskflow API

The Taskflow API provides a simple approach for defining Python tasks and their dependencies, using a syntax that is closer to using regular Python functions than the more object-oriented operator API. This allows the API to dramatically simplify DAGs that make heavy use of `PythonOperators` and pass data between the resulting tasks using XComs. The API also addresses one of our previous criticisms of using XComs by ensuring that values are passed explicitly between tasks, rather than hiding dependencies between tasks within the corresponding functions.

However, one drawback of the Taskflow API is that its use is currently limited to Python tasks that would otherwise be implemented using the `PythonOperator`. As such, tasks involving any other Airflow operators will require using the regular API to define tasks and their dependencies. Although this does not prevent you from mixing and matching the two styles, the resulting code can become confusing if you're not careful. For example, when combining our new `train`/`deploy` tasks back into our original DAG (figure 5.19), we need to define a dependency between the `join_data-sets` task and the `model_id` reference, which is not incredibly intuitive.

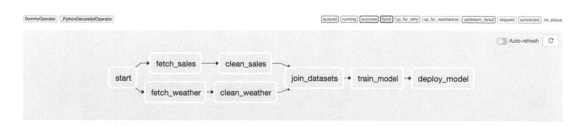

Figure 5.19   Combining the Taskflow-style `train`/`deploy` tasks back into the original DAG, which also contains other (non-`PythonOperator`-based) operators

Listing 5.29   Combining other operators with Taskflow (dags/13_taskflow_full.py)

```
with DAG(...) as dag:
    start = DummyOperator(task_id="start")        ◁──  Defining tasks and
    ...                                                dependencies using
    [clean_sales, clean_weather] >> join_datasets ◁── the regular API


    @task
    def train_model():                    ◁─┐
        model_id = str(uuid.uuid4())        │
        return model_id                     │
                                            │  Using the Taskflow
    @task                                   │  API for Python tasks
    def deploy_model(model_id: str):    ◁───  and dependencies
        print(f"Deploying model {model_id}")│
                                            │
    model_id = train_model()            ◁─┘
    deploy_model(model_id)
                                     ┌─  Mixing the two styles with a dependency
    join_datasets >> model_id    ◁──┘   between a Taskflow style and a regular task
```

Any data passed between Taskflow-style tasks will be stored as XComs. This means that
all passed values are subject to the technical limitations of XComs (i.e., they must be
serializable). Moreover, the size of data sets passed between tasks may be limited by the
XCom backend used by your Airflow deployment, as discussed in the previous section.

Summary

- Airflow's basic task dependencies can be used to define linear task dependencies and fan-in/fan-out structures in Airflow DAGs.
- Using the `BranchPythonOperator`, you can build branches into your DAGs, allowing you to choose multiple execution paths depending on certain conditions.
- Using conditional tasks, you can execute tasks depending on specific conditions.
- Explicitly encoding branches/conditions in your DAG structure provides substantial benefits in terms of the interpretability of how your DAG was executed.
- The triggering of Airflow tasks is controlled by trigger rules, which govern behaviors and can be configured to allow tasks to respond to different situations.
- State can be shared between tasks using XComs.
- The Taskflow API can help simplify DAGs containing Python-heavy DAGs.

Part 2

Beyond the basics

Now that you're familiar with Airflow's basics and able to build some of your own data pipelines, you're ready to learn some more advanced techniques that allow you to build more complex cases involving external systems, custom components, and more.

In chapter 6, we'll examine how you can trigger pipelines in ways that don't involve fixed schedules. This allows you to trigger pipelines in response to certain events, such as new files coming in or a call from an HTTP service.

Chapter 7 will demonstrate how to use Airflow's built-in functionality to run tasks on external systems. This is an extremely powerful feature of Airflow that allows you to build pipelines that coordinate data flows across many different systems, such as databases, computational frameworks such as Apache Spark, and storage systems.

Next, chapter 8 will show you how you can build custom components for Airflow, allowing you to execute tasks on systems not supported by Airflow's built-in functionality. This functionality can also be used to build components that can easily be reused across your pipelines to support common workflows.

To help increase the robustness of your pipelines, chapter 9 elaborates on different strategies you can use to test your data pipelines and custom components. This has been a commonly recurring topic in Airflow meet-ups, so we'll spend some time exploring it.

Finally, chapter 10 dives into using container-based approaches for implementing tasks in your pipelines. We'll show you how you can run tasks using both Docker and Kubernetes and discuss several advantages and drawbacks of using containers for your tasks.

After completing part 2, you should be well underway to becoming an advanced Airflow user, being able to write complex (and testable) pipelines that optionally involve custom components and/or containers. However, depending on your interests, you may want to pick specific chapters to focus on, as not all chapters may be relevant to your use case.

Triggering workflows

6

This chapter covers

- Waiting for certain conditions to be met with sensors
- Deciding how to set dependencies between tasks in different DAGs
- Executing workflows via the CLI and REST API

In chapter 3, we explored how to schedule workflows in Airflow based on a time interval. The time intervals can be given as convenience strings (e.g., `"@daily"`), timedelta objects (e.g., `timedelta(days=3)`), or cron strings (e.g., `"30 14 * * *"`). These are all notations to instruct the workflow to trigger at a certain time or interval. Airflow will compute the next time to run the workflow given the interval and start the first task(s) in the workflow at the next date and time.

In this chapter, we explore other ways to trigger workflows. This is often desired following a certain action, in contrast to the time-based intervals, which start workflows at predefined times. Trigger actions are often the result of external events; think of a file being uploaded to a shared drive, a developer pushing their code to a repository, or the existence of a partition in a Hive table, any of which could be a reason to start running your workflow.

6.1   *Polling conditions with sensors*

One common use case to start a workflow is the arrival of new data; imagine a third party delivering a daily dump of its data on a shared storage system between your company and the third party. Assume we're developing a popular mobile couponing app and are in contact with all supermarket brands to deliver a daily export of their promotions that are going to be displayed in our couponing app. Currently, the promotions are mostly a manual process: most supermarkets employ pricing analysts to take many factors into account and deliver accurate promotions. Some promotions are well thought out weeks in advance, and some are spontaneous one-day flash sales. The pricing analysts carefully study competitors, and sometimes promotions are made late at night. Hence, the daily promotions data often arrives at random times. We saw data arrive on the shared storage between 16:00 and 2:00 the next day, although the daily data can be delivered at any time of the day.

Let's develop the initial logic for such a workflow (figure 6.1).

Figure 6.1   Initial logic for processing supermarket promotions data

In this workflow, we copy the supermarkets' (1–4) delivered data into our own raw storage from which we can always reproduce results. The `process_supermarket_{1,2,3,4}` tasks then transform and store all raw data in a results database that can be read by the app. And finally, the `create_metrics` task computes and aggregates several metrics that give insights in the promotions for further analysis.

With data from the supermarkets arriving at varying times, the timeline of this workflow could look like figure 6.2.

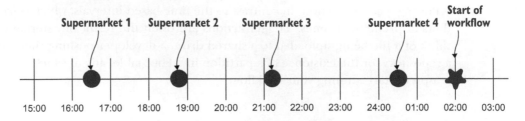

Figure 6.2   Timeline of processing supermarket promotion data

Here we see the data delivery times of the supermarkets and the start time of our workflow. Since we've experienced supermarkets delivering data as late as 2:00, a safe bet would be to start the workflow at 2:00 to be certain all supermarkets have delivered their data. However, this results in lots of waiting time. Supermarket 1 delivered its data at 16:30, while the workflow starts processing at 2:00 but does nothing for 9.5 hours (figure 6.3).

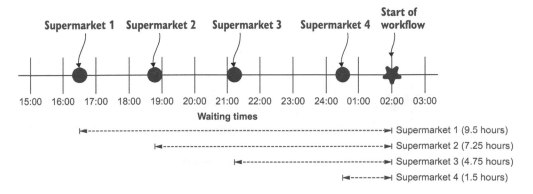

Figure 6.3 Timeline of supermarket promotion workflow with waiting times

One way to solve this in Airflow is with the help of *sensors*, which are a special type (subclass) of operators. Sensors continuously poll for certain conditions to be true and succeed if so. If false, the sensor will wait and try again until either the condition is true or a timeout is eventually reached.

Listing 6.1 A FileSensor waits for a filepath to exist

```
from airflow.sensors.filesystem import FileSensor

wait_for_supermarket_1 = FileSensor(
    task_id="wait_for_supermarket_1",
    filepath="/data/supermarket1/data.csv",
)
```

This `FileSensor` will check for the existence of /data/supermarket1/data.csv and return true if the file exists. If not, it returns false and the sensor will wait for a given period (default 60 seconds) and try again. Both operators (sensors are also operators) and DAGs have configurable timeouts, and the sensor will continue checking the condition until a timeout is reached. We can inspect the output of sensors in the task logs:

```
{file_sensor.py:60} INFO - Poking for file /data/supermarket1/data.csv
{file_sensor.py:60} INFO - Poking for file /data/supermarket1/data.csv
{file_sensor.py:60} INFO - Poking for file /data/supermarket1/data.csv
{file_sensor.py:60} INFO - Poking for file /data/supermarket1/data.csv
{file_sensor.py:60} INFO - Poking for file /data/supermarket1/data.csv
```

Here we see that approximately once a minute,[1] the sensor *pokes* for the availability of the given file. *Poking* is Airflow's name for running the sensor and checking the sensor condition.

When incorporating sensors into this workflow, one change should be made. Now that we know we won't wait until 2:00 and assume all data is available, but instead start continuously, checking if the data is available, the DAG start time should be placed at the start of the data arrival boundaries (figure 6.4).

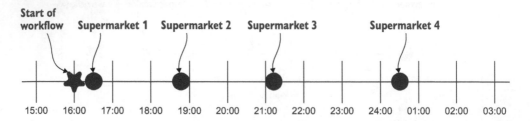

Figure 6.4   Supermarket promotions timeline with sensors

The corresponding DAG will have a task (`FileSensor`) added to the start of processing each supermarket's data and would look like figure 6.5.

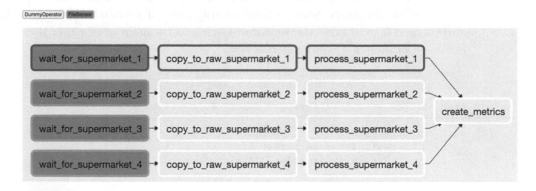

Figure 6.5   Supermarket promotion DAG with sensors in Airflow

In figure 6.5, sensors were added at the start of the DAG and the DAG's `schedule_interval` was set to start *before* the expected delivery of data. This way, sensors at the start of the DAG would continuously poll for the availability of data and continue to the next task once the condition has been met (i.e., once the data is available in the given path).

---

[1] Configurable with the `poke_interval` argument.

Here we see supermarket 1 has already delivered data, which sets the state of its corresponding sensor to success and continues processing its downstream tasks. As a result, data was processed directly after delivery, without unnecessarily waiting until the end of the expected time of delivery.

6.1.1   Polling custom conditions

Some data sets are large and consist of multiple files (e.g., data-01.csv, data-02.csv, data-03.csv, etc.). Airflow's FileSensor supports wildcards to match, for example, data-*.csv, which will match any file matching the pattern. So, if, for example, the first file data-01.csv is delivered while others are still being uploaded to the shared storage by the supermarket, the FileSensor would return true and the workflow would continue to the copy_to_raw task, which is undesirable.

Therefore, we agreed with the supermarkets to write a file named _SUCCESS as the last part of uploading, to indicate the full daily data set was uploaded. The data team decided they want to check for both the existence of one or more files named data-*.csv and one file named _SUCCESS. Under the hood the FileSensor uses *globbing* (https://en.wikipedia.org/wiki/Glob) to match patterns against file or directory names. While globbing (similar to regex but more limited in functionality) would be able to match multiple patterns with a complex pattern, a more readable approach is to implement the two checks with the PythonSensor.

The PythonSensor is similar to the PythonOperator in the sense that you supply a Python callable (function, method, etc.) to execute. However, the PythonSensor callable is limited to returning a Boolean value: true to indicate the condition is met successfully, false to indicate it is not. Let's check out a PythonSensor callable checking these two conditions.

Listing 6.2   Implementing a custom condition with the PythonSensor

```
from pathlib import Path

from airflow.sensors.python import PythonSensor

def _wait_for_supermarket(supermarket_id):            Initialize Path object.
    supermarket_path = Path("/data/" + supermarket_id)
    data_files = supermarket_path.glob("data-*.csv")       Collect data-*.csv files.
    success_file = supermarket_path / "_SUCCESS"       Collect _SUCCESS file.
    return data_files and success_file.exists()

                                                       Return whether both
                                                       data and success files
                                                       exist.
wait_for_supermarket_1 = PythonSensor(
    task_id="wait_for_supermarket_1",
    python_callable=_wait_for_supermarket,
    op_kwargs={"supermarket_id": "supermarket1"},
    dag=dag,
)
```

The callable supplied to the PythonSensor is executed and expected to return a Boolean true or false. The callable shown in listing 6.2 now checks two conditions, namely

if both the data and the success file exist. Other than using a different color, the
`PythonSensor` tasks appear the same in the UI (figure 6.6).

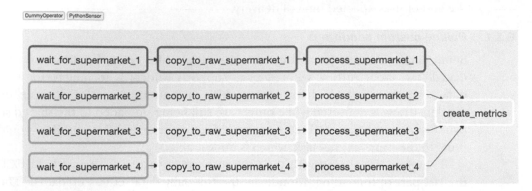

Figure 6.6   Supermarket promotion DAG using `PythonSensors` for custom conditions

6.1.2   *Sensors outside the happy flow*

Now that we've seen sensors running successfully, what happens if a supermarket one
day doesn't deliver its data? By default, sensors will fail just like operators (figure 6.7).

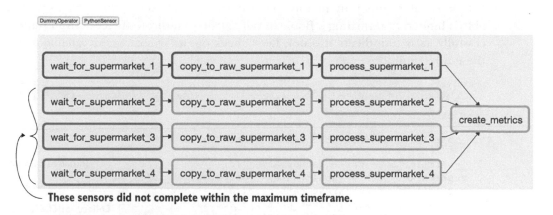

Figure 6.7   Sensors exceeding the maximum timeframe will fail.

Sensors accept a `timeout` argument, which holds the maximum number of seconds a
sensor is allowed to run. If, at the start of the next poke, the number of running seconds turns out to be higher than the number set to timeout, the sensor will fail:

```
INFO - Poking callable: <function wait_for_supermarket at 0x7fb2aa1937a0>
INFO - Poking callable: <function wait_for_supermarket at 0x7fb2aa1937a0>
ERROR - Snap. Time is OUT.
```

```
Traceback (most recent call last):
  ➥ File "/usr/local/lib/python3.7/site-
    packages/airflow/models/taskinstance.py", line 926, in _run_raw_task
    result = task_copy.execute(context=context)
  ➥ File "/usr/local/lib/python3.7/site-
    packages/airflow/sensors/base_sensor_operator.py", line 116, in execute
    raise AirflowSensorTimeout('Snap. Time is OUT.')
airflow.exceptions.AirflowSensorTimeout: Snap. Time is OUT.
INFO - Marking task as FAILED.
```

By default, the sensor timeout is set to seven days. If the DAG `schedule_interval` is set to once a day, this will lead to an undesired snowball effect—which is surprisingly easy to encounter with many DAGs! The DAG runs once a day, and supermarkets 2, 3, and 4 will fail after seven days, as shown in figure 6.7. However, new DAG runs are added every day and the sensors for those respective days are started, and as a result more and more tasks start running. Here's the catch: there's a limit to the number of tasks Airflow can handle and will run (on various levels).

It is important to understand there are limits to the maximum number of running tasks on various levels in Airflow; the number of tasks per DAG, the number of tasks on a global Airflow level, the number of DAG runs per DAG, and so on. In figure 6.8, we see 16 running tasks (which are all sensors). The DAG class has a `concurrency` argument, which controls how many simultaneously running tasks are allowed within that DAG.

Listing 6.3 Setting the maximum number of concurrent tasks in a DAG

```
dag = DAG(
    dag_id="couponing_app",
    start_date=datetime(2019, 1, 1),
    schedule_interval="0 0 * * *",
    concurrency=50,          ◁─┐ This DAG allows 50
)                                concurrently running tasks.
```

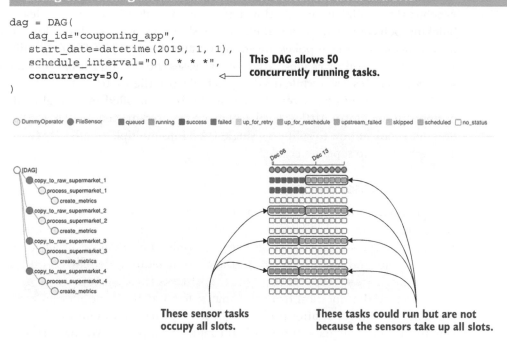

These sensor tasks occupy all slots. **These tasks could run but are not because the sensors take up all slots.**

Figure 6.8 Sensor deadlock: the running tasks are all sensors waiting for a condition to be true, which never happens and thus occupy all slots.

In figure 6.8, we ran the DAG with all defaults, which is 16 concurrent tasks per DAG. The following snowball effect happened:

- Day 1: Supermarket 1 succeeded; supermarkets 2, 3, and 4 are polling, occupying 3 tasks.
- Day 2: Supermarket 1 succeeded; supermarkets 2, 3, and 4 are polling, occupying 6 tasks.
- Day 3: Supermarket 1 succeeded; supermarkets 2, 3, and 4 are polling, occupying 9 tasks.
- Day 4: Supermarket 1 succeeded; supermarkets 2, 3, and 4 are polling, occupying 12 tasks.
- Day 5: Supermarket 1 succeeded; supermarkets 2, 3, and 4 are polling, occupying 15 tasks.
- Day 6: Supermarket 1 succeeded; supermarkets 2, 3, and 4 are polling, occupying 16 tasks; two new tasks cannot run, and any other task trying to run is blocked.

This behavior is often referred to as *sensor deadlock*. In this example, the maximum number of running tasks in the supermarket couponing DAG is reached, and thus the impact is limited to that DAG, while other DAGs can still run. However, once the global Airflow limit of maximum tasks is reached, your entire system is stalled, which is obviously undesirable. This issue can be solved in various ways.

The sensor class takes an argument `mode`, which can be set to either `poke` or `reschedule` (available since Airflow 1.10.2). By default, it's set to `poke`, leading to the blocking behavior. This means the sensor task occupies a task slot as long as it's running. Once in a while, it pokes the condition and then does nothing, but still occupies a task slot. The sensor `reschedule` mode releases the slot after it has finished poking, so it *only* occupies a slot while it's doing actual work (figure 6.9).

The number of concurrent tasks can also be controlled by several configuration options on the global Airflow level, which are covered in section 12.6. In the next section, let's look at how to split up a single DAG into multiple smaller DAGs, which trigger each other to separate concerns.

6.2   *Triggering other DAGs*

At some point in time, more supermarkets are added to our couponing service. More and more people would like to gain insights in the supermarket's promotions and the `create_metrics` step at the end is executed only once a day, after all supermarkets' data was delivered and processed. In the current setup, it depends on the successful state of the `process_supermarket_{1,2,3,4}` tasks (figure 6.10).

We received a question from the analyst team about if the metrics could also be made available directly after processing instead of having to wait for other supermarkets to deliver their data and run it through the pipeline. We have several options

```
wait_for_supermarket1 = PythonSensor(
task_id="wait_for_supermarket_1",
python_callable=_wait_for_supermarket,
op_kwargs={"supermarket_id": "supermarket1"},
mode="reschedule",
dag=dag,
)

mode="reschedule"  applies a new state "up_for_reschedule"
```

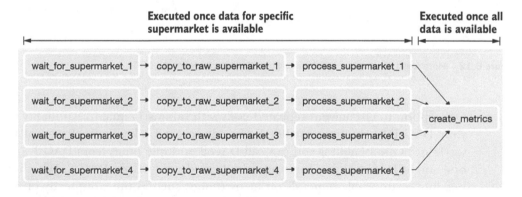

These sensors now release their slots after poking. . .

. . . allowing these tasks to continue running.

Figure 6.9 Sensors with `mode="reschedule"` release their slot after poking, allowing other tasks to run.

Executed once data for specific supermarket is available

Executed once all data is available

wait_for_supermarket_1 → copy_to_raw_supermarket_1 → process_supermarket_1

wait_for_supermarket_2 → copy_to_raw_supermarket_2 → process_supermarket_2

wait_for_supermarket_3 → copy_to_raw_supermarket_3 → process_supermarket_3

wait_for_supermarket_4 → copy_to_raw_supermarket_4 → process_supermarket_4

create_metrics

Figure 6.10 Different execution logic between the supermarket-specific tasks and the `create_metrics` task indicates a potential split in separate DAGs.

here (depending on the logic it performs). We could set the create_metrics task as a downstream task after every process_supermarket_* task (figure 6.11).

Figure 6.11 Replicating tasks to avoid waiting for completion of all processes

Suppose the create_metrics task evolved into multiple tasks, making the DAG structure more complex and resulting in more repeated tasks (figure 6.12).

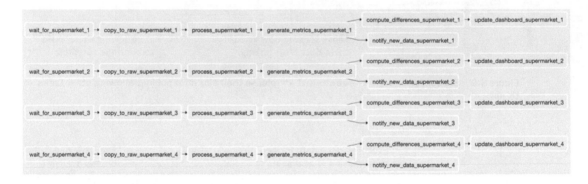

Figure 6.12 More logic once again indicates a potential split in separate DAGs.

One option to circumvent repeated tasks with (almost) equal functionality is to split your DAG into multiple smaller DAGs where each takes care of part of the total workflow. One benefit is you can call DAG 2 multiple times from DAG 1, instead of one single DAG holding multiple (duplicated) tasks from DAG 2. Whether this is possible or desirable depends on many things, such as the complexity of the workflow. If, for example, you'd like to be able to create the metrics without having to wait for the workflow to complete according to its schedule, but instead trigger it manually whenever you'd like, then it could make sense to split it into two separate DAGs.

This scenario can be achieved with the `TriggerDagRunOperator`. This operator allows triggering other DAGs, which you can apply to decouple parts of a workflow.

> **Listing 6.4 Triggering other DAGs using the TriggerDagRunOperator**

```
import airflow.utils.dates
from airflow import DAG
from airflow.operators.dummy import DummyOperator
from airflow.operators.trigger_dagrun import TriggerDagRunOperator

dag1 = DAG(
    dag_id="ingest_supermarket_data",
    start_date=airflow.utils.dates.days_ago(3),
    schedule_interval="0 16 * * *",
)

for supermarket_id in range(1, 5):
    # ...
    trigger_create_metrics_dag = TriggerDagRunOperator(
        task_id=f"trigger_create_metrics_dag_supermarket_{supermarket_id}",
        trigger_dag_id="create_metrics",          ◁┐
        dag=dag1,                                      dag_id
    )                                                  should
                                                       align.
dag2 = DAG(
    dag_id="create_metrics",                      ◁─┘
    start_date=airflow.utils.dates.days_ago(3),
    schedule_interval=None,                       ◁── No schedule_interval
)                                                     required if only triggered
# ...
```

The string provided to the `trigger_dag_id` argument of the `TriggerDagRunOperator` must match the `dag_id` of the DAG to trigger. The end result is that we now have two DAGs, one for ingesting data from the supermarkets and one for computing metrics on the data (figure 6.13).

Figure 6.13 DAGs split in two, with DAG 1 triggering DAG 2 using the `TriggerDagRunOperator`. The logic in DAG 2 is now defined just once, simplifying the situation shown in figure 6.12.

Visually, in the Airflow UI there is almost no difference between a scheduled DAG, manually triggered DAG, or an automatically triggered DAG. Two small details in the tree view tell you whether a DAG was triggered or started by a schedule. First, scheduled DAG runs and their task instances show a black border (figure 6.14).

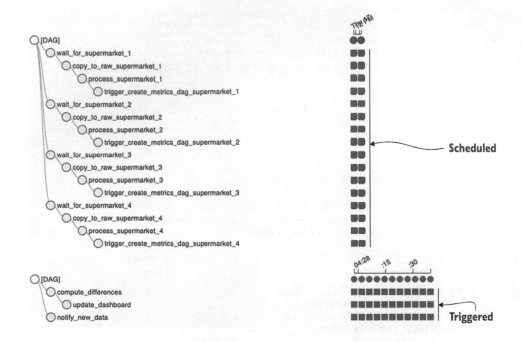

Figure 6.14   **Black borders indicate a scheduled run; no borders are triggered.**

Second, each DAG run holds a field `run_id`. The value of the `run_id` starts with one of the following:

- `scheduled__` to indicate the DAG run started because of its schedule
- `backfill__` to indicate the DAG run started by a backfill job
- `manual__` to indicate the DAG run started by a manual action (e.g., pressing the Trigger Dag button, or triggered by a `TriggerDagRunOperator`)

Hovering over the DAG run circle displays a tooltip showing the `run_id` value, telling us how the DAG started running (figure 6.15).

6.2.1   *Backfilling with the TriggerDagRunOperator*

What if you changed some logic in the `process_*` tasks and wanted to rerun the DAGs from there on? In a single DAG you could clear the state of the `process_*` and corresponding downstream tasks. However, clearing tasks *only* clears tasks within the same DAG. Tasks downstream of a `TriggerDagRunOperator` in another DAG are not cleared, so be well aware of this behavior.

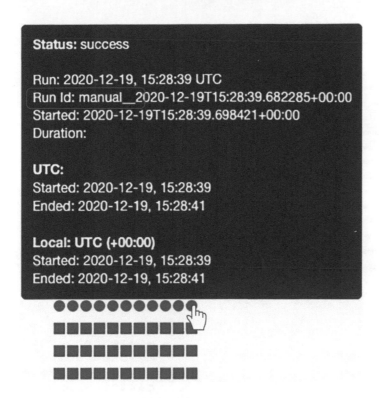

Figure 6.15 The `run_id` tells us the origin of the DAG run.

Clearing tasks in a DAG, including a `TriggerDagRunOperator`, will trigger a new DAG run instead of clearing the corresponding previously triggered DAG runs (figure 6.16).

6.2.2 Polling the state of other DAGs

The example in figure 6.13 works as long as there is no dependency from the to be triggered DAGs back to the triggering DAG. In other words, the first DAG can trigger the downstream DAG whenever, without having to check any conditions.

   If the DAGs become very complex, for clarity the first DAG could be split across multiple DAGs, and a corresponding `TriggerDagRunOperator` task could be made for each corresponding DAG, as seen in figure 6.17 in the middle. Also, one DAG triggering multiple downstream DAGs is a possible scenario with the `TriggerDagRunOperator`, as seen in figure 6.17 on the right.

   But what if multiple triggering DAGs must complete before another DAG can start running? For example, what if DAGs 1, 2, and 3 each extract, transform, and load a data set, and you'd like to run DAG 4 *only* once all three DAGs have completed, for example to compute a set of aggregated metrics? Airflow manages dependencies

Figure 6.16   Clearing `TriggerDagRunOperators` **does not clear tasks in the triggered DAG; instead, new DAG runs are created.**

Figure 6.17   Various inter-DAG dependencies possible with the `TriggerDagRunOperator`

between tasks within one single DAG; however, it does *not* provide a mechanism for inter-DAG dependencies (figure 6.18).[2]

---

[2] This Airflow plug-in visualizes inter-DAG dependencies by scanning all your DAGs for usage of the `Trigger-DagRunOperator` and `ExternalTaskSensor`: https://github.com/ms32035/airflow-dag-dependencies.

DAGs 1, 2, and 3

etl

DAG 4

etl ← ? report

etl

Figure 6.18   Illustration of inter-DAG dependency, which cannot be solved with the `TriggerDagRunOperator`

For this situation we could apply the `ExternalTaskSensor`, which is a sensor poking the state of tasks in other DAGs, as shown in figure 6.19. This way the `wait_for_etl_dag{1,2,3}` tasks act as a proxy to ensure the completed state of all three DAGs before finally executing the report task.

DAGs 1, 2, and 3   **DAG 4**

etl ←------ wait_for_etl_dag1

etl ←------ wait_for_etl_dag2 → report

etl ←------ wait_for_etl_dag3

Figure 6.19   Instead of pushing execution with the `TriggerDagRunOperator`, in some situations such as ensuring completed state for DAGs 1, 2, and 3, we must pull execution toward DAG 4 with the `ExternalTaskSensor`.

The way the `ExternalTaskSensor` works is by pointing it to a task in another DAG to check its state (figure 6.20).

```
import airflow.utils.dates
from airflow  import DAG
from airflow.operators.dummy  import DummyOperator
from airflow.sensors.external_task  import ExternalTaskSensor

dag1 = DAG(dag_id="ingest_supermarket_data", schedule_interval="0 16 * * *", ...)
dag2 = DAG(schedule_interval="0 16 * * *", ...)

DummyOperator(task_id="copy_to_raw", dag=dag1) >> DummyOperator(task_id="process_supermarket", dag=dag1)

wait = ExternalTaskSensor(
    task_id="wait_for_process_supermarket",
    external_dag_id="ingest_supermarket_data",
    external_task_id="process_supermarket", ------------------------
    dag=dag2,
)
report = DummyOperator(task_id="report", dag=dag2)
wait >> report
```

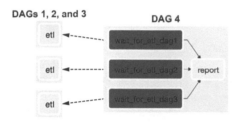

copy_to_raw → process_supermarket   wait_for_process_supermarket → report

Figure 6.20   Example usage of the `ExternalTaskSensor`

Since there is no event from DAG 1 to DAG 2, DAG 2 is polling for the state of a task in DAG 1, but this comes with several downsides. In Airflow's world, DAGs have no notion of other DAGs. While it's technically possible to query the underlying metastore (which is what the ExternalTaskSensor does), or read DAG scripts from disk and infer the execution details of other workflows, they are not coupled in Airflow in any way. This requires a bit of alignment between DAGs in case the ExternalTaskSensor is used. The default behavior is such that the ExternalTaskSensor simply checks for a successful state of a task with the exact same execution date as itself. So, if an ExternalTaskSensor runs with an execution date of 2019-10-12T18:00:00, it would query the Airflow metastore for the given task, also with an execution date of 2019-10-12T18:00:00. Now let's say both DAGs have a different schedule interval; then these would not align and thus the ExternalTaskSensor would never find the corresponding task! (See figure 6.21.)

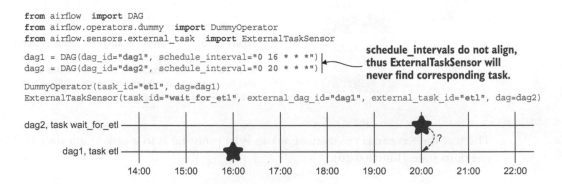

Figure 6.21 An ExternalTaskSensor checks for the completion of a task in another DAG, following its own schedule_interval, which will never be found if the intervals do not align.

In case the schedule intervals do not align we can offset, by which the ExternalTaskSensor must search for the task in the other DAG. This offset is controlled by the execution_delta argument on the ExternalTaskSensor. It expects a timedelta object, and it's important to know it operates counterintuitive from what you expect. The given timedelta is subtracted from the execution_date, meaning that a positive timedelta actually looks back in time (figure 6.22).

Note that checking a task using the ExternalTaskSensor where the other DAG has a different interval period, for example, DAG 1 runs once a day and DAG 2 runs every five hours, complicates setting a good value for execution_delta. For this use case, it's possible to provide a function returning a list of timedeltas via the execution_date_fn argument. Refer to the Airflow documentation for the details.

```
from airflow  import DAG
from airflow.operators.dummy  import DummyOperator
from airflow.sensors.external_task  import ExternalTaskSensor
dag1 = DAG(dag_id="dag1", schedule_interval="0 16 * * *")
dag2 = DAG(dag_id="dag2", schedule_interval="0 20 * * *")
DummyOperator(task_id="etl", dag=dag1)
ExternalTaskSensor(
    task_id="wait_for_etl",
    external_dag_id="dag1",
    external_task_id="etl",
    execution_delta=datetime.timedelta(hours=4),
    dag=dag2,
)
```

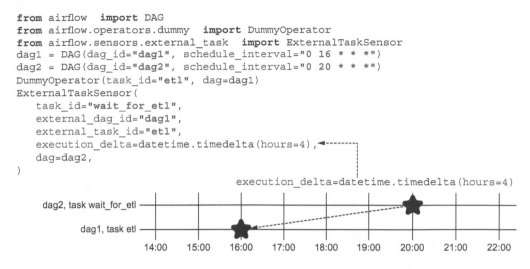

Figure 6.22 An `ExternalTaskSensor` can be offset with `execution_delta` to match with the intervals of other DAGs.

6.3 *Starting workflows with REST/CLI*

In addition to triggering DAGs from other DAGs, they can also be triggered via the REST API and CLI. This can be useful if you want to start workflows from outside Airflow (e.g., as part of a CI/CD pipeline). Or, data arriving at random times in an AWS S3 bucket can be processed by setting a Lambda function to call the REST API, triggering a DAG, instead of having to run sensors polling all the time.

Using the Airflow CLI, we can trigger a DAG as follows.

Listing 6.5 Triggering a DAG using the Airflow CLI

```
airflow dags trigger dag1
```

➥ [2019-10-06 14:48:54,297] {cli.py:238} INFO - Created <DagRun dag1 @ 2019-
    10-06 14:48:54+00:00: manual__2019-10-06T14:48:54+00:00, externally
    triggered: True>

This triggers dag1 with the execution date set to the current date and time. The DAG run id is prefixed with "manual__" to indicate it was triggered manually, or from outside Airflow. The CLI accepts additional configuration to the triggered DAG.

Listing 6.6 Triggering a DAG with additional configuration

```
airflow dags trigger -c '{"supermarket_id": 1}' dag1
airflow dags trigger --conf '{"supermarket_id": 1}' dag1
```

This piece of configuration is then available in all tasks of the triggered DAG run via the task context variables.

Listing 6.7   Applying configuration DAG run

```
import airflow.utils.dates
from airflow import DAG
from airflow.operators.python import PythonOperator

dag = DAG(
    dag_id="print_dag_run_conf",
    start_date=airflow.utils.dates.days_ago(3),
    schedule_interval=None,
)


def print_conf(**context):
    print(context["dag_run"].conf)


process = PythonOperator(
    task_id="process",
    python_callable=print_conf,
    dag=dag,
)
```

> **Configuration supplied when triggering DAGs is accessible in the task context**

These tasks print the conf provided to the DAG run, which can be applied as a variable throughout the task:

```
{cli.py:516} INFO - Running <TaskInstance: print_dag_run_conf.process 2019-
    10-15T20:01:57+00:00 [running]> on host ebd4ad13bf98
{logging_mixin.py:95} INFO - {'supermarket': 1}
{python_operator.py:114} INFO - Done. Returned value was: None
{logging_mixin.py:95} INFO - [2019-10-15 20:03:09,149]
    {local_task_job.py:105} INFO - Task exited with return code 0
```

As a result, if you have a DAG in which you run copies of tasks simply to support different variables, this becomes a whole lot more concise with the DAG run conf, since it allows you to insert variables into the pipeline (figure 6.23). However, note that the DAG in listing 6.8 has no schedule interval (i.e., it only runs when triggered). If the logic in your DAG relies on a DAG run conf, then it won't be possible to run on a schedule since that doesn't provide any DAG run conf.

Figure 6.23   Simplifying DAGs by providing payload at runtime

Similarly, it is also possible to use the REST API for the same result (e.g., in case you have no access to the CLI but your Airflow instance can be reached over HTTP).

Listing 6.8 Triggering a DAG using the Airflow REST API

```
# URL is /api/v1

curl \
-u admin:admin \          ◁——  Sending a plaintext username/password is not
-X POST \                       desirable; consult the Airflow API authentication
"http://localhost:8080/api/v1/dags/print_dag_run_conf/dagRuns" \   documentation for other authentication methods.
-H  "Content-Type: application/json" \
-d '{"conf": {}}'         ◁——  The endpoint requires a piece
                                of data, even if no additional
{                               configuration is given.
  "conf": {},
  "dag_id": "print_dag_run_conf",
  "dag_run_id": "manual__2020-12-19T18:31:39.097040+00:00",
  "end_date": null,
  "execution_date": "2020-12-19T18:31:39.097040+00:00",
  "external_trigger": true,
  "start_date": "2020-12-19T18:31:39.102408+00:00",
  "state": "running"
}


curl \
-u admin:admin \
-X POST \
"http://localhost:8080/api/v1/dags/print_dag_run_conf/dagRuns" \
-H  "Content-Type: application/json" \
-d '{"conf": {"supermarket": 1}}'

{
  "conf": {
    "supermarket": 1
  },
  "dag_id": "listing_6_08",
  "dag_run_id": "manual__2020-12-19T18:33:58.142200+00:00",
  "end_date": null,
  "execution_date": "2020-12-19T18:33:58.142200+00:00",
  "external_trigger": true,
  "start_date": "2020-12-19T18:33:58.153941+00:00",
  "state": "running"
}
```

This could be convenient when triggering DAG from outside Airflow, for example from your CI/CD system.

Summary

- Sensors are a special type of operators that continuously poll for a given condition to be true.
- Airflow provides a collection of sensors for various systems/use cases; a custom condition can also be made with the PythonSensor.
- The TriggerDagRunOperator can trigger a DAG from another DAG, while the ExternalTaskSensor can poll the state in another DAG.
- Triggering DAGs is possible from outside Airflow with the REST API and/or CLI.

Communicating with external systems

7

This chapter covers

- Working with Airflow operators performing actions on systems outside Airflow
- Applying operators specific to external systems
- Implementing operators in Airflow doing A-to-B operations
- Testing tasks connecting to external systems

In all previous chapters, we've focused on various aspects of writing Airflow code, mostly demonstrated with examples using generic operators such as the Bash-Operator and PythonOperator. While these operators can run arbitrary code and thus could run any workload, the Airflow project also holds other operators for more specific use cases, for example, running a query on a Postgres database. These operators have one and only one specific use case, such as running a query. As a result, they are easy to use by simply providing the query to the operator, and the operator internally handles the querying logic. With a PythonOperator, you would have to write such querying logic yourself.

For the record, with the phrase *external system* we mean any technology other than Airflow and the machine Airflow is running on. This could be, for example,

Microsoft Azure Blob Storage, an Apache Spark cluster, or a Google BigQuery data warehouse.

To see when and how to use such operators, in this chapter we'll develop two DAGs connecting to external systems and moving and transforming data between these systems. We will inspect the various options Airflow holds (and does not hold)[1] to deal with this use case and the external systems.

In section 7.1, we develop a machine learning model on AWS, working with AWS S3 buckets and AWS SageMaker, a solution for developing and deploying machine learning models. Next, in section 7.2, we demonstrate how to move data between various systems with a Postgres database containing Airbnb places to stay in Amsterdam. The data comes from Inside Airbnb (http://insideairbnb.com), a website and public data managed by Airbnb, with records about listings, reviews, and more. Once a day we will download the latest data from the Postgres database into our AWS S3 bucket. From there, we will run a Pandas job inside a Docker container to determine the price fluctuations, and the result is saved back to S3.

7.1   *Connecting to cloud services*

A large portion of software runs on cloud services nowadays. Such services can generally be controlled via an API—an interface to connect and send requests to your cloud provider. The API typically comes with a client in the form of a Python package, for example, AWS's client is named boto3 (https://github.com/boto/boto3), GCP's client is named the Cloud SDK (https://cloud.google.com/sdk), and Azure's client is appropriately named the Azure SDK for Python (https://docs.microsoft.com/azure/python). Such clients provide convenient functions where, bluntly said, you enter the required details for a request and the clients handle the technical internals of handling the request and response.

In the context of Airflow, to the programmer the interface is an operator. Operators are the convenience classes to which you can provide the required details to make a request to a cloud service, and the operator internally handles the technical implementation. These operators internally make use of the Cloud SDK to send requests and provide a small layer around the Cloud SDK, which provides certain functionality to the programmer (figure 7.1).

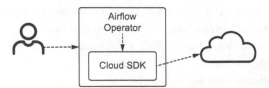

Figure 7.1   An Airflow operator translates given arguments to operations on the Cloud SDK.

---

[1] Operators are always under development. This chapter was written in 2020; please note at the time of reading there might be new operators that suit your use case that were not described in this chapter.

7.1.1 Installing extra dependencies

The `apache-airflow` Python package includes a few essential operators but no components to connect with any cloud. For the cloud services, you can install the provider packages in table 7.1.

Table 7.1 Extra packages to install for additional cloud provider Airflow components

Cloud	Pip install command
AWS	pip install `apache-airflow-providers-amazon`
GCP	pip install `apache-airflow-providers-google`
Azure	pip install `apache-airflow-providers-microsoft-azure`

This goes not only for the cloud providers but also for other external services. For example, to install operators and corresponding dependencies required for running the `PostgresOperator`, install the `apache-airflow-providers-postgres` package. For a full list of all available additional packages, refer to the Airflow documentation (https://airflow.apache.org/docs).

Let's look at an operator to perform an action on AWS. Take, for example, the `S3CopyObjectOperator`. This operator copies an object from one bucket to another. It accepts several arguments (skipping the irrelevant arguments for this example).

Listing 7.1 The S3CopyObjectOperator only requires you to fill the necessary details

```
from airflow.providers.amazon.aws.operators.s3_copy_object import
    S3CopyObjectOperator

S3CopyObjectOperator(
    task_id="...",
    source_bucket_name="databucket",          The bucket to copy from
    source_bucket_key="/data/{{ ds }}.json",   The object name to copy
    dest_bucket_name="backupbucket",           The bucket to copy to
    dest_bucket_key="/data/{{ ds }}-backup.json",   The target object name
)
```

This operator makes copying an object on S3 to a different location on S3 a simple exercise of filling in the blanks, without needing to dive into the details of AWS's boto3 client.[2]

7.1.2 Developing a machine learning model

Let's look at a more complex example and work with a number of AWS operators by developing a data pipeline building a handwritten numbers classifier. The model will be trained on the MNIST (http://yann.lecun.com/exdb/mnist) data set, containing approximately 70,000 handwritten digits 0–9 (figure 7.2).

---

[2] If you check the implementation of the operator, internally it calls `copy_object()` on boto3.

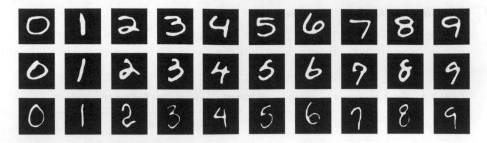

Figure 7.2   Example handwritten digits in the MNIST data set

After training the model, we should be able to feed it a new, previously unseen, handwritten number, and the model should classify the handwritten number (figure 7.3).

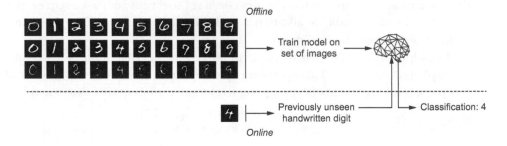

Figure 7.3   Rough outline of how a machine learning model is trained in one stage and classifies previously unseen samples in another

There are two parts to the model: an offline and an online part. The offline part takes a large set of handwritten digits, trains a model to classify these handwritten digits, and the result (a set of model parameters) is stored. This process can be done periodically when new data is collected. The online part is responsible for loading the model and classifying previously unseen digits. This should run instantaneously, as users expect direct feedback.

Airflow workflows are typically responsible for the offline part of a model. Training a model comprises data loading, preprocessing it into a format suitable for the model, and training the model, which can become complex. Also, periodically retraining the model fits nicely with Airflow's batch-processing paradigm. The online part is typically an API, such as a REST API or HTML page with REST API calls under the hood. Such an API is typically deployed only once or as part of a CI/CD pipeline. There is no use case for redeploying an API every week, and therefore it's typically not part of an Airflow workflow.

For training a handwritten digit classifier, we'll develop an Airflow pipeline. The pipeline will use AWS SageMaker, an AWS service facilitating the development and deployment of machine learning models. In the pipeline, we first copy sample data from a public location to our own S3 bucket. Next, we transform the data into a format usable for the model, train the model with AWS SageMaker, and finally, deploy the model to classify a given handwritten digit. The pipeline will look figure 7.4.

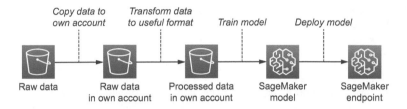

Figure 7.4   Logical steps to create a handwritten digit classifier

The depicted pipeline could run just once and the SageMaker model could be deployed just once. The strength of Airflow is the ability to schedule such a pipeline and rerun (partial) pipelines if desired in case of new data or changes to the model. If the raw data is continuously updated, the Airflow pipeline will periodically reload the raw data and redeploy the model, trained on the new data. Also, a data scientist could tune the model to their liking, and the Airflow pipeline could automatically redeploy the model without having to manually trigger anything.

Airflow holds several operators on various services of the AWS platform. While the list is never complete because services are continuously added, changed, or removed, most AWS services are supported by an Airflow operator. AWS operators are provided by the `apache-airflow-providers-amazon` package.

Let's look at the pipeline (figure 7.5).

Figure 7.5   Logical steps implemented in Airflow DAG

Even though there are just four tasks, there's quite a lot to configure on AWS Sage-Maker, and hence the DAG code is lengthy. No worries, though; we'll break it down afterward.

Listing 7.2   DAG to train and deploy a handwritten digit classifier

```
import gzip
import io
import pickle

import airflow.utils.dates
from airflow import DAG
from airflow.operators.python import PythonOperator
from airflow.providers.amazon.aws.hooks.s3 import S3Hook
from airflow.providers.amazon.aws.operators.s3_copy_object import
    S3CopyObjectOperator
from airflow.providers.amazon.aws.operators.sagemaker_endpoint import
    SageMakerEndpointOperator
from airflow.providers.amazon.aws.operators.sagemaker_training import
    SageMakerTrainingOperator
from sagemaker.amazon.common import write_numpy_to_dense_tensor

dag = DAG(
    dag_id="chapter7_aws_handwritten_digits_classifier",
    schedule_interval=None,
    start_date=airflow.utils.dates.days_ago(3),
)
```

The S3CopyObjectOperator copies objects between two S3 locations.

```
download_mnist_data = S3CopyObjectOperator(
    task_id="download_mnist_data",
    source_bucket_name="sagemaker-sample-data-eu-west-1",
    source_bucket_key="algorithms/kmeans/mnist/mnist.pkl.gz",
    dest_bucket_name="[your-bucket]",
    dest_bucket_key="mnist.pkl.gz",
    dag=dag,
)
```

Sometimes your desired functionality is not supported by any operator and you have to implement the logic yourself.

```
def _extract_mnist_data():
    s3hook = S3Hook()
```

We can use the S3Hook for operations on S3.

```
    # Download S3 dataset into memory
    mnist_buffer = io.BytesIO()
    mnist_obj = s3hook.get_key(
        bucket_name="[your-bucket]",
        key="mnist.pkl.gz",
    )
```

Download the S3 object.

```
    mnist_obj.download_fileobj(mnist_buffer)

    # Unpack gzip file, extract dataset, convert, upload back to S3
    mnist_buffer.seek(0)
    with gzip.GzipFile(fileobj=mnist_buffer, mode="rb") as f:
        train_set, _, _ = pickle.loads(f.read(), encoding="latin1")
        output_buffer = io.BytesIO()
        write_numpy_to_dense_tensor(
            file=output_buffer,
            array=train_set[0],
            labels=train_set[1],
        )
```

```
            output_buffer.seek(0)
            s3hook.load_file_obj(          ←──┐ Upload the extracted
                output_buffer,                 │ data back to S3.
                key="mnist_data",
                bucket_name="[your-bucket]",
                replace=True,
            )
```

Sometimes your desired functionality is not supported by any operator and you have to implement it yourself and call with the PythonOperator.

```
    extract_mnist_data = PythonOperator(     ←──┘
        task_id="extract_mnist_data",
        python_callable=_extract_mnist_data,
        dag=dag,
    )
```

The SageMakerTraining-Operator creates a Sage-Maker training job.

```
    sagemaker_train_model = SageMakerTrainingOperator(   ←──
        task_id="sagemaker_train_model",
```

The config is a JSON holding the training job configuration.

```
        config={
            "TrainingJobName": "mnistclassifier-{{ execution_date.strftime('%Y-
    %m-%d-%H-%M-%S') }}",
            "AlgorithmSpecification": {
                "TrainingImage": "438346466558.dkr.ecr.eu-west-
    1.amazonaws.com/kmeans:1",
                "TrainingInputMode": "File",
            },
            "HyperParameters": {"k": "10", "feature_dim": "784"},
            "InputDataConfig": [
                {
                    "ChannelName": "train",
                    "DataSource": {
                        "S3DataSource": {
                            "S3DataType": "S3Prefix",
                            "S3Uri": "s3://[your-bucket]/mnist_data",
                            "S3DataDistributionType": "FullyReplicated",
                        }
                    },
                }
            ],
            "OutputDataConfig": {"S3OutputPath": "s3://[your-bucket]/
    mnistclassifier-output"},
            "ResourceConfig". {
                "InstanceType": "ml.c4.xlarge",
                "InstanceCount": 1,
                "VolumeSizeInGB": 10,
            },
            "RoleArn": "arn:aws:iam::297623009465:role/service-role/
    AmazonSageMaker-ExecutionRole-20180905T153196",
            "StoppingCondition": {"MaxRuntimeInSeconds": 24 * 60 * 60},
        },
        wait_for_completion=True,
        print_log=True,
        check_interval=10,
        dag=dag,
    )
```

The operator conveniently waits until the training job is completed and prints CloudWatch logs while training.

```
sagemaker_deploy_model = SageMakerEndpointOperator(
    task_id="sagemaker_deploy_model",
    wait_for_completion=True,
    config={
        "Model": {
            "ModelName": "mnistclassifier-{{ execution_date.strftime('%Y-
%m-%d-%H-%M-%S') }}",
            "PrimaryContainer": {
                "Image": "438346466558.dkr.ecr.eu-west-1.amazonaws.com/
kmeans:1",
                "ModelDataUrl": (
                    "s3://[your-bucket]/mnistclassifier-output/"
                    "mnistclassifier-{{ execution_date.strftime('%Y-%m-%d-
%H-%M-%S') }}/"
                    "output/model.tar.gz"
                ),  # this will link the model and the training job
            },
            "ExecutionRoleArn": "arn:aws:iam::297623009465:role/service-
role/AmazonSageMaker-ExecutionRole-20180905T153196",
        },
        "EndpointConfig": {
            "EndpointConfigName": "mnistclassifier-{{
execution_date.strftime('%Y-%m-%d-%H-%M-%S') }}",
            "ProductionVariants": [
                {
                    "InitialInstanceCount": 1,
                    "InstanceType": "ml.t2.medium",
                    "ModelName": "mnistclassifier",
                    "VariantName": "AllTraffic",
                }
            ],
        },
        "Endpoint": {
            "EndpointConfigName": "mnistclassifier-{{
execution_date.strftime('%Y-%m-%d-%H-%M-%S') }}",
            "EndpointName": "mnistclassifier",
        },
    },
    dag=dag,
)
```

The SageMakerEndpoint-Operator deploys the trained model, which makes it available behind an HTTP endpoint.

```
download_mnist_data >> extract_mnist_data >> sagemaker_train_model >>
    sagemaker_deploy_model
```

With external services, the complexity often does not lie within Airflow but with ensuring the correct integration of various components in your pipeline. There's quite a lot of configuration involved with SageMaker, so let's break down the tasks piece by piece.

Listing 7.3   Copying data between two S3 buckets

```
download_mnist_data = S3CopyObjectOperator(
    task_id="download_mnist_data",
    source_bucket_name="sagemaker-sample-data-eu-west-1",
```

```
    source_bucket_key="algorithms/kmeans/mnist/mnist.pkl.gz",
    dest_bucket_name="[your-bucket]",
    dest_bucket_key="mnist.pkl.gz",
    dag=dag,
)
```

After initializing the DAG, the first task copies the MNIST data set from a public bucket to our own bucket. We store it in our own bucket for further processing. The S3CopyObjectOperator asks for both the bucket and object name on the source and destination and will copy the selected object for you. So, while developing, how do we verify this works correctly, without first coding the full pipeline and keeping fingers crossed to see if it works in production?

7.1.3 Developing locally with external systems

Specifically for AWS, if you have access to the cloud resources from your development machine with an access key, you can run Airflow tasks locally. With the help of the CLI command airflow tasks test, we can run a single task for a given execution date. Since the download_mnist_data task doesn't use the execution date, it doesn't matter what value we provide. However, say the dest_bucket_key was given as mnist-{{ ds }} .pkl.gz; then we'd have to think wisely about what execution date we test with. From your command line, complete the steps in the following listing.

Listing 7.4 Setting up for locally testing AWS operators

```
# Add secrets in ~/.aws/credentials:
 # [myaws]
 # aws_access_key_id=AKIAEXAMPLE123456789
 # aws_secret_access_key=supersecretaccesskeydonotshare!123456789

export AWS_PROFILE=myaws
export AWS_DEFAULT_REGION=eu-west-1          Initialize a local
export AIRFLOW_HOME=[your project dir]       Airflow metastore.
airflow db init
airflow tasks test chapter7_aws_handwritten_digits_classifier
    download_mnist_data 2020-01-01          Run a single task.
```

This will run the task download_mnist_data and display logs.

Listing 7.5 Verifying a task manually with airflow tasks test

```
$ airflow tasks test chapter7_aws_handwritten_digits_classifier
    download_mnist_data 2019-01-01

INFO - Using executor SequentialExecutor
INFO - Filling up the DagBag from .../dags
INFO - Dependencies all met for <TaskInstance:
    chapter7_aws_handwritten_digits_classifier.download_mnist_data 2019-01-
    01T00:00:00+00:00 [None]>
-------------------------------------------------------------------------
```

```
INFO - Starting attempt 1 of 1
--------------------------------------------------------------------------
⇒  INFO - Executing <Task(PythonOperator): download_mnist_data> on 2019-01-
    01T00:00:00+00:00
INFO - Found credentials in shared credentials file: ~/.aws/credentials
INFO - Done. Returned value was: None
⇒  INFO - Marking task as SUCCESS.dag_id=chapter7_aws_handwritten_digits
    _classifier, task_id=download_mnist_data, execution_date=20190101T000000,
    start_date=20200208T110436, end_date=20200208T110541
```

After this, we can see the data was copied into our own bucket (figure 7.6).

Name ▾	Last modified ▾	Size ▾	Storage class ▾
☐ 🗋 mnist.pkl.gz	Feb 8, 2020 10:02:15 AM GMT+0100	15.4 MB	Standard

Figure 7.6   After running the task locally with `airflow tasks test`, the data is copied to our own AWS S3 bucket.

What just happened? We configured the AWS credentials to allow us to access the cloud resources from our local machine. While this is specific to AWS, similar authentication methods apply to GCP and Azure. The AWS boto3 client used internally in Airflow operators will search in various places for credentials on the machine where a task is run. In listing 7.4, we set the AWS_PROFILE environment variable, which the boto3 client picks up for authentication. After this, we set another environment variable: AIRFLOW_HOME. This is the location where Airflow will store logs and such. Inside this directory, Airflow will search for a /dags directory. If that happens to live elsewhere, you can point Airflow there with another environment variable: AIRFLOW__CORE__DAGS_FOLDER.

Next, we run `airflow db init`. Before doing this, ensure you either have not set AIRFLOW__CORE__SQL_ALCHEMY_CONN (a URI that points to a database for storing all state), or set it to a database URI specifically for testing purposes. Without AIRFLOW__CORE__SQL_ALCHEMY_CONN set, `airflow db init` initializes a local SQLite database (a single file, no configuration required, database) inside AIRFLOW_HOME.[3] `airflow tasks test` exists for running and verifying a single task and does not record any state in the database; however, it does require a database for storing logs, and therefore we must initialize one with `airflow db init`.

After all this, we can run the task from the command line with `airflow tasks test chapter7_aws_handwritten_digits_classifier extract_mnist_data 2020-01-01`.

---

[3] The database will be generated in a file name airflow.db in the directory set by AIRFLOW_HOME. You can open and inspect it with, for example, DBeaver.

After we've copied the file to our own S3 bucket, we need to transform it into a format the SageMaker KMeans model expects, which is the RecordIO format.[4]

> **Listing 7.6 Transforming MNIST data to RecordIO format for SageMaker KMeans model**

```
import gzip
import io
import pickle

from airflow.operators.python import PythonOperator
from airflow.providers.amazon.aws.hooks.s3 import S3Hook
from sagemaker.amazon.common import write_numpy_to_dense_tensor


def _extract_mnist_data():                          Initialize S3Hook to
    s3hook = S3Hook()               ◁─────          communicate with S3.

    # Download S3 dataset into memory              Download data into in-
    mnist_buffer = io.BytesIO()                    memory binary stream.
    mnist_obj = s3hook.get_key(     ◁─────
        bucket_name="your-bucket",
        key="mnist.pkl.gz",
    )
    mnist_obj.download_fileobj(mnist_buffer)

    # Unpack gzip file, extract dataset, convert, upload back to S3
    mnist_buffer.seek(0)
    with gzip.GzipFile(fileobj=mnist_buffer, mode="rb") as f:
        train_set, _, _ = pickle.loads(f.read(), encoding="latin1")
        output_buffer = io.BytesIO()
        write_numpy_to_dense_tensor(     ◁───   Convert Numpy array
            file=output_buffer,                 to RecordIO records.
            array=train_set[0],
            labels=train_set[1],
        )
        output_buffer.seek(0)
        s3hook.load_file_obj(        ◁─┤   Upload result
            output_buffer,                 to S3.
            key="mnist_data",
            bucket_name="your-bucket",
            replace=True,
        )


extract_mnist_data = PythonOperator(
    task_id="extract_mnist_data",
    python_callable=_extract_mnist_data,
    dag=dag,
)
```

Annotations (left margin): **Unzip and unpickle** → `with gzip.GzipFile(fileobj=mnist_buffer, mode="rb") as f:`

---

[4] Mime type `application/x-recordio-protobuf` documentation: https://docs.aws.amazon.com/sagemaker/latest/dg/cdf-inference.html.

Airflow in itself is a general-purpose orchestration framework with a manageable set of features to learn. However, working in the data field often takes time and experience to know about all technologies and to know which dots to connect in which way. You never develop Airflow alone; oftentimes you're connecting to other systems and reading the documentation for that specific system. While Airflow will trigger the job for such a task, the difficulty in developing a data pipeline often lies outside Airflow and with the system that you're communicating with. While this book focuses solely on Airflow, due to the nature of working with other data-processing tools, we try to demonstrate, via these examples, what it's like to develop a data pipeline.

For this task, there is no existing functionality in Airflow for downloading data and extracting, transforming, and uploading the result back to S3. Therefore, we must implement our own function. The function downloads the data into an in-memory binary stream (io.BytesIO) so that the data is never stored in a file on the filesystem and so that no remaining files are left after the task. The MNIST data set is small (15 MB) and will therefore run on any machine. However, think wisely about the implementation; for larger data it might be wise to opt for storing the data on disks and processing in chunks.

Similarly, this task can also be run/tested locally with

```
airflow tasks test chapter7_aws_handwritten_digits_classifier extract_mnist_data
    2020-01-01
```

Once completed, the data will be visible in S3 (figure 7.7).

Name ▼	Last modified ▼	Size ▼	Storage class ▼
📄 mnist.pkl.gz	Feb 8, 2020 10:02:15 AM GMT+0100	15.4 MB	Standard
📄 mnist_data	Feb 8, 2020 10:55:17 AM GMT+0100	151.8 MB	Standard

Figure 7.7 Gzipped and pickled data was read and transformed into a usable format.

The next two tasks train and deploy the SageMaker model. The SageMaker operators take a config argument, which entails configuration specific to SageMaker and is not in the scope of this book. Let's focus on the other arguments.

Listing 7.7 Training an AWS SageMaker model

```
sagemaker_train_model = SageMakerTrainingOperator(
    task_id="sagemaker_train_model",
    config={
        "TrainingJobName": "mnistclassifier-{{ execution_date.strftime('%Y-
        %m-%d-%H-%M-%S') }}",
```

```
      ...
    },
    wait_for_completion=True,
    print_log=True,
    check_interval=10,
    dag=dag,
)
```

Many of the details in config are specific to SageMaker and can be discovered by reading the SageMaker documentation. Two lessons applicable to working with any external system can be made, though.

First, AWS restricts the `TrainingJobName` to be unique within an AWS account and region. Running this operator with the same `TrainingJobName` twice will return an error. Say we provided a fixed value, `mnistclassifier`, to the `TrainingJobName`; running it a second time would result in failure:

```
botocore.errorfactory.ResourceInUse: An error occurred (ResourceInUse) when
calling the CreateTrainingJob operation: Training job names must be unique
within an AWS account and region, and a training job with this name already
exists (arn:aws:sagemaker:eu-west-1:[account]:training-job/mnistclassifier)
```

The config argument can be templated, and, hence, if you plan to retrain your model periodically, you must provide it a unique `TrainingJobName`, which we can do by templating it with the `execution_date`. This way we ensure our task is idempotent and existing training jobs do not result in conflicting names.

Second, note the arguments `wait_for_completion` and `check_interval`. If `wait_for_completion` were set to false, the command would simply *fire and forget* (that's how the boto3 client works): AWS would start a training job, but we'd never know if the training job completed successfully. Therefore, all SageMaker operators wait (default `wait_for_completion=True`) for the given task to complete. Internally, the operators poll every X seconds, checking to see if the job is still running. This ensures our Airflow tasks only complete once finished (figure 7.8). If you have downstream tasks and want to ensure the correct behavior and order of your pipeline, you'll want to wait for completion.

Figure 7.8 The SageMaker operators only succeed once the job is completed successfully in AWS.

Once the full pipeline is complete, we have successfully deployed a SageMaker model and endpoint to expose it (figure 7.9).

However, in AWS, a SageMaker endpoint is not exposed to the outside world. It is accessible via the AWS APIs, but not, for example, via a worldwide accessible HTTP

Name	▼	ARN	Creation time	▼	Status	▼	Last updated
○	mnistclassifier	arn:aws:sagemaker:eu-west-1:[accountid]:endpoint/mnistclassifier	Feb 07, 2020 12:15 UTC		⊘ InService		Feb 09, 2020 12:47 UTC

Figure 7.9 In the SageMaker model menu, we can see the model was deployed and the endpoint is operational.

endpoint. Of course, to complete the data pipeline we'd like to have a nice interface or API to feed handwritten digits and receive a result. In AWS, in order to make it accessible to the internet, we could deploy a lambda (https://aws.amazon.com/lambda) to trigger the SageMaker endpoint and an API gateway (https://aws.amazon.com/api-gateway) to create an HTTP endpoint, forwarding requests to the Lambda,[5] so why not integrate them into our pipeline (figure 7.10)?

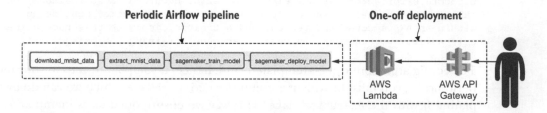

Figure 7.10 The handwritten digit classifier exists of more components than just the Airflow pipeline.

The reason for not deploying infrastructure is the fact the Lambda and API Gateway will be deployed as one-offs, not periodically. They operate in the online stage of the model and therefore are better deployed as part of a CI/CD pipeline. For the sake of completeness, the API can be implemented with Chalice.

Listing 7.8 An example user-facing API using AWS Chalice

```
import json
from io import BytesIO

import boto3
import numpy as np
from PIL import Image
from chalice import Chalice, Response
from sagemaker.amazon.common import numpy_to_record_serializer

app = Chalice(app_name="number-classifier")
```

---

[5] Chalice (https://github.com/aws/chalice) is a Python framework similar to Flask for developing an API and automatically generating the underlying API gateway and lambda resources in AWS.

```
@app.route("/", methods=["POST"], content_types=["image/jpeg"])
def predict():
    """
    Provide this endpoint an image in jpeg format.
    The image should be equal in size to the training images (28x28).
    """
    img = Image.open(BytesIO(app.current_request.raw_body)).convert("L")
    img_arr = np.array(img, dtype=np.float32)
    runtime = boto3.Session().client(
        service_name="sagemaker-runtime",
        region_name="eu-west-1",
    )
    response = runtime.invoke_endpoint(
        EndpointName="mnistclassifier",
        ContentType="application/x-recordio-protobuf",
        Body=numpy_to_record_serializer()(img_arr.flatten()),
    )
    result = json.loads(response["Body"].read().decode("utf-8"))
    return Response(
        result,
        status_code=200,
        headers={"Content-Type": "application/json"},
)
```

Convert input image to grayscale numpy array.

Invoke the SageMaker endpoint deployed by the Airflow DAG.

The SageMaker response is returned as bytes.

The API holds one single endpoint, which accepts a JPEG image.

Listing 7.9   Classifying a handwritten image by submitting it to the API

```
curl --request POST \
  --url http://localhost:8000/ \
  --header 'content-type: image/jpeg' \
  --data-binary @'/path/to/image.jpeg'
```

The result, if trained correctly, looks like figure 7.11.

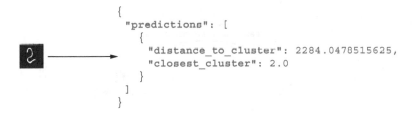

```
{
  "predictions": [
    {
      "distance_to_cluster": 2284.0478515625,
      "closest_cluster": 2.0
    }
  ]
}
```

Figure 7.11   Example API input and output. A real product could display a nice UI for uploading images and displaying the predicted number.

The API transforms the given image into RecordIO format, just like the SageMaker model was trained on. The RecordIO object is then forwarded to the SageMaker endpoint deployed by the Airflow pipeline, and finally returns a prediction for the given image.

7.2   *Moving data from between systems*

A classic use case for Airflow is a periodic ETL job, where data is downloaded daily and transformed elsewhere. Such a job is often for analytical purposes, where data is exported from a production database and stored elsewhere for processing later. The production database is most often (depending on the data model) not capable of returning historical data (e.g., the state of the database as it was one month ago). Therefore, a periodic export is often created and stored for later processing. Historic data dumps will grow your storage requirements quickly and require distributed processing to crunch all data. In this section, we'll explore how to orchestrate such a task with Airflow.

We developed a GitHub repository with code examples to go along with this book. It contains a Docker Compose file for deploying and running the next use case, where we extract Airbnb listings data and process it in a Docker container with Pandas. In a large-scale data processing job, the Docker container could be replaced by a Spark job, which distributes the work over multiple machines. The Docker Compose file contains the following:

- One Postgres container holding the Airbnb Amsterdam listings.
- One AWS S3-API-compatible container. Since there is no AWS S3-in-Docker, we created a MinIO container (AWS S3 API compatible object storage) for reading/writing data.
- One Airflow container.

Visually, the flow will look like figure 7.12.

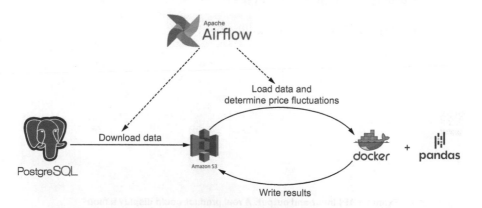

Figure 7.12   Airflow managing jobs moving data between various systems

Airflow acts as the "spider in the web," starting and managing jobs and ensuring all finish successfully in the correct order, failing the pipeline if not.

The Postgres container is a custom-built Postgres image holding a database filled with Inside Airbnb data, available on Docker Hub as airflowbook/ insideairbnb. The database holds one single table named "listings," which contains records of places in Amsterdam listed on Airbnb between April 2015 and December 2019 (figure 7.13).

Let's first query the database and export data to S3. From there we will read and process the data with Pandas.

A common task in Airflow is a data transfer between two systems, possibly with a transformation in between. Querying a MySQL database and storing the result on Google Cloud Storage, copying data from an SFTP server to your data lake on AWS S3, or calling an HTTP REST API and storing the output have one thing in common, namely that they deal with two systems: one for the input and one for the output.

Figure 7.13 Table structure of example Inside Airbnb database

In the Airflow ecosystem, this has led to the development of many such A-to-B operators. For these examples, we have the MySql-ToGoogleCloudStorageOperator, SFTPToS3Operator, and the SimpleHttpOperator. While there are many use cases to cover with the operators in the Airflow ecosystem, there is no Postgres-query-to-AWS-S3 operator (at the time of writing this book). So, what to do?

7.2.1 *Implementing a PostgresToS3Operator*

First, we could take note of how other similar operators work and develop our own PostgresToS3Operator. Let's look at an operator closely related to our use case, the MongoToS3Operator in airflow.providers.amazon.aws.transfers.mongo_to_s3 (after installing apache-airflow-providers-amazon). This operator runs a query on a MongoDB database and stores the result in an AWS S3 bucket. Let's inspect it and figure out how to replace MongoDB with Postgres. The execute() method is implemented as follows (some code was obfuscated).

Listing 7.10 Implementation of the MongoToS3Operator

```
def execute(self, context):
    s3_conn = S3Hook(self.s3_conn_id)          ◁——  An S3Hook is
                                                      instantiated.

    results = MongoHook(self.mongo_conn_id).find(   ◁——  A MongoHook is
        mongo_collection=self.mongo_collection,          instantiated and used
        query=self.mongo_query,                          to query for data.
        mongo_db=self.mongo_db
    )
```

```
docs_str = self._stringify(self.transform(results))          ◁─┐ Results are
                                                               transformed.

# Load Into S3
s3_conn.load_string(            ◁─┐ load_string() is called on
    string_data=docs_str,           the S3Hook to write the
    key=self.s3_key,                transformed results.
    bucket_name=self.s3_bucket,
    replace=self.replace
)
```

It's important to note that this operator does not use any of the filesystems on the Airflow machine but keeps all results in memory. The flow is basically

```
MongoDB → Airflow in operator memory → AWS S3.
```

Since this operator keeps the intermediate results in memory, think wisely about the memory implications when running very large queries, because a very large result could potentially drain the available memory on the Airflow machine. For now, let's keep the MongoToS3Operator implementation in mind and look at one other A-to-B operator, the S3ToSFTPOperator.

Listing 7.11   Implementation of the S3ToSFTPOperator

```
def execute(self, context):
    ssh_hook = SSHHook(ssh_conn_id=self.sftp_conn_id)
    s3_hook = S3Hook(self.s3_conn_id)

    s3_client = s3_hook.get_conn()                             NamedTemporaryFile is used
    sftp_client = ssh_hook.get_conn().open_sftp()              for temporarily downloading
                                                               a file, which is removed after
                                                               the context exits.
    with NamedTemporaryFile("w") as f:            ◁─────────────┘
        s3_client.download_file(self.s3_bucket, self.s3_key, f.name)
        sftp_client.put(f.name, self.sftp_path)
```

This operator, again, instantiates two hooks: SSHHook (SFTP is FTP over SSH) and S3Hook. However, in this operator, the intermediate result is written to a NamedTemporaryFile, which is a temporary place on the local filesystem of the Airflow instance. In this situation, we do not keep the entire result in memory, but we must ensure enough disk space is available.

Both operators have two hooks in common: one for communicating with system A and one for communicating with system B. However, how data is retrieved and transferred between systems A and B is different and up to the person implementing the specific operator. In the specific case of Postgres, database cursors can iterate to fetch and upload chunks of results. However, this implementation detail is not in the scope of this book. Keep it simple and assume the intermediate result fits within the resource boundaries of the Airflow instance.

A very minimal implementation of a PostgresToS3Operator could look as follows.

Listing 7.12 Example implementation of a PostgresToS3Operator

```
def execute(self, context):
    postgres_hook = PostgresHook(postgres_conn_id=self._postgres_conn_id)
    s3_hook = S3Hook(aws_conn_id=self._s3_conn_id)

    results = postgres_hook.get_records(self._query)        ◄─┤ Fetch records from the
    s3_hook.load_string(                     ◄─┐               PostgreSQL database.
        string_data=str(results),              │ Upload records
        bucket_name=self._s3_bucket,           │ to S3 object.
        key=self._s3_key,
    )
```

Let's inspect this code. The initialization of both hooks is straightforward; we initialize them, providing the name of the connection ID the user provides. While it is not necessary to use keyword arguments, you might notice the S3Hook takes the argument aws_conn_id (and not s3_conn_id as you might expect). During the development of such an operator, and the usage of such hooks, it is inevitable to sometimes dive into the source code or carefully read the documentation to view all available arguments and understand how things are propagated into classes. In the case of the S3Hook, it subclasses the AwsHook and inherits several methods and attributes, such as the aws_conn_id.

The PostgresHook is also a subclass, namely of the DbApiHook. By doing so, it inherits several methods, such as get_records(), which executes a given query and returns the results. The return type is a sequence of sequences (more precisely a list of tuples[6]). We then *stringify* the results and call load_string(), which writes encoded data to the given bucket/key on AWS S3. You might think this is not very practical, and you are correct. Although this is a minimal flow to run a query on Postgres and write the result to AWS S3, the list of tuples is stringified, which no data processing framework is able to interpret as an ordinary file format such as CSV or JSON (figure 7.14).

Figure 7.14 Exporting data from a Postgres database to stringified tuples

The tricky part of developing data pipelines is often not the orchestration of jobs with Airflow, but ensuring all bits and pieces of various jobs are configured correctly and fit together like puzzle pieces. So, let's write the results to CSV; this will allow

---

[6] As specified in PEP 249, the Python Database API Specification.

data-processing frameworks such as Apache Pandas and Spark to easily interpret the output data.

For uploading data to S3, the S3Hook provides various convenience methods. For file-like objects,[7] we can apply load_file_obj().

Listing 7.13 In-memory conversion of Postgres query results to CSV and upload to S3

```
def execute(self, context):
    postgres_hook = PostgresHook(postgres_conn_id=self._postgres_conn_id)
    s3_hook = S3Hook(aws_conn_id=self._s3_conn_id)

    results = postgres_hook.get_records(self.query)

    data_buffer = io.StringIO()
    csv_writer = csv.writer(data_buffer, lineterminator=os.linesep)
    csv_writer.writerows(results)
    data_buffer_binary = io.BytesIO(data_buffer.getvalue().encode())
    s3_hook.load_file_obj(
        file_obj=data_buffer_binary,
        bucket_name=self._s3_bucket,
        key=self._s3_key,
        replace=True,
    )
```

For convenience, we first create a string buffer, which is like a file in memory to which we can write strings. After writing, we convert it to binary.

It requires a file-like object in binary mode.

Ensure idempotency by replacing files if they already exist.

Buffers live in memory, which can be convenient because memory leaves no remaining files on the filesystem after processing. However, we have to realize that the output of the Postgres query must fit into memory. The key to idempotency is setting replace=True. This ensures existing files are overwritten. We can rerun our pipeline after, for example, a code change, and then the pipeline will fail without replace=True because of the existing file.

With these few extra lines, we can now store CSV files on S3. Let's see it in practice.

Listing 7.14 Running the PostgresToS3Operator

```
download_from_postgres = PostgresToS3Operator(
    task_id="download_from_postgres",
    postgres_conn_id="inside_airbnb",
    query="SELECT * FROM listings WHERE download_date={{ ds }}",
    s3_conn_id="s3",
    s3_bucket="inside_airbnb",
    s3_key="listing-{{ ds }}.csv",
    dag=dag,
)
```

With this code, we now have a convenient operator that makes querying Postgres and writing the result to CSV on S3 an exercise of filling in the blanks.

---

[7] In-memory objects with file-operation methods for reading/writing.

7.2.2 Outsourcing the heavy work

A common discussion in the Airflow community is whether to view Airflow as not only a task orchestration system but also a task execution system since many DAGs are written with the BashOperator and PythonOperator, which execute work within the same Python runtime as Airflow. Opponents of this mindset argue for viewing Airflow only as a task-triggering system and suggest no actual work should be done inside Airflow itself. Instead, all work should be offloaded to a system intended for dealing with data, such as Apache Spark.

Let's imagine we have a very large job that would take all resources on the machine Airflow is running on. In this case, it's better to run the job elsewhere; Airflow will start the job and wait for it to complete. The idea is that there should be a strong separation between orchestration and execution, which we can achieve by Airflow starting the job and waiting for completion and a data-processing framework such as Spark performing the actual work.

In Spark, there are various ways to start a job:

- *Using the* SparkSubmitOperator—This requires a spark-submit binary and YARN client config on the Airflow machine to find the Spark instance.
- *Using the* SSHOperator—This requires SSH access to a Spark instance but does not require Spark client config on the Airflow instance.
- *Using the* SimpleHTTPOperator—This requires running Livy, a REST API for Apache Spark, to access Spark.

The key to working with any operator in Airflow is reading the documentation and figuring out which arguments to provide. Let's look at the DockerOperator, which starts the Docker container for processing the Inside Airbnb data using Pandas.

Listing 7.15 Running a Docker container with the DockerOperator

```
crunch_numbers = DockerOperator(
    task_id="crunch_numbers",
    image="airflowbook/numbercruncher",
    api_version="auto",
    auto_remove=True,
    docker_url="unix://var/run/docker.sock",
    network_mode="host",
    environment={
        "S3_ENDPOINT": "localhost:9000",
        "S3_ACCESS_KEY": "[insert access key]",
        "S3_SECRET_KEY": "[insert secret key]",
    },
    dag=dag,
)
```

Remove the container after completion.

To connect to other services on the host machine via http:// localhost, we must share the host network namespace by using host network mode.

The DockerOperator wraps around the Python Docker client and, given a list of arguments, enables starting Docker containers. In listing 7.15, the docker_url is set to a Unix socket, which requires Docker running on the local machine. It starts the Docker image `airflowbook/numbercruncher`, which includes a Pandas script loading the Inside Airbnb data from S3, processing it, and writing back the results to S3.

Listing 7.16   Sample results from the numbercruncher script

```
[
  {
    "id": 5530273,
    "download_date_min": 1428192000000,
    "download_date_max": 1441238400000,
    "oldest_price": 48,
    "latest_price": 350,
    "price_diff_per_day": 2
  },
  {
    "id": 5411434,
    "download_date_min": 1428192000000,
    "download_date_max": 1441238400000,
    "oldest_price": 48,
    "latest_price": 250,
    "price_diff_per_day": 1.3377483444
  },
  ...
]
```

Airflow manages the starting of the container, fetching logs, and eventually removing the container if required. The key is to ensure no state is left behind such that your tasks can run idempotently and no remainders are left.

Summary

- Operators for external systems expose functionality by calling the client for a given system.
- Sometimes these operators are merely passing through arguments to the Python client.
- Other times they provide additional functionality, such as the `SageMaker-TrainingOperator`, which continuously polls AWS and blocks until completion.
- If access to external services from the local machine is possible, we can test tasks using the CLI command `airflow tasks test`.

Building custom components

This chapter covers

- Making your DAGs more modular and succinct with custom components
- Designing and implementing a custom hook
- Designing and implementing a custom operator
- Designing and implementing a custom sensor
- Distributing your custom components as a basic Python library

One strong feature of Airflow is that it can be easily extended to coordinate jobs across many different types of systems. We have already seen some of this function ality in earlier chapters, where we were able to execute a job on for training a machine learning model on Amazon's SageMaker service using the S3CopyObject-Operator, but you can (for example) also use Airflow to run jobs on an ECS (Elastic Container Service) cluster in AWS using the ECSOperator to perform queries on a Postgres database with the PostgresOperator, and much more.

However, at some point, you may want to execute a task on a system that is not supported by Airflow, or you may have a task that you can implement using the

PythonOperator but that requires a lot of boilerplate code, which prevents others from easily reusing your code across different DAGs. How should you go about this?

Fortunately, Airflow allows you to easily create new operators for implementing your custom operations. This enables you to run jobs on otherwise unsupported systems or simply to make common operations easy to apply across DAGs. In fact, this is exactly how many of the operators in Airflow were implemented: someone needed to run a job on a certain system and built an operator for it.

In this chapter, we will show you how you can build your own operators and use them in your DAGs. We will also explore how you can package your custom components into a Python package, making them easy to install and reuse across environments.

8.1   *Starting with a PythonOperator*

Before building any custom components, let's try solving our problem using the (by now familiar) PythonOperator. In this case, we're interested in building a recommender system, which will recommend new movie(s) to watch depending on our view history. However, as an initial pilot project, we decide to focus on simply getting in our data, which concerns past ratings of users for a given set of movies and recommending the movies that seem most popular overall based on their ratings.

The movie ratings data will be supplied via an API, which we can use to obtain user ratings in a certain time period. This allows us, for example, to fetch new ratings daily and to use this for training our recommender. For our pilot, we want to set up this daily import process and create a ranking of the most popular movies. This ranking will be used downstream to start recommending popular movies (figure 8.1).

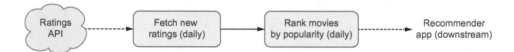

Figure 8.1   **Building a simple pilot MVP for movie recommender project**

8.1.1   *Simulating a movie rating API*

To simulate data for this use case, we use data from the 25M MovieLens data set (https://grouplens.org/datasets/movielens/), which is freely available and contains 25 million ratings for 62,000 movies by 162,000 users. As the data set itself is provided as a flat file, we built a small REST API using Flask,[1] which serves parts of the data set at different endpoints.

---

[1] The code for the API is available in the code repository accompanying this book.

To start serving the API, we've provided a smaller Docker Compose file that creates multiple containers: one for our REST API and a couple for running Airflow itself. You can start both containers using the following commands:

```
$ cd chapter08
$ docker-compose up
```

After both containers have finished starting up, you should be able to access our movie rating API at port 5000 on localhost (http://localhost:5000). Visiting this URL should show you a hello from our movie rating API (figure 8.2).

Figure 8.2   Hello from the movie rating API

For this use case, we are mainly interested in obtaining movie ratings, which are provided by the /ratings endpoint of the API. To access this endpoint, visit http://localhost:5000/ratings. This should result in an authentication prompt (figure 8.3), as this part of the API returns data that could contain (potentially) sensitive user information. By default, we use airflow/airflow as a username and password combination.

Figure 8.3   Authenticating to the ratings endpoint

Figure 8.4   Ratings returned by the ratings endpoint of the API

After you enter the credentials, you should get an initial list of ratings (figure 8.4). As you can see, the ratings are returned in a JSON format. In this JSON, the actual ratings are contained in the `result` key, while two additional fields, `limit` and `offset`, indicate that we are only looking at a single page of the results (the first 100 ratings) and that there are potentially more ratings available (indicated by the total field, which describes the total number of records available for a query).

To step through the paginated result of a query, you can use the `offset` parameter of the API. For example, to fetch the next set of 100 records, we can add the `offset` parameter with a value of 100:

http://localhost:5000/ratings?offset=100

We can also increase the number of records retrieved in a single query using the `limit` parameter:

http://localhost:5000/ratings?limit=1000

By default, the ratings endpoint returns all ratings available in the API. To fetch ratings for a specific time period, we can select ratings between a given start/end date using the `start_date` and `end_date` parameters:[2]

http://localhost:5000/ratings?start_date=2019-01-01&end_date=2019-01-02

---

[2] The API only goes back 30 days, so make sure to update the start/end date parameters to more recent dates than this example to get results.

This API filtering functionality will allow us to load data from the API on an incremental (daily) basis, without having to load the full data set.

8.1.2 *Fetching ratings from the API*

Now that we've seen the basics of the MovieLens API, we want to start fetching ratings programmatically so that we can (later) automate this fetching using Airflow.

For accessing our API from Python, we can use requests (https://requests.readthe docs.io/en/master/), which is a popular and easy-to-use library for performing HTTP requests in Python. To start firing requests at our API, we first need to create a requests session using the Session class:

```
import requests
session = requests.Session()
```

This session will then allow us to fetch ratings from our API by using its get method, which performs a GET HTTP request on our API:

```
response = session.get("http://localhost:5000/ratings")
```

The get method also allows us to pass extra arguments, such as parameters (e.g., start/end date), to include in the query:

```
response = session.get(
    "http://localhost:5000/ratings",
    params={
        "start_date": "2019-01-01",
        "end_date": "2019-01-02",
    },
)
```

Our call to get will return a *response object*, representing the result of the request. This response object can be used to check whether the query was successful using the raise_for_status method, which raises an exception if the query returned an unexpected status code. We can access the result of the query using the content attribute or, in this case, using the json method (as we know that our API returns JSON):

```
response.raise_for_status()
response.json()
```

If we perform this query, we should see that our requests fail, as we forgot to include any authentication in our request. Because our API is using basic HTTP authentication, we can configure our session to include our authentication details as follows:

```
movielens_user = "airflow"
movielens_password = "airflow"

session.auth = (movielens_user, movielens_password)
```

This will make sure that the requests session includes our username/password authentication with its requests.

Let's encapsulate this functionality in a _get_session function, which will handle setting up the session with authentication so that we don't have to worry about this in other parts of our code. We'll also let this function return the base URL of the API so that this is also defined in a single place.

Listing 8.1   Function that builds the API HTTP session

```
def _get_session():
    """Builds a requests Session for the Movielens API."""


    session = requests.Session()          ⟵┘  Create a requests
    session.auth = ("airflow", "airflow")  ⟵   session.

    base_url = "http://localhost:5000"

    return session, base_url   ⟵
```

Create a requests session.

Configure the session for basic HTTP authentication with this username and password.

Return the session together with the API's base URL, so we also know where to reach the API.

To make this a bit more configurable, we can also specify our username/password and the different parts of our URL using environment variables.

Listing 8.2   Making _get_session configurable (dags/01_python.py)

Retrieve the API configuration details from optional environment variables.

```
MOVIELENS_HOST = os.environ.get("MOVIELENS_HOST", "movielens")   ⟵
MOVIELENS_SCHEMA = os.environ.get("MOVIELENS_SCHEMA", "http")
MOVIELENS_PORT = os.environ.get("MOVIELENS_PORT", "5000")

MOVIELENS_USER = os.environ["MOVIELENS_USER"]          ⟵
MOVIELENS_PASSWORD = os.environ["MOVIELENS_PASSWORD"]

def _get_session():
    """Builds a requests Session for the Movielens API."""

    session = requests.Session()
    session.auth = (MOVIELENS_USER, MOVIELENS_PASSWORD)

    base_url = f"{MOVIELENS_SCHEMA}://{MOVIELENS_HOST}:{MOVIELENS_PORT}"

    return session, base_url

session, base_url = _get_session()
```

Fetch the username/ password from two required environment variables.

Use the retrieved configuration to build our session and base URL.

This will later allow us to easily change these parameters when running our script by defining values for these environment variables.

Now that we have a rudimentary setup for our requests session, we need to implement some functionality that will transparently handle the pagination of the API.

One way to do this is to wrap our call to `session.get` with some code that inspects the API response and keeps requesting new pages until we reach the total number of rating records.

Listing 8.3 Helper function for handling pagination (dags/01_python.py)

```python
def _get_with_pagination(session, url, params, batch_size=100):
    """
    Fetches records using a GET request with given URL/params,
    taking pagination into account.
    """
    offset = 0
    total = None
    while total is None or offset < total:
        response = session.get(
            url,
            params={
                **params,
                **{"offset": offset, "limit": batch_size}
            }
        )
        response.raise_for_status()
        response_json = response.json()

        yield from response_json["result"]

        offset += batch_size
        total = response_json["total"]
```

- **Keep track of how many records we've retrieved and how many we should expect.** → `offset = 0` / `total = None`
- **Keep looping until we've retrieved all records. Note that the None check is for the first loop, as the total number of records is unknown until after the first loop.** → `while total is None or offset < total:`
- **Fetch a new page, starting from the given offset.**
- **Check the result status and parse the result JSON.** → `response_json = response.json()`
- **Yield any retrieved records to the caller.** → `yield from response_json["result"]`
- **Update our current offset and the total number of records.**

By using `yield from` to return our results, this function effectively returns a generator of individual rating records, meaning that we don't have to worry about pages of results anymore.[3]

The only thing missing is a function that ties this all together and allows us to perform queries to the ratings endpoint while specifying start and end dates for the desired date range.

Listing 8.4 Tying things together in _get_ratings (dags/01_python.py)

Get the requests session (with authentication) plus base URL for the API.

```python
def _get_ratings(start_date, end_date, batch_size=100):
    session, base_url = _get_session()

    yield from _get_with_pagination(
        session=session,
        url=base_url + "/ratings",
```

- **Make sure we're using the ratings endpoint.**
- **Use our pagination function to transparently fetch a collection of records.**

---

[3] An additional advantage of this implementation is that it is lazy: it will only fetch a new page when the records from the current page have been exhausted.

```
        params="start_date": start_date, "end_date": end_date},     ◄──┐  Fetch records
        batch_size=batch_size,     ◄──┐  Limit pages to a                   between the
    )                                     specific batch size.              given start/end
                                                                            dates.
ratings = _get_ratings(session, base_url + "/ratings")     ◄──────┐
next(ratings)     ◄──────┐  Fetch a single record...              │  Example usage of
list(ratings)     ◄──────┘                                        │  the _get_ratings
                         └── ... or fetch the entire batch.        │  function
```

This provides us with a nice, concise function for fetching ratings, which we can start using in our DAG.

8.1.3 Building the actual DAG

Now that we have our _get_ratings function, we can call it using the PythonOperator to fetch ratings for each schedule interval. Once we have the ratings, we can dump the results into a JSON output file, partitioned by date so that we can easily rerun fetches if needed.

We can implement this functionality by writing a small wrapper function that takes care of supplying the start/end dates and writing the ratings to an output function.

Listing 8.5 Using the _get_ratings function (dags/01_python.py)

```
def _fetch_ratings(templates_dict, batch_size=1000, **_):     ┌── Use logging to provide
    logger = logging.getLogger(__name__)     ◄──────             │  some useful feedback
                                                                 │  about what the function
    start_date = templates_dict["start_date"]     ◄──┐         │  is doing.
    end_date = templates_dict["end_date"]             │
    output_path = templates_dict["output_path"]       │  Extract the templated start/end
                                                      └── dates and output path.
    logger.info(f"Fetching ratings for {start_date} to {end_date}")
    ratings = list(                           ◄──┐  Use the _get_ratings
        _get_ratings(                              │  function to fetch
            start_date=start_date,                 │  rating records.
            end_date=end_date,
            batch_size=batch_size,
        )
    )
    logger.info(f"Fetched {len(ratings)} ratings")

    logger.info(f"Writing ratings to {output_path}")     ┌── Create the output
                                                          │  directory if it
    output_dir = os.path.dirname(output_path)     ◄──────┘  doesn't exist.
    os.makedirs(output_dir, exist_ok=True)
                                              ┌── Write the output
                                              │  data as JSON.
    with open(output_path, "w") as file_:     ◄──┘
        json.dump(ratings, fp=file_)


fetch_ratings = PythonOperator(     ◄──┐  Create the
    task_id="fetch_ratings",              │  task using the
    python_callable=_fetch_ratings,       │  PythonOperator.
    templates_dict={
        "start_date": "{{ds}}",
```

```
        "end_date": "{{next_ds}}",
        "output_path": "/data/python/ratings/{{ds}}.json",
    },
)
```

Note that the start_date/end_date/output_path parameters are passed using templates_dict, which allows us to reference context variables, such as the execution date, in their values.

After fetching our ratings, we include another step, rank_movies, to produce our rankings. This step uses the PythonOperator to apply our rank_movies_by_rating function, which ranks movies by their average rating, optionally filtering for a minimum number of ratings.

Listing 8.6 Helper function for ranking movies (dags/custom/ranking.py)

```
import pandas as pd

def rank_movies_by_rating(ratings, min_ratings=2):          Calculate the average
    ranking = (                                             rating and the total
        ratings.groupby("movieId")                          number of ratings.
        .agg(
            avg_rating=pd.NamedAgg(column="rating", aggfunc="mean"),
            num_ratings=pd.NamedAgg(column="userId", aggfunc="nunique"),
        )
        .loc[lambda df: df["num_ratings"] > min_ratings]
        .sort_values(["avg_rating", "num_ratings"], ascending=False)
    )
    return ranking
                                                            Sort by average rating.
```

Filter for the minimum number required ratings.

Listing 8.7 Adding the rank_movies task (dags/01_python.py)

```
def _rank_movies(templates_dict, min_ratings=2, **_):
    input_path = templates_dict["input_path"]
    output_path = templates_dict["output_path"]         Read ratings from the
                                                        given (templated)
    ratings = pd.read_json(input_path)                  input path.
    ranking = rank_movies_by_rating(ratings, min_ratings=min_ratings)

    output_dir = os.path.dirname(output_path)           Create the output
    os.makedirs(output_dir, exist_ok=True)              directory if it
                                                        doesn't exist.
    ranking.to_csv(output_path, index=True)

                                                   Use the _rank_movies
rank_movies = PythonOperator(                      function within a
    task_id="rank_movies",                         PythonOperator.
    python_callable=_rank_movies,
    templates_dict={
        "input_path": "/data/python/ratings/{{ds}}.json",
        "output_path": "/data/python/rankings/{{ds}}.csv",
    },
)
                                                   Connect the fetch
fetch_ratings >> rank_movies                       and rank tasks.
```

Use the helper function to rank movies.

Write ranked movies to CSV.

This results in a DAG comprising two steps: one for fetching ratings and one for ranking movies. As such, by scheduling this DAG to run daily, it provides a ranking of the most popular movies for that day. (Of course, a smarter algorithm might take some history into account, but we have to start somewhere, right?)

8.2 Building a custom hook

As you can see, it takes some effort (and code) to actually start fetching ratings from our API and to use them for our ranking. Interestingly, the majority of our code concerns the interaction with the API, in which we have to get our API address and authentication details, set up a session for interacting with the API, and include extra functionality for handling details of the API, such as pagination.

One way of dealing with the complexity of interacting with the API is encapsulating all this code into a reusable Airflow hook. By doing so, we can keep all the API-specific code in one place and simply use this hook in different places in our DAGs, which allows us to reduce the effort of fetching ratings to something like this.

> **Listing 8.8   Using a MovielensHook for fetching ratings**

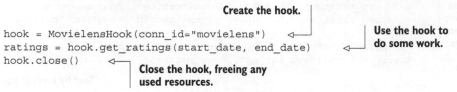

```
                                      Create the hook.
hook = MovielensHook(conn_id="movielens")     ◁             Use the hook to
ratings = hook.get_ratings(start_date, end_date)   ◁        do some work.
hook.close()   ◁
                 Close the hook, freeing any
                 used resources.
```

Hooks also allow us to leverage Airflow's functionality for managing connection credentials via the database and UI, meaning that we don't have to manually supply our API credentials to our DAG. In the next few sections, we'll explore how to write a custom hook and set about building a hook for our movie API.

8.2.1 Designing a custom hook

In Airflow, all hooks are created as subclasses of the abstract `BaseHook` class.

> **Listing 8.9   Skeleton for a custom hook**

```
from airflow.hooks.base_hook import BaseHook

class MovielensHook(BaseHook):
    ...
```

To start building a hook, we need to define an `__init__` method that specifies which connection the hook uses (if applicable) and any other extra arguments our hook might need. In this case, we want our hook to get its connection details from a specific connection but don't need any extra arguments.

Listing 8.10 Start of the MovielensHook class (dags/custom/hooks.py)

```
from airflow.hooks.base_hook import BaseHook

class MovielensHook(BaseHook):
    def __init__(self, conn_id):
        super().__init__()
        self._conn_id = conn_id
```

The parameter conn_id tells the hook which connection to use.

Call the constructor of the BaseHook class.[4]

Don't forget to store our connection ID.

Most Airflow hooks are expected to define a get_conn method, which is responsible for setting up a connection to an external system. In our case, this means that we can reuse most of our previously defined _get_session function, which already provides us with a preconfigured session for the movie API. That means a naive implementation of get_conn could look something like this.

Listing 8.11 Initial implementation of the get_conn method

```
class MovielensHook(BaseHook):

    ...

    def get_conn(self):
        session = requests.Session()
        session.auth = (MOVIELENS_USER, MOVIELENS_PASSWORD)

        schema = MOVIELENS_SCHEMA
        host = MOVIELENS_HOST
        port = MOVIELENS_PORT

        base_url = f"{schema}://{host}:{port}"

        return session, base_url
```

However, instead of hardcoding our credentials, we prefer to fetch them from the Airflow credentials store, which is more secure and easier to manage. To do so, we first need to add our connection to the Airflow metastore, which we can do by opening the "Admin > Connections" section using the Airflow web UI and clicking Create to add a new connection.

In the connection create screen (figure 8.5), we need to fill in the connection details of our API. In this case, we'll call the connection "movielens." We'll use this ID later in our code to refer to the connection. Under connection type, we select HTTP for our rest API. Under host, we need to refer to the hostname of the API in our Docker Compose setup, which is "movielens." Next, we can (optionally) indicate what schema we'll use for the connection (HTTP) and add the required login credentials

---

[4] In Airflow 1, the constructor of the BaseHook class requires a source argument to be passed. Typically you can just pass source=None, as you won't be using it anywhere.

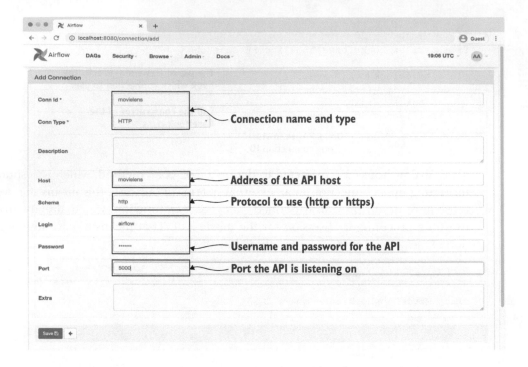

Figure 8.5   Adding our movie API connection in the Airflow web UI

(user: "airflow", password: "airflow"). Finally, we need to say under which port our API will be available, which is port 5000 in our Docker Compose setup (as we saw earlier when manually accessing the API).

Now that we have our connection, we need to modify our get_conn to fetch the connection details from the metastore. To do so, the BaseHook class provides a convenience method called get_connection, which can retrieve the connection details for a given connection ID from the metastore:

```
config = self.get_connection(self._conn_id)
```

This connection configuration object has fields that map to the different details we just filled in when creating our connection. As such, we can use the config object to start determining the host/port and user/password for our API. First, we use the schema, host, and port fields to determine our API URL as before:

```
schema = config.schema or self.DEFAULT_SCHEMA
host = config.host or self.DEFAULT_HOST
port = config.port or self.DEFAULT_PORT

base_url = f"{schema}://{host}:{port}/"
```

Note that we define default values in our class (similar to the constants we defined before) in case these fields are not specified in the connection. If we want to require them to be specified in the connection itself, we can raise an error instead of supplying defaults.

Now that we have obtained our base URL from the metastore, we only need to configure authentication details on our session:

```
if config.login:
    session.auth = (config.login, config.password)
```

This gives us the following new implementation for get_conn.

Listing 8.12 Making get_conn configurable (dags/custom/hooks.py)

```
class MovielensHook(BaseHook):
    DEFAULT_HOST = "movielens"          Default connection values,
    DEFAULT_SCHEMA = "http"             as stored class variables
    DEFAULT_PORT = 5000                 for convenience

    def __init__(self, conn_id):
        super().__init__()
        self._conn_id = conn_id

    def get_conn(self):
        config = self.get_connection(self._conn_id)    Fetching the connection
                                                        configuration using the
                                                        given ID

        schema = config.schema or self.DEFAULT_SCHEMA    Building the base URL
        host = config.host or self.DEFAULT_HOST          using the connection
        port = config.port or self.DEFAULT_PORT          config and defaults

        base_url = f"{schema}://{host}:{port}"

        session = requests.Session()                Creating the requests
                                                    session using login/
        if config.login:                            password from the
            session.auth = (config.login, config.password)   connection config

        return session, base_url      Returning the requests
                                      session and base URL
```

One drawback of this implementation is that each call to get_conn will result in a call to the Airflow metastore, as get_conn needs to fetch the credentials from the database. We can avoid this limitation by also caching session and base_url on our instance as protected variables.

Listing 8.13 Adding caching for the API session (dags/custom/hooks.py)

```
class MovielensHook(BaseHook):

    def __init__(self, conn_id, retry=3):
        ...
        self._session = None        Two extra instance variables, used for
        self._base_url = None       caching the session and base URL
```

```
def get_conn(self):
    """
    Returns the connection used by the hook for querying data.
    Should in principle not be used directly.
    """

    if self._session is None:
        config = self.get_connection(self._conn_id)
        ...
        self._base_url = f"{schema}://{config.host}:{port}"

        self._session = requests.Session()
        ...

    return self._session, self._base_url
```

Check if we already have an active session before creating one.

This way, the first time get_conn gets called, self._session is None, so we end up fetching our connection details from the metastore and setting up our base URL and session. By storing these objects in the _session and _base_url instance variables, we make sure that these objects are cached for later calls. As such, a second call to get_conn will see that self._session no longer is None and will return the cached session and base URL.

> **NOTE** Personally, we're not fans of using the get_conn method directly outside of the hook, even though it is publicly exposed, because this method exposes the internal details of how your hook accesses the external system, breaking encapsulation. This will give you substantial headaches if you ever want to change this internal detail, as your code will be strongly coupled to the internal connection type. This has been an issue in the Airflow codebase as well, for example, in the case of the HdfsHook, where the implementation of the hook was tightly coupled to a Python 2.7–only library (snakebite).

Now that we have completed our implementation of get_conn, we are able to build an authenticated connection to our API. This means we can finally start building some useful methods into our hook, which we can then use to do something useful with our API.

For fetching ratings, we can reuse the code from our previous implementation, which retrieved ratings from the /ratings endpoint of the API and used our get_with_pagination function to handle pagination. The main difference from the previous version is that we now use get_conn within the pagination function to get our API session.

Listing 8.14   Adding a get_ratings method (dags/custom/hooks.py)

```
class MovielensHook(BaseHook):
    ...

    def get_ratings(self, start_date=None, end_date=None, batch_size=100):
        """
        Fetches ratings between the given start/end date.
```

Public method that will be called by users of the hook

```
        Parameters
        ----------
        start_date : str
            Start date to start fetching ratings from (inclusive). Expected
            format is YYYY-MM-DD (equal to Airflow"s ds formats).
        end_date : str
            End date to fetching ratings up to (exclusive). Expected
            format is YYYY-MM-DD (equal to Airflow"s ds formats).
        batch_size : int
            Size of the batches (pages) to fetch from the API. Larger values
            mean less requests, but more data transferred per request.
        """

        yield from self._get_with_pagination(
            endpoint="/ratings",
            params={"start_date": start_date, "end_date": end_date},
            batch_size=batch_size,
        )

    def _get_with_pagination(self, endpoint, params, batch_size=100):      ◁──┐
        """                                                                   │
        Fetches records using a get request with given url/params,           │
        taking pagination into account.                                      │
        """                                                  Our internal helper
                                                             method that handles
        session, base_url = self.get_conn()                    pagination (same
                                                                 implementation
        offset = 0                                                  as before)
        total = None
        while total is None or offset < total:
            response = session.get(
                url, params={
                    **params,
                    **{"offset": offset, "limit": batch_size}
                }
            )
            response.raise_for_status()
            response_json = response.json()

            yield from response_json["result"]

            offset += batch_size
            total = response_json["total"]
```

Altogether, this gives us a basic Airflow hook that handles connections to the Movie-Lens API. Adding extra functionality (other than just fetching ratings) can be easily done by adding extra methods to the hook.

Although it may seem like a lot of effort to build a hook, most of the work was shifting around the functions we wrote before into a single, consolidated hook class. An advantage of our new hook is that it provides nice encapsulation of the MovieLens API logic in a single class, which is easy to use across different DAGs.

8.2.2   *Building our DAG with the MovielensHook*

Now that we have our hook, we can start using it to a fetch ratings in our DAG. However, first we need to save our hook class somewhere so that we can import it into our DAG. One way is by creating a package in the same directory as our DAGs folder[5] and save our hook in a hooks.py module inside this package.

> **Listing 8.15   Structure for a DAG directory with a custom package**

```
chapter08
├── dags                        Example package
│   ├── custom        ◄────      named "custom"
│   │   ├── __init__.py
│   │   └── hooks.py   ◄──       Module containing
│   ├── 01_python.py            the custom hook
│   └── 02_hook.py              code
├── docker-compose.yml
└── ...
```

Once we have this package, we can import our hook from the new custom package, which contains our custom hook code:

```
from custom.hooks import MovielensHook
```

After importing the hook, fetching ratings becomes quite simple. We only need to instantiate the hook with the proper connection ID and then call the hook's get_ratings method with the desired start/end dates.

> **Listing 8.16   Using our MovielensHook to fetch ratings**

```
hook = MovielensHook(conn_id=conn_id)
ratings = hook.get_ratings(
    start_date=start_date,
    end_date=end_date,
    batch_size=batch_size
)
```

This gives back a generator of rating records, which we then write to an output (JSON) file.

To use the hook in our DAG, we still need to wrap this code in a PythonOperator that takes care of supplying the correct start/end dates for the given DAG run, as well as actually writing the ratings to the desired output file. For this, we can essentially use the same _fetch_ratings function we defined for our initial DAG, changing the call to _get_ratings with the call to our new hook.

---

[5] We'll show another package-based approach later in this chapter.

Listing 8.17   Using the MovielensHook in the DAG (dags/02_hook.py)

Create an instance of the MovielensHook with the appropriate connection ID.

```
def _fetch_ratings(conn_id, templates_dict, batch_size=1000, **_):
    logger = logging.getLogger(__name__)

    start_date = templates_dict["start_date"]
    end_date = templates_dict["end_date"]
    output_path = templates_dict["output_path"]

    logger.info(f"Fetching ratings for {start_date} to {end_date}")
    hook = MovielensHook(conn_id=conn_id)          ←
    ratings = list(
        hook.get_ratings(
            start_date=start_date, end_date=end_date, batch_size=batch_size
        )
    )
    logger.info(f"Fetched {len(ratings)} ratings")

    logger.info(f"Writing ratings to {output_path}")

    output_dir = os.path.dirname(output_path)
    os.makedirs(output_dir, exist_ok=True)

    with open(output_path, "w") as file_:
        json.dump(ratings, fp=file_)


PythonOperator(
    task_id="fetch_ratings",
    python_callable=_fetch_ratings,
    op_kwargs={"conn_id": "movielens"},          ←
    templates_dict={
        "start_date": "{{ds}}",
        "end_date": "{{next_ds}}",
        "output_path": "/data/custom_hook/{{ds}}.json",
    },
)
```

Use the hook to fetch ratings from the API.

Write the fetched ratings like before.

Specify which connection to use.

Note that we added the parameter conn_id to fetch_ratings, which specifies the connection to use for the hook. As such, we also need to include this parameter when calling _fetch_ratings from the PythonOperator.

This gives us the same behavior as before, but with a much simpler and smaller DAG file, as most of the complexity surrounding the MovieLens API is now outsourced to the MovielensHook.

8.3   *Building a custom operator*

Although building a MovielensHook has allowed us to move a lot of complexity from our DAG into the hook, we still have to write a considerable amount of boilerplate code for defining start/end dates and writing the ratings to an output file. This means that, if we want to reuse this functionality in multiple DAGs, we will still have some considerable code duplication and extra effort involved.

Fortunately, Airflow also allows us to build custom operators, which can be used to perform repetitive tasks with a minimal amount of boilerplate code. In this case, we could, for example, use this functionality to build a `MovielensFetchRatingsOperator`, which would allow us to fetch movie ratings using a specialized operator class.

8.3.1   *Defining a custom operator*

In Airflow, all operators are built as subclasses of the `BaseOperator` class.

Listing 8.18   Skeleton for a custom operator

```
from airflow.models import BaseOperator
from airflow.utils.decorators import apply_defaults


class MyCustomOperator(BaseOperator):
    @apply_defaults
    def __init__(self, conn_id, **kwargs):
        super.__init__(self, **kwargs)
        self._conn_id = conn_id
        ...
```

Inherit from the Base-Operator class.

Decorator that makes sure default DAG arguments are passed to our operator

Pass any extra keyword arguments to the BaseOperator constructor.

Any arguments specific to your operator (such as `conn_id` in this example) can be specified explicitly in the `__init__` constructor method. How you use these arguments is, of course, up to you. Operator-specific arguments vary between different operators, but typically include connection IDs (for operators involving remote systems) and any details required for the operation (such as start/end dates, queries, etc.).

The `BaseOperator` class also takes a large number of (mostly optional) generic arguments that define the basic behavior of the operator. Examples of generic arguments include the `task_id` the operator created for the task, but also many arguments such as `retries` and `retry_delay` that affect the scheduling of the resulting task. To avoid having to list all these generic tasks explicitly, we use Python's `**kwargs` syntax to forward these generic arguments to the `__init__` of the `BaseOperator` class.

Thinking back to earlier DAGs in this book, you may remember that Airflow also provides the option of defining certain arguments as default arguments for the entire DAG. This is done using the `default_args` parameter to the DAG object itself.

Listing 8.19   Applying default arguments to operators

```
default_args = {
    "retries": 1,
    "retry_delay": timedelta(minutes=5),
}

with DAG(
    ...
    default_args=default_args
```

```
) as dag:
    MyCustomOperator(
        ...
    )
```

To ensure that these default arguments are applied to your custom operator, Airflow supplies the `apply_defaults` decorator, which is applied to the `__init__` method of your operator (as shown in our initial example). In practice, this means that you should always include the `apply_defaults` decorator when defining custom operators; otherwise, you will inadvertently break this Airflow behavior for your operator.

Now that we have our basic custom operator class, we still need to define what our operator actually does by implementing the `execute` method, the main method Airflow calls when the operator is actually being executed as part of a DAG run.

Listing 8.20   The operator's execute method

```
class MyCustomOperator(BaseOperator):
    ...

    def execute(self, context):   ◁─────┐  Main method called when
        ...                              executing our operator
```

As you can see, the `execute` method takes a single parameter, `context`, which is a dict containing all the Airflow context variables. The method can then continue to perform whatever function the operator was designed to do, taking variables from the Airflow context (such as execution dates, etc.) into account.

8.3.2   Building an operator for fetching ratings

Now that we know the basics of building an operator, let's see how we can start building a custom one for fetching ratings. The idea is that this operator fetches ratings from the MovieLens API between a given start/end date and writes these ratings to a JSON file, similar to what our `_fetch_ratings` function was doing in our previous DAG.

We can start by filling in the required parameters for the operator in its `__init__` method, which include the start/end dates, which connection to use, and an output path to write to.

Listing 8.21   Start of the custom operator (dags/custom/operators.py)

```
class MovielensFetchRatingsOperator(BaseOperator):
    """
    Operator that fetches ratings from the Movielens API.

    Parameters
    ----------
    conn_id : str
        ID of the connection to use to connect to the Movielens
        API. Connection is expected to include authentication
        details (login/password) and the host that is serving the API.
```

```
    output_path : str
        Path to write the fetched ratings to.
    start_date : str
        (Templated) start date to start fetching ratings from (inclusive).
        Expected format is YYYY-MM-DD (equal to Airflow"s ds formats).
    end_date : str
        (Templated) end date to fetching ratings up to (exclusive).
        Expected format is YYYY-MM-DD (equal to Airflow"s ds formats).
    """

    @apply_defaults
    def __init__(
        self, conn_id, output_path, start_date, end_date, **kwargs,
    ):
        super(MovielensFetchRatingsOperator, self).__init__(**kwargs)

        self._conn_id = conn_id
        self._output_path = output_path
        self._start_date = start_date
        self._end_date = end_date
```

Next, we have to implement the body of the operator, which actually fetches the ratings and writes them to an output file. To do this, we can essentially fill in the execute method of the operator with a modified version of our implementation for _fetch _ratings.

Listing 8.22 Adding the execute method (dags/custom/operators.py)

```
class MovielensFetchRatingsOperator(BaseOperator):
    ...

    def execute(self, context):                          Create an instance of
        hook = MovielensHook(self._conn_id)  ◁─────────  the MovielensHook.

        try:
            self.log.info(
                f"Fetching ratings for {self._start_date} to {self._end_date}"
            )
            ratings = list(
                hook.get_ratings(
                    start_date=self._start_date,
                    end_date=self._end_date,
                )
            )
            self.log.info(f"Fetched {len(ratings)} ratings")
        finally:
            hook.close()

        self.log.info(f"Writing ratings to {self._output_path}")

        output_dir = os.path.dirname(self._output_path)
        os.makedirs(output_dir, exist_ok=True)
```

Use the hook to fetch ratings.

Close the hook to release any resources.

Create the output directory if it doesn't exist.

```
with open(self._output_path, "w") as file_:        ◁——  Write out
    json.dump(ratings, fp=file_)                          the results.
```

As you can see, porting our code to a custom operator required relatively few changes to our code. Similar to the `_fetch_ratings` function, this `execute` method starts by creating an instance of our `MovielensHook` and using this hook to fetch ratings between the given start/end dates. One difference is that the code now takes its parameters from `self`, making sure to use the values passed when instantiating the operator. We also switched our logging calls to use the logger provided by the `BaseOperator` class, which is available in the `self.log` property. Finally, we added some exception handling to make sure our hook is always closed properly, even if the call to `get_ratings` fails. This way, we don't waste any resources by forgetting to close our API sessions , which is good practice when implementing code that uses hooks.

Using this operator is relatively straightforward, as we can simply instantiate the operator and include it in our DAG.

Listing 8.23   Using the MovielensFetchRatingsOperator

```
fetch_ratings = MovielensFetchRatingsOperator(
    task_id="fetch_ratings",
    conn_id="movielens",
    start_date="2020-01-01",
    end_date="2020-01-02",
    output_path="/data/2020-01-01.json"
)
```

A drawback of this implementation is that it takes predefined dates for which the operator will fetch ratings. As such, the operator will only fetch ratings for a single hardcoded time period, without taking the execution date into account.

Fortunately, Airflow also allows us to make certain operator variables templateable, meaning that they can refer to context variables such as the execution date. To allow specific instance variables to be templated, we need to tell Airflow to template them using the `templates_field` class variable.

Listing 8.24   Adding template fields (dags/custom/operators.py)

```
class MovielensFetchRatingsOperator(BaseOperator):
    ...
    template_fields = ("_start_date", "_end_date", "_output_path")      ◁——
    ...
                                                        Tell Airflow to template
                                                        these instance variables
    @apply_defaults                                          on our operator.
    def __init__(
        self,
        conn_id,
        output_path,
        start_date="{{ds}}",
```

```
        end_date="{{next_ds}}",
        **kwargs,
    ):
        super(MovielensFetchRatingsOperator, self).__init__(**kwargs)

        self._conn_id = conn_id
        self._output_path = output_path
        self._start_date = start_date
        self._end_date = end_date
```

This effectively tells Airflow that the variables _start_date, _end_date, and _output _path (which are created in __init__) are available for templating. This means that if we use any Jinja templating in these string parameters, Airflow will make sure that these values are templated before our execute method is called. As a result, we can now use our operator with templated arguments as follows.

Listing 8.25   Using templating in the operator (dags/03_operator.py)

```
from custom.operators import MovielensFetchRatingsOperator

fetch_ratings = MovielensFetchRatingsOperator(
    task_id="fetch_ratings",
    conn_id="movielens",
    start_date="{{ds}}",
    end_date="{{next_ds}}",
    output_path="/data/custom_operator/{{ds}}.json"
)
```

This way, Airflow will fill in the values of the start of the execution window (ds) for the start date and the end of the execution window (next_ds) for the end date. It will also make sure the output is written to a file tagged with the start of the execution window (ds).

8.4   *Building custom sensors*

With all this talk about operators, you may be wondering how much effort it takes to build a custom sensor. In case you skipped over them in previous chapters, a sensor is a special type of operator that can be used to wait for a certain condition to be fulfilled before executing any downstream tasks in the DAG. For example, you may want to use a sensor for checking if certain files or data are available in a source system before trying to use the data in any downstream analysis.

Regarding their implementation, sensors are very similar to operators, except that they inherit from the BaseSensorOperator class instead of the BaseOperator.

Listing 8.26   Skeleton for a custom sensor

```
from airflow.sensors.base import BaseSensorOperator

class MyCustomSensor(BaseSensorOperator):
    ...
```

As the name suggests, this shows that sensors are in fact a special type of operator. The `BaseSensorOperator` class provides the basic functionality for a sensor and requires sensors to implement a special poke method rather than the execute method.

```
class MyCustomSensor(BaseSensorOperator):

    def poke(self, context):
        ...
```

The signature of the poke method is similar to execute in that it takes a single argument containing the Airflow context. However, in contrast to the execute method, poke is expected to return a Boolean value that indicates if the sensor condition is true. If it is, the sensor finishes its execution, allowing downstream tasks to start executing. If the condition is false, the sensor sleeps for several seconds before checking the condition again. This process repeats until the condition becomes true or the sensor hits its timeout.

Although Airflow has many built-in sensors, you can essentially build your own to check any type of condition. For example, in our use case, we may want to implement a sensor that first checks if rating data is available for a given date before continuing with the execution of our DAG.

To start building our `MovielensRatingsSensor`, we first need to define the `__init__` of our custom sensor class, which should take a connection ID (that species which connection details to use for the API) and a range of start/end dates, which specifies for which date range we want to check if there are ratings. This would look something like the following.

```
from airflow.sensors.base import BaseSensorOperator
from airflow.utils.decorators import apply_defaults

class MovielensRatingsSensor(BaseSensorOperator):
    """
    Sensor that waits for the Movielens API to have
    ratings for a time period.

    start_date : str
        (Templated) start date of the time period to check for (inclusive).
        Expected format is YYYY-MM-DD (equal to Airflow"s ds formats).
    end_date : str
        (Templated) end date of the time period to check for (exclusive).
        Expected format is YYYY-MM-DD (equal to Airflow"s ds formats).
    """
```

```
    template_fields = ("_start_date", "_end_date")    ◁─────┐
                                                            │   Since sensors are a special type
    @apply_defaults                                    ◁────┤   of operator, we can use the
    def __init__(self, conn_id, start_date="{{ds}}",        │   same basic setup as we used
                 end_date="{{next_ds}}", **kwargs):         │   for implementing an operator.
        super().__init__(**kwargs)                     ◁────┘
        self._conn_id = conn_id
        self._start_date = start_date
        self._end_date = end_date
```

After specifying the constructor, the only thing we need to implement is our `poke` method. In this method, we can check if there are ratings for a specific date range by simply requesting ratings between the given start/end dates that return true if there are any records. Note that this does not require fetching all rating records; we only need to demonstrate that there is at least one record in the range.

Using our `MovielensHook`, implementing this algorithm is pretty straightforward. First, we instantiate the hook and then call `get_ratings` to start fetching records. As we are only interested in seeing if there is at least one record, we can try calling next on the generator returned by `get_ratings`, which will raise a `StopIteration` if the generator is empty. As such, we can test for the exception using try/except, returning `True` if no exception is raised and `False` if it is (indicating that there were no records).

Listing 8.29   Implementing the poke method (dags/custom/sensors.py)

```
class MovielensRatingsSensor(BaseSensorOperator):
    def poke(self, context):
        hook = MovielensHook(self._conn_id)

        try:
            next(
                hook.get_ratings(
                    start_date=self._start_date,
                    end_date=self._end_date,
                    batch_size=1
                )
            )
            self.log.info(
                f"Found ratings for {self._start_date} to {self._end_date}"
            )
            return True
        except StopIteration:
            self.log.info(
                f"Didn't find any ratings for {self._start_date} "
                f"to {self._end_date}, waiting..."
            )
            return False
        finally:
            hook.close()
```

Try to fetch one record from the hook (using next to fetch the first record).

If this succeeds, we have at least one record, so return true.

If this fails with a StopIteration, the collection of records is empty, so return false.

Makes sure to close the hook to free resources

Note that the reuse of our `MovielensHook` makes this code relatively short and succinct, demonstrating the power of containing the details of interacting with the MovieLens API within the hook class.

This sensor class can now be used to make the DAG check and wait for new ratings to come in before continuing with the execution of the rest of the DAG.

Listing 8.30 Using the sensor to wait for ratings (dags/04_sensor.py)

```
...

from custom.operators import MovielensFetchRatingsOperator
from custom.sensors import MovielensRatingsSensor

with DAG(
    dag_id="04_sensor",
    description="Fetches ratings with a custom sensor.",
    start_date=airflow_utils.dates.days_ago(7),
    schedule_interval="@daily",
) as dag:
    wait_for_ratings = MovielensRatingsSensor(       ◁─┐  Sensor that waits for
        task_id="wait_for_ratings",                        records to be available
        conn_id="movielens",
        start_date="{{ds}}",
        end_date="{{next_ds}}",
    )

    fetch_ratings = MovielensFetchRatingsOperator(   ◁─┐  Operator that fetches
        task_id="fetch_ratings",                           records once the sensor
        conn_id="movielens",                               has completed
        start_date="{{ds}}",
        end_date="{{next_ds}}",
        output_path="/data/custom_sensor/{{ds}}.json"
    )

    ...

    wait_for_ratings >> fetch_ratings >> rank_movies
```

8.5 *Packaging your components*

Up to now, we've relied on including our custom components in a subpackage within the DAGs directory to make them importable by our DAGs. However, this approach is not necessarily ideal if you want to be able to use these components in other projects, want to share them with other people, or want to perform more rigorous testing on them.

A better approach for distributing your components is to put your code into a Python package. Although this requires a bit of extra overhead in terms of setup, it gives you the benefit of being able to install your components into your Airflow environment, as with any other package. Moreover, keeping the code separate from your DAGs allows you to set up a proper CI/CD process for your custom code and makes it easier to share/collaborate on the code with others.

8.5.1   *Bootstrapping a Python package*

Unfortunately, packaging can be a complicated topic in Python. In this case, we'll focus on the most basic example of Python packaging, which involves using `setuptools` to create a simple Python package.[6] Using this approach, we aim to create a small package called `airflow_movielens`, which will contain the hook, operator, and sensor classes written in the previous sections.

To start building our package, lets first create a directory for our package:

```
$ mkdir -p airflow-movielens
$ cd airflow-movielens
```

Next, let's start including our code by creating the base of our package. To do this, we'll contain a `src` subdirectory in our `airflow-movielens` directory and create a directory, `airflow_movielens` (the name of our package), inside this `src` directory. To make `airflow_movielens` into a package, we also create an `__init__.py` file inside the directory:[7]

```
$ mkdir -p src/airflow_movielens
$ touch src/airflow_movielens/__init__.py
```

Next, we can start including our code by creating the files `hooks.py`, `sensors.py`, and `operators.py` in the `airflow_movielens` directory and copying the implementations of our custom hook, sensor, and operator classes into their respective files. Once done, you should end up with a result that looks something like this:

```
$ tree airflow-movielens/
airflow-movielens/
└── src
    └── airflow_movielens
        ├── __init__.py
        ├── hooks.py
        ├── operators.py
        └── sensors.py
```

Now that we have the basic structure of our package, all we need to do to turn this into a package is to include a `setup.py` file, which tells `setuptools` how to install it. A basic setup.py file typically looks something like the following listing.

> **Listing 8.31   Example setup.py file (package/airflow-movielens/setup.py)**

```
#!/usr/bin/env python
import setuptools
```

---

[6] More in-depth discussions of Python packaging and different packaging approaches are outside the scope of this book and explained more elaborately in many Python books and/or online articles.

[7] Technically the `__init__.py` file is no longer necessary with PEP420, but we like to be explicit.

```
                requirements = ["apache-airflow", "requests"]          ◄──┐  List of Python
                                                                          │  packages that our
  Name,                                                                   │  package depends on
  version, and   setuptools.setup(
  description of      name="airflow_movielens",
  our package        version="0.1.0",
                     description="Hooks, sensors and operators for the Movielens API.",
                     author="Anonymous",
  Author details     author_email="anonymous@example.com",        Informs setuptools about
  (metadata)         install_requires=requirements,          ◄──┘  our dependencies
                     packages=setuptools.find_packages("src"),
                     package_dir={"": "src"},                                          Package
                     url="https://github.com/example-repo/airflow_movielens",  ◄──┘    home page
                     license="MIT license",              ◄──┐
                )                                            └─ License of the code

  Tells setuptools where to look
  for our package's Python files
```

The most important part of this file is the call to `setuptools.setup`, which gives `set-uptools` detailed metadata about our package. The most important fields in this call are as follows:

- *name*—Defines the name of your package (what it will be called when installed).
- *version*—The version number of your package.
- *install_requires*—A list of dependencies required by your package.
- *packages/package_dir*—Tells setuptools which packages to include when installing and where to look for these packages. In this case, we use a src directory layout for our Python package.[8]

Additionally, `setuptools` allows you to include many optional fields[9] for describing your package, including the following:

- *author*—The name of the package author (you).
- *author_email*—Contact details for the author.
- *description*—A short, readable description of your package (typically one line). A longer description can be given using the `long_description` argument.
- *url*—Where to find your package online.
- *license*—The license under which your package code is released (if any).

Looking at the `setup.py` implementation, this means that we tell `setuptools` that our dependencies include `apache-airflow` and `requests`, that our package should be called `airflow_movielens` with a version of 0.1, and that it should include files from the `airflow_movielens` package situated in the `src` directory, while including some extra details about ourselves and the package description license.

---

[8] See this blog for more details on src- versus non-src-based layouts: https://blog.ionelmc.ro/2014/05/25/python-packaging/#the-structure.

[9] For a full reference of parameters that you can pass to `setuptools.setup`, please refer to the `setuptools` documentation.

Once we have finished writing our `setup.py`, our package should look like this:

```
$ tree airflow-movielens
airflow-movielens
├── setup.py
└── src
    └── airflow_movielens
        ├── __init__.py
        ├── hooks.py
        ├── operators.py
        └── sensors.py
```

This means we now have a setup for our basic `airflow_movielens` Python package, which we can try installing in the next section.

Of course, more elaborate packages will typically include tests, documentation, and so on, which we don't describe here. If you want to see extensive setups for Python packaging, we recommend checking out the many templates available online (e.g., https://github.com/audreyr/cookiecutter-pypackage), which provide excellent starting points for bootstrapping Python package development.

8.5.2   *Installing your package*

Now that we have our basic package, we should be able to install `airflow_movielens` into our Python environment. You can try this by running pip to install the package in your active environment:

```
$ python -m pip install ./airflow-movielens
Looking in indexes: https://pypi.org/simple
Processing ./airflow-movielens
Collecting apache-airflow
...
Successfully installed ... airflow-movielens-0.1.0 ...
```

Once pip is done installing your package and dependencies, you can check whether your package was installed by starting Python and trying to import one of the classes from your package:

```
$ python
Python 3.7.3 | packaged by conda-forge | (default, Jul  1 2019, 14:38:56)
[Clang 4.0.1 (tags/RELEASE_401/final)] :: Anaconda, Inc. on darwin
Type "help", "copyright", "credits" or "license" for more information.
>>> from airflow_movielens.hooks import MovielensHook
>>> MovielensHook
<class 'airflow_movielens.hooks.MovielensHook'>
```

Deploying your package to your Airflow environment shouldn't require much more effort than installing your package in Airflow's Python environment. However, depending on your setup, you should make sure that your package and all its dependencies are installed in all of the environments Airflow uses (that is, the scheduler, webserver, and worker environments).

Distribution of your package can be handled by either installing directly from a GitHub repository,

```
$ python -m pip install git+https://github.com/...
```

or by using a pip package feed such as PyPI (or a private feed),

```
$ python -m pip install airflow_movielens
```

or by installing from a file-based location (as we initially did here). In the latter case, you do need to make sure that the Airflow environment can access the directory from which you want to install the package.

Summary

- You can extend Airflow's built-in functionality by building custom components that fit your specific use cases. In our experience, two use cases in which custom operators are particularly powerful are as follows:
  - Running tasks on systems that are not natively supported by Airflow (e.g., new cloud services, databases, etc.)
  - Providing operators/sensors/hooks for commonly performed operations, such that these are easy to implement by people in your team across DAGs

  Of course, this is by no means an exhaustive list, and there may be many other situations in which you would want to build your own components.
- Custom hooks allow you to interact with systems that do not have support built into Airflow.
- Custom operators can be created to perform tasks that are specific to your workflows and are not covered by built-in operators.
- Custom sensors allow you to build components for waiting on (external) events.
- Code containing custom operators, hooks, sensors, and so on can be structured by implementing them in a (distributable) Python library.
- Custom hooks/operators/sensors require you to install them with their dependencies on your Airflow cluster before they can be used. This can be tricky if you do not have permission to install software on the cluster or if you have software with conflicting dependencies.
- Some people prefer to rely on generic operators such as the built-in `Docker-Operator` and the `KubernetesPodOperator` to execute their tasks. An advantage of this approach is that you can keep your Airflow installation lean, as Airflow is only coordinating containerized jobs; you can keep all dependencies of specific tasks with the container. We'll focus on this approach further in a future chapter.

Testing

9

> ## This chapter covers
> - Testing Airflow tasks in a CI/CD pipeline
> - Structuring a project for testing with pytest
> - Mimicking a DAG run to test tasks that apply templating
> - Faking external system events with mocking
> - Testing behavior in external systems with containers

In all previous chapters, we focused on various parts of developing Airflow. So how do you ensure the code you've written is valid before deploying it into a production system? Testing is an integral part of software development, and nobody wants to write code, take it through a deployment process, and keep their fingers crossed for all to be okay. Such a way of development is obviously inefficient and provides no guarantees on the correct functioning of the software, both in valid and invalid situations.

This chapter will dive into the gray area of testing Airflow, which is often regarded as a tricky subject. This is because of Airflow's nature of communicating with many external systems and the fact that it's an orchestration system, which starts and stops tasks performing logic, while Airflow itself (often) does not perform any logic.

9.1 *Getting started with testing*

Tests can be applied on various levels. Small individual units of work (i.e., single functions) can be tested with unit tests. While such tests might validate the correct behavior, they do not validate the behavior of a system composed of multiple such units altogether. For this purpose, we write integration tests, which validate the behavior of multiple components together. In testing literature, the next used level of testing is acceptance testing (evaluating fit with business requirements), which does not apply to this chapter. Here, we will dive into unit and integration testing.

Throughout this chapter, we demonstrate various code snippets written with pytest (https://pytest.org). While Python has a built-in framework for testing named unittest, pytest is one of the most popular third-party testing frameworks for various features such as fixtures, which we'll take advantage of in this chapter. No prior knowledge of pytest is assumed.

Since the supporting code with this book lives in GitHub, we'll demonstrate a CI/CD pipeline running tests with GitHub Actions (https://github.com/features/actions), the CI/CD system that integrates with GitHub. With the ideas and code from the GitHub Actions examples, you should be able to get your CI/CD pipeline running in any system. All popular CI/CD systems, such as GitLab, Bitbucket, CircleCI, Travis CI, and so on, work by defining the pipeline in YAML format in the root of the project directory, which we'll also do in the GitHub Actions examples.

9.1.1 *Integrity testing all DAGs*

In the context of Airflow, the first step for testing is generally a *DAG integrity test*, a term made known by a blog post titled "Data's Inferno: 7 Circles of Data Testing Hell with Airflow" (http://mng.bz/1rOn). Such a test verifies all your DAGs for their *integrity* (i.e., the correctness of the DAG, for example, validating if the DAGs do not contain cycles; if the task IDs in the DAG are unique, etc.). The DAG integrity test often filters simple mistakes. For example, a mistake is often made when generating tasks in a for loop with a fixed task ID instead of a dynamically set task ID, resulting in each generated task having the same ID. Upon loading DAGs, Airflow also performs such checks itself and will display an error if found (figure 9.1). To avoid going through a deployment cycle to discover in the end your DAG contains a simple mistake, it is wise to perform DAG integrity tests in your test suite.

The following DAG in listing 9.1 would display an error in the UI because there is a cycle between t1 > t2 > t3 > back to t1. This violates the property that a DAG should have finite start and end nodes.

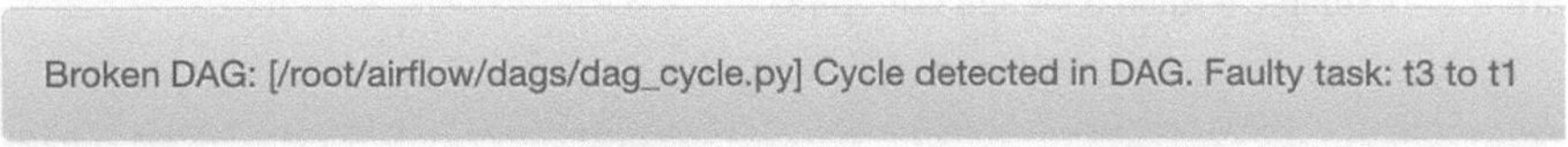

Broken DAG: [/root/airflow/dags/dag_cycle.py] Cycle detected in DAG. Faulty task: t3 to t1

Figure 9.1 DAG cycle error displayed by Airflow

Listing 9.1   Example cycle in DAG, resulting in an error

```
t1 = DummyOperator(task_id="t1", dag=dag)
t2 = DummyOperator(task_id="t2", dag=dag)
t3 = DummyOperator(task_id="t3", dag=dag)

t1 >> t2 >> t3 >> t1
```

Now let's catch this error in a DAG integrity test. First, let's install pytest.

Listing 9.2   Installing pytest

```
pip install pytest

Collecting pytest
...............
Installing collected packages: pytest
Successfully installed pytest-5.2.2
```

This gives us a pytest CLI utility. To see all available options, run `pytest --help`. For now, there's no need to know all the options; knowing you can run tests with `pytest [file/directory]` (where the directory contains test files) is enough. Let's create such a file. A convention is to create a tests/ folder at the root of the project that holds all the tests and mirrors the same directory structure as in the rest of the project.[1] So, if your project structure is like the one shown in figure 9.2,

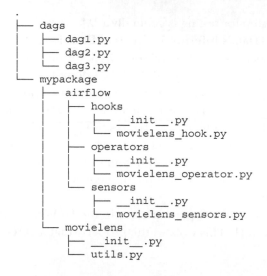

```
.
├── dags
│   ├── dag1.py
│   ├── dag2.py
│   └── dag3.py
└── mypackage
    ├── airflow
    │   ├── hooks
    │   │   ├── __init__.py
    │   │   └── movielens_hook.py
    │   ├── operators
    │   │   ├── __init__.py
    │   │   └── movielens_operator.py
    │   └── sensors
    │       ├── __init__.py
    │       └── movielens_sensors.py
    └── movielens
        ├── __init__.py
        └── utils.py
```

Figure 9.2   Example Python package structure

---

[1] Pytest calls this structure "Tests outside application code." The other supported structure by pytest is to store test files directly next to your application code, which it calls "tests as part of your application code."

then the tests/ directory structure would look like the one shown in figure 9.3:

```
.
├── dags
├── mypackage
└── tests
    ├── dags
    │   └── test_dag_integrity.py
    └── mypackage
        ├── airflow
        │   ├── hooks
        │   │   └── test_movielens_hook.py
        │   ├── operators
        │   │   └── test_movielens_operator.py
        │   └── sensors
        │       └── test_movielens_sensor.py
        └── movielens
            └── test_utils.py
```

Figure 9.3 Test directory structure following the structure in figure 9.2

Note all test files mirror the filenames that are (presumably) being tested, prefixed with test_. Again, while mirroring the name of the file to test is not required, is it an evident convention to tell something about the contents of the file. Tests that overlap multiple files or provide other sorts of tests (such as the DAG integrity test) are conventionally placed in files named according to whatever they're testing. However, the test_ prefix here is required; pytest scans through given directories and searches for files prefixed with test_ or suffixed with _test.[2] Also, note there are no __init__.py files in the tests/ directory; the directories are not modules, and tests should be able to run independently of each other without importing each other. Pytest scans directories and files and auto-discovers tests; there's no need to create modules with __init__.py files.

Let's create a file named tests/dags/test_dag_integrity.py.

Listing 9.3 DAG integrity test

```
import glob
import importlib.util
import os

import pytest
from airflow.models import DAG

DAG_PATH = os.path.join(
    os.path.dirname(__file__), "..", "..", "dags/**/*.py"
)
DAG_FILES = glob.glob(DAG_PATH, recursive=True)
```

---

[2] Test discovery settings are configurable in pytest if you want to support, for example, test files named check_*.

```
@pytest.mark.parametrize("dag_file", DAG_FILES)
def test_dag_integrity(dag_file):
    module_name, _ = os.path.splitext(dag_file)
    module_path = os.path.join(DAG_PATH, dag_file)
    ➥ mod_spec = importlib.util.spec_from_file_location(module_name,
      module_path)
    module = importlib.util.module_from_spec(mod_spec)
    mod_spec.loader.exec_module(module)

    ➥ dag_objects = [var for var in vars(module).values() if isinstance(var,
      DAG)]

    assert dag_objects

    for dag in dag_objects:
        dag.test_cycle()
```

Here, we see one function named `test_dag_integrity`, which performs the test. The code might look a little obscure at first sight, so let's break it down. Remember the folder structure previously explained? There's a dags/ folder that holds all DAG files, and the file test_dag_integrity.py, which lives in tests/dags/test_dag_integrity.py. This DAG integrity test is pointed to a folder holding all DAG files, in which it then searches recursively for *.py files (figure 9.4).

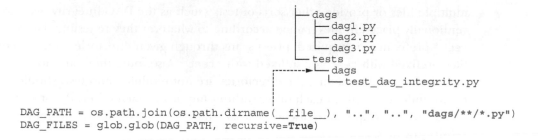

```
DAG_PATH = os.path.join(os.path.dirname(__file__), "..", "..", "dags/**/*.py")
DAG_FILES = glob.glob(DAG_PATH, recursive=True)
```

Figure 9.4   `DAG_PATH` points to the directory holding all DAG files.

The `dirname()` returns the directory of `test_dag_integrity.py`, and then we browse two directories up, first to tests/, second to the root, and from there we search for anything matching the pattern `dags/**/*.py`. `"**"` will search recursively, so DAG files in, for example, dags/dir1/dir2/dir3/mydag.py, will also be found. Finally, the variable `DAG_FILES` holds a list of files found in dags/ ending in .py. Next, the decorator `@pytest.mark.parametrize` runs the test for every found Python file (figure 9.5).

```
@pytest.mark.parametrize("dag_file", DAG_FILES)
def test_dag_integrity(dag_file):
```
Run test for every element in DAG_FILES.

Figure 9.5   A parameterized test runs a test for every `dag_file`.

The first part of the test is a little obscure. We won't go into details, but it boils down to loading and executing the file, just like Python itself would do, and extracting the DAG objects from it.

Listing 9.4 The DAG integrity test trying to instantiate every DAG object found

Load file.

```
module_name, _ = os.path.splitext(dag_file)
module_path = os.path.join(DAG_PATH, dag_file)
mod_spec = importlib.util.spec_from_file_location(module_name, module_path)
module = importlib.util.module_from_spec(mod_spec)
mod_spec.loader.exec_module(module)

dag_objects = [var for var in vars(module).values() if isinstance(var, DAG)]
```

All objects of class DAG found in file

Now that the DAG objects are extracted from the file, we can apply certain checks on it. In the code, we applied two checks. First was an assertion: `assert dag_objects`, checking if DAG objects were found in the file (making it successful). Adding this assertion validates all Python files found in /dags if they contain at least one DAG object. For example, Scripts utility functions stored in /dags, in which no DAG objects are instantiated, therefore fail. Whether this is desirable is up to you, but having one directory holding only DAG files and nothing else does provide a clear separation of duties.

The second check (`for dag in dag_objects: dag.test_cycle()`) validates whether there are no cycles in the DAG objects. This is called explicitly for a reason. Before Airflow 1.10.0, DAGs were checked for cycles with every change to their structure. This check becomes computationally heavier as more and more tasks are added. For DAGs with a large number of tasks, this became a burden, because for every new task a DAG cycle check was performed, causing long reading times. Therefore, the DAG cycle check was moved to the point where DAGs are parsed and cached by Airflow (into a structure called the DagBag) such that the cycle check is performed only once after parsing the complete DAG, reducing reading time. As a result, it's perfectly fine to declare `t1 >> t2 >> t1` and evaluate it. Only once a live running Airflow instance will read your script will it complain about the cycle. So, to avoid going through a deployment cycle, we call `test_cycle()` explicitly on each DAG found in the test.

These are two example checks, but you can add your own, of course. If, say, you want each DAG name to start with "import" or "export," you can check the `dag_ids`:

```
assert dag.dag_id.startswith(("import", "export"))
```

Now let's run the DAG integrity test. On the command line, run pytest (optionally hinting pytest where to search with `pytest tests/` to avoid scanning other directories).

Listing 9.5   Output of running pytest

```
$ pytest tests/
========================= test session starts =========================
....
collected 1 item

tests/dags/test_dag_integrity.py F
[100%]

============================= FAILURES =============================
_____ test_dag_integrity[..../dag_cycle.py] _____

dag_file = '..../dag_cycle.py'

    @pytest.mark.parametrize("dag_file", DAG_FILES)
    def test_dag_integrity(dag_file):
        """Import DAG files and check for DAG."""
        module_name, _ = os.path.splitext(dag_file)
        module_path = os.path.join(DAG_PATH, dag_file)
    ➡   mod_spec = importlib.util.spec_from_file_location(module_name,
    module_path)
        module = importlib.util.module_from_spec(mod_spec)
        mod_spec.loader.exec_module(module)

    ➡   dag_objects = [
            var for var in vars(module).values() if isinstance(var, DAG)
        ]

        assert dag_objects

        for dag in dag_objects:
            # Test cycles
>           dag.test_cycle()

tests/dags/test_dag_integrity.py:29:
_ _ _ _ _ _ _ _ _ _ _ _ _ _ _ _ _ _ _ _ _ _ _ _ _ _ _ _ _ _ _ _ _
.../site-packages/airflow/models/dag.py:1427: in test_cycle
    self._test_cycle_helper(visit_map, task_id)
.../site-packages/airflow/models/dag.py:1449: in _test_cycle_helper
    self._test_cycle_helper(visit_map, descendant_id)
.../site-packages/airflow/models/dag.py:1449: in _test_cycle_helper
    self._test_cycle_helper(visit_map, descendant_id)
_ _ _ _ _ _ _ _ _ _ _ _ _ _ _ _ _ _ _ _ _ _ _ _ _ _ _ _ _ _ _ _ _

➡ self = <DAG: chapter8_dag_cycle>, visit_map = defaultdict(<class 'int'>,
    {'t1': 1, 't2': 1, 't3': 1}), task_id = 't3'

    def _test_cycle_helper(self, visit_map, task_id):
        """
        Checks if a cycle exists from the input task using DFS traversal
        ...

        task = self.task_dict[task_id]
        for descendant_id in task.get_direct_relative_ids():
```

```
                  if visit_map[descendant_id] == DagBag.CYCLE_IN_PROGRESS:
                      msg = "Cycle detected in DAG. Faulty task: {0} to
       {1}".format(
                          task_id, descendant_id)
       >              raise AirflowDagCycleException(msg)
       E                  airflow.exceptions.AirflowDagCycleException: Cycle
          detected in DAG. Faulty task: t3 to t1

  ..../airflow/models/dag.py:1447: AirflowDagCycleException
  ========================== 1 failed in 0.21s ==========================
```

The result of the test is quite lengthy, but typically you search for answers at the top and bottom. Near the top you find which test failed, and at the bottom, answers why the test failed.

Listing 9.6 Exception reason found in listing 9.5

```
airflow.exceptions.AirflowDagCycleException: Cycle detected in DAG.
Faulty task: t3 to t1
```

This example shows us (as expected) a cycle was detected from t3 to t1. Upon instantiation of DAGs and operators, several other checks are performed out of the box. Say you are using a BashOperator but forgot to add the (required) bash_command argument. The DAG integrity test will evaluate all statements in the script and fail when evaluating the BashOperator.

Listing 9.7 Faulty instantiation of a BashOperator

```
BashOperator(task_id="this_should_fail", dag=dag)
```

The DAG integrity test will encounter an exception and fail.

Listing 9.8 Exception raised by the faulty instantiation in listing 9.7

```
airflow.exceptions.AirflowException: Argument ['bash_command'] is required
```

With the DAG integrity test in place, let's run it automatically in a CI/CD pipeline.

9.1.2 Setting up a CI/CD pipeline

In a one-liner, a CI/CD pipeline is a system that runs predefined scripts when you make a change to your code repository. The *continuous integration* (CI) denotes checking and validating the changed code to ensure it complies with coding standards and a test suite. For example, upon pushing code, you could check for Flake8 (http://flake8.pycqa.org), Pylint (https://www.pylint.org), and Black (https://github.com/psf/black), and run a series of tests. The *continuous deployment* (CD) indicates automatically deploying the code into production systems, completely automated and without human interference. The goal is to maximize coding productivity without having to deal with manually validating and deploying it.

There is a wide range of CI/CD systems. In this chapter we will cover GitHub Actions (https://github.com/features/actions); the general ideas should apply to any CI/CD system. Most CI/CD systems start with a YAML configuration file in which a pipeline is defined: a series of steps to execute upon changing code. Each step should complete successfully to make the pipeline successful. In the Git repository, we can then enforce rules such as "only merge to master with a successful pipeline."

The pipeline definitions typically live in the root of your project; GitHub Actions requires YAML files stored in a directory: .github/workflows. With GitHub Actions, the name of the YAML doesn't matter, so we could create a file named airflow-tests .yaml with the following content.

Listing 9.9   Example GitHub Actions pipeline for Airflow project

```yaml
name: Python static checks and tests

on: [push]

jobs:
 testing:
   runs-on: ubuntu-18.04
   steps:
     - uses: actions/checkout@v1
     - name: Setup Python
       uses: actions/setup-python@v1
       with:
         python-version: 3.6.9
         architecture: x64

     - name: Install Flake8
       run: pip install flake8
     - name: Run Flake8
       run: flake8

     - name: Install Pylint
       run: pip install pylint
     - name: Run Pylint
       run: find . -name "*.py" | xargs pylint --output-format=colorized

     - name: Install Black
       run: pip install black
     - name: Run Black
       run: find . -name "*.py" | xargs black --check

     - name: Install dependencies
       run: pip install apache-airflow pytest

     - name: Test DAG integrity
       run: pytest tests/
```

The keywords shown in this YAML file are unique to GitHub Actions, although the general ideas apply to other CI/CD systems too. Important things to note are the tasks in GitHub Actions defined under "steps." Each step runs a piece of code. For example, Flake8 performs static code analysis and will fail if any issues are encountered, such as an unused import. On row 3, we state on: [push], which tells GitHub to run the complete CI/CD pipeline every time it receives a push. In a completely automated CD system, it would contain filters for steps on specific branches, such as master, to only run steps and deploy code if the pipeline succeeds on that branch.

9.1.3 *Writing unit tests*

Now that we have a CI/CD pipeline up and running, which initially checks the validity of all DAGs in the project, it's time to dive a bit deeper into the Airflow code and start unit testing individual bits and pieces.

Looking at the custom components demonstrated in chapter 8; there are several things we could test to validate correct behavior. The saying goes, "Never trust user input," so we'd like to be certain our code works correctly in both valid and invalid situations. Take, for example, the MovielensHook from chapter 8, which holds a method, get_ratings(). The method accepts several arguments; one of them is batch_size, which controls the size of batches requested from the API. You can imagine valid input would be any positive number (maybe with some upper limit). But what if the user provides a negative number (e.g., –3)? Maybe the API handles the invalid batch size correctly and returns an HTTP error, such as 400 or 422, but how does the MovielensHook respond to that? Sensible options might be input value handling before even sending the request, or proper error handling if the API returns an error. This behavior is what we want to check.

Let's continue with the work of chapter 8 and implement a MovielensPopularity-Operator, which is an operator returning the top N popular movies between two given dates.

Listing 9.10 Example operator MovielensPopularityOperator

```
class MovielensPopularityOperator(BaseOperator):
    def __init__(
        self,
        conn_id,
        start_date,
        end_date,
        min_ratings=4,
        top_n=5,
        **kwargs,
    ):
        super().__init__(**kwargs)
        self._conn_id = conn_id
        self._start_date = start_date
        self._end_date = end_date
        self._min_ratings = min_ratings
        self._top_n = top_n
```

```
def execute(self, context):
    with MovielensHook(self._conn_id) as hook:
        ratings = hook.get_ratings(
            start_date=self._start_date,
            end_date=self._end_date,
        )

        rating_sums = defaultdict(Counter)
        for rating in ratings:
            rating_sums[rating["movieId"]].update(count=1,
rating=rating["rating"])

        averages = {
            movie_id: (rating_counter["rating"] /
rating_counter["count"], rating_counter["count"])
            for movie_id, rating_counter in rating_sums.items()
            if rating_counter["count"] >= self._min_ratings
        }
        return sorted(averages.items(), key=lambda x: x[1],
reverse=True)[: self._top_n]
```

Get raw ratings.

Sum up ratings per movie_id.

Filter min_ratings and calculate mean rating per movie_id.

Return top_n ratings sorted by mean ratings and number of ratings.

How do we test the correctness of this `MovielensPopularityOperator`? First, we could test it as a whole by simply running the operator with given values and check if the result is as expected. To do this, we require a couple of pytest components to run the operator by itself, outside a live Airflow system and inside a unit test. This allows us to run the operator under different circumstances and validate whether it behaves correctly.

9.1.4 *Pytest project structure*

With pytest, a test script requires to be prefixed with `test_`. Just like the directory structure, we also mimic the filenames, so a test for code in `movielens_operator.py` would be stored in a file named test_movielens_operator.py. Inside this file, we create a function to be called as a test.

Listing 9.11   Example test function testing the BashOperator

```
def test_example():
    task = BashOperator(
        task_id="test",
        bash_command="echo 'hello!'",
        xcom_push=True,
    )
    result = task.execute(context={})
    assert result == "hello!"
```

In this example, we instantiate the `BashOperator` and call the `execute()` function, given an empty context (empty dict). When Airflow runs your operator in a live setting, several things happen before and after, such as rendering templated variables and setting up the task instance context and providing it to the operator. In this test, we are not running in a live setting but calling the execute() method directly. This is the lowest level function you can call to run an operator and it's the method every operator implements to perform its functionality. We don't need any task instance context to run the BashOperator; therefore, we provide it an empty context. In the case the test depends on processing something from the task instance context, we could fill it with the required keys and values.[3]

Let's run this test.

Listing 9.12 Output of running the test in listing 9.11

```
$ pytest tests/dags/chapter9/custom/test_operators.py::test_example
========================= test session starts =========================
platform darwin -- Python 3.6.7, pytest-5.2.2, py-1.8.0, pluggy-0.13.0
rootdir: .../data-pipelines-with-apache-airflow
collected 1 item

tests/dags/chapter9/custom/test_operators.py
```

Now let's apply this to the MovielensPopularityOperator.

Listing 9.13 Example test function testing the MovielensPopularityOperator

```
def test_movielenspopularityoperator():
    task = MovielensPopularityOperator(
        task_id="test_id",
        start_date="2015-01-01",
        end_date="2015-01-03",
        top_n=5,
    )
    result = task.execute(context={})
    assert len(result) == 5
```

The first thing that appears is red text telling us the operator is missing a required argument.

Listing 9.14 Output of running the test in listing 9.13

```
$ pytest tests/dags/chapter9/custom/test_operators.py::test
  _movielenspopularityoperator
========================= test session starts =========================
platform darwin -- Python 3.6.7, pytest-5.2.2, py-1.8.0, pluggy-0.13.0
rootdir: /.../data-pipelines-with-apache-airflow
collected 1 item

tests/dags/chapter9/custom/test_operators.py F
[100%]
```

---

[3] The xcom_push=True argument returns stdout in the Bash_command as string, which we use in this test to fetch and validate the Bash_command. In a live Airflow setup, any object returned by an operator is automatically pushed to XCom.

```
================================ FAILURES ================================
_____ test_movielenspopularityoperator _____

mocker = <pytest_mock.plugin.MockFixture object at 0x10fb2ea90>

    def test_movielenspopularityoperator(mocker: MockFixture):
        task = MovielensPopularityOperator(
>               task_id="test_id", start_date="2015-01-01", end_date="2015-01-
    03", top_n=5
        )
E       TypeError: __init__() missing 1 required positional argument:
    'conn_id'

tests/dags/chapter9/custom/test_operators.py:30: TypeError
========================= 1 failed in 0.10s =========================
```

Now we see the test failed because we're missing the required argument conn_id, which points to the connection ID in the metastore. But how do you provide this in a test? Tests should be isolated from each other; they should not be able to influence the results of other tests, so a database shared between tests is not an ideal situation. In this case, *mocking* comes to the rescue.

Mocking is "faking" certain operations or objects. For example, the call to a database that is expected to exist in a production setting but not while testing could be faked, or *mocked*, by telling Python to return a certain value instead of making the actual call to the (nonexistent during testing) database. This allows you to develop and run tests without requiring a connection to external systems. It requires insight into the internals of whatever it is you're testing, and thus sometimes requires you to dive into third-party code.

Pytest has a set of supporting plug-ins (not officially by pytest), which ease the usage of concepts such as mocking. For this, we can install the pytest-mock Python package:

```
pip install pytest-mock
```

pytest-mock is a Python package that provides a tiny convenience wrapper around the built-in mock package. To use it, pass an argument named "mocker"[4] to your test function, which is the entry point for using anything in the pytest-mock package.

> **Listing 9.15   Mocking an object in a test**

```
def test_movielenspopularityoperator(mocker):
    mocker.patch.object(
        MovielensHook,
        "get_connection",
        return_value=Connection(
            conn_id="test",
            login="airflow",
```

---

[4] If you want to type your arguments, mocker is of type pytest_mock.MockFixture.

```
                password="airflow",
        ),
    )
    task = MovielensPopularityOperator(
        task_id="test_id",
        conn_id="test",
        start_date="2015-01-01",
        end_date="2015-01-03",
        top_n=5,
    )
    result = task.execute(context=None)
    assert len(result) == 5
```

With this code, the get_connection() call on the MovielensHook is *monkey-patched* (substituting its functionality at runtime to return the given object instead of querying the Airflow metastore), and executing MovielensHook.get_connection() won't fail when running the test since no call to the nonexistent database is made during testing, but instead, the predefined, expected connection object is returned.

Listing 9.16 Substituting a call to an external system in a test

The mocker object magically exists
at runtime; no import required.

Patch an attribute on an
object with a mock object.

The object
to patch

```
def test_movielenspopularityoperator(mocker):
    mock_get = mocker.patch.object(
        MovielensHook,
        "get_connection",
            return_value=Connection(conn_id="test", login="airflow",
    password="airflow"),
    )
    task = MovielensPopularityOperator(...)
```

The function to patch

The value
to return

This example shows how to substitute a call to an external system (the Airflow metastore) at test time by returning a predefined Connection object. What if you want to validate the call is actually made in your test? We can assign the patched object to a variable that holds several properties collected when calling the patched object. Say we would like to ensure the get_connection() method is called once and only once, and the conn_id argument provided to get_connection() holds the same value as provided to the MovielensPopularityOperator.

Listing 9.17 Validating the behavior of a mocked function

```
mock_get = mocker.patch.object(
    MovielensHook,
    "get_connection",
    return_value=Connection(...),
)
task = MovielensPopularityOperator(..., conn_id="testconn")
task.execute(...)
```

Assign mock to variable
to capture behavior.

```
        assert mock_get.call_count == 1
        mock_get.assert_called_with("testconn")
```

Assert it was
called only once.

Assert it was called with the expected conn_id.

Assigning the return value of `mocker.patch.object` to a variable named `mock_get` will capture all calls made to the mocked object and gives us the possibility of verifying the given input, number of calls, and more. In this example, we assert if `call_count` can verify that the `MovielensPopularityOperator` doesn't accidentally make multiple calls to the Airflow metastore in a live setting. Also, since we provide the `conn_id` "testconn" to the `MovielensPopularityOperator`, we expect this `conn_id` to be requested from the Airflow metastore, which we validate with `assert_called_with()`.[5] The `mock_get` object holds more properties to verify (e.g., a called property to simply assert whether the object was called [any number of times]) (figure 9.6).

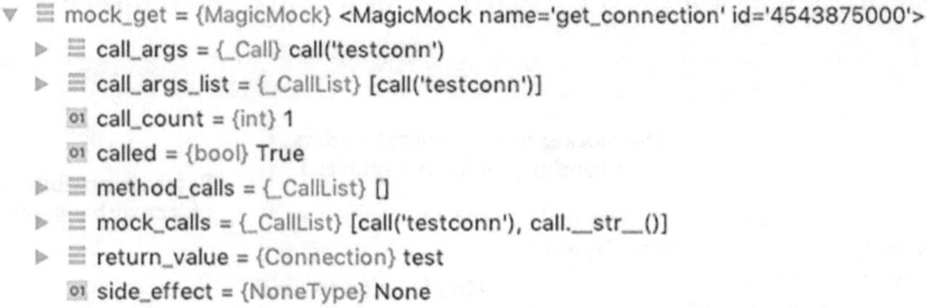

```
▼ ≣ mock_get = {MagicMock} <MagicMock name='get_connection' id='4543875000'>
  ▶ ≣ call_args = {_Call} call('testconn')
  ▶ ≣ call_args_list = {_CallList} [call('testconn')]
    01 call_count = {int} 1
    01 called = {bool} True
  ▶ ≣ method_calls = {_CallList} []
  ▶ ≣ mock_calls = {_CallList} [call('testconn'), call.__str__()]
  ▶ ≣ return_value = {Connection} test
    01 side_effect = {NoneType} None
```

Figure 9.6 `mock_get` contains several properties that can be used to validate the behavior. (Screenshot was taken using the Python debugger in PyCharm.)

One of the biggest pitfalls with mocking in Python is mocking the incorrect object. In the example code, we are mocking the `get_connection()` method. This method is called on the `MovielensHook`, which inherits from the `BaseHook` (`airflow.hooks .base` package). The `get_connection()` method is defined on the `BaseHook`. Intuitively, you would therefore probably mock `BaseHook.get_connection()`. However, this is incorrect.

The correct way to mock in Python is to mock the location where it is being called and not where it is defined.[6] Let's illustrate this in code.

---

[5] A convenience method exists for these two asserts named `assert_called_once_with()`.

[6] This is explained in the Python documentation: https://docs.python.org/3/library/unittest.mock.html#where-to-patch. It is also demonstrated in http://alexmarandon.com/articles/python_mock_gotchas.

Listing 9.18   Paying attention to the correct import location when mocking in Python

```
from airflowbook.operators.movielens_operator import (
    MovielensPopularityOperator,
    MovielensHook,
)
```
We must import the method to mock from where it's called.

```
def test_movielenspopularityoperator(mocker):
    mock_get = mocker.patch.object(
        MovielensHook,
        "get_connection",
        return_value=Connection(...),
    )
    task = MovielensPopularityOperator(...)
```
Inside the Movielens-PopularityOperator code, MovielensHook.get_connection() is called.

9.1.5   *Testing with files on disk*

Consider an operator that reads one file holding a list of JSONs and writes these to CSV format (figure 9.7).

```
[
    {"name": "bob", "age": 41, "sex": "M"},
    {"name": "alice", "age": 24, "sex": "F"},      name,age,sex
    {"name": "carol", "age": 60, "sex": "F"}        bob,41,M
]                                                   alice,24,F
                                                    carol,60,F
```

Figure 9.7   Converting JSON to CSV format

The operator for this operation could look as follows.

Listing 9.19   Example operator using local disk

```
class JsonToCsvOperator(BaseOperator):
    def __init__(self, input_path, output_path, **kwargs):
        super().__init__(**kwargs)
        self._input_path = input_path
        self._output_path = output_path

    def execute(self, context):
        with open(self._input_path, "r") as json_file:
            data = json.load(json_file)

        columns = {key for row in data for key in row.keys()}

        with open(self._output_path, mode="w") as csv_file:
            writer = csv.DictWriter(csv_file, fieldnames=columns)
            writer.writeheader()
            writer.writerows(data)
```

This `JsonToCsvOperator` takes two input arguments: the input (JSON) path and the output (CSV) path. To test this operator, we could store a static file in our test directory to use as input for the test, but where do we store the output file?

In Python, we have the tempfile module for tasks involving temporary storage. It leaves no remainders on your file system since the directory and its contents are wiped after usage. Once again, pytest provides a convenient access point to this module named `tmp_dir` (gives `os.path` object) and `tmp_path` (gives `pathlib` object). Let's view an example using `tmp_path`.

Listing 9.20   Testing using temporary paths

```python
import csv
import json
from pathlib import Path

from airflowbook.operators.json_to_csv_operator import JsonToCsvOperator


def test_json_to_csv_operator(tmp_path: Path):          ◁── Use tmp_path fixture.
    input_path = tmp_path / "input.json"          │ Define paths.
    output_path = tmp_path / "output.csv"         │

    input_data = [
        {"name": "bob", "age": "41", "sex": "M"},
        {"name": "alice", "age": "24", "sex": "F"},     Save input file.
        {"name": "carol", "age": "60", "sex": "F"},
    ]
    with open(input_path, "w") as f:
        f.write(json.dumps(input_data))

    operator = JsonToCsvOperator(
        task_id="test",
        input_path=input_path,
        output_path=output_path,
    )                                              Execute
    operator.execute(context={})           ◁──    JsonToCsvOperator.

    with open(output_path, "r") as f:
        reader = csv.DictReader(f)                 Read output file.
        result = [dict(row) for row in reader]

    assert result == input_data      ◁── Assert content.
```

◁── After the test, the tmp_path and its contents are removed.

Upon starting the test, a temporary directory is created. The `tmp_path` argument actually refers to a function, which is executed for each test it is called in. In pytest, these are called *fixtures* (https://docs.pytest.org/en/stable/fixture.html). While fixtures bear some resemblance with unittest's `setUp()` and `tearDown()` methods, they allow for greater flexibility because fixtures can be mixed and matched (e.g., one fixture could initialize a temporary directory for all tests in a class, while another fixture only initializes for a single test).[7] The default scope of fixtures is every test function. We can see this by printing the path and running different tests, or even the same test twice:

```
print(tmp_path.as_posix())
```

This will print, respectively,

- /private/var/folders/n3/g5l6d1j10gxfsdkphhgkgn4w0000gn/T/pytest-of-basharenslak/pytest-**19**/test_json_to_csv_operator0
- /private/var/folders/n3/g5l6d1j10gxfsdkphhgkgn4w0000gn/T/pytest-of-basharenslak/pytest-**20**/test_json_to_csv_operator0

There are other fixtures to use, and pytest fixtures have many features that are not demonstrated this book. If you're serious about all pytest features, it helps to go over the documentation.

9.2 *Working with DAGs and task context in tests*

Some operators require more context (e.g., templating of variables) or usage of the task instance context for execution. We cannot simply run operator.execute(context={}) like we did in the previous examples, because we provide no task context to the operator, which it needs to perform its code.

In these cases, we would like to run the operator in a more realistic scenario, as if Airflow were to actually run a task in a live system, and thus create a task instance context, template all variables, and so on. Figure 9.8 shows the steps that are performed when a task is executed in Airflow.[8]

As you can see, step 5 is the only one we've run in the examples so far (listings 9.15, 9.17, and 9.20). If running a live Airflow system, many more steps are performed when executing an operator, some of which we need to execute to test, for example, correct templating.

Say we implemented an operator that pulls movie ratings between two given dates, which the user can provide via templated variables.

Listing 9.21 Example operator using templated variables

```
class MovielensDownloadOperator(BaseOperator):
    template_fields = ("_start_date", "_end_date", "_output_path")

    def __init__(
        self,
        conn_id,
        start_date,
        end_date,
        output_path,
        **kwargs,
    ):
```

---

[7] Look up "pytest scope" if you're interested in learning how to share fixtures across tests.
[8] In TaskInstance, _run_raw_task().

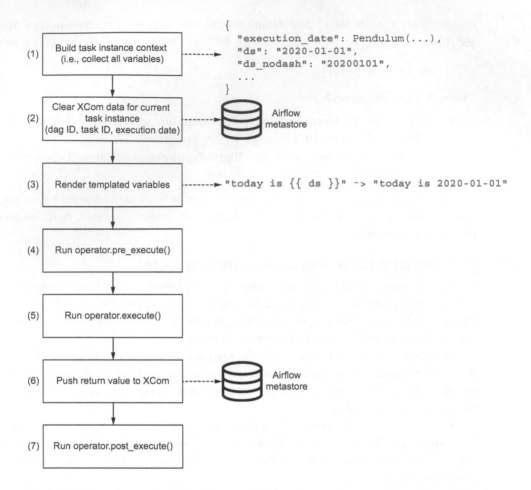

Figure 9.8   Running an operator involves several steps. In section 9.1, we test only step 5 and manually provide runtime task context to `operator.execute()` if needed.

```
        super().__init__(**kwargs)
        self._conn_id = conn_id
        self._start_date = start_date
        self._end_date = end_date
        self._output_path = output_path

    def execute(self, context):
        with MovielensHook(self._conn_id) as hook:
            ratings = hook.get_ratings(
                start_date=self._start_date,
                end_date=self._end_date,
            )

        with open(self._output_path, "w") as f:
            f.write(json.dumps(ratings))
```

This operator is not testable, as in the previous examples, since it (potentially) requires the task instance context to execute. For example, the output_path argument could be provided as /output/{{ ds }}.json, and the ds variable is not available when testing with operator.execute(context={}).

So, for this, we'll call the actual method Airflow itself also uses to start a task, which is operator.run() (a method on the BaseOperator class). To use it, the operator must be assigned to a DAG. While the previous example could be run as-is, without creating a DAG for testing purposes, in order to use run() we need to provide a DAG to the operator, because when Airflow runs a task, it refers to the DAG object on several occasions (e.g., when building up the task instance context).

We could define a DAG in our tests as follows.

Listing 9.22 DAG with default arguments for testing purposes

```
dag = DAG(
    "test_dag",
    default_args={
        "owner": "airflow",
        "start_date": datetime.datetime(2019, 1, 1),
    },
    schedule_interval="@daily",
)
```

The values we provide to the test DAG don't matter, but we'll refer to these while asserting the results of the operator. Next, we can define our task and run it.

Listing 9.23 Testing with a DAG to render templated variables

```
def test_movielens_operator(tmp_path, mocker):
    mocker.patch.object(
        MovielensHook,
        "get_connection",
        return_value=Connection(
            conn_id="test", login="airflow", password="airflow"
        ),
    )

    dag = DAG(
        "test_dag",
        default_args={
            "owner": "airflow",
            "start_date": datetime.datetime(2019, 1, 1),
        },
        schedule_interval="@daily",
    )

    task = MovielensDownloadOperator(
        task_id="test",
        conn_id="testconn",
        start_date="{{ prev_ds }}",
        end_date="{{ ds }}",
```

```
        output_path=str(tmp_path / "{{ ds }}.json"),
        dag=dag,
    )

    task.run(
        start_date=dag.default_args["start_date"],
        end_date=dag.default_args["start_date"],
    )
```

If you run the test as we've defined it now, you will probably encounter an error similar to the following listing.

Listing 9.24   First time running a test including a DAG

```
.../site-packages/sqlalchemy/engine/default.py:580: OperationalError

The above exception was the direct cause of the following exception:

➡ > task.run(start_date=dag.default_args["start_date"],
      end_date=dag.default_args["start_date"])

...
cursor = <sqlite3.Cursor object at 0x1110fae30>
➡ statement = 'SELECT task_instance.try_number AS task_instance_try_number,
      task_instance.task_id AS task_instance_task_id, task_ins...\nWHERE
      task_instance.dag_id = ? AND task_instance.task_id = ? AND
      task_instance.execution_date = ?\n LIMIT ? OFFSET ?'
parameters = ('test_dag', 'test', '2015-01-01 00:00:00.000000', 1, 0)
...

    def do_execute(self, cursor, statement, parameters, context=None):
>       cursor.execute(statement, parameters)
➡ E       sqlalchemy.exc.OperationalError: (sqlite3.OperationalError) no such
      column: task_instance.max_tries
➡ E       [SQL: SELECT task_instance.try_number AS task_instance_try_number,
      task_instance.task_id AS task_instance_task_id, task_instance.dag_id AS
      task_instance_dag_id, task_instance.execution_date AS
      task_instance_execution_date, task_instance.start_date AS
      task_instance_start_date, task_instance.end_date AS task_instance_end_date,
      task_instance.duration AS task_instance_duration, task_instance.state AS
      task_instance_state, task_instance.max_tries AS task_instance_max_tries,
      task_instance.hostname AS task_instance_hostname, task_instance.unixname AS
      task_instance_unixname, task_instance.job_id AS task_instance_job_id,
      task_instance.pool AS task_instance_pool, task_instance.queue AS
      task_instance_queue, task_instance.priority_weight AS
      task_instance_priority_weight, task_instance.operator AS
      task_instance_operator, task_instance.queued_dttm AS
      task_instance_queued_dttm, task_instance.pid AS task_instance_pid,
      task_instance.executor_config AS task_instance_executor_config
E        FROM task_instance
➡ E        WHERE task_instance.dag_id = ? AND task_instance.task_id = ? AND
      task_instance.execution_date = ?
E        LIMIT ? OFFSET ?]
➡ E        [parameters: ('test_dag', 'test', '2015-01-01 00:00:00.000000', 1, 0)]
E        (Background on this error at: http://sqlalche.me/e/e3q8)
```

As you can tell from the error message, there's something wrong in the Airflow metastore. To run a task, Airflow queries the database for several pieces of information, such as previous task instances with the same execution date. But, if you haven't initialized the Airflow database (airflow db init) in the path AIRFLOW_HOME is set to (~/airflow if not set), or configured Airflow to a running database, then it will have no database to read or write. So also when testing, we will need a metastore. There are several approaches to deal with the metastore during testing.

First, hypothetically, we could mock every single database call, as shown before, when querying for connection credentials. While this is possible, it is very cumbersome. A more practical approach is to run a real metastore that Airflow can query while running the tests.

To do this, you run airflow db init, which initializes the database. Without any configuration, the database will be a SQLite database, stored in ~/airflow/airflow .db. If you set the AIRFLOW_HOME environment variable, Airflow will store the database in that given directory. Ensure that while running tests you provide the same AIRFLOW_HOME value so that Airflow can find your metastore.[9]

Now, once you've set up a metastore for Airflow to query, we can run the test and see it succeed. Also, we can now see a row was written to the Airflow metastore during the test (figure 9.9).[10]

	ᴬᴮᶜ task_id	ᴬᴮᶜ dag_id	ᴬᴮᶜ execution_date	ᴬᴮᶜ start_date	ᴬᴮᶜ end_date	123 duration	ᴬᴮᶜ state	123 try_number
1	test	test_dag	2019-01-01 00:00:00.000000	2019-12-22 21:52:13.111447	2019-12-22 21:52:13.283970	0,172523	success	1

Figure 9.9 Calling `task.run()` results in task run details stored in the database.

There are two things to point out in this test. If you have multiple tests using a DAG, there is a neat way to reuse it with pytest. We've covered pytest fixtures, and these can be reused over multiple files in (sub)directories using a file named conftest.py. This file can hold a fixture for instantiating a DAG.

Listing 9.25 Example pytest fixture to reuse DAG throughout tests

```
import datetime

import pytest
from airflow.models import DAG
```

---

[9] To ensure your tests run isolated from anything else, a Docker container with an empty initialized Airflow database can be convenient.

[10] DBeaver is a free SQLite database browser.

```
@pytest.fixture
def test_dag():
    return DAG(
        "test_dag",
        default_args={
            "owner": "airflow",
            "start_date": datetime.datetime(2019, 1, 1),
        },
        schedule_interval="@daily",
    )
```

Now every test requiring a DAG object can simply instantiate it by adding test_dag as an argument to the test, which executes the test_dag() function at the start of the test.

Listing 9.26 Creating required objects by including fixtures with a test

```
def test_movielens_operator(tmp_path, mocker, test_dag):
    mocker.patch.object(
        MovielensHook,
        "get_connection",
        return_value=Connection(
            conn_id="test",
            login="airflow",
            password="airflow",
        ),
    )

    task = MovielensDownloadOperator(
        task_id="test",
        conn_id="testconn",
        start_date="{{ prev_ds }}",
        end_date="{{ ds }}",
        output_path=str(tmp_path / "{{ ds }}.json"),
        dag=test_dag,
    )

    task.run(
        start_date=dag.default_args["start_date"],
        end_date=dag.default_args["start_date"],
    )
```

task.run() is a method on the BaseOperator class. run() takes two dates and, given the DAG's schedule_interval, computes instances of the task to run between the two given dates. Since we provide the same two dates (the DAGs' starting date), there will be only one single task instance to execute.

9.2.1 Working with external systems

Assume we're working with an operator that connects to a database, say a Movielens-ToPostgresOperator, which reads MovieLens ratings and writes the results to a Postgres database. This is an often-seen use case, when a source only provides data as it is at the time of requesting but cannot provide historical data, and people would like to build up history of the source. For example, if you queried the MovieLens API today, where John rated *The Avengers* with four stars yesterday but today changed his rating to five, the API would only return his five-star rating. An Airflow job could, once a day, fetch all data and store the daily export together with the time of the writing.

The operator for such an operation could look like this.

Listing 9.27 Example operator connecting with a PostgreSQL database

```python
from airflow.hooks.postgres_hook import PostgresHook
from airflow.models import BaseOperator

from airflowbook.hooks.movielens_hook import MovielensHook


class MovielensToPostgresOperator(BaseOperator):
    template_fields = ("_start_date", "_end_date", "_insert_query")

    def __init__(
        self,
        movielens_conn_id,
        start_date,
        end_date,
        postgres_conn_id,
        insert_query,
        **kwargs,
    ):
        super().__init__(**kwargs)
        self._movielens_conn_id = movielens_conn_id
        self._start_date = start_date
        self._end_date = end_date
        self._postgres_conn_id = postgres_conn_id
        self._insert_query = insert_query

    def execute(self, context):
        with MovielensHook(self._movielens_conn_id) as movielens_hook:
            ratings = list(movielens_hook.get_ratings(
                start_date=self._start_date,
                end_date=self._end_date),
            )

        postgres_hook = PostgresHook(
            postgres_conn_id=self._postgres_conn_id
        )
        insert_queries = [
            self._insert_query.format(",".join([str(_[1]) for _ in
    sorted(rating.items())]))
            for rating in ratings
        ]
        postgres_hook.run(insert_queries)
```

Let's break down the `execute()` method. It connects the MovieLens API and Postgres database by fetching data and transforming the results into queries for Postgres (figure 9.10).

Get all ratings between given start_date and end_date using MovielensHook.

Create PostgresHook for communicating with Postgres.

```
def execute(self, context):
    with MovielensHook(self._movielens_conn_id) as movielens_hook:
        ratings = list(movielens_hook.get_ratings(start_date=self._start_date, end_date=self._end_date))

    postgres_hook = PostgresHook(postgres_conn_id=self._postgres_conn_id)
    insert_queries = [
        self._insert_query.format(",".join([str(_[1]) for _ in sorted(rating.items())]))
        for rating in ratings
    ]
    postgres_hook.run(insert_queries)
```

Create list of insert queries. Ratings return as a list of dicts:
```
{'movieId': 51935, 'userId': 21127, 'rating': 4.5,  'timestamp': 1419984001}
```

For each rating, we:

1. sort by key for deterministic results:
```
sorted(ratings[0].items())
[('movieId', 51935), ('rating', 4.5), ('timestamp',  1419984001), ('userId', 21127)]
```

2. create list of values, casted to string for .join()
```
[str(_[1]) for _ in sorted(ratings[0].items())]
['51935', '4.5', '1419984001', '21127']
```

3. join all values to string with comma
```
",".join([str(_[1]) for _ in sorted(rating.items())])
'51935,4.5,1419984001,21127'
```

4. provide result to insert_query.format(...)
```
self._insert_query.format(",".join([str(_[1]) for _ in sorted(rating.items())]))
'INSERT INTO movielens (movieId,rating,ratingTimest amp,userId,...) VALUES (51935,4.5,1419984001,21127,  ...)'
```

Figure 9.10   Breakdown of converting JSON data to Postgres queries

How do we test this, assuming we cannot access our production Postgres database from our laptops? Luckily, it's easy to spin a local Postgres database for testing with Docker. Several Python packages exist that provide convenient functions for controlling Docker containers within the scope of pytest tests. For the following example, we'll use pytest-docker-tools (https://github.com/Jc2k/pytest-docker-tools). This package provides a set of convenient helper functions with which we can create a Docker container for testing.

We won't go into all the details of the package but will demonstrate how to create a sample Postgres container for writing MovieLens results. If the operator works correctly, we should have results written to the Postgres database in the container at the end of the test. Testing with Docker containers allows us to use the real methods of hooks, without having to mock calls, with the aim of testing as realistic as possible.

First, install pytest-docker-tools in your environment with `pip install pytest_docker_tools`. This provides us a few helper functions, such as *fetch* and *container*. First, we will fetch the container.

Listing 9.28   Fetching a Docker image for testing with pytest_docker_tools

```
from pytest_docker_tools import fetch

postgres_image = fetch(repository="postgres:11.1-alpine")
```

The fetch function triggers docker pull on the machine it's running on (and therefore requires Docker to be installed) and returns the pulled image. Note the fetch function itself is a pytest fixture, which means we cannot call it directly but must provide it as a parameter to a test.

Listing 9.29   Using a Docker image in a test with pytest_docker_tools fixtures

```python
from pytest_docker_tools import fetch

postgres_image = fetch(repository="postgres:11.1-alpine")

def test_call_fixture(postgres_image):
    print(postgres_image.id)
```

Running this test will print

```
Fetching postgres:11.1-alpine
PASSED                      [100%]
sha256:b43856647ab572f271decd1f8de88b590e157bfd816599362fe162e8f37fb1ec
```

We can now use this image ID to configure and start a Postgres container.

Listing 9.30   Starting a Docker container for a test with pytest_docker_tools fixtures

```python
from pytest_docker_tools import container

postgres_container = container(
    image="{postgres_image.id}",
    ports={"5432/tcp": None},
)

def test_call_fixture(postgres_container):
    print(
        f"Running Postgres container named {postgres_container.name} "
        f"on port {postgres_container.ports['5432/tcp'][0]}."
    )
```

The container function in pytest_docker_tools is also a fixture, so that too can only be called by providing it as an argument to a test. It takes several arguments that configure the container to start, in this case the image ID, which was returned from the fetch() fixture and the ports to expose. Just like running Docker containers on the command line, we could also configure environment variables, volumes, and more.

The ports configuration requires a bit of explanation. You typically map a container port to the same port on the host system (i.e., docker run -p 5432:5432 postgres). A container for tests is not meant to be a container running until infinity, and we also don't want to conflict with any other ports in use on the host system.

Providing a dict to the ports keyword argument, where keys are container ports and values map to the host system, and leaving the values to None, will map the host port to a random open port on the host (just like running docker run -P). Providing the fixture to a test will execute the fixture (i.e., run the container), and pytest-docker-tools then internally maps the assigned ports on the host system to a ports attribute on the fixture itself. `postgres_container.ports['5432/tcp'][0]` gives us the assigned port number on the host, which we can then use in the test to connect to.

In order to mimic a real database as much as possible, we'd like to set a username and password and initialize it with a schema and data to query. We can provide both to the container fixture.

Listing 9.31   Initializing a Postgres container for testing against a real database

```
postgres_image = fetch(repository="postgres:11.1-alpine")
postgres = container(
    image="{postgres_image.id}",
    environment={
        "POSTGRES_USER": "testuser",
        "POSTGRES_PASSWORD": "testpass",
    },
    ports={"5432/tcp": None},
    volumes={
        os.path.join(os.path.dirname(__file__), "postgres-init.sql"): {
            "bind": "/docker-entrypoint-initdb.d/postgres-init.sql"
        }
    },
)
```

Database structure and data can be initialized in `postgres-init.sql`.

Listing 9.32   Initializing a schema for the test database

```
SET SCHEMA 'public';
CREATE TABLE movielens (
    movieId integer,
    rating float,
    ratingTimestamp integer,
    userId integer,
    scrapeTime timestamp
);
```

In the container fixture, we provide a Postgres username and password via environment variables. This is a feature of the Postgres Docker image; it allows us to configure several settings via environment variables. Read the Postgres Docker image documentation for all environment variables. Another feature of the Docker image is the ability to initialize a container with a startup script by placing a file with extension *.sql, *.sql.gz or *.sh in the directory /docker-entrypoint-initdb.d. These are executed while booting the container, before starting the actual Postgres service, and we can use these to initialize our test container with a table to query.

In listing 9.31, we mount a file named `postgres-init.sql` to the container with the `volumes` keyword to the container fixture:

```
volumes={
        os.path.join(os.path.dirname(__file__), "postgres-init.sql"): {
            "bind": "/docker-entrypoint-initdb.d/postgres-init.sql"
        }
    }
```

We provide it a dict where the keys show the (absolute) location on the host system. In this case, we saved a file named `postgres-init.sql` in the same directory as our test script, so `os.path.join(os.path.dirname(__file__), "postgres-init.sql")` will give us the absolute path to it. The values are also a dict where the key indicates the mount type (bind) and the value of the location inside the container, which should be in `/docker-entrypoint-initdb.d` in order to run the *.sql script at boot-time of the container.

Put all this together in a script and we can finally test against a real Postgres database.

Listing 9.33   Completing the test using a Docker container for testing external systems

```
import os

import pytest
from airflow.models import Connection
from pytest_docker_tools import fetch, container

from airflowbook.operators.movielens_operator import MovielensHook,
    MovielensToPostgresOperator, PostgresHook

postgres_image = fetch(repository="postgres:11.1-alpine")
postgres = container(
    image="{postgres_image.id}",
    environment={
        "POSTGRES_USER": "testuser",
        "POSTGRES_PASSWORD": "testpass",
    },
    ports={"5432/tcp": None},
    volumes={
        os.path.join(os.path.dirname(__file__), "postgres-init.sql"): {
            "bind": "/docker-entrypoint-initdb.d/postgres-init.sql"
        }
    },
)


def test_movielens_to_postgres_operator(mocker, test_dag, postgres):
    mocker.patch.object(
        MovielensHook,
        "get_connection",
        return_value=Connection(
            conn_id="test",
            login="airflow",
            password="airflow",
        ),
    )
```

```
    mocker.patch.object(
        PostgresHook,
        "get_connection",
        return_value=Connection(
            conn_id="postgres",
            conn_type="postgres",
            host="localhost",
            login="testuser",
            password="testpass",
            port=postgres.ports["5432/tcp"][0],
        ),
    )

    task = MovielensToPostgresOperator(
        task_id="test",
        movielens_conn_id="movielens_id",
        start_date="{{ prev_ds }}",
        end_date="{{ ds }}",
        postgres_conn_id="postgres_id",
        insert_query=(
            "INSERT INTO movielens
    (movieId,rating,ratingTimestamp,userId,scrapeTime) "
            "VALUES ({0}, '{{ macros.datetime.now() }}')"
        ),
        dag=test_dag,
    )

    pg_hook = PostgresHook()

    row_count = pg_hook.get_first("SELECT COUNT(*) FROM movielens")[0]
    assert row_count == 0

    task.run(
        start_date=test_dag.default_args["start_date"],
        end_date=test_dag.default_args["start_date"],
    )

    row_count = pg_hook.get_first("SELECT COUNT(*) FROM movielens")[0]
    assert row_count > 0
```

The full test turns out a bit lengthy because of the container initialization and the connection mocking we have to do. After this, we instantiate a PostgresHook (which uses the same mocked get_connection() as in the MovielensToPostgresOperator and thus connects to the Docker Postgres container). We first assert if the number of rows is zero, run the operator, and finally test if any data was inserted.

Outside the test logic itself, what happens? During test startup, pytest figures out which tests use a fixture, and will execute only if the given fixture is used (figure 9.11).

At the time pytest decides to start the container fixture, it will fetch, run, and initialize the container. This takes a couple of seconds, so there will be a small delay of a few seconds in the test suite. After the tests finish, the fixtures are terminated. Pytest-docker-tools puts a small wrapper around the Python Docker client, providing a couple of convenient constructs and fixtures to use in tests.

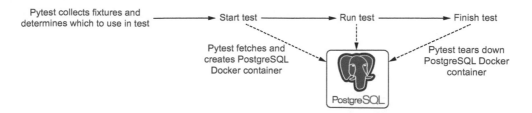

Figure 9.11 Process of running a test with pytest-docker-tools. Running Docker containers during tests enables testing against real systems. The life cycle of the Docker container is managed by pytest-docker-tools, and the user must implement the test.

9.3 *Using tests for development*

Tests not only help for verifying the correctness of your code. They are also helpful during development because they allow you to run a small snippet of code without having to use a live system. Let's see how they can help us while developing workflows. We will show a couple of screenshots of PyCharm, but any modern IDE will allow us to set breakpoints and debug.

Let's go back to the MovielensPopularityOperator shown in section 9.1.3. In the execute() method, it runs a series of statements, and we would like to know the state halfway through. With PyCharm, we can do this by placing a breakpoint and running a test that hits the line of code the breakpoint is set to (figure 9.12).

```python
class MovielensPopularityOperator(BaseOperator):
    def __init__(self, conn_id, start_date, end_date, min_ratings=4, top_n=5, **kwargs):
        super().__init__(**kwargs)
        self._conn_id = conn_id
        self._start_date = start_date
        self._end_date = end_date
        self._min_ratings = min_ratings
        self._top_n = top_n

    def execute(self, context):
        with MovielensHook(self._conn_id) as hook:
            ratings = hook.get_ratings(start_date=self._start_date, end_date=self._end_date)

            rating_sums = defaultdict(Counter)
            for rating in ratings:
                rating_sums[rating["movieId"]].update(count=1, rating=rating["rating"])

            averages = {
                movie_id: (rating_counter["rating"] / rating_counter["count"], rating_counter["count"])
                for movie_id, rating_counter in rating_sums.items()
                if rating_counter["count"] >= self._min_ratings
            }
            return sorted(averages.items(), key=lambda x: x[1], reverse=True)[: self._top_n]
```

Click in the border to set a breakpoint.
The debugger will pause once it reaches this statement.

Figure 9.12 Setting a breakpoint in an IDE. This screenshot was taken in PyCharm, but any IDE allows you to set breakpoints and debug.

Now run the `test_movielenspopularityoperator` test and start it in debug mode (figure 9.13).

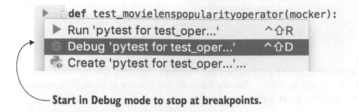

def test_movielenspopularityoperator(mocker):
Run 'pytest for test_oper...' ^⇧R
Debug 'pytest for test_oper...' ^⇧D
Create 'pytest for test_oper...'...
Start in Debug mode to stop at breakpoints.

Figure 9.13 Starting a test in debug mode so that it stops at breakpoints

Once the test reaches the line of code on which you've set a breakpoint, you can inspect the current state of variables but also execute code at that moment. Here, we can, for example, inspect the task instance context halfway through the `execute()` method (figure. 9.14).

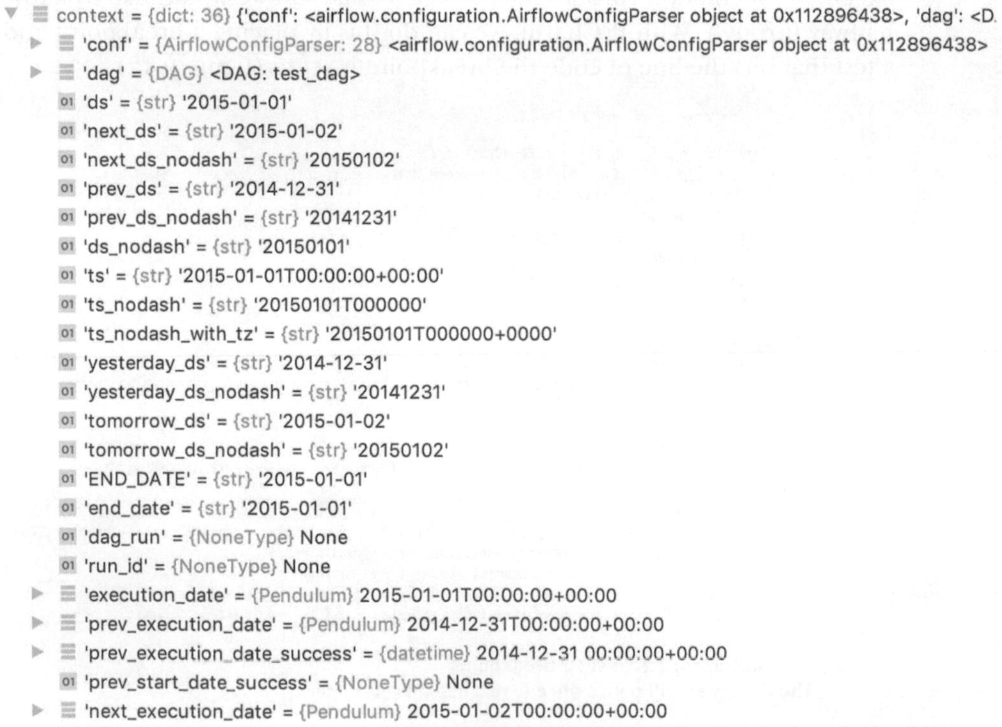

context = {dict: 36} {'conf': <airflow.configuration.AirflowConfigParser object at 0x112896438>, 'dag': <D.
'conf' = {AirflowConfigParser: 28} <airflow.configuration.AirflowConfigParser object at 0x112896438>
'dag' = {DAG} <DAG: test_dag>
'ds' = {str} '2015-01-01'
'next_ds' = {str} '2015-01-02'
'next_ds_nodash' = {str} '20150102'
'prev_ds' = {str} '2014-12-31'
'prev_ds_nodash' = {str} '20141231'
'ds_nodash' = {str} '20150101'
'ts' = {str} '2015-01-01T00:00:00+00:00'
'ts_nodash' = {str} '20150101T000000'
'ts_nodash_with_tz' = {str} '20150101T000000+0000'
'yesterday_ds' = {str} '2014-12-31'
'yesterday_ds_nodash' = {str} '20141231'
'tomorrow_ds' = {str} '2015-01-02'
'tomorrow_ds_nodash' = {str} '20150102'
'END_DATE' = {str} '2015-01-01'
'end_date' = {str} '2015-01-01'
'dag_run' = {NoneType} None
'run_id' = {NoneType} None
'execution_date' = {Pendulum} 2015-01-01T00:00:00+00:00
'prev_execution_date' = {Pendulum} 2014-12-31T00:00:00+00:00
'prev_execution_date_success' = {datetime} 2014-12-31 00:00:00+00:00
'prev_start_date_success' = {NoneType} None
'next_execution_date' = {Pendulum} 2015-01-02T00:00:00+00:00

Figure 9.14 Debugging allows us to inspect the state of the program at the set breakpoint. Here we inspect the values of the context.

Sometimes your code works locally but returns an error on a production machine. How would we debug on a production machine? There is a way to debug remotely, but that's beyond the scope of this book. It allows you to connect your local PyCharm (or other IDE) debugger to a remote running Python process. (Search for "PyCharm remote debugging" for more information.)

Another alternative, if for whatever reason you cannot use a real debugger, is to resort to a command line debugger (for this, you need access to the command line on the remote machine). Python has a built-in debugger named pdb (Python Debugger). It works by adding this line of code on the location you want to debug.[11]

Listing 9.34 Setting a breakpoint in code

```
import pdb; pdb.set_trace()
```

Now you can start your code from the command line, either by running a test with pytest or by starting an Airflow task in a DAG with the CLI, by running

```
airflow tasks test [dagid] [taskid] [execution date]
```

Here's an example:

```
airflow tasks test movielens_download fetch_data 2019-01-01T12:00:00
```

`airflow tasks test` runs the task without registering any records in the metastore. It's useful for running and testing individual tasks in a production setting. Once the pdb breakpoint is reached, you can execute code and control the debugger with certain keys such as n for executing the statement and going to the next line, and l for displaying the surrounding lines (figure 9.15). (See the full list of commands by searching for "pdb cheat sheet" on the internet.)

9.3.1 Testing complete DAGs

So far, we've focused on various aspects of testing individual operators: testing with and without task instance context, operators using the local filesystem, and operators using external systems with the help of Docker. But all these focused on testing a single operator. A large and important aspect of the development of workflows is ensuring all building blocks fit together nicely. While one operator might run correctly from a logical point of view, it could, for example, transform data in an unexpected way, which makes the subsequent operator fail. How do we ensure all operators in a DAG work together as expected?

Unfortunately, this is not an easy question to answer. Mimicking a real environment is not always possible, for various reasons. For example, with a DTAP (development, test,

---

[11] With Python 3.7 and PEP553, a new way to set breakpoints was introduced, simply by calling `breakpoint()`.

The statement where pdb pauses
"1" to inspect surrounding lines
-> shows next line to execute.

```
>>>>>>>>>>>>>>>>>>>>>>>>>>>>>>>>>>>>>>>>>> PDB   set_trace >>>>>>>>>>>>>>>>>>>>>>>>>>>>>>>>>>>>>>>>>>>>> >>>>>
> /src/airflowbook/operators/movielens_operator.py( 70)execute()
-> postgres_hook = PostgresHook(postgres_conn_id=se lf._postgres_conn_id)
(Pdb) l
65 with MovielensHook(self._movielens_conn_id) as m ovielens_hook:
66 ratings = list(movielens_hook.get_ratings(start_ date=self._start_date, end_date=self._end_date))
67
68 import pdb; pdb.set_trace()
69
70 -> postgres_hook = PostgresHook(postgres_conn_id =self._postgres_conn_id)
71 insert_queries = [
72 self._insert_query.format(",".join([str(_[1]) fo r _ in sorted(rating.items())]))
73 for rating in ratings
74 ]
75 postgres_hook.run(insert_queries)
(Pdb) len(ratings)
3103
(Pdb) n
> /src/airflowbook/operators/movielens_operator.py( 72)execute()
-> self._insert_query.format(",".join([str(_[1]) fo r _ in sorted(rating.items())]))
```

Check if the variable ratings holds any values by printing the length.

Evaluate line and go to the next.

Figure 9.15   Debugging on the command line with PDB

acceptance, production) separated system, we often cannot create a perfect replica of production in the development environment because of privacy regulations or the size of the data. Say the production environment holds a petabyte of data; then it would be impractical (to say the least) to keep the data in sync on all four environments. Therefore, people have been creating production environments that are as real as possible, which we can use for developing and validating the software. With Airflow, this is no different, and we've seen several approaches to this problem. We briefly describe two approaches in sections 9.4 and 9.5.

9.4   *Emulate production environments with Whirl*

One approach to recreating a production environment is a project named Whirl (https://github.com/godatadriven/whirl). Its idea is to simulate all components of your production environment in Docker containers and manage all these with Docker Compose. Whirl comes with a CLI utility to easily control these environments. While Docker is a great tool for development, one downside is that not everything is available as a Docker image. For example, there is no Google Cloud Storage available as a Docker image.

9.5   *Create DTAP environments*

Simulating your production environment locally with Docker, or working with a tool such as Whirl, is not always possible. One reason for that is security (e.g., it's sometimes not possible to connect your local Docker setup with an FTP server used in your production DAGs because the FTP server is IP allowlisted).

One approach that is often more negotiable with a security officer is to set up isolated DTAP environments. Four fully-fledged environments are sometimes cumbersome to set up and manage, so in smaller projects with few people, sometimes just two (development and production) are used. Each environment can have specific requirements, such as dummy data in the development and test environments. The implementation of such a DTAP street is often very specific to the project and infrastructure, and is not in the scope of this book.

In the context of an Airflow project, it is wise to create one dedicated branch in your GitHub repository per environment: development environment > development branch, production environment > production/main, and so on. This way you can develop locally in branches. Then, first merge into the development branch and run DAGs on the development environment. Once satisfied with the results, you would then merge your changes into the next branch, say main, and run the workflows in the corresponding environment.

Summary

- A DAG integrity test filters basic errors in your DAGs.
- Unit testing verifies the correctness of individual operators.
- Pytest and plug-ins provide several useful constructs for testing, such as temporary directories and plug-ins for managing Docker containers during tests.
- Operators that don't use task instance context can simply run with `execute()`.
- Operators that do use task instance context must run together with a DAG.
- For integration testing, you must simulate your production environment as closely as possible.

Running tasks in containers

10

This chapter covers

- Identifying some challenges involved in managing Airflow deployments
- Examining how containerized approaches can help simplify Airflow deployments
- Running containerized tasks in Airflow on Docker
- Establishing a high-level overview of workflows in developing containerized DAGs

In previous chapters, we implemented several DAGs using different Airflow operators, each specialized to perform a specific type of task. In this chapter, we touch on some of the drawbacks of using many different operators, especially with an eye on creating Airflow DAGs that are easy to build, deploy, and maintain. In light of these issues, we look at how we can use Airflow to run tasks in containers using Docker and Kubernetes and some of the benefits this containerized approach can bring.

220

10.1 Challenges of many different operators

Operators are arguably one of the strong features of Airflow, as they provide great flexibility to coordinate jobs across many different types of systems. However, creating and managing DAGs with many different operators can be quite challenging due to the complexity involved.

To see why, consider the DAG in figure 10.1, which is based on our recommender use case from chapter 8. The DAG consists of three different tasks: fetching movie recommendations from our movie API, ranking movies based on the fetched recommendations, and pushing these movies to a MySQL database for further use downstream. Note that this relatively simple DAG already uses three different operators: an `HttpOperator` (or some other API operator) for accessing the API, a `PythonOperator` for executing the Python recommender function, and a `MySQLOperator` for storing the results.

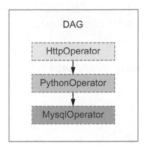

1. Fetch data from API.

2. Aggregate data to calculate stats.

3. Load into MySQL for analytics.

Figure 10.1 Illustration of our movie recommender DAG. The DAG fetches movie recommendations, uses them to rank movies, and stores the result in a database. Each of these steps involves a different operator, thus adding complexity to the development and maintenance of the DAG.

10.1.1 Operator interfaces and implementations

A drawback of using different operators for each of these tasks is that we need to familiarize ourselves with the interfaces and inner workings of each operator to use them effectively. Additionally, if we were to encounter bugs in any of the operators[1] we would need to spend valuable time and resources on tracking down the underlying issues and fixing them. While these efforts may seem tractable for this small example, imagine maintaining an Airflow deployment with many different DAGs, which together use a multitude of different operators. In such a scenario, working with all these operators may seem a bit more daunting.

---

[1] This is unfortunately not unheard of, especially for more esoteric and less frequently used Airflow operators.

10.1.2 *Complex and conflicting dependencies*

Another challenge in using many different operators is that each generally requires its own set of dependencies (Python or otherwise). For example, the HttpOperator depends on the Python library requests for doing HTTP requests, while the MySQL-Operator depends on Python- and/or system-level dependencies for talking to MySQL. Similarly, the recommender code being called by the PythonOperator is likely to have its own slew of dependencies (such as pandas, scikit-learn, etc., if machine learning were involved).

Because of the way that Airflow is set up, all of these dependencies need to be installed in the environment that runs the Airflow scheduler, as well as the Airflow workers themselves. When using many different operators, this requires many dependencies to be installed,[2] leading to potential conflicts (figure 10.2) and a great deal of complexity in setting up and maintaining these environments (not to mention the potential security risks with installing so many different software packages). Conflicts are particularly a problem in Python environments, as Python does not provide any mechanism for installing multiple versions of the same package in the same environment.

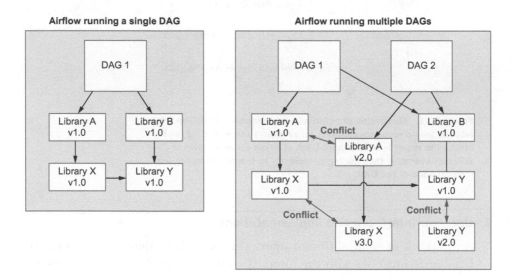

Figure 10.2 Complex and conflicting dependencies between Airflow tasks or DAGs. Running many DAGs in a single environment can lead to conflicts when DAGs depend on different versions of the same (or related) packages. Python in particular does not support installing different versions of the same package in the same environment. This means that any conflicts in packages (right) would need to be resolved by rewriting the DAGs (or their dependencies) to use the same package versions.

---

[2] Just look at Airflow's setup.py file for an idea of the sheer number of dependencies involved in supporting all of Airflow's operators.

10.1.3 *Moving toward a generic operator*

Because of these challenges in using and maintaining many different operators and their dependencies, some have argued it would be better to focus on using a single generic operator for running Airflow tasks. An upside of this approach is that we only have to be familiar with one kind of operator, which means that our many different Airflow DAGs suddenly become much easier to understand, as they only consist of one type of task. Moreover, if everyone uses the same operator to run their tasks, we are less likely to run into bugs in this heavily used operator. Finally, having only one operator means we only have to worry about one set of Airflow dependencies—those required for this single operator.

But where would we find such a generic operator capable of running many different tasks that at the same time doesn't require us to install and manage dependencies for each? That's where containers come in.

10.2 *Introducing containers*

Containers have been touted as one of the major recent developments that allow applications to be easily packed with the required dependencies and to be easily deployed in different environments uniformly. Before going into how we can use containers within Airflow, we'll first give a short[3] introduction to containers to make sure we're all on the same page. If you're already familiar with Docker and the concepts behind containers, feel free to skip ahead to section 10.3.

10.2.1 *What are containers?*

Historically, one of the biggest challenges in developing software applications has been their deployment (i.e., ensuring that your application[s] can run correctly and stably on the target machine[s]). This typically involves juggling and accounting for many different factors, including differences between operating systems, variation in installed dependencies and libraries, differing hardware, and so on.

One approach to managing this complexity is to use virtualization, in which applications are installed into a virtual machine (VM) that is running on top of the client's operating host operating system (figure 10.3). Using this type of approach, applications see just the VM's operating system (OS), meaning that we only have to ensure the virtual OS meets the requirements of our application rather than modifying the host OS. As such, to deploy our application we can simply install our application with any required dependencies into the virtual OS, which we can then ship to our clients.

A drawback of VMs is that they are quite heavy because they require running an entire operating system (the virtual or guest OS) on top of the host operating system. Moreover, every new VM will be running its own guest operating system, meaning

---

[3] For a full introduction, we happily refer you to the many, many books written about container-based virtualization and related technologies, such as Docker/Kubernetes.

that considerable resources are required to run multiple applications in VMs on a single machine.

This limitation led to the development of container-based virtualization, which is a much more lightweight approach than VMs (figure 10.3). In contrast to VMs, container-based virtualization approaches use kernel-level functionality in the host operating system to virtualize applications. This means containers can segregate applications and their dependencies in the same fashion as VMs, but without requiring each application to run its own operating system; they can simply leverage this functionality from the host OS.

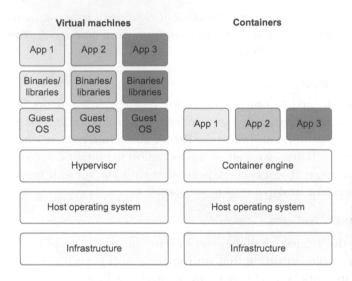

Figure 10.3   Comparison between virtual machines (VMs) and containers. Note that containers are much more lightweight as they don't require running a full guest OS for each application.

Interaction between containers and the host operating system is often managed by a service called the container engine, which provides an API for managing and running the different application containers and their images. This service often also provides command-line tooling that helps users build and interact with their containers. The most well-known container engine is Docker, which has gained a lot of popularity over the years due to its being relatively easy to use and its large community.

10.2.2 *Running our first Docker container*

To explore the lifecycle of building and running a container, let's try to build a small container using Docker. This will hopefully give you a feel for working with containers and the involved development workflow. Before getting started, make sure you have Docker installed. You can find instructions for installing Docker Desktop at https://www.docker.com/get-started. Once you have Docker installed and running, we can run our first container using the following command in your terminal.

> **Listing 10.1   Running a Docker container**

```
$ docker run debian:buster-slim echo Hello, world!
```

Running this command should give you something like the following output:

```
Unable to find image 'debian:buster-slim' locally
latest: Pulling from library/debian
...
Digest: sha256:76c15066d7db315b42dc247b6d439779d2c6466f
 7dc2a47c2728220e288fc680
Status: Downloaded newer image for debian:buster-slim
Hello, world!
```

What happened when we ran this command? In short, Docker performed the following steps for us:

1 The docker client contacted the Docker daemon (the container service running on our local machine).
2 The Docker daemon pulled a Debian Docker image, which contains the base Debian binaries and libraries, from the Docker hub registry (an online service for storing Docker images).
3 The Docker daemon created a new container using that image.
4 The container executed our command echo Hello, world inside the container.
5 The Docker daemon streamed the output from the command to the Docker client, showing it on our terminal.

This means that we were able to execute our command echo Hello, world inside an Ubuntu container on our local machine, independent of our host operating system. Pretty cool!

Similarly, we can run commands in Python using the following command.

> **Listing 10.2   Running a command inside a Python container**

```
$ docker run python:3.8 python -c 'import sys; print(sys.version)'
```

This effectively runs our Python command inside the Python container. Note that here we specify a tag for the image (3.8), which in this case makes sure we use a version of the Python image that contains Python 3.8.

10.2.3 Creating a Docker image

Although running an existing image is pretty straightforward, what if we want to include our own application in an image so that we can run it using Docker? Let's illustrate the process with a small example.

In this example, we have a small script (fetch_weather.py) that fetches weather predictions from the wttr.in API (http://wttr.in) and writes the output of this API to an output file. This script has a couple of dependencies (Python and the Python packages' clicks and requests), and we want to package the whole thing as a Docker image so that it is easy for end users to run.

We can start building a Docker image by creating a Dockerfile, which is essentially a text-based file that describes to Docker how to build the image. The basic structure of a Dockerfile is something like this.

Listing 10.3   Dockerfile for fetching weather from the wttr API

```
FROM python:3.8-slim                                        ◁──┐ Tell Docker which image to use as
                                                                  a base for building our image.

COPY requirements.txt /tmp/requirements.txt                 ◁──┐ Copy requirements file and run
RUN pip install -r /tmp/requirements.txt                         pip to install the requirements.

COPY scripts/fetch_weather.py /usr/local/bin/fetch-weather  ◁──┐ Copy our script and make
RUN chmod +x /usr/local/bin/fetch-weather                        sure it's executable.

ENTRYPOINT [ "/usr/local/bin/fetch-weather" ]               ◁──┐ Tell Docker which
CMD [ "--help" ]   ◁──┐ Tell Docker which default                 command to run when
                        arguments to include                      starting the container.
                        with the command.
```

Each line of the Dockerfile is essentially an instruction that tells Docker to perform a specific task when building the image. Most Dockerfiles start with a `FROM` instruction that tells Docker which base image to use as a starting point. The remaining instructions (`COPY`, `ADD`, `ENV`, etc.) then tell Docker how to add extra layers to the base image that contains your application and its dependencies.

To actually build an image using this Dockerfile, we can use the following `docker build` command.

Listing 10.4   Building a Docker image using the Dockerfile

```
$ docker build --tag manning-airflow/wttr-example .
```

This effectively tells Docker to build a Docker image using the current directory (.) as a build context. Docker will then look inside this directory for the Dockerfile and also search for any files included in `ADD`/`COPY` statements (such as our script and the requirements file). The `--tag` argument tells Docker which name to assign to the built image (in this case `manning-airflow/wttr-example`).

Running this `build` command will give something like the following output:

```
Sending build context to Docker daemon    5.12kB
Step 1/7 : FROM python:3.8-slim
 ---> 9935a3c58eae
Step 2/7 : COPY requirements.txt /tmp/requirements.txt
 ---> 598f16e2f9f6
Step 3/7 : RUN pip install -r /tmp/requirements.txt
 ---> Running in c86b8e396c98
Collecting click
...
```

```
Removing intermediate container c86b8e396c98
 ---> 102aae5e3412
Step 4/7 : COPY scripts/fetch_weather.py /usr/local/bin/fetch-weather
 ---> 7380766da370
Step 5/7 : RUN chmod +x /usr/local/bin/fetch-weather
 ---> Running in 7d5bf4d184b5
Removing intermediate container 7d5bf4d184b5
 ---> cae6f678e8f8
Step 6/7 : ENTRYPOINT [ "/usr/local/bin/fetch-weather" ]
 ---> Running in 785fe602e3fa
Removing intermediate container 785fe602e3fa
 ---> 3a0b247507af
Step 7/7 : CMD [ "--help" ]
 ---> Running in bad0ef960f30
Removing intermediate container bad0ef960f30
 ---> ffabdb642077
Successfully built ffabdb642077
Successfully tagged wttr-example:latest
```

This essentially shows the entire build process involved in creating our image, starting with the Python base image (step 1) up until our final CMD instruction (step 7), finished by Docker stating it tagged the built image with the provided name.

To do a test run of the built image, we can use the following command.

Listing 10.5 Running a Docker container using the wttr image

```
$ docker run manning-airflow/wttr-example:latest
```

This should print the following help message from our script inside the container:

```
Usage: fetch-weather [OPTIONS] CITY

  CLI application for fetching weather forecasts from wttr.in.

Options:
  --output_path FILE  Optional file to write output to.
  --help              Show this message and exit.
```

Now that we have our container image, we can start using it to fetch weather forecasts from the wttr API in the next section.

10.2.4 Persisting data using volumes

We can run the wttr-example image we built in the previous section to fetch the weather for a city like Amsterdam using the following Docker command.

Listing 10.6 Running the wttr container for a specific city

```
$ docker run wttr-example:latest Amsterdam
```

Assuming everything goes correctly, this should print some weather forecasts for Amsterdam in the terminal, together with some fancy graphs (figure 10.4).

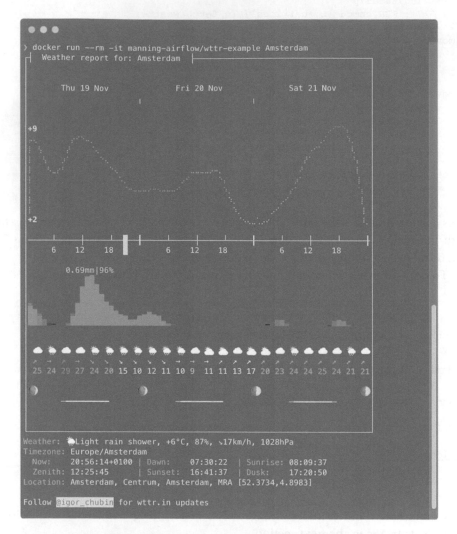

Figure 10.4   Example output from the `wttr-example` container for Amsterdam

To build some history of weather forecasts, we may also want to write the forecasts to some output file(s) that we can use for future reference or analysis. Fortunately, our CLI script includes an extra argument, `--output_path`, which allows us to specify an output file path to write the forecasts to, instead of writing them to the console.

However, if you try to run this command with a local file path, you will see that it doesn't actually create any JSON output on your local file system:

```
$ docker run wttr-example:latest Amsterdam --output_path amsterdam.json
$ ls amsterdam.json
ls: amsterdam.json: No such file or directory
```

This is because your container environment is isolated from your host operating system, which means that it (among other things) has an isolated file system separated from the host file system.

To share files with your container you need to make sure that the files are available in a file system your container has access to. One commonly used option is to read/write files using storage that can be accessed via the internet (such as Amazon's S3 storage) or the local network. Alternatively, you can mount files or folders from your host system into the container to make them accessible from within the container.

To mount a file or folder into your container, you need to supply a --volume argument to docker run that specifies the file/folder to mount and the desired path inside the container.

Listing 10.7 Mounting a volume when running a container

```
$ docker run --volume `pwd`/data:/data wttr-example ...          ◄──┐
```
Mount the local directory data (left) in the container under /data.

This effectively tells Docker to mount the local folder data under the path /data within the container. This means that we can now write our weather output to the mounted data volume using the following command.

Listing 10.8 Persisting output from the wttr container

```
$ docker run --rm --volume `pwd`/data:/data \
➥ wttr-example Amsterdam --output_path /data/amsterdam.json      ◄──┐
```
Pass extra arguments from Amsterdam and --output_path to the container.

We can verify everything worked by checking if the text file indeed exists after our container finished running:

```
$ ls data/amsterdam.json
data/amsterdam.json
```

When you're done with running containers, you can use the following command to check if any containers are still secretly running:

```
$ docker ps
```

You can stop any running containers with Docker's stop command, using the container IDs obtained from the previous command to reference the running containers:

```
$ docker stop <container_id>
```

Stopped docker containers still hang around in a suspended state in the background in case you want to start them again at a later point in time. If you don't need the container anymore, you can fully remove the container using Docker's rm command:

```
$ docker rm <container_id>
```

Note that stopped containers aren't visible by default when using Docker's ps command to look for running containers. You can view stopped containers by including the -a flag when running the ps command:

```
$ docker ps -a
```

10.3   Containers and Airflow

Now that we have a basic understanding of what Docker containers are and how they can be used, let's turn back to Airflow. In this section, we'll dive into how containers can be used within Airflow and what potential benefits they can bring.

10.3.1   Tasks in containers

Airflow allows you to run your tasks as containers. In practice, this means that you can use container-based operators (such as the DockerOperator and the Kubernetes-PodOperators) to define tasks. These operators will, when executed, start running a container and wait for it to finish running whatever it was supposed to (similar to docker run).

The result of each task depends on the executed command and the software inside the container image. As an example, consider our recommender DAG (figure 10.1). The original example uses three operators to perform three different tasks, namely fetching ratings (using the HttpOperator), ranking movies (using the PythonOperator), and posting the results (using a MySQL-based operator). Using a Docker-based approach (figure 10.5), we could replace these different tasks using the DockerOperator and use it to execute commands in three different Docker containers with the appropriate dependencies.

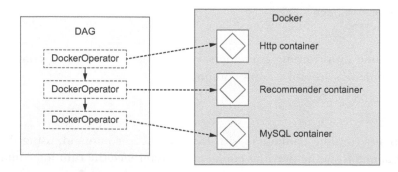

Figure 10.5   Docker version of the recommender DAG from figure 10.1

10.3.2 *Why use containers?*

Of course, this kind of container-based approach does require building images for each of the tasks (although sometimes you might be able to share images between related or similar tasks). As such, you might wonder why you would go through the hassle of building and maintaining these Docker images instead of implementing everything in a few scripts or Python functions.

EASIER DEPENDENCY MANAGEMENT

One of the biggest advantages of using (Docker) containers is that they provide an easier approach for managing dependencies. By creating different images for different tasks, you can install the exact dependencies required by each of the tasks into their respective image. As tasks then run in isolation within these images, you no longer have to deal with conflicts in dependencies between tasks (figure 10.6). As an additional advantage, you don't have to install any task dependencies in the Airflow worker environment (only in Docker), as the tasks are no longer run directly on the workers.

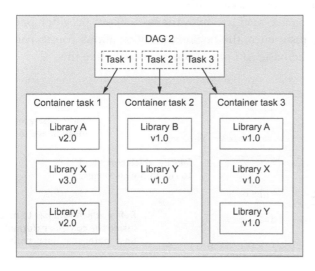

Figure 10.6 Managing dependencies across different tasks using containers

UNIFORM APPROACH FOR RUNNING DIFFERENT TASKS

Another advantage of using containers for tasks is that each containerized task has the same interface, as they're all effectively the same operation (running a container) executed by the same operator (e.g., the DockerOperator). The only differences are the involved images, with some slight variation in their configuration and executed command. This uniformity makes it easier to develop DAGs, as you only have to learn one operator. And, if any operator-related issues pop up, we only have to debug and fix issues in this one operator instead of having to be intimately familiar with many different ones.

IMPROVED TESTABILITY

Finally, another benefit of using container images is that they can be developed and maintained separately from the Airflow DAG in which they run. This means that each image can have its own development life cycle and can be subjected to a dedicated test suite (e.g., running on mock data), which verifies whether the software in the image does what we expect. The separation into containers makes this testing easier than, for example, using the PythonOperator, which often involves tasks that are tightly coupled to the DAG itself, thus making it hard to test the functions separate from Airflow's orchestration layer.

10.4 Running tasks in Docker

After this introduction, it's time to implement a part of our recommender DAG in containers. In this section, we'll dive into how to run the existing DAG in containers using Docker.

10.4.1 Introducing the DockerOperator

The easiest way to run a task in a container with Airflow is to use the DockerOperator, which is available in the apache-airflow-providers-docker[4] provider package. As the name of the operator insinuates, the DockerOperator allows you to run tasks in containers using Docker. The basic API of the operator looks like this.

Listing 10.9   Example use of the DockerOperator

```
rank_movies = DockerOperator(
      task_id="rank_movies",
      image="manning-airflow/movielens-ranking",        ◁──┐ Tell the
      command=[                                              DockerOperator
          "rank_movies.py",              ◁──┐ Specify which command  which image to use.
          "--input_path",                    to run in the container.
          "/data/ratings/{{ds}}.json",
          "--output_path",
          "/data/rankings/{{ds}}.csv",         ┌── Define which volumes to mount
      ],                                       │   inside the container (format:
      volumes=["/tmp/airflow/data:/data"],  ◁─┘   host_path: container_path).
  )
```

The idea behind the DockerOperator is that it performs the equivalent of a docker run command (as shown in the previous section) to run a specified container image with specific arguments and wait for the container to finish doing its work. In this case, we're telling Airflow to run the rank_movies.py script inside the manning-airflow/movielens-ranking Docker image, with some extra arguments indicating where the script should read/write its data. Note that we also provide an extra volumes argument that mounts a data directory into the container so that we can provide input data to the container and also keep the results after the task/container finishes.

---

[4] For Airflow 1.10.x, you can install the DockerOperator using the apache-airflow-backport-providers-docker backport package.

What happens when this operator is actually executed? In essence, what happens is illustrated in figure 10.7. First, Airflow tells a worker to execute the task by scheduling it (1). Next, the DockerOperator executes a docker run command on the Worker machine with the appropriate arguments (2). Then, if needed, the Docker daemon fetches the required Docker image from the registry (3). Finally, Docker creates a container running the image (4) and mounts the local volume into the container (5). As soon as the command finishes, the container is terminated and the DockerOperator retrieves the results in the Airflow worker.

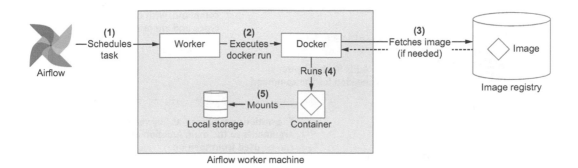

Figure 10.7 Illustration of what happens when a task is executed using the DockerOperator. The image registry stores a collection of Docker images This can be a private registry (containing our own images), or a public registry like DockerHub (which is used by default when fetching images). Images are cached locally when fetched so that you only have to do it once (barring any updates to the image).

10.4.2 Creating container images for tasks

Before we can run tasks using the DockerOperator, we need to build any required Docker images for the various tasks. To build an image for any given task, we need to determine exactly which software (and corresponding dependencies) are required to execute the task. Once this is clear, we can start creating a Dockerfile (together with any supporting files) and use docker build to actually create the required image.

As an example, let's look at the first task in our movie recommender DAG: the task for fetching ratings (figure 10.1). This task needs to contact an external API to fetch movie ratings from users for a given range of dates so that we can use these ratings as input for our recommender model in the next task.

To be able to run this process within a container, we first need to convert the code we wrote for fetching ratings in chapter 8 into a script that can be easily run inside the container. The first step toward building this script is using a small scaffold to create a CLI script in Python, which we can then fill in with the required functionality. Using the popular click Python library,[5] such a scaffold could look something like listing 10.10.

---

[5] You can, of course, also use the built-in argparse library, but we personally quite like the brevity of the click library's API for building CLI applications.

Listing 10.10   Skeleton for a Python CLI script, based on the click library

```
#!/usr/bin/env python                       Shebang telling Linux to execute
                                            this script using Python
import logging
import click
                                            Setup logging to provide
logging.basicConfig(level=logging.INFO)     feedback to the user

@click.command()                            Converts the main function
@click.option(                              to a click CLI command
    "--start_date",
    type=click.DateTime(formats=["%Y-%m-%d"]),   Adds an option to the CLI
    required=True,                               command, with corresponding
    help="Start date for ratings.",              types and annotations
)
@click.option(          Adds further options
    ...                 needed for the command
)
@click.option(
    ...                                     The options are passed as keyword
)                                           arguments to the main function and
...                                         can be used from then on.
def main(start_date, ...):
    """CLI script for fetching ratings from the movielens API."""
    ...
                                            Python's way of ensuring that the
if __name__ == "__main__":                  main function/command is called
    main()                                  when this script is executed
```

In this scaffold, we define one function, main, which is executed when our script runs and should therefore implement our rating fetching functionality. We also use the click.command decorator to convert the main function into a click CLI command, which will take care of parsing any arguments from the command line and presenting useful feedback to the user. The click.option decorators are used to tell the click library which arguments our CLI should accept and what types of values to expect. The nice thing about this is that click will also handle parsing and validating arguments for us, so we don't have to handle this type of logic ourselves.

Using the scaffold, we can start filling in the main function with the same logic we started with in chapter 8.[6]

Listing 10.11   Ratings script (docker/images/movielens-fetch/scripts/fetch_ratings.py)

```
...
from pathlib import Path
                              Define the different CLI arguments for click.
@click.command()             Omitted here for brevity; full Implementation
@click.option(...)           is available in the code samples.
...
```

---

[6] Code is adapted from the PythonOperator-based example we started with in chapter 8.

```
def main(start_date, end_date, output_path,
        host, user, password, batch_size):
    """CLI script for fetching ratings from the movielens API."""

    session = requests.Session()              ◄——┐  Sets up the requests session for
    session.auth = (user, password)               │  performing HTTP requests, with
                                                   │  the correct authentication details

    logging.info("Fetching ratings from %s (user: %s)", host, user)   ◄——┐
    ratings = list(                                                       │
        _get_ratings(                ◄——┐  Uses our _get_ratings      Logging is used to
            session=session,             │  function (omitted for     provide feedback
            host=host,                   │  brevity) for fetching ratings      to the user.
            start_date=start_date,       │  using the provided session
            end_date=end_date,           │
            batch_size=batch_size,       │
        )
    )
    logging.info("Retrieved %d ratings!", len(ratings))

    output_path = Path(output_path)          ┐  Makes sure the output
                                             │  directory exists
    output_dir = output_path.parent      ◄——┘
    output_dir.mkdir(parents=True, exist_ok=True)

    logging.info("Writing to %s", output_path)   ┐  Writes the output as JSON
    with output_path.open("w") as file_:      ◄——┘  to the output directory
        json.dump(ratings, file_)
```

In short, this code starts with setting up a requests session for performing HTTP requests and then uses the _get_ratings function[7] to retrieve ratings for the defined time period from the API. The result from this function call is a list of records (as dicts), which is then written to the output path in JSON format. We also use some logging statements in between to provide feedback to the user.

Now that we have our script, we can start building the Docker image. To do this, we need to create a Dockerfile that installs the dependencies for our script (click and requests), copies our script into the image, and makes sure this script is in our PATH.[8] This should give us something like the following Dockerfile.

Listing 10.12 Embedding the ratings script (docker/images/movielens-fetch/Dockerfile)

```
FROM python:3.8-slim                                          ┐  Install the required
RUN pip install click==7.1.1 requests==2.23.0         ◄——┘  dependencies.
COPY scripts/fetch_ratings.py /usr/bin/local/fetch-ratings    ◄——┐  Copy the
RUN chmod +x /usr/bin/local/fetch-ratings                          │  fetch_ratings
ENV PATH="/usr/local/bin:${PATH}"      ◄——┐                         │  script and make
                                                                    │  it executable.
        Ensure the script is on the PATH (so it can be run
        without having to specify the full path to the script).
```

---

[7] The _get_ratings function is omitted here for brevity but is available in the source code accompanying this book.

[8] This is so that we can run the script using the fetch-ratings command instead of having to specify the full path to the script.

Note that this assumes we put our script `fetch_ratings.py` in a scripts directory next to our Dockerfile. Our dependencies are installed by specifying them directly in the Dockerfile, although you may also want to use a `requirements.txt` file instead, which you copy into the image before running pip.

> **Listing 10.13 Using requirements.txt (docker/images/movielens-fetch-reqs/Dockerfile)**

```
COPY requirements.txt /tmp/requirements.txt
RUN pip install -r /tmp/requirements.txt
```

With this Dockerfile, we can finally build our image for fetching ratings:

```
$ docker build -t manning-airflow/movielens-fetch .
```

To test the built image, we can try executing it with `docker run`:

```
$ docker run --rm manning-airflow/movielens-fetch fetch-ratings --help
```

This command should print the help message from our script, which looks something like this:

```
Usage: fetch-ratings [OPTIONS]

  CLI script for fetching movie ratings from the movielens API.

Options:
  --start_date [%Y-%m-%d]  Start date for ratings.  [required]
  --end_date [%Y-%m-%d]    End date for ratings.  [required]
  --output_path FILE       Output file path.  [required]
  --host TEXT              Movielens API URL.
  --user TEXT             Movielens API user.  [required]
  --password TEXT         Movielens API password.  [required]
  --batch_size INTEGER    Batch size for retrieving records.
  --help                 Show this message and exit.
```

This means that we now have a container image for our first task. We can use a similar approach to build different images for each of the other tasks as well. Depending on the amount of shared code, you may also want to create images that are shared between tasks but that can run with different arguments or even with different scripts. How you organize this is up to you.

10.4.3 *Building a DAG with Docker tasks*

Now that we know how to build Docker images for each of our tasks, we can start building the DAG for running the Docker tasks. The process for building such a Docker-based DAG is relatively simple: we only need to replace our existing tasks with `DockerOperators` and make sure that each `DockerOperator` runs its task with the correct arguments. We also need to think about how to exchange data between tasks, as the Docker containers' filesystems will not exist past the duration of the task.

Starting with the fetching of the ratings, the first part of our DAG is simply a `Docker-Operator` that calls the `fetch-ratings` script inside the `manning-airflow/movielens-fetch` container, which we built in the previous section.

Listing 10.14   Running the fetch container (docker/dags/01_docker.py)

```
import datetime as dt

from airflow import DAG
from airflow.providers.docker.operators.docker import DockerOperator

with DAG(
    dag_id="01_docker",
    description="Fetches ratings from the Movielens API using Docker.",
    start_date=dt.datetime(2019, 1, 1),
    end_date=dt.datetime(2019, 1, 3),
    schedule_interval="@daily",
) as dag:
    Fetch
ratings = DockerOperator(
        task_id="fetch_ratings",
        image="manning-airflow/movielens-fetch",          ← Tell the DockerOperator to
        command=[                                            use the movielens-fetch
            "fetch-ratings",        ←                        image.
            "--start_date",            Run the fetch-ratings script
            "{{ds}}",                  in the container with the
            "--end_date",              required arguments.
            "{{next_ds}}",
            "--output_path",
            "/data/ratings/{{ds}}.json",     Provide host and
            "--user",                        authentication details
            os.environ["MOVIELENS_USER"],  ← for our API.
            "--password",
            os.environ["MOVIELENS_PASSWORD"],
            "--host",
            os.environ["MOVIELENS_HOST"],          Mount a volume to store data. Note
        ],                                         that this host path is on the Docker
        volumes=["/tmp/airflow/data:/data"],  ←    host, not the Airflow container.
        network_mode="airflow",     ←
)                               Make sure the container is attached to the
                                airflow Docker network so that it can reach the
                                API (which is running on the same network).
```

When running the container from the operator, make sure to include arguments that tell the operator how to connect to the MovieLens API (host, user, password), which range of dates to fetch ratings for (start_date/end_date), and where to write the retrieved ratings to (output_path).

We also tell Docker to mount a host file system path into the container under /data so that we can persist the fetched ratings outside the container. Additionally, we tell Docker to run the container on a specific (Docker) network called Airflow, which is where our MovieLens API container is running if you're using our docker-compose templates to run Airflow.[9]

For our second movie ranking task, we can follow a similar approach to build a Docker container for the task, which we can then run using the DockerOperator.

Listing 10.15   Adding the ranking task to the DAG (docker/dags/01_docker.py)

```
rank_movies = DockerOperator(
    task_id="rank_movies",
    image="manning-airflow/movielens-ranking",        ◁──┐  Use the
    command=[                                               movielens-ranking
        "rank-movies",              ◁──┐                    image.
        "--input_path",                │  Call the rank-movies
        "/data/ratings/{{ds}}.json",   │  script with the required
        "--output_path",               │  input/output paths.
        "/data/rankings/{{ds}}.csv",
    ],
    volumes=["/tmp/airflow/data:/data"],
)
fetch_ratings >> rank_movies
```

Here you can also see one of the big advantages of using the DockerOperator: even though these tasks do different things, the interface for running the tasks is the same (save for the command arguments that are passed to the container). As such, this task now runs the rank-movies command inside the manning-airflow/movielens-ranking image, making sure to read and write data to the same host path mount as the previous task. This allows the ranking task to read the output from the fetch_ratings task and persist the ranked movies in the same directory structure.

Now that we have our first two tasks[10] in the DAG, we can try running it from within Airflow. To do so, open the Airflow web UI and activate the DAG. After waiting for it to finish running, you should see a couple of successful runs for the past few days (figure 10.8).

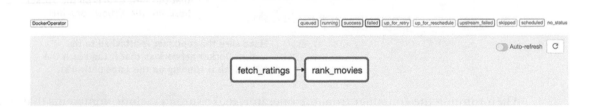

Figure 10.8   The Docker-based DAG in the Airflow UI

---

[9] We won't go any deeper into Docker networking here, as it's a bit of an implementation detail; you wouldn't need to configure networking if you were accessing an API on the internet. If you're interested, check out Docker networking in a good Docker book or the online documentation.

[10] We'll leave the third task of loading recommendations into a database as an exercise.

You can check the result of the run by clicking on the task and then opening the logs by clicking on View logs. For the fetch_ratings task, this should show something like the following log entries, in which you can see that the DockerOperator started our image and logged the output logs from the container.

Listing 10.16   Log output from the fetch_ratings task

```
[2020-04-13 11:32:56,780] {docker.py:194} INFO -
➥ Starting docker container from image manning-airflow/movielens-fetch
[2020-04-13 11:32:58,214] {docker.py:244} INFO -
➥ INFO:root:Fetching ratings from http://movielens:5000 (user: airflow)
 [2020-04-13 11:33:01,977] {docker.py:244} INFO -
➥ INFO:root:Retrieved 3299 ratings!
 [2020-04-13 11:33:01,979] {docker.py:244} INFO -
➥ INFO:root:Writing to /data/ratings/2020-04-12.json
```

You can also check the output files from the DAG run by looking at the output files, which (in our example) were written to the /tmp/airflow/data directory on the Docker host.

Listing 10.17   Movie ranking output from the DAG

```
$ head /tmp/airflow/data/rankings/*.csv | head
==> /tmp/airflow/data/rankings/2020-04-10.csv <==
movieId,avg_rating,num_ratings
912,4.833333333333333,6
38159,4.833333333333333,3
48516,4.833333333333333,3
4979,4.75,4
7153,4.75,4
```

10.4.4 *Docker-based workflow*

As we have seen, the workflow for building DAGs using Docker containers is a bit different than the approach we have used for other DAGs. The biggest difference in the Docker-based approach is that you first need to create Docker containers for your different tasks. As such, the overall workflow typically consists of several steps (illustrated in figure 10.9).

1 A developer creates Dockerfile(s) for the required image(s), which install the required software and dependencies. The developer (or a CI/CD process) then tells Docker to build the image(s) using the Dockerfile(s).
2 The Docker daemon builds the corresponding image(s) on the development machine (or a machine in the CI/CD environment).
3 The Docker daemon pushes the built image(s) to a container registry to expose the image for further use downstream.
4 A developer creates the DAG using DockerOperators that reference the built image(s).
5 After the DAG is activated, Airflow starts running the DAG and scheduling DockerOperator tasks for the respective runs.

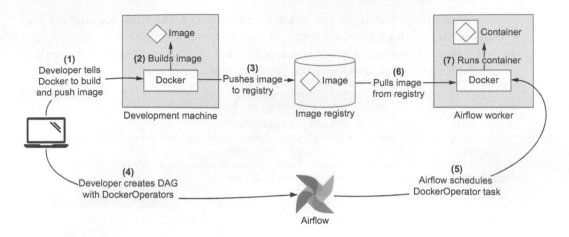

Figure 10.9   Common workflow for working with Docker images in Airflow

6 Airflow workers pick up the `DockerOperator` task(s) and pull the required
image(s) from the container registry.

7 For each task, the Airflow worker runs a container with the corresponding
image and arguments using the Docker daemon installed on the worker.

One benefit of this approach is that it effectively decouples the development of the software for running the task, which is now stored inside the Docker image, from the development of the overall DAG. This allows the development of the images to occur within
their own life cycle and allows you to test the images separate from the DAG itself.

10.5   *Running tasks in Kubernetes*

Although Docker provides a convenient approach for running containerized tasks on
a single machine, it does not help you with orchestrating and distributing the work
over multiple machines, thus limiting the scalability of the approach. This limitation
of Docker has led to the development of container orchestration systems such as
Kubernetes, which help scale containerized applications across computer clusters. In
this section, we'll show how you can run your containerized tasks on Kubernetes
instead of Docker and illustrate some of the benefits and drawbacks of using Kubernetes on top of Docker.

10.5.1   *Introducing Kubernetes*

As Kubernetes is an entire subject in itself, we won't give a full account of what it is but
aim to give you a high-level understanding of what it can do for you.[11]

---

[11] For a full overview of Kubernetes, we recommend you read a comprehensive book on the subject, such as
Kubernetes in Action by Marko Lukša (Manning, 2018).

Kubernetes is an open source container orchestration platform that focuses on the deployment, scaling, and management of containerized applications. Compared to the more vanilla Docker, Kubernetes helps you scale your containers by managing their deployment across multiple worker nodes while also taking things like required resources (CPU and/or memory), storage, and special hardware requirements (e.g., GPU access) into account when scheduling containers onto nodes.

Kubernetes is essentially organized into two main components: the Kubernetes master (or control plane) and the nodes (figure 10.10). The Kubernetes master is responsible for running many of the different components, including the API server, the scheduler, and other services responsible for managing deployments, storage, and so on. The Kubernetes API server is used by clients such as kubectl (Kubernetes's main CLI interface) or the Kubernetes Python SDK to query Kubernetes and run commands to initiate deployments. This makes the Kubernetes master the main contact point for managing your containerized applications on a Kubernetes cluster.

The Kubernetes worker nodes are responsible for running the container applications assigned to them by the scheduler. In Kubernetes, these applications are referred to as *pods*, which can contain one or multiple containers that need to be run together

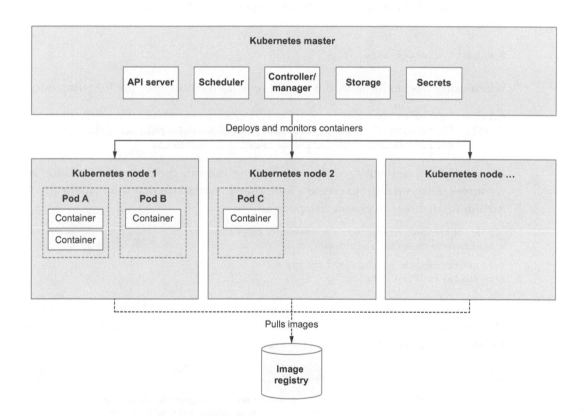

Figure 10.10 High-level overview of Kubernetes

on a single machine. For now, all you need to know is that a pod is the smallest unit of work inside Kubernetes. In the context of Airflow, each task will run as a container inside a single pod.

Kubernetes also provides built-in functionality for managing secrets and storage. In essence, this means that we can, for example, request a storage volume from the Kubernetes master and mount this as persistent storage inside the container. As such, these storage volumes function similarly to the Docker volume mounts we saw in the previous section, but are managed by Kubernetes. This means that we don't have to worry about where the storage comes from (unless you are responsible for operating the cluster, of course), but can simply request and use the volume provided.

10.5.2 *Setting up Kubernetes*

Before we dive into adjusting our DAG to run in Kubernetes, let's start with setting up the required resources we need in Kubernetes. First, make sure you have access to a Kubernetes cluster and have the `kubectl` client installed locally. The easiest way to get access is to install one locally (using, for example, Docker for Mac/Windows or Minikube), or to set one up in one of the cloud providers.

Once you have Kubernetes set up properly, you can verify if it is functioning by running

```
$ kubectl cluster-info
```

When using Docker for Mac, this should return something like the following output:

```
Kubernetes master is running at https://kubernetes.docker.internal:6443
KubeDNS is running at https://kubernetes.docker.internal:6443/api/v1/
    namespaces/kube-system/services/kube-dns:dns/proxy
```

If your Kubernetes cluster is up and running, we can continue with creating some resources. First, we need to create a Kubernetes namespace that will contain all of our Airflow-related resources and task pods.

> **Listing 10.18   Creating a Kubernetes namespace**

```
$ kubectl create namespace airflow
namespace/airflow created
```

Next, we're going to create some storage resources for our Airflow DAG, which will allow us to store the results of our tasks. These resources are defined as follows using Kubernetes's YAML syntax for specifying resources.

> **Listing 10.19   YAML specification for storage (kubernetes/resources/data-volume.yml)**

```
apiVersion: v1
kind: PersistentVolume
metadata:
```
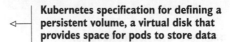
Kubernetes specification for defining a persistent volume, a virtual disk that provides space for pods to store data

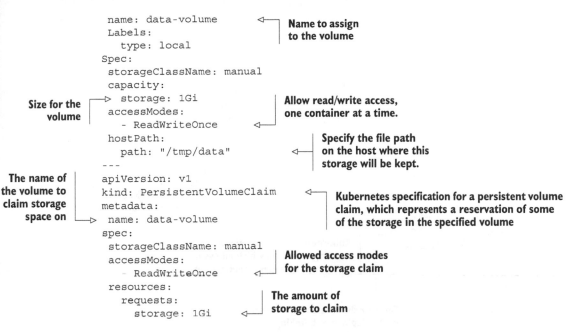

```
name: data-volume
Labels:
  type: local
Spec:
storageClassName: manual
capacity:
  storage: 1Gi
accessModes:
  - ReadWriteOnce
hostPath:
  path: "/tmp/data"
---
apiVersion: v1
kind: PersistentVolumeClaim
metadata:
  name: data-volume
spec:
storageClassName: manual
accessModes:
  - ReadWriteOnce
resources:
  requests:
    storage: 1Gi
```

Name to assign to the volume

Size for the volume

Allow read/write access, one container at a time.

Specify the file path on the host where this storage will be kept.

The name of the volume to claim storage space on

Kubernetes specification for a persistent volume claim, which represents a reservation of some of the storage in the specified volume

Allowed access modes for the storage claim

The amount of storage to claim

In essence, this specification defines two resources used for storage. The first is a Kubernetes volume, and the second is a storage claim, which essentially tells Kubernetes that we need some storage to be used for our containers. This claim can be used by any of the Kubernetes pods run by Airflow to store data (as we'll see in the next section).

Using this YAML, we can create the required storage resources.

Listing 10.20   Deploying the storage resources using kubectl

```
$ kubectl --namespace airflow apply -f resources/data-volume.yml
persistentvolumeclaim/data-volume created
persistentvolume/data-volume created
```

We also need to create a deployment of our MovieLens API, which we will be querying using our DAG. The following YAML allows us to create deployment and service resources for the MovieLens API, which tell Kubernetes how to start running our API service.

Listing 10.21   YAML specification for the API (kubernetes/resources/api.yml)

```
apiVersion: apps/v1
kind: Deployment
metadata:
 name: movielens-deployment
 labels:
   app: movielens
spec:
 replicas: 1
```

Kubernetes specification for creating a deployment of a container

Name of the deployment

Labels for the deployment (which are matched in the service)

```
selector:
  matchLabels:
    app: movielens
template:
  metadata:
    Labels:
      app: movielens
  spec:
    containers:
    - name: movielens
      image: manning-airflow/movielens-api
      ports:
      - containerPort: 5000
      env:
      - name: API_USER
        value: airflow
      - name: API_PASSWORD
        value: airflow
---
apiVersion: v1
kind: Service
metadata:
  name: movielens
spec:
  selector:
    app: movielens
  ports:
    - protocol: TCP
      port: 80
      targetPort: 5000
```

Specify which containers to include in the deployment, together with their respective ports, environment variables, etc.

Tell Kubernetes to use the latest version of the movielens-api image. (Latest is the default image tag used by Docker/Kubernetes if no specific version tag is specified.)

Kubernetes specification for creating a service, which allows us to connect to a given deployment

Selector that matches the labels of the deployment, linking this service to the deployment

Mapping the service port (80) to the port exposed by the container in the deployment (5000)

We can create the service in the same manner we used for the storage resources.

Listing 10.22   Deploying the MovieLens API

```
$ kubectl --namespace airflow apply -f resources/api.yml
deployment.apps/movielens-deployment created
service/movielens created
```

After waiting for a couple of seconds, you should see the pods for the API coming online:

```
$ kubectl --namespace airflow get pods
NAME                        READY   STATUS    RESTARTS   AGE
movielens-deployment-...    1/1     Running   0          11s
```

You can check if the API service is working by running

```
$ kubectl --namespace airflow port-forward svc/movielens 8000:80
```

and then opening http://localhost:8000 in a browser. If everything is working correctly, you should now see the "hello world" from the API displayed in your browser.

10.5.3 *Using the KubernetesPodOperator*

After creating the required Kubernetes resources, we can now start adjusting our Docker-based recommender DAG to use the Kubernetes cluster instead of Docker.

To start running our tasks on Kubernetes, we need to replace our `DockerOperators` with instances of the `KubernetesPodOperator`, which are available in the `apache-airflow-providers-cncf-kubernetes` providers package.[12] As the name implies, the `KubernetesPodOperator` runs tasks within pods on a Kubernetes cluster. The basic API of the operator is as follows.

Listing 10.23   Using the KubernetesPodOperator (kubernetes/dags/02_kubernetes.py)

```
fetch_ratings = KubernetesPodOperator(
        task_id="fetch_ratings",
        image="manning-airflow/movielens-fetch",          ◀── Which image to use
        cmds=["fetch-ratings"],          ◀── The executable to run inside the container
        arguments=[          ◀── Arguments to pass to the executable (specified separately here, in contrast to the DockerOperator)
            "--start_date",
            "{{ds}}",
            "--end_date",
            "{{next_ds}}",
            "--output_path",
            "/data/ratings/{{ds}}.json",
            "--user",
            os.environ["MOVIELENS_USER"],
            "--password",
            os.environ["MOVIELENS_PASSWORD"],
            "--host",
            os.environ["MOVIELENS_HOST"],
        ],
        namespace="airflow",          ◀── Kubernetes namespace to run the pod in
        name="fetch-ratings",          ◀── Name to use for the pod
        cluster_context="docker-desktop",          ◀── Name of the cluster to use (in case you have multiple Kubernetes clusters registered)
        in_cluster=False,          ◀── Specifies that we're not running Airflow itself inside Kubernetes
        volumes=[volume],
        volume_mounts=[volume_mount],          ◀── Volumes and volume mounts to use in the pod
        image_pull_policy="Never",          ◀── Specify an image pull policy that requires Airflow to use our locally built images rather than trying to pull images from Docker Hub.
        is_delete_operator_pod=True,          ◀── Automatically deletes pods when they finish running
)
```

Similar to the `DockerOperator`, the first few arguments tell the `KubernetesPodOperator` how to run our task as a container: the `image` argument tells Kubernetes which Docker image to use, while the `cmds` and `arguments` parameters define which executable to run (`fetch-ratings`) and which arguments to pass to the executable. The remaining arguments tell Kubernetes which cluster to use (`cluster_context`), in which namespace to run the pod (`namespace`), and what name to use for the container (`name`).

---

[12] For Airflow 1.10.x, you can install the `KubernetesPodOperator` using the `apache-airflow-backport-providers-cncf-kubernetes backport` package.

We also supply two extra arguments, `volumes` and `volume_mounts`, which specify how the volumes we created in the previous section should be mounted into the tasks in the Kubernetes pod. These configuration values are created using two config classes from the Kubernetes Python SDK: `V1Volume` and `V1VolumeMount`.

Listing 10.24 Volumes and volume mounts (kubernetes/dags/02_kubernetes.py)

```
from kubernetes.client import models as k8s

...

volume_claim = k8s.V1PersistentVolumeClaimVolumeSource(      <-- References to the
    claim_name="data-volume"                                     previously created
)                                                                storage volume
volume = k8s.V1Volume(                                  <------   and claim
    name="data-volume",
    persistent_volume_claim=volume_claim
)
volume_mount = k8s.V1VolumeMount(
    name="data-volume",                          Where to mount
    mount_path="/data",          <-------        the volume
    sub_path=None,
    read_only=False,         <---|  Mount the volume
)                                   as writable.
```

Here, we first create a `V1Volume` configuration object, which references the persistent volume claim `data-volume`, which we created as a Kubernetes resource in the previous section. Next, we create a `V1VolumeMount` configuration object, which refers to the volume configuration we just created (`data-volume`) and specifies where this volume should be mounted in the pod's container. These configuration objects can then be passed to the `KubernetesPodOperators` using the `volumes` and `volume_mounts` arguments.

Now the only thing remaining is to create a second task for the movie ranking task.

Listing 10.25 Adding the movie ranking task (kubernetes/dags/02_kubernetes.py)

```
rank_movies = KubernetesPodOperator(
    task_id="rank_movies",
    image="manning-airflow/movielens-rank",
    cmds=["rank-movies"],
    arguments=[
        "--input_path",
        "/data/ratings/{{ds}}.json",
        "--output_path",
        "/data/rankings/{{ds}}.csv",
    ],
    namespace="airflow",
    name="fetch-ratings",
    cluster_context="docker-desktop",
    in_cluster=False,
    volumes=[volume],
```

```
        volume_mounts=[volume_mount],
        image_pull_policy="Never",
        is_delete_operator_pod=True,
    )
```

Then we tie all this together into the final DAG.

```python
import datetime as dt
import os

from kubernetes.client import models as k8s

from airflow import DAG
from airflow.providers.cncf.kubernetes.operators.kubernetes_pod import (
    KubernetesPodOperator,
)

with DAG(
    dag_id="02_kubernetes",
    description="Fetches ratings from the Movielens API using kubernetes.",
    start_date=dt.datetime(2019, 1, 1),
    end_date=dt.datetime(2019, 1, 3),
    schedule_interval="@daily",
) as dag:
    volume_claim = k8s.V1PersistentVolumeClaimVolumeSource(...)
    volume = k8s.V1Volume(...)
    volume_mount = k8s.V1VolumeMount(...)

    fetch_ratings = KubernetesPodOperator(...)
    rank_movies = KubernetesPodOperator(...)

    fetch_ratings >> rank_movies
```

After finishing the DAG, we can start running it by enabling it from the Airflow web
UI. After waiting a few moments, we should see Airflow starting to schedule and run
our tasks (figure 10.11). For more detail, you can open the log of an individual task
instance by clicking on the task and then clicking View logs. This shows you the output
of the task, which should look something like this.

Figure 10.11   Several successful runs of the recommender DAG based on the `KubernetesPodOperator`

```
Listing 10.27   Logs from the Kubernetes-based fetch_ratings task
```

```
...
[2020-04-13 20:28:45,067] {logging_mixin.py:95} INFO -
➥  [[34m2020-04-13 20:28:45,067[0m] {[34mpod_launcher.py:[0m122}
➥  INFO[0m - Event: [1mfetch-ratings-0a31c089[0m had an event
➥  of type [1mPending[0m[0m
[2020-04-13 20:28:46,072] {logging_mixin.py:95} INFO -
➥  [[34m2020-04-13 20:28:46,072[0m] {[34mpod_launcher.py:[0m122}
➥  INFO[0m - Event: [1mfetch-ratings-0a31c089[0m had an event
➥  of type [1mRunning[0m[0m
[2020-04-13 20:28:48,926] {logging_mixin.py:95} INFO -
➥   [[34m2020-04-13 20:28:48,926[0m] {[34mpod_launcher.py:[0m105}
➥  INFO[0m - b'Fetching ratings from
➥  http://movielens.airflow.svc.cluster.local:80 (user: airflow)\n'[0m
[2020-04-13 20:28:48,926] {logging_mixin.py:95} INFO -
➥  [[34m2020-04-13 20:28:48,926[0m] {[34mpod_launcher.py:[0m105}
➥  INFO[0m - b'Retrieved 3372 ratings!\n'[0m
[2020-04-13 20:28:48,927] {logging_mixin.py:95} INFO -
➥  [[34m2020-04-13 20:28:48,927[0m] {[34mpod_launcher.py:[0m105}
➥  INFO[0m - b'Writing to /data/ratings/2020-04-10.json\n'[0m
[2020-04-13 20:28:49,958] {logging_mixin.py:95} INFO -
➥  [[34m2020-04-13 20:28:49,958[0m] {[34mpod_launcher.py:[0m122}
➥  INFO[0m - Event: [1mfetch-ratings-0a31c089[0m had an event
➥  of type [1mSucceeded[0m[0m
...
```

10.5.4 *Diagnosing Kubernetes-related issues*

If you're unlucky, you may see that your tasks get stuck in the running state instead of finishing correctly. This usually happens because Kubernetes is unable to schedule the tasks pod, which means that the pod will be stuck in the pending state rather than running on the cluster. To check if this is indeed the case, you can look at the logs of the corresponding task(s), which can tell you more about the state of the pods on the cluster.

```
Listing 10.28   Log output showing a task stuck in a pending state
```

```
[2020-04-13 20:27:01,301] {logging_mixin.py:95} INFO -
➥  [[34m2020-04-13 20:27:01,301[0m] {[34mpod_launcher.py:[0m122}
➥  INFO[0m - Event: [1mfetch-ratings-0a31c089[0m had an event of type
➥  [1mPending[0m[0m
[2020-04-13 20:27:02,308] {logging_mixin.py:95} INFO -
➥  [[34m2020-04-13 20:27:02,308[0m] {[34mpod_launcher.py:[0m122}
➥  INFO[0m - Event: [1mfetch-ratings-0a31c089[0m had an event
➥  of type [1mPending[0m[0m
[2020-04-13 20:27:03,315] {logging_mixin.py:95} INFO -
➥  [[34m2020-04-13 20:27:03,315[0m] {[34mpod_launcher.py:[0m122}
➥  INFO[0m - Event: [1mfetch-ratings-0a31c089[0m had an event
➥  of type [1mPending[0m[0m
...
```

Here, you can see that the pods are indeed still pending on the cluster.

To diagnose the underlying issue, you can look up the task pods using

```
$ kubectl --namespace airflow get pods
```

Once you have identified the name of the corresponding pod, you can ask Kubernetes for more details on the state of the pod using the `describe` subcommand in `kubectl`.

Listing 10.29 Describing a specific pod to identify any issues.

```
$ kubectl --namespace describe pod [NAME-OF-POD]
...
Events:
  Type      Reason          Age   From              Message
  ----      ------          ----  ----              -------
  Warning   FailedScheduling 82s  default-scheduler persistentvolumeclaim
➡ "data-volume" not found
```

This command produces a great amount of detail about the corresponding pod, including recent events (in the `Events` section shown). Here, we can see that our pod was not being scheduled because the required persistent volume claim was not created properly.

To fix this, we can try fixing the resources by properly applying our resource specification (which we probably forgot to do), and then checking for new events.

Listing 10.30 Fixing the issue by creating the missing resources

```
$ kubectl --namespace airflow apply -f resources/data-volume.yml
persistentvolumeclaim/data-volume created
persistentvolume/data-volume created

$ kubectl --namespace describe pod [NAME-OF-POD]
...
Events:
  Type      Reason          Age  From              Message
  ----      ------          ---- ----              ------
  Warning  FailedScheduling 33s  default-scheduler persistentvolumeclaim
➡ "data-volume" not found
  Warning  FailedScheduling 6s   default-scheduler pod has unbound
➡ immediate PersistentVolumeClaims
  Normal   Scheduled       3s   default-scheduler Successfully assigned
➡ airflow/fetch-ratings-0a31c089 to docker-desktop
  Normal   Pulled          2s   kubelet, ...      Container image
➡ "manning-airflow/movielens-fetch" already present on machine
  Normal   Created         2s   kubelet, ...      Created container base
  Normal   Started         2s   kubelet, ...      Started container base
```

This shows that Kubernetes was indeed able to schedule our pod after creating the required volume claim, thus fixing our previous issue.

> **NOTE**   In general, we recommend that you start diagnosing any issues by first checking the Airflow logs for any useful feedback. If you see anything that

looks like scheduling issues, kubectl is your best hope for identifying any issues with your Kubernetes cluster or configuration.

Although far from comprehensive, this example hopefully gives you some idea of the approaches you can use for debugging Kubernetes-related issues when using the KubernetesPodOperator.

10.5.5 Differences with Docker-based workflows

The Kubernetes-based workflow (figure 10.12) is relatively similar to that of the Docker-based approach (figure 10.9). However, in addition to having to set up and maintain a Kubernetes cluster (which is not necessarily trivial), there are some other differences to keep in mind.

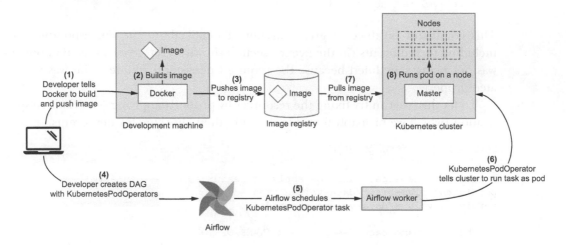

Figure 10.12   Workflow for building DAGs using the KubernetesPodOperator

One is that the task containers are no longer executed on the Airflow worker node but on a separate (Kubernetes) node within the Kubernetes cluster. This means that any resources used on the worker are fairly minimal, and you can use functionality in Kubernetes to make sure your task is deployed to a node with the correct resources (e.g., CPU, memory, GPU).

Second, any storage will no longer be accessed from the Airflow worker but needs to be made available to the Kubernetes pod. Typically this means using storage provided via Kubernetes (as we have shown with Kubernetes volumes and storage claims); however, you can also use different types of network/cloud storage, as long as the pod has the appropriate access to the storage.

Overall, Kubernetes provides considerable advantages over Docker, especially w.r.t. scalability, flexibility (e.g., providing different resources/nodes for different workloads), and managing other resources such as storage, secrets, and so on. Additionally,

Airflow itself can be run on top of Kubernetes, meaning that you can have your entire Airflow setup running on a single, scalable, container-based infrastructure.

Summary

- Airflow deployments can be difficult to manage if they involve many different operators, as this requires knowledge of the different APIs and complicates debugging and dependency management.
- One way of tackling this issue is to use container technologies such as Docker to encapsulate your tasks inside container images and run these images from within Airflow.
- This containerized approach has several advantages, including easier dependency management, a more uniform interface for running tasks, and improved testability of tasks.
- Using the DockerOperator, you can run tasks in container images directly using Docker, similar to the docker run CLI command.
- You can use the KubernetesPodOperator to run containerized tasks in pods on a Kubernetes cluster.
- Kubernetes allows you to scale your containerized tasks across a compute cluster, which provides (among other things) greater scalability and more flexibility in terms of computing resources.

Part 3

Airflow in practice

Now that you've learned how to build complex pipelines, let's start using them in production! To help you get started, part 3 discusses several topics in using Airflow in production.

First, chapter 11 reviews some of the practices we've seen for implementing pipelines and highlights several best practices that should help you build efficient and maintainable pipelines.

Chapter 12 and 13 dive into details to consider for running Airflow in a production setting. Chapter 12 describes how to deploy Airflow, touching on topics such as architectures for scaling Airflow, monitoring, logging, and alerting. Chapter 13 focuses specifically on securing Airflow to avoid unwanted access and minimizing the impact of security breaches.

Finally, chapter 14 ties all previous chapters together in a summary use case.

After completing part 3, you should be able to write efficient and maintainable pipelines in Airflow. You should also have a good idea of how to deploy Airflow and which implementation details to consider for a robust and secure deployment.

Best practices

This chapter covers

- Writing clean, understandable DAGs using style conventions

- Using consistent approaches for managing credentials and configuration options

- Generating repeated DAGs and tasks using factory functions

- Designing reproducible tasks by enforcing idempotency and determinism constraints

- Handling data efficiently by limiting the amount of data processed in your DAG

- Using efficient approaches for handling/storing (intermediate) data sets

- Managing managing concurrency using resource pools

In previous chapters, we have described most of the basic elements that go into building and designing data processes using Airflow DAGs. In this chapter, we dive a bit deeper into some best practices that can help you write well-architected DAGs that are both easy to understand and efficient in terms of how they handle your data and resources.

11.1 *Writing clean DAGs*

Writing DAGs can easily become a messy business. For example, DAG code can quickly become overly complicated or difficult to read—especially if DAGs are written by team members with very different styles of programming. In this section, we touch on some tips to help you structure and style your DAG code, hopefully providing some (often needed) clarity for your intricate data processes.

11.1.1 *Use style conventions*

As in all programming exercises, one of the first steps to writing clean and consistent DAGs is to adopt a common, clean programming style and apply this style consistently across all your DAGs. Although a thorough exploration of clean coding practices is well outside the scope of this book, we can provide several tips as starting points.

FOLLOWING STYLE GUIDES

The easiest way to make your code cleaner and easier to understand is to use a commonly used style when writing your code. There are multiple style guides available in the community, including the widely known PEP8 style guide (https://www.python.org/dev/peps/pep-0008/) and guides from companies such as Google (https://google.github.io/styleguide/pyguide.html). These generally include recommendations for indentation, maximum line lengths, naming styles for variables/classes/functions, and so on. By following these guides, other programmers will be better able to read your code.

Listing 11.1   Examples of non-PEP8-compliant code

```
spam( ham[ 1 ], { eggs: 2 } )

i=i+1
submitted +=1

my_list = [
    1, 2, 3,
    4, 5, 6,
    ]
```

Listing 11.2   Making the examples in listing 11.1 PEP-8 compliant

```
spam(ham[1], {eggs: 2})        ⟵  Less unnecessary whitespace

i = i + 1                      Consistent whitespace
submitted += 1                 around operators

my_list = [                    ⟵  More readable indenting
    1, 2, 3,                       around list brackets
    4, 5, 6,
]
```

USING STATIC CHECKERS TO CHECK CODE QUALITY

The Python community has also produced a plethora of software tools that can be used to check whether your code follows proper coding conventions and/or styles. Two popular tools are Pylint and Flake8, which both function as static code checkers, meaning that you can run them over your code to get a report of how well (or not) your code adheres to their envisioned standards.

For example, to run Flake8 over your code, you can install it using pip and run it by pointing it at your codebase.

Listing 11.3 Installing and running Flake8

```
python -m pip install flake8
python -m flake8 dags/*.py
```

This command will run Flake8 on all of the Python files in the DAGs folder, giving you a report on the perceived code quality of these DAG files. The report will typically look something like this.

Listing 11.4 Example output from Flake8

```
$ python -m flake8 chapter08/dags/
chapter08/dags/04_sensor.py:2:1: F401
➥ 'airflow.operators.python.PythonOperator' imported but unused
chapter08/dags/03_operator.py:2:1: F401
➥ 'airflow.operators.python.PythonOperator' imported but unused
```

Both Flake8 and Pylint are used widely within the community, although Pylint is generally considered to have a more extensive set of checks in its default configuration.[1] Of course, both tools can be configured to enable/disable certain checks, depending on your preferences, and can be combined to provide comprehensive feedback. For more details, we refer you to the respective websites of both tools.

USING CODE FORMATTERS TO ENFORCE COMMON FORMATTING

Although static checkers give you feedback on the quality of your code, tools such as Pylint or Flake8 do not impose overly strict requirements on how you format your code (e.g., when to start a new line, how to indent your function headers, etc.). As such, Python code written by different people can still follow very different formatting styles, depending on the preferences of the author.

One approach to reducing the heterogeneity of code formatting within teams is to use a code formatter to surrender control (and worry) to the formatting tool, which will ensure that your code is reformatted according to its guidelines. As such, applying a formatter consistently across your project will ensure all code follows one consistent formatting style: the style implemented by the formatter.

---

[1] This can be considered to be a strength or weakness of `pylint`, depending on your preferences, as some people consider it overly pedantic.

Two commonly used code Python formatters are YAPF (https://github.com/google/yapf) and Black (https://github.com/psf/black). Both tools adopt a similar style of taking your Python code and reformatting it to their styles, with slight differences in the styles enforced by both. As such, the choice between Black and YAPF may depend on personal preference, although Black has gained much popularity within the Python community over the past few years.

To show a small example, consider the following (contrived) example of an ugly function.

Listing 11.5   Code example before Black formatting

```
def my_function(
    arg1, arg2,
    arg3):
    """Function to demonstrate black."""
    str_a = 'abc'
    str_b = "def"
    return str_a + \
        str_b
```

Applying Black to this function will give you the following (cleaner) result.

Listing 11.6   The same code example after Black formatting

```
def my_function(arg1, arg2, arg3):        ◄──  More consistent
    """Function to demonstrate black."""       indenting for arguments
    str_a = "abc"
    str_b = "def"                          Consistent use of double quotes
    return str_a + str_b   ◄──  Unnecessary line
                                break removed
```

To run Black yourself, install it using pip and apply it to your Python files using the following.

Listing 11.7   Installing and running black

```
python -m pip install black
python -m black dags/
```

This should give you something like the following output, indicating whether Black reformatted any Python files for you.

Listing 11.8   Example output from black

```
reformatted dags/example_dag.py
All done! 💥 🍰 💥
1 file reformatted.
```

Note that you can also perform a dry run of Black using the --check flag, which will cause Black to indicate only whether it would reformat any files rather than doing any actual reformatting.

Many editors (such as Visual Studio Code, Pycharm) support integration with these tools, allowing you to reformat your code from within your editor. For details on how to configure this type of integration, see the documentation of the respective editor.

AIRFLOW-SPECIFIC STYLE CONVENTIONS

It's also a good idea to agree on style conventions for your Airflow code, particularly in cases where Airflow provides multiple ways to achieve the same results. For example, Airflow provides two different styles for defining DAGs.

Listing 11.9 Two styles for defining DAGs

```
with DAG(...) as dag:               ◁──┐ Using a context
    task1 = PythonOperator(...)         │ manager
    task2 = PythonOperator(...)


dag = DAG(...)                      ◁──┐ Without a context
task1 = PythonOperator(..., dag=dag)    │ manager
task2 = PythonOperator(..., dag=dag)
```

In principle, both these DAG definitions do the same thing, meaning that there is no real reason to choose one over the other, outside of style preferences. However, within your team it may be a good idea to choose one of the two styles and follow them throughout your codebase, keeping things more consistent and understandable.

This consistency is even more important when defining dependencies between tasks, as Airflow provides several different ways for defining the same task dependency.

Listing 11.10 Different styles for defining task dependencies

```
task1 >> task2
task1 << task2
[task1] >> task2
task1.set_downstream(task2)
task2.set_upstream(task1)
```

Although these different definitions have their own merits, combining different styles of dependency definitions within a single DAG can be confusing.

Listing 11.11 Mixing different task dependency notations

```
task1 >> task2
task2 << task3
task5.set_upstream(task3)
task3.set_downstream(task4)
```

As such, your code will generally be more readable if you stick to a single style for defining dependencies across tasks.

Listing 11.12 Using a consistent style for defining task dependencies

```
task1 >> task2 >> task3 >> [task4, task5]
```

As before, we don't necessarily have a clear preference for any given style; just make sure that you pick one that you (and your team) like and apply it consistently.

11.1.2 Manage credentials centrally

In DAGs that interact with many different systems, you may find yourself juggling with many different types of credentials—databases, compute clusters, cloud storage, and so on. As we've seen in previous chapters, Airflow allows you to maintain these credentials in its connection store, which ensures your credentials are maintained securely[2] in a central location.

Although the connection store is the easiest place to store credentials for built-in operators, it can be tempting to store secrets for your custom `PythonOperator` functions (and other functions) in less secure places for ease of accessibility. For example, we have seen quite a few DAG implementations with security keys hardcoded into the DAG itself or in external configuration files.

Fortunately, it is relatively easy to use the Airflow connections store to maintain credentials for your custom code too, by retrieving the connection details from the store in your custom code and using the obtained credentials to do your work.

Listing 11.13 Fetching credentials from the Airflow metastore

```
from airflow.hooks.base_hook import BaseHook

def _fetch_data(conn_id, **context)
    credentials = BaseHook.get_connection(conn_id)      ◁─── Fetching credentials
    ...                                                       using the given ID

fetch_data = PythonOperator(
    task_id="fetch_data",
    op_kwargs={"conn_id": "my_conn_id"},
    dag=dag
)
```

An advantage of this approach is that it uses the same method of storing credentials as all other Airflow operators, meaning that credentials are managed in one single place. As a consequence, you only have to worry about securing and maintaining credentials in this central database.

Of course, depending on your deployment you may want to maintain your secrets in other external systems (e.g., Kubernetes secrets, cloud secret stores) before passing

---

[2] Assuming Airflow has been configured securely. See chapters 12 and 13 for more information on configuring Airflow deployments and security in Airflow.

them into Airflow. In this case, it is still a good idea to make sure these credentials are passed into Airflow (using environment variables, for example) and that your code accesses them using the Airflow connection store.

11.1.3 *Specify configuration details consistently*

You may have other parameters you need to pass in as configuration to your DAG, such as file paths, table names, and so on. Because they are written in Python, Airflow DAGs provide you with many different options for configuration options, including global variables (within the DAG), configuration files (e.g., YAML, INI, JSON), environment variables, Python-based configuration modules, and so on. Airflow also allows you to store configurations in the metastore using Variables (https://airflow.apache .org/docs/stable/concepts.html#variables) .

For example, to load some configuration options from a YAML file[3] you might use something like the following.

Listing 11.14   Loading configuration options from a YAML file

```
import yaml

with open("config.yaml") as config_file:
    config = yaml.load(config_file)       ◁── Read config file
...                                           using PyYAML.
fetch_data = PythonOperator(
    task_id="fetch_data",
    op_kwargs={
        "input_path": config["input_path"],
        "output_path": config["output_path"],
    },
    ...
)
```

Listing 11.15   Example YAML configuration file

```
input_path: /data
output_path: /output
```

Similarly, you could also load the config using Airflow Variables, which is essentially an Airflow feature for storing (global) variables in the metastore.[4]

---

[3] Note that you should be careful to not store any sensitive secrets in such configuration files, as these are typically stored in plain text. If you do store sensitive secrets in configuration files, make sure that only the correct people have permissions to access the file. Otherwise, consider storing secrets in more secure locations such as the Airflow metastore.

[4] Note that fetching Variables like this in the global scope of your DAG is generally bad for the performance of your DAG. Read the next subsection to find out why.

Listing 11.16 Storing configuration options in Airflow Variables

```
from airflow.models import Variable

input_path = Variable.get("dag1_input_path")         Fetching global variables
output_path = Variable.get("dag1_output_path")       using Airflow's Variable
                                                     mechanism
fetch_data = PythonOperator(
    task_id="fetch_data",
    op_kwargs={
        "input_path": input_path,
        "output_path": output_path,
    },
    ...
)
```

Note that fetching Variables in the global scope like this can be a bad idea, as this means Airflow will refetch them from the database every time the scheduler reads your DAG definition.

In general, we don't have any real preference for how you store your config, as long as you are consistent about it. For example, if you store your configuration for one DAG as a YAML file, it makes sense to follow the same convention for other DAGs as well.

For configuration that is shared across DAGs, it is highly recommended to specify the configuration values in a single location (e.g., a shared YAML file), following the DRY (don't repeat yourself) principle. This way, you will be less likely to run into issues where you change a configuration parameter in one place and forget to change it in another.

Finally, it is good to realize that configuration options can be loaded in different contexts depending on where they are referenced within your DAG. For example, if you load a config file in the main part of your DAG, as follows.

Listing 11.17 Loading configuration options in the DAG definition (inefficient)

```
import yaml

with open("config.yaml") as config_file:
    config = yaml.load(config_file)        In the global scope, this config
                                           will be loaded on the scheduler.
fetch_data = PythonOperator(...)
```

The `config.yaml` file is loaded from the local file system of the machine(s) running the Airflow webserver and/or scheduler. This means that both these machines should have access to the config file path. In contrast, you can also load the config file as part of a (Python) task.

Listing 11.18 Loading configuration options within a task (more efficient)

```
import yaml

def _fetch_data(config_path, **context):
    with open(config_path) as config_file:
        config = yaml.load(config_file)          ◁──  In task scope, this config
        ...                                            will be loaded on the
                                                       worker.
fetch_data = PythonOperator(
    op_kwargs={"config_path": "config.yaml"},
    ...
)
```

In this case, the config file won't be loaded until your function is executed by an Airflow worker, meaning that the config is loaded in the context of the Airflow worker. Depending on how you set up your Airflow deployment, this may be an entirely different environment (with access to different file systems, etc.), leading to erroneous results or failures. Similar situations may occur with other configuration approaches as well.

You can avoid these types of situations by choosing one configuration approach that works well and sticking with it across DAGs. Also, be mindful of where different parts of your DAG are executed when loading configuration options and preferably use approaches that are accessible to all Airflow components (e.g., nonlocal file systems, etc.).

11.1.4 Avoid doing any computation in your DAG definition

Airflow DAGs are written in Python, which gives you a great deal of flexibility when writing them. However, a drawback of this approach is that Airflow needs to execute your Python DAG file to derive the corresponding DAG. Moreover, to pick up any changes you may have made to your DAG, Airflow has to reread the file at regular intervals and sync any changes to its internal state.

As you can imagine, this repeated parsing of your DAG files can lead to problems if any of them take a long time to load. This can happen, for example, if you do any long-running or heavy computations when defining your DAG.

Listing 11.19 Performing computations in the DAG definition (inefficient)

```
...                                        This long computation
task1 = PythonOperator(...)                will be computed every
my_value = do_some_long_computation()  ◁── time the DAG is parsed.
task2 = PythonOperator(op_kwargs={"my_value": my_value})
...
```

This kind of implementation will cause Airflow to execute do_some_long_computation every time the DAG file is loaded, blocking the entire DAG parsing process until the computation has finished.

One way to avoid this issue to postpone the computation to the execution of the task that requires the computed value.

Listing 11.20   Performing computations within tasks (more efficient)

```
def _my_not_so_efficient_task(value, ...):
    ...


PythonOperator(
    task_id="my_not_so_efficient_task",
    ...
    op_kwargs={
        "value": calc_expensive_value()
    }
)
```

Here, the value will be computed every time the DAG is parsed.

```
def _my_more_efficient_task(...):
    value = calc_expensive_value()
    ...

PythonOperator(
    task_id="my_more_efficient_task",
    python_callable=_my_more_efficient_task,
    ...
)
```

By moving the computation into the task, the value will only be calculated when the task is executed.

Another approach would be to write our own hook/operator, which only fetches credentials when needed for execution, but this may require a bit more work.

Something similar may occur in more subtle cases, in which a configuration is loaded from an external data source or file system in your main DAG file. For example, we may want to load credentials from the Airflow metastore and share them across a few tasks by doing something like this.

Listing 11.21   Fetching credentials from the metastore in the DAG definition (inefficient)

```
from airflow.hooks.base_hook import BaseHook

api_config = BaseHook.get_connection("my_api_conn")
api_key = api_config.login
api_secret = api_config.password

task1 = PythonOperator(
    op_kwargs={"api_key": api_key, "api_secret": api_secret},
    ...
)
...
```

This call will hit the database every time the DAG is parsed.

However, a drawback of this approach is that it fetches credentials from the database every time our DAG is parsed instead of only when the DAG is executed. As such, we will see repeated queries every 30 seconds or so (depending on the Airflow config) against our database, simply for retrieving these credentials.

These types of performance issues can generally be avoided by postponing the fetching of credentials to the execution of the task function.

Listing 11.22 Fetching credentials within a task (more efficient)

```
from airflow.hooks.base_hook import BaseHook

def _task1(conn_id, **context):
    api_config = BaseHook.get_connection(conn_id)    ◄─┐  This call will only hit
    api_key = api_config.login                          the database when
    api_secret = api_config.password                    the task is executed.
    ...

task1 = PythonOperator(op_kwargs={"conn_id": "my_api_conn"})
```

This way, credentials are only fetched when the task is actually executed, making our DAG much more efficient. This type of *computation creep*, in which you accidentally include computations in your DAG definitions, can be subtle and requires some vigilance to avoid. Also, some cases may be worse than others: you may not mind repeatedly loading a configuration file from a local file system, but repeatedly loading from a cloud storage or database may be less preferable.

11.1.5 Use factories to generate common patterns

In some cases, you may find yourself writing variations of the same DAG over and over again. This often occurs in situations where you are ingesting data from related data sources, with only small variations in source paths and any transformations applied to the data. Similarly, you may have common data processes within your company that require many of the same steps/transformations and as a result are repeated across many different DAGs.

One effective way to speed up the process of generating these common DAG structures is to write a *factory function*. The idea behind such a function is that it takes any required configuration for the respective steps and generates the corresponding DAG or set of tasks (thus producing it, like a factory). For example, if we have a common process that involves fetching some data from an external API and preprocessing this data using a given script, we could write a factory function that looks a bit like this.

Listing 11.23 Generating sets of tasks with a factory function (dags/01_task_factory.py)

File paths used by   Parameters that configure the tasks that
the different tasks   will be created by the factory function

```
def generate_tasks(dataset_name, raw_dir, processed_dir,
                   preprocess_script, output_dir, dag):    ◄─┘
    raw_path = os.path.join(raw_dir, dataset_name, "{ds_nodash}.json")
    processed_path = os.path.join(
        processed_dir, dataset_name, "{ds_nodash}.json"
    )
    output_path = os.path.join(output_dir, dataset_name, "{ds_nodash}.json")
```

```
fetch_task = BashOperator(                          ◁─┐ Creating the individual tasks
    task_id=f"fetch_{dataset_name}",
    bash_command=f"echo 'curl http://example.com/{dataset_name}.json
    ➡ > {raw_path}.json'",
    dag=dag,
)

preprocess_task = BashOperator(
    task_id=f"preprocess_{dataset_name}",
    bash_command=f"echo '{preprocess_script} {raw_path}
    ➡ {processed_path}'",
    dag=dag,
)

export_task = BashOperator(
    task_id=f"export_{dataset_name}",
    bash_command=f"echo 'cp {processed_path} {output_path}'",
    dag=dag,
)
                                                    ┌─ Defining task
fetch_task >> preprocess_task >> export_task    ◁───┘   dependencies

return fetch_task, export_task    ◁──┐ Return the first and last tasks in the chain
                                     │ so that we can connect them to other
                                     │ tasks in the larger graph (if needed).
```

We could then use this factory function to ingest multiple data sets like this.

Listing 11.24   Applying the task factory function (dags/01_task_factory.py)

```
import airflow.utils.dates
from airflow import DAG

with DAG(
    dag_id="01_task_factory",
    start_date=airflow.utils.dates.days_ago(5),
    schedule_interval="@daily",
) as dag:                                  ┌─ Creating sets of
    for dataset in ["sales", "customers"]: │  tasks with different
        generate_tasks(              ◁─────┘  configuration values
            dataset_name=dataset,
            raw_dir="/data/raw",
            processed_dir="/data/processed",
            output_dir="/data/output",              ┌ Passing the DAG
            preprocess_script=f"preprocess_{dataset}.py", │ instance to connect
            dag=dag,                        ◁───────┘ the tasks to the DAG
        )
```

This should give us a DAG similar to the one in figure 11.1. Of course, for independent data sets, it would probably not make sense to ingest the two in a single DAG. You can, however, easily split the tasks across multiple DAGs by calling the generate_tasks factory method from different DAG files.

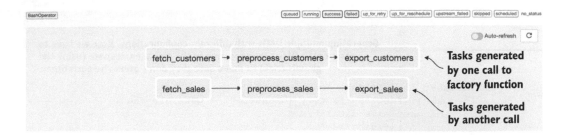

Figure 11.1 Generating repeated patterns of tasks using factory methods. This example DAG contains multiple sets of almost identical tasks, which were generated from a configuration object using a task factory method.

You can also write factory methods for generating entire DAGs, as shown in listing 11.25.

Listing 11.25 Generating DAGs with a factory function (dags/02_dag_factory.py)

```
def generate_dag(dataset_name, raw_dir, processed_dir, preprocess_script):
    with DAG(
        dag_id=f"02_dag_factory_{dataset_name}",
        start_date=airflow.utils.dates.days_ago(5),
        schedule_interval="@daily",
    ) as dag:                          ◁──  Generating the DAG
        raw_file_path = ...                 instance within the
        processed_file_path = ...           factory function

        fetch_task = BashOperator(...)
        preprocess_task = BashOperator(...)

        fetch_task >> preprocess_task

    return dag
```

This would allow you to generate a DAG using the following, minimalistic DAG file.

Listing 11.26 Applying the DAG factory function

```
...
                         Creating the DAG using
                         the factory function
dag = generate_dag(      ◁──
    dataset_name="sales",
        raw_dir="/data/raw",
        processed_dir="/data/processed",
        preprocess_script="preprocess_sales.py",
)
```

You can also use this kind of approach to generate multiple DAGs using a DAG file.

Listing 11.27 Generating multiple DAGs with a factory function (dags/02_dag_factory.py)

> Generating multiple DAGs with different configurations. Note we have to
> assign each DAG a unique name in the global namespace (using the
> globals trick) to make sure they don't overwrite each other.

```
...
for dataset in ["sales", "customers"]:
    globals()[f"02_dag_factory_{dataset}"] = generate_dag(   ◀──────
        dataset_name=dataset,
        raw_dir="/data/raw",
        processed_dir="/data/processed",
        preprocess_script=f"preprocess_{dataset}.py",
    )
```

This loop effectively generates multiple DAG objects in the global scope of your DAG
file, which Airflow picks up as separate DAGs (figure 11.2). Note that the objects need
to have different variable names to prevent them from overwriting each other; otherwise, Airflow will only see a single DAG instance (the last one generated by the loop).

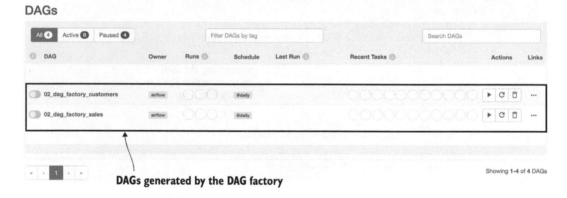

DAGs generated by the DAG factory

**Figure 11.2 Multiple DAGs generated from a single file using a DAG factory function. (Screenshot taken from
the Airflow UI, showing multiple DAGs that were generated from a single DAG file using a DAG factory function.)**

We recommend some caution when generating multiple DAGs from a single DAG file,
as it can be confusing if you're not expecting it. (The more general pattern is to have
one file for each DAG.) As such, this pattern is best used sparingly when it provides
significant benefits.

Task or DAG factory methods can be particularly powerful when combined with
configuration files or other forms of external configuration. This allows you to, for
example, build a factory function that takes a YAML file as input and generates a DAG
based on the configuration defined in that file. This way, you can configure repetitive
ETL processes using a bunch of relatively simple configuration files, which can also be
edited by users who have little knowledge of Airflow.

11.1.6 *Group related tasks using task groups*

Complex Airflow DAGs, particularly those generated using factory methods, can often become difficult to understand due to complex DAG structures or the sheer number of tasks involved. To help organize these complex structures, Airflow 2 has a new feature called *task groups*. Task groups effectively allow you to (visually) group sets of tasks into smaller groups, making your DAG structure easier to oversee and comprehend.

You can create task groups using the TaskGroup context manager. For example, taking our previous task factory example, we can group the tasks generated for each data set as follows.

> **Listing 11.28 Using TaskGroups to visually group tasks (dags/03_task_groups.py)**

```
...
for dataset in ["sales", "customers"]:
    with TaskGroup(dataset, tooltip=f"Tasks for processing {dataset}"):
        generate_tasks(
            dataset_name=dataset,
            raw_dir="/data/raw",
            processed_dir="/data/processed",
            output_dir="/data/output",
            preprocess_script=f"preprocess_{dataset}.py",
            dag=dag,
        )
```

This effectively groups the set of tasks generated for the sales and customers data sets into two task groups, one for each data set. As a result, the grouped tasks are shown as a single condensed task group in the web interface, which can be expanded by clicking on the respective group (figure 11.3).

Although this is a relatively simple example, the task group feature can be quite effective in reducing the amount of visual noise in more complex cases. For example, in our DAG for training machine learning models in chapter 5, we created a considerable

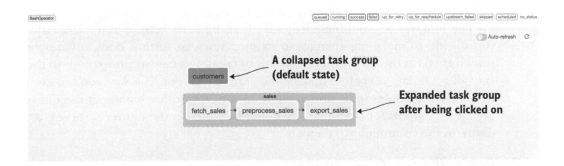

Figure 11.3 Task groups can help organize DAGs by grouping related tasks. Initially, task groups are depicted as single nodes in the DAG, as shown for the customers **task group in this figure. By clicking on a task group you can expand it and view the tasks within the group, as shown here for the** sales **task group. Note that task groups can be nested, meaning that you can have task groups within task groups.**

number of tasks for fetching and cleaning weather and sales data from different systems. Task groups allow us to reduce the apparent complexity of this DAG by grouping the sales- and weather-related tasks into their respective task groups. This allows us to hide the complexity of the data set fetching tasks by default but still zoom in on the individual tasks when needed (figure 11.4).

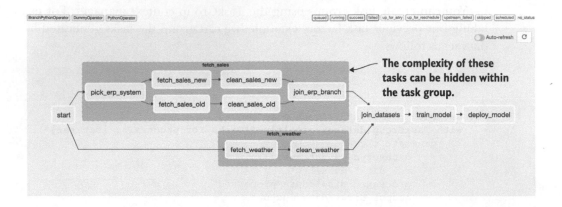

Figure 11.4   Using task groups to organize the umbrella DAG from chapter 5. Here, grouping the tasks for fetching and cleaning the weather and sales data sets helps greatly simplify the complex task structures involved in these processes. (Code example is given in dags/04_task_groups_umbrella.py.)

11.1.7 *Create new DAGs for big changes*

Once you've started running a DAG, the scheduler database contains instances of the runs of that DAG. Big changes to the DAG, such as to the start date and/or schedule interval, may confuse the scheduler, as the changes no longer fit with previous DAG runs. Similarly, removing or renaming tasks will prevent you from accessing the history of those tasks from the UI, as they will no longer match the current state of the DAG and will therefore no longer be displayed.

The best way to avoid these issues is to create a new version of the DAG whenever you decide to make big changes to existing ones, as Airflow does not support versioned DAGs at this time. You can do this by creating a new versioned copy of the DAG (i.e., dag_v1, dag_v2) before making the desired changes. This way, you can avoid confusing the scheduler while also keeping historical information about the old version available. Support for versioned DAGs may be added in the future, as there is a strong desire in the community to do so.

11.2 *Designing reproducible tasks*

Aside from your DAG code, one of the biggest challenges in writing a good Airflow DAG is designing your tasks to be reproducible, meaning that you can easily rerun a task and expect the same result—even if the task is run at different points in time. In this section, we revisit some key ideas and offer some advice on ensuring your tasks fit into this paradigm.

11.2.1 *Always require tasks to be idempotent*

As briefly discussed in chapter 3, one of the key requirements for a good Airflow task is that the task is idempotent, meaning that rerunning the same task multiple times gives the same overall result (assuming the task itself has not changed).

Idempotency is an important characteristic because there are many situations in which you or Airflow may rerun a task. For example, you may want to rerun some DAG runs after changing some code, leading to the re-execution of a given task. In other cases, Airflow itself may rerun a failed task using its retry mechanism, even though the given task did manage to write some results before failing. In both cases, you want to avoid introducing multiple copies of the same data in your environment or running into other undesirable side effects.

Idempotency can typically be enforced by requiring that any output data is overwritten when a task is rerun, as this ensures any data written by a previous run is overwritten by the new result. Similarly, you should carefully consider any other side effects of a task (such as sending notifications, etc.) and determine whether these violate the idempotency of your task in any detrimental way.

11.2.2 *Task results should be deterministic*

Tasks can only be reproducible if they are deterministic. This means that a task should always return the same output for a given input. In contrast, nondeterministic tasks prevent us from building reproducible DAGs, as every run of the task may give us a different result, even for the same input data.

Nondeterministic behavior can be introduced in various ways:

- Relying on the implicit ordering of your data or data structures inside the function (e.g., the implicit ordering of a Python dict or the order of rows in which a data set is returned from a database, without any specific ordering)
- Using external state within a function, including random values, global variables, external data stored on disk (not passed as input to the function), and so on
- Performing data processing in parallel (across multiple processes/threads), without doing any explicit ordering on the result
- Race conditions within multithreaded code
- Improper exception handling

In general, issues with nondeterministic functions can be avoided by carefully thinking about sources of nondeterminism that may occur within your function. For example, you can avoid nondeterminism in the ordering of your data set by applying an explicit sort to it. Similarly, any issues with algorithms that include randomness can be avoided by setting the random seed before performing the corresponding operation.

11.2.3 Design tasks using functional paradigms

One approach that may help in creating your tasks is to design them according to the paradigm of functional programming. Functional programming is an approach to building computer programs that essentially treats computation as the application of mathematical functions while avoiding changing state and mutable data. Additionally, functions in functional programming languages are typically required to be pure, meaning that they may return a result but otherwise do not have any side effects.

One of the advantages of this approach is that the result of a pure function in a functional programming language should always be the same for a given input. As such, pure functions are generally both idempotent and deterministic—exactly what we are trying to achieve for our tasks in Airflow functions. Therefore, proponents of the functional paradigm have argued that similar approaches can be applied to data-processing applications, introducing the functional data engineering paradigm.

Functional data engineering approaches essentially aim to apply the same concepts from functional programming languages to data engineering tasks. This includes requiring tasks to not have any side effects and to always have the same result when applied to the same input data set. The main advantage of enforcing these constraints is that they go a long way toward achieving our ideals of idempotent and deterministic tasks, thus making our DAGs and tasks reproducible.

For more details, refer to this blog post by Maxime Beauchemin (one of the key people behind Airflow), which provides an excellent introduction to the concept of functional data engineering for data pipelines in Airflow: http://mng.bz/2eqm.

11.3 Handling data efficiently

DAGs that are meant to handle large amounts of data should be carefully designed to do so in the most efficient manner possible. In this section, we'll discuss a couple of tips on how to handle large data volumes efficiently.

11.3.1 Limit the amount of data being processed

Although this may sound a bit trivial, the best way to efficiently handle data is to limit your processing to the minimal data required to obtain the desired result. After all, processing data that is going to be discarded anyway is a waste of both time and resources.

In practice, this means carefully thinking about your data sources and determining if they are all required. For the data sets that are needed, you can try to see if you can reduce the size of them by discarding rows/columns that aren't used. Performing aggregations early on can also substantially increase performance, as the right aggregation can greatly reduce the size of an intermediate data set—thus decreasing the amount of work that needs to be done downstream.

To give an example, imagine a data process in which we are interested in calculating the monthly sales volumes of our products among a particular customer base (figure 11.5). In this example, we can calculate the aggregate sales by first joining the

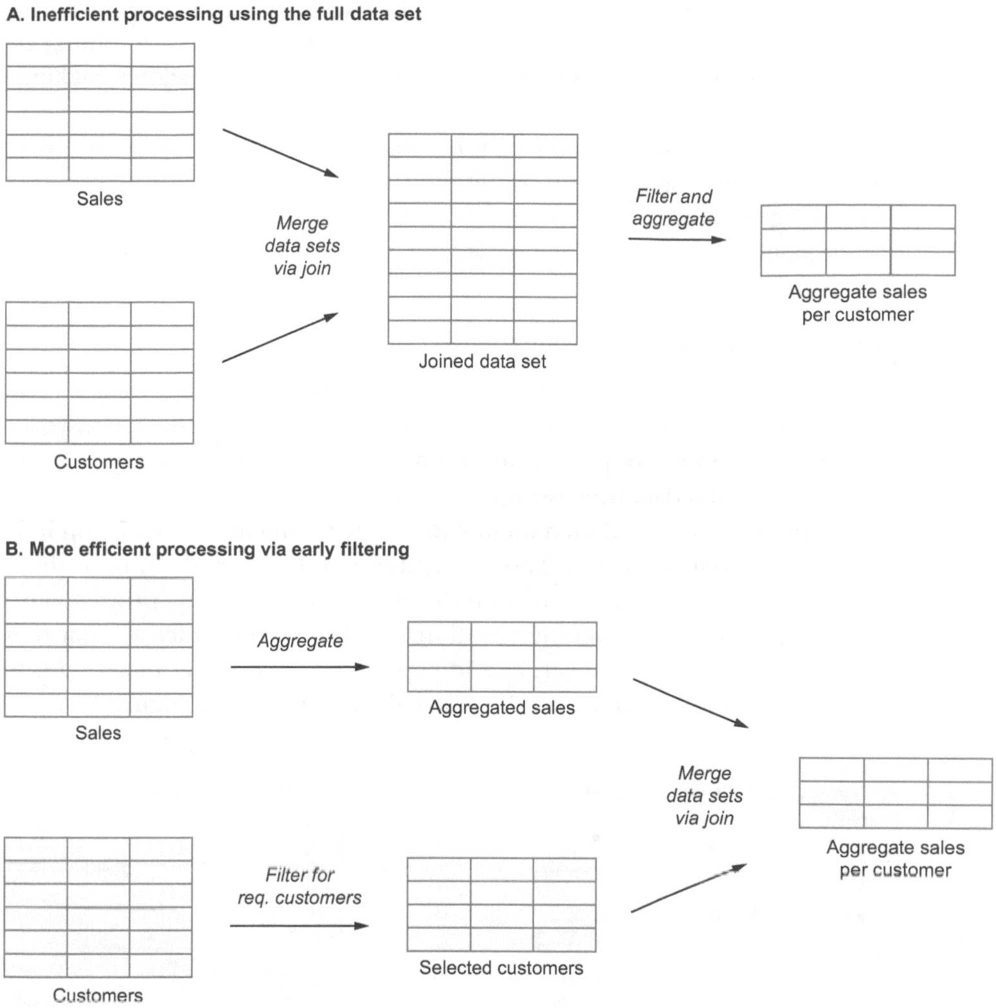

A. Inefficient processing using the full data set

B. More efficient processing via early filtering

Figure 11.5 Example of an inefficient data process compared to a more efficient one. (A) One way to calculate the aggregate sales per customer is to first fully join both data sets and then aggregate sales to the required granularity and filter for the customers of interest. Although this may give the desired result, it is not very efficient due to the potentially large size of the joined table. (B) A more efficient approach is to first filter/aggregate the sales and customer tables down to the minimum required granularity, allowing us to join the two smaller data sets.

two data sets, followed by an aggregation and filtering step in which we aggregate our sales to the required granularity then filtered for the required customers. A drawback of this approach is that we are joining two potentially large data sets to get our result, which may take considerable time and resources.

A more efficient approach is to push the filtering/aggregation steps forward, allowing us to reduce the size of the customer and sales data sets before joining them. This potentially allows us to greatly reduce the size of the joined data set, making our computation much more efficient.

Although this example may be a bit abstract, we have encountered many similar cases where smart aggregation or the filtering of data sets (both in terms of rows and columns) greatly increased the performance of the involved data processes. As such, it may be beneficial to carefully look at your DAGs and see if they are processing more data than needed.

11.3.2 *Incremental loading/processing*

In many cases, you may not be able to reduce the size of your data set using clever aggregation or filtering. However, especially for time series data sets, you can often also limit the amount of processing you need to do in each run of your processing by using incremental data processing.

The main idea behind incremental processing (which we touched on in chapter 3) is to split your data into (time-based) partitions and process them individually in each of your DAG runs. This way, you limit the amount of data being processed in each run to the size of the corresponding partition, which is usually much smaller than the size of the entire data set. However, by adding each run's results as increments to the output data set, you'll still build up the entire data set over time (figure 11.6).

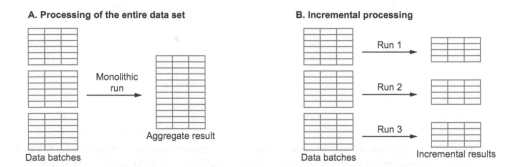

Figure 11.6   Illustration of monolithic processing (A), in which the entire data set is processed on every run, compared to incremental processing (B), in which the data set is analyzed in incremental batches as data comes in

An advantage of designing your process to be incremental is that any error in one of the runs won't require you to redo your analysis for the entire data set; you can simply restart the run that failed. Of course, in some cases you may still have to do analyses on the entire data set. However, you can still benefit from incremental processing by performing filtering/aggregation steps in the incremental part of your process and doing the large-scale analysis on the reduced result.

11.3.3 *Cache intermediate data*

In most data-processing workflows, DAGs consist of multiple steps that each perform additional operations on data coming from preceding steps. An advantage of this approach (as described earlier in this chapter) is that it breaks our DAG down into clear, atomic steps, which are easy to rerun if we encounter any errors.

However, to be able to rerun any steps in such a DAG efficiently, we need to make sure that the data required for those steps is readily available (figure 11.7). Otherwise, we wouldn't be able to rerun any individual step without also rerunning all its dependencies, which defeats part of the purpose of splitting our workflow into tasks in the first place.

Figure 11.7 **Storing intermediate data from tasks ensures that each task can easily be rerun independently of other tasks. In this case, cloud storage (indicated by the bucket) is used to store intermediate results of the *fetch/preprocess* tasks.**

A drawback of caching intermediate data is that this may require excessive amounts of storage if you have several intermediate versions of large data sets. In this case, you may consider making a trade-off in which you only keep intermediate data sets for a limited amount of time, providing you with some time to rerun individual tasks should you encounter problems in recent runs.

Regardless, we recommend always keeping the rawest version of your data available (e.g., the data you just ingested from an external API). This ensures you always have a copy of the data as it was at that point in time. This type of snapshot/versioning of data is often not available in source systems, such as databases (assuming no snapshots are made) or APIs. Keeping this raw copy of your data around ensures you can always reprocess it as needed, for example, whenever you make changes to your code or if any problems occurred during the initial processing.

11.3.4 *Don't store data on local file systems*

When handling data within an Airflow job, it can be tempting to write intermediate data to a local file system. This is especially the case when using operators that run locally on the Airflow worker, such as the Bash and Python operators, as the local file system is easily accessible from within them.

However, a drawback of writing files to local systems is that downstream tasks may not be able to access them because Airflow runs its tasks across multiple workers, which allows it to run multiple tasks in parallel. Depending on your Airflow deployment, this can mean that two dependent tasks (i.e., one task expects data from the other) can run on two different workers, which do not have access to each other's file systems and are therefore not able to access each other's files.

The easiest way to avoid this issue is to use shared storage that can be accessed in the same manner from every Airflow worker. For example, a commonly used pattern is to write intermediate files to a shared cloud storage bucket, which can be accessed from each worker using the same file URLs and credentials. Similarly, shared databases or other storage systems can be used to store data, depending on the type of data involved.

11.3.5 *Offload work to external/source systems*

In general, Airflow really shines when it's used as an orchestration tool rather than using the Airflow workers themselves to perform actual data processing. For example, with small data sets, you can typically get away with loading data directly on the workers using the PythonOperator. However, for larger data sets, this can become problematic, as they will require you to run Airflow workers on increasingly larger machines.

In these cases, you can get much more performance out of a small Airflow cluster by offloading your computations or queries to external systems that are best suited for that type of work. For example, when querying data from a database, you can make your work more efficient by pushing any required filtering/aggregation to the database system itself rather than fetching data locally and performing the computations in Python on your worker. Similarly, for big data applications, you can typically get better performance by using Airflow to run your computation on an external Spark cluster.

The key message here is that Airflow was primarily designed as an orchestration tool, so you'll get the best results if you use it that way. Other tools are generally better suited for performing the actual data processing, so be sure to use them for doing so, allowing the different tools to each play to their strengths.

11.4 *Managing your resources*

When working with large volumes of data, it can be easy to overwhelm your Airflow cluster or other systems used for processing the data. In this section, we'll dive into a few tips for managing your resources effectively, hopefully providing some ideas for managing these kinds of problems.

11.4.1 *Managing concurrency using pools*

When running many tasks in parallel, you may run into situations where multiple tasks need access to the same resource. This can quickly overwhelm said resource if it is not designed to handle this kind of concurrency. Examples can include shared resources like a database or GPU system, but can also include Spark clusters if, for example, you want to limit the number of jobs running on a given cluster.

Airflow allows you to control how many tasks have access to a given resource using *resource pools*, where each pool contains a fixed number of *slots*, which grant access to the corresponding resource. Individual tasks that need access to the resource can be assigned to the resource pool, effectively telling the Airflow scheduler that it needs to obtain a slot from the pool before it can schedule the corresponding task.

You can create a resource pool by going to the "Admin > Pools" section in the Airflow UI. This view will show you an overview of the pools that have been defined within Airflow (figure 11.8). To create a new resource pool, click Create. In the new screen (figure 11.9), you can enter a name and description for the new resource pool, together with the number of slots you want to assign to it. The number of slots defines the degree of concurrency for the resource pool. This means that a resource pool with 10 slots will allow 10 tasks to access the corresponding resource simultaneously.

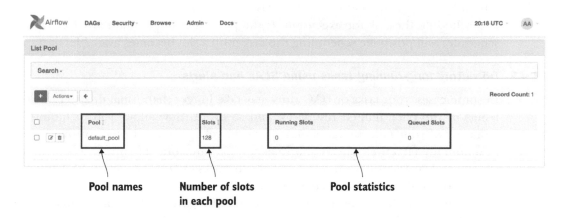

Figure 11.8 Overview of Airflow resource pools in the web UI

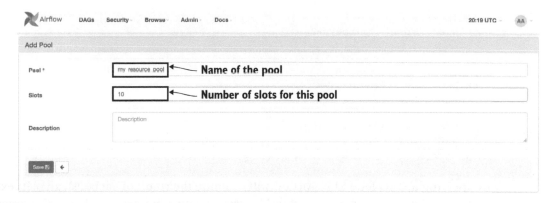

Figure 11.9 Creating a new resource pool in the Airflow web UI

To make your tasks use the new resource pool, you need to assign the resource pool when creating the task.

Listing 11.29   Assigning a specific resource pool to a task

```
PythonOperator(
    task_id="my_task",
    ...
    pool="my_resource_pool"
)
```

This way, Airflow will check to see if any slots are still available in `my_resource_pool` before scheduling the task in a given run. If the pool still contains free slots, the scheduler will claim an empty slot (decreasing the number of available slots by one) and schedule the task for execution. If the pool does not contain any free slots, the scheduler will postpone scheduling the task until a slot becomes available.

11.4.2 *Detecting long-running tasks using SLAs and alerts*

In some cases, your tasks or DAG runs may take longer than usual due to unforeseen issues in the data, limited resources, and so on. Airflow allows you to monitor the behavior of your tasks using its *SLA* (service-level agreement) mechanism. This SLA functionality effectively allows you to assign SLA timeouts to your DAGs or tasks, in which case Airflow will warn you if any of your tasks or DAGs misses its SLA (i.e., takes longer to run than the specified SLA timeout).

At the DAG level, you can assign an SLA by passing the `sla` argument to the `default_args` of the DAG.

```
from datetime import timedelta

default_args = {
    "sla": timedelta(hours=2),
    ...
}

with DAG(
    dag_id="...",
    ...
    default_args=default_args,
) as dag:
    ...
```

By applying a DAG-level SLA, Airflow will examine the result of each task after its execution to determine whether the task's start or end time exceeded the SLA (compared to the start time of the DAG). If the SLA was exceeded, Airflow will generate an SLA miss alert, notifying users it was missed. After generating the alert, Airflow will continue executing the rest of the DAG, generating similar alerts for other tasks that exceed the SLA.

By default, SLA misses are recorded in the Airflow metastore and can be viewed using the web UI under Browse > SLA misses. Alert emails are also sent to any email addresses defined on the DAG (using the `email` DAG argument), warning users that the SLA was exceeded for the corresponding task.

You can also define custom handlers for SLA misses by passing a handler function to the DAG using the `sla_miss_callback` parameter.

Listing 11.31   Custom callback for SLA misses (dags/05_sla_misses.py)

```
def sla_miss_callback(context):
    send_slack_message("Missed SLA!")

...

with DAG(
    ...
    sla_miss_callback=sla_miss_callback
) as dag:
    ...
```

It is also possible to specify task-level SLAs by passing an `sla` argument to a task's operator.

Listing 11.32   Assigning an SLA to specific tasks

```
PythonOperator(
    ...
    sla=timedelta(hours=2)
)
```

This will only enforce the SLA for the corresponding tasks. However, it's important to note that Airflow will still compare the end time of the task to the start time of the DAG when enforcing the SLA, rather than the start time of the task. This is because Airflow SLAs are always defined relative to the start time of the DAG, not to individual tasks.

Summary

- Adopting common style conventions together with supporting linting/formatting tools can greatly increase the readability of your DAG code.
- Factory methods allow you to efficiently generate recurring DAGs or task structures while capturing differences between instances in small configuration objects or files.
- Idempotent and deterministic tasks are key to building reproducible tasks and DAGs, which are easy to rerun and backfill from within Airflow. Concepts from functional programming can help you design tasks with these characteristics.

- Data processes can be implemented efficiently by carefully considering how data is handled (i.e., processing in the appropriate systems, limiting the amount of data that is loaded, and using incremental loading) and by caching intermediate data sets in available file systems that are available across workers.
- You can manage/limit access to your resources in Airflow using resource pools.
- Long-running tasks/DAGs can be detected and flagged using SLAs.

Operating Airflow
in production

12

This chapter covers

- Dissecting the Airflow scheduler
- Configuring Airflow to scale horizontally using different executors
- Monitoring the status and performance of Airflow visually
- Sending out alerts in case of task failures

In most of the previous chapters, we focused on various parts of Airflow from a programmer's perspective. In this chapter, we aim to explore Airflow from an operations perspective. A general understanding of concepts such as (distributed) software architecture, logging, monitoring, and alerting is assumed. However, no specific technology is required.

Configuring Airflow

Throughout this chapter, we often refer to the Airflow configuration. Configuration in Airflow is interpreted in this order of preference:

1   Environment variable (AIRFLOW__[SECTION]__[KEY])
2   Command environment variable (AIRFLOW__[SECTION]__[KEY]_CMD)
3   In airflow.cfg
4   Command in airflow.cfg
5   Default value

Whenever referring to configuration options, we will demonstrate option 1. For example, take the configuration item `web_server_port` in the `webserver` section. This will be demonstrated as `AIRFLOW__WEBSERVER__WEB_SERVER_PORT`.

To find the current value of any configuration item, you can scroll down in the Configurations page in the Airflow UI down to the table "Running Configuration," which shows all configuration options, their current value, and from which of the five options the configuration was set.

12.1   Airflow architectures

At a minimum, Airflow consists of three components (figure 12.1):

- Webserver
- Scheduler
- Database

Figure 12.1   **The most basic Airflow architecture**

Webserver   Database   Scheduler   DAGs

The webserver and scheduler are both Airflow processes. The database is a separate service you have to provide to Airflow for storing metadata from the webserver and scheduler. A folder with DAG definitions must be accessible by the scheduler.

Webserver and DAGs deployment in Airflow 1

In Airflow 1, the DAG files must be accessible to *both* the webserver and scheduler. This complicates deployment because sharing files between multiple machines or processes is not a trivial task.

In Airflow 2, DAGs are written in a serialized format in the database. The webserver reads this serialized format from the database and does not require access to the DAG files.

Serialization of DAGs has been possible since Airflow 1.10.10, although it is optional. To enable DAG serialization in Airflow 1 (≥1.10.10 only), you must configure the following:

- AIRFLOW__CORE__STORE_DAG_CODE=True
- AIRFLOW__CORE__STORE_SERIALIZED_DAGS=True

The webserver's responsibility is to visually display information about the current status of the pipelines and allow the user to perform certain actions, such as triggering a DAG.

The scheduler's responsibility is twofold:

1 Parse DAG files (i.e., read DAG files, extract bits and pieces, and store these in the metastore).
2 Determine tasks to run and place these tasks on a queue.

We will dive deeper into the scheduler's responsibilities in section 12.1.3. Airflow can be installed in various ways: from a single machine (which requires minimal effort to set up but is not scalable), to multiple machines (which requires more initial work but has horizontal scalability). In Airflow, the different execution modes are configured by the type of *executor*. At the time of writing, there are four types of executors:

- SequentialExecutor (default)
- LocalExecutor
- CeleryExecutor
- KubernetesExecutor

The type of executor is configurable by setting AIRFLOW__CORE__EXECUTOR to one of the executor types from the list (table 12.1). Let's look at how these four executors operate internally.

Table 12.1 Overview of the Airflow executor modes

Executor	Distributed	Ease of installation	Good fit
SequentialExecutor	No	Very easy	Demoing/testing
LocalExecutor	No	Easy	When running on a single machine is good enough
CeleryExecutor	Yes	Moderate	If you need to scale out over multiple machines
KubernetesExecutor	Yes	Complex	When you're familiar with Kubernetes and prefer a containerized setup

12.1.1 *Which executor is right for me?*

The `SequentialExecutor` is the simplest and the one you get automatically with Airflow. As the name implies, it runs tasks sequentially. It is mainly used for testing and demo purposes and will run tasks rather slowly. It will only operate on a single machine.

The next step, while remaining on a single machine, is the `LocalExecutor`, which is not limited to a single task at a time but can run multiple tasks in parallel. Internally, it registers tasks to execute in a Python *FIFO* (first in, first out) queue, which worker processes read and execute. By default, the `LocalExecutor` can run up to 32 parallel processes (this number is configurable).

If you want to distribute your workloads over multiple machines, you have two options: the `CeleryExecutor` and the `KubernetesExecutor`. Distributing work over multiple machines can be done for various reasons: you're hitting the resource limits of a single machine, you want redundancy by running jobs on multiple machines, or you simply want to run workloads faster by distributing the work across multiple machines.

The `CeleryExecutor` internally applies Celery (http://www.celeryproject.org) as the mechanism for queueing tasks to run, and workers read and process tasks from the queue. From a user's perspective, it works the same as the `LocalExecutor` by sending tasks to a queue, and workers read tasks to process from the queue. However, the main difference is that all components can run on different machines, spreading the workload. Currently, Celery supports RabbitMQ, Redis, and AWS SQS for the queuing mechanism (called the *broker* in Celery terms). Celery also comes with a monitoring tool named Flower for inspecting the state of the Celery system. Celery is a Python library and thus nicely integrates with Airflow. For example, the CLI command `airflow celery worker` will actually start a Celery worker. The only real external dependency for this setup is the queuing mechanism.

Lastly, the `KubernetesExecutor`, as the name implies, runs workloads on Kubernetes (https://kubernetes.io). It requires the setup and configuration of a Kubernetes cluster on which to run Airflow, and the executor integrates with the Kubernetes APIs for distributing Airflow tasks. Kubernetes is the de facto solution for running containerized workloads, which implies every task in an Airflow DAG is run in a Kubernetes pod. Kubernetes is highly configurable and scalable and is often already in use within an organization; therefore, many happily use Kubernetes in combination with Airflow.

12.1.2 *Configuring a metastore for Airflow*

Everything that happens in Airflow is registered in a database, which we also refer to as the *metastore* in Airflow. A workflow script consists of several components, which the scheduler interprets and stores in the metastore. Airflow performs all database operations with the help of SQLAlchemy, a Python *ORM* (object relational mapper) framework, for conveniently writing Python objects directly to a database without having to manually write out SQL queries. As a result of using SQLAlchemy internally, only databases supported by it are also supported by Airflow. From all supported databases, Airflow recommends using PostgreSQL or MySQL. SQLite is also supported, but only in combination with the SequentialExecutor as it does not support concurrent writes and is therefore not suitable for a production system. It is, however, very convenient for testing and development purposes due to its easy setup.

Without any configuration, running airflow db init creates a SQLite database in $AIRFLOW_HOME/airflow.db. In case you want to set up a production system and go with MySQL or Postgres, you must first create the database separately. Next, you must point Airflow to the database by setting AIRFLOW__CORE__SQL_ALCHEMY_CONN.

The value of this configuration item should be given in URI format (protocol: //[username:password@]host[:port]/path). See the following examples:

- MySQL: mysql://username:password@localhost:3306/airflow
- PostgreSQL: postgres://username:password@localhost:5432/airflow

The Airflow CLI provides three commands for configuring the database:

- airflow db init: Create the Airflow database schema on an empty database.
- airflow db reset: Wipe any existing database and create a new, empty, database. This is a destructive operation!
- airflow db upgrade: Apply missing database schema upgrades (if you've upgraded the Airflow version) to the database. Running db upgrade on an already upgraded database schema will result in no action and is therefore safe to execute multiple times. In the case no database has been initialized, the effect will be the same as db init. Note, however, that it does not create default connections as db init does.

Running any of the these database commands will print something like the following.

Listing 12.1 Initializing the Airflow metastore

```
$ airflow db init
DB: sqlite:////home/airflow/airflow.db
[2020-03-20 08:39:17,456] {db.py:368} INFO - Creating tables
INFO [alembic.runtime.migration] Context impl SQLiteImpl.
INFO [alembic.runtime.migration] Will assume non-transactional DDL.
... Running upgrade  -> e3a246e0dc1, current schema
... Running upgrade e3a246e0dc1 -> 1507a7289a2f, create is_encrypted
...
```

What you see is the output of Alembic, another Python database framework, for scripting database migrations. Each line in listing 12.1 is the output of one single database migration. If you upgrade to a newer Airflow version that contains database migrations (whether or not a new version contains database upgrades is listed in the release notes), you must also upgrade the corresponding database. Running airflow db upgrade will check at which migration step your current database lives and apply the migration steps that were added in the new release.

At this stage, you have a fully functional Airflow database and can run airflow webserver and airflow scheduler. When opening the webserver on http://localhost:8080, you will see many example_* DAGs and connections (figure 12.2).

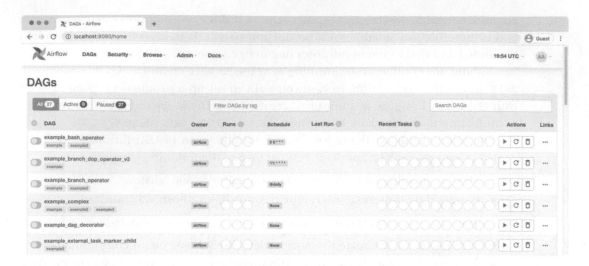

Figure 12.2   By default, Airflow will load example DAGs (and connections, not displayed here).

These examples might come in handy during development but are likely not desirable for a production system. You can exclude example DAGs by setting AIRFLOW__ CORE__LOAD_EXAMPLES=False.

However, upon restarting the scheduler and webserver, you will probably be surprised to still see the DAGs and connections. The reason is that setting load_examples to False tells Airflow to not load example DAGs (does not apply to connections!), and Airflow will not reload them. However, already loaded DAGs remain in the database and are not deleted. The same behavior applies to default connections, which can be excluded by setting AIRFLOW__CORE__LOAD_DEFAULT_CONNECTIONS=False.

With this in mind, a "clean" (i.e., no examples) database is achieved by the completing the following steps:

1   Install Airflow.
2   Set AIRFLOW__CORE__LOAD_EXAMPLES=False.
3   Set AIRFLOW__CORE__LOAD_DEFAULT_CONNECTIONS=False.
4   Run airflow db init.

12.1.3   *A closer look at the scheduler*

To understand how and when tasks are executed, let's take a closer look at the scheduler. The scheduler has multiple responsibilities:

- Parsing DAG files and storing extracted information in the database
- Determining which tasks are ready to execute and placing these in the queued state
- Fetching and executing tasks in the queued state

Airflow runs all tasks in DAGs within a *job*. Although job classes are internal to Airflow, you can view the running jobs in the Airflow UI. The scheduler also runs in a job, albeit its own special job, namely a SchedulerJob. All jobs can be inspected in the Airflow UI under Browse → Jobs (figure 12.3).

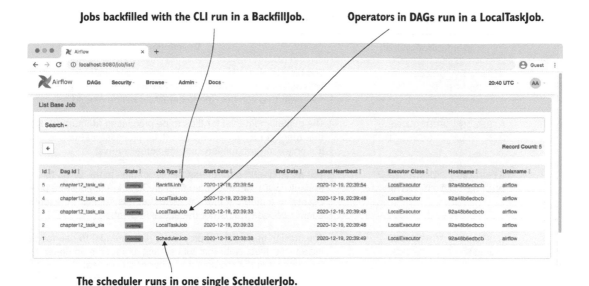

Figure 12.3   The scheduler, regular tasks, and backfill tasks are run within a job in Airflow. All jobs can be viewed in the Airflow UI.

The SchedulerJob has three responsibilities. First, it's responsible for parsing DAG files and storing extracted information in the database. Let's inspect what that entails.

THE DAG PROCESSOR

The Airflow scheduler periodically processes Python files in the DAGs directory (the directory set by `AIRFLOW__CORE__DAGS_FOLDER`). This means that even if no change was made to a DAG file,[1] it periodically evaluates each DAG file and persists the found DAGs in the Airflow metastore because you can create dynamic DAGs (that change structure based on an external source in Airflow) while the code stays the same. An example is a DAG in which a YAML file is read and tasks are generated based on the content of it. In order to pick up changes in dynamic DAGs, the scheduler reprocesses DAG files periodically.

---

[1] While there are ongoing discussions in the Airflow community to make the DAG parsing event-based by listening for file changes on DAG files and explicitly configuring DAGs for reprocessing if required, which could alleviate the CPU usage of the scheduler, this does not exist at the time of writing.

Processing DAGs takes processing power. The more you re-process your DAG files, the faster changes will be picked up, but at the cost of taking more CPU power. If you know your DAGs do not change dynamically, it's safe to raise default intervals to alleviate the CPU. The interval of DAG processing is related to four configurations (shown in table 12.2).

Table 12.2   Airflow configuration options related to DAG processing

Configuration item	Description
AIRFLOW__SCHEDULER__ PROCESSOR_POLL_INTERVAL	The time to wait after completing a scheduler loop. Inside a scheduler loop (among other operations) DAGs are parsed, so the lower this number, the faster DAGs will be parsed.
AIRFLOW__SCHEDULER__ MIN_FILE_PROCESS_INTERVAL	The minimum interval for files to be processed (default: 0). Note that there is no guarantee files will be processed at this interval; it's only a lower boundary, not the actual interval.
AIRFLOW__SCHEDULER__ DAG_DIR_LIST_INTERVAL	The minimum time to refresh the list of files in the DAGs folder (default: 300). Already listed files are kept in memory and processed at a different interval. Note that this setting represents a lower boundary; it is not the actual interval.
AIRFLOW__SCHEDULER__ PARSING_PROCESSES	The maximum number of processes (not threads) to use for parsing all DAG files. Note that this setting represents an upper boundary; it is not the actual number of processes.

An optimal configuration for your system depends on the number of DAGs, the size of your DAGs (i.e., how long it takes for the DAG processor to evaluate them), and the available resources on the machine on which the scheduler is running. All intervals define a boundary for how often to perform a process; at times the interval value is compared, but it's possible, for example, that the DAG_DIR_LIST_INTERVAL is checked after 305 seconds while the value is set to 300 seconds.

AIRFLOW__SCHEDULER__DAG_DIR_LIST_INTERVAL is particularly useful to lower. If you find yourself often adding new DAGs and waiting for them to appear, the issue can be addressed by lowering this value.

All DAG processing happens within a while True loop, in which Airflow loops over a series of steps for processing DAG files over and over. In the log files, you will see the output of DAG processing in /logs/dag_processor_manager/dag_processor_manager.log.

Listing 12.2   Example output of DAG processor manager

```
================================================================
DAG File Processing Stats

File Path   PID Runtime # DAGs # Errors Last Runtime Last Run
----------- --- ------- ------ -------- ------------ -----------
.../dag1.py             1        0  0.09s       ... 18:55:15
```

```
.../dag2.py                    1      0  0.09s    ... 18:55:15
.../dag3.py                    1      0  0.10s    ... 18:55:15
.../dag4.py 358 0.00s          1      0  0.08s    ... 18:55:15
.../dag5.py 359 0.07s          1      0  0.08s    ... 18:55:15
================================================================
... - Finding 'running' jobs without a recent heartbeat
... - Failing jobs without heartbeat after 2020-12-20 18:50:22.255611
... - Finding 'running' jobs without a recent heartbeat
... - Failing jobs without heartbeat after 2020-12-20 18:50:32.267603
... - Finding 'running' jobs without a recent heartbeat
... - Failing jobs without heartbeat after 2020-12-20 18:50:42.320578
```

Note that these file processing stats are not printed with every iteration but every X number of seconds that `AIRFLOW__SCHEDULER__PRINT_STATS_INTERVAL` is set to (default: 30 seconds). Also note that the displayed statistics represent the information from the last run, not the results of the last number of `PRINT_STATS_INTERVAL` seconds.

THE TASK SCHEDULER

Second, the scheduler is responsible for determining which task instances may be executed. A `while True` loop periodically checks for each task instance if a set of conditions are met, such as (among others) if all upstream dependencies are satisfied, if the end of an interval is reached, if the task instance in the previous DAG ran successfully if `depends_on_past=True`, and so on. Whenever a task instance meets all conditions, it is set to a scheduled state, which means the scheduler decided it met all conditions and is okay to execute.

Another loop in the scheduler determines another set of conditions in which tasks go from a scheduled to queued state. Here, conditions include (among others) if there are enough open slots and if certain tasks have priority over others (given the `priority_weight` argument). Once all these conditions have been met, the scheduler will push a command to a queue to run the task and set the state of the task instance to queued. This means once the task instance has been placed on a queue, it's no longer the responsibility of the scheduler. At this point, tasks are now the responsibility of the executor that will read the task instance from the queue and start the task on a worker.

> **NOTE** The task scheduler is responsible for tasks up to the queued state. Once a task is given the queued state, it becomes the responsibility of the executor to run the task.

The type of queue and how a task instance is processed once it's been placed on a queue is contained in the process named *executor*. The executor part of the scheduler can be configured in various ways, from a single process on a single machine to multiple processes distributed over multiple machines, as explained in section 12.1.1.

THE TASK EXECUTOR

In general, the task executor process will wait for the task scheduler process to place task instances to execute on a queue. Once placed on this queue, the executor will fetch the task instance from the queue and execute it. Airflow registers each state change in the metastore. The message placed on the queue contains several details of the task instance. In the executor, *executing* tasks means creating a new process for the task to run in so that it doesn't bring down Airflow if something fails. In the new process, it executes the CLI command `airflow tasks run` to run a single task instance, such as the following example (using the LocalExecutor).

> **Listing 12.3   The command executed for any given task**

```
airflow tasks run [dag_id] [task_id] [execution date] –local –pool [pool
    id] -sd [dag file path]
```

```
For example:
airflow tasks run chapter12_task_sla sleeptask 2020-04-04T00:00:00+00:00
    --local --pool default_pool -sd /..../dags/chapter12/task_sla.py
```

Right before executing the command, Airflow registers the state of the task instance as running in the metastore. After this, it executes the task and periodically checks in by sending a heartbeat to the metastore. The heartbeat is yet another `while True` loop in which Airflow does the following:

- Checks if the task has finished.
- If finished and the exit code is zero, the task is successful.
- If finished and the exit code does not equal zero, the task failed.
- If not finished,
    - Register the heartbeat and wait X seconds, configured with `AIRFLOW__SCHEDULER__JOB_HEARTBEAT_SEC` (default 5).
    - Repeat.

For a successful task, this process repeats a certain number of times, until the task is completed. If no error occurred, the state of the task is changed to success. The ideal flow of a task is depicted in figure 12.4.

12.2   *Installing each executor*

There are many ways to install and configure Airflow; hence, it's impractical to elaborate on all ways in this book. However, we demonstrate the main items required for getting each executor up and running.

As explained in section 12.1, the executor is part of Airflow's scheduler. The DAG processor and task scheduler can only be run in a single way, by starting `airflow scheduler`. However, the task executor can be installed in different ways, from a single

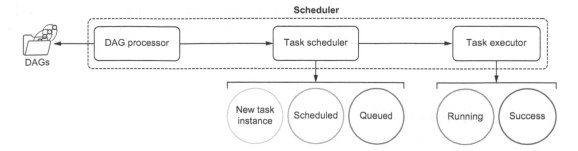

Figure 12.4 The ideal flow of a task and the task state for which the components of the scheduler are responsible. The dotted line represents the full scheduler responsibility. When running the `SequentialExecutor`/`LocalExecutor` mode, this is a single process. The `CeleryExecutor` and `KubernetesExecutor` run the task executor in separate processes, designed to scale over multiple machines.

process on a single machine to multiple processes on multiple machines, for performance and/or redundancy.

The executor type is set in Airflow with `AIRFLOW__CORE__EXECUTOR`, where the value is one of the following:

- `SequentialExecutor` (default)
- `LocalExecutor`
- `CeleryExecutor`
- `KubernetesExecutor`

You can validate the correct installation of any executor by running a DAG. If any task makes it to the running state, it means it went through the cycle of being scheduled, queued, and running, which means it is picked up by the executor.

12.2.1 Setting up the SequentialExecutor

The default executor in Airflow is the `SequentialExecutor` (figure 12.5). The task executor part of the scheduler is run in a single subprocess, within which tasks are run one by one, so it's the slowest method of task execution. However, it is convenient for testing because it requires no configuration.

Figure 12.5 With the `SequentialExecutor`, all components must run on the same machine.

The `SequentialExecutor` works with a SQLite database. Running `airflow db init` without any configuration will initialize a SQLite database in your `$AIRFLOW_HOME` directory, which is a single file named airflow.db. After that, start two processes:

- `airflow scheduler`
- `airflow webserver`

12.2.2 *Setting up the LocalExecutor*

Setting up Airflow with the `LocalExecutor` is not much different from the `Sequential-Executor` setup (figure 12.6). Its architecture is similar to the `SequentialExecutor` but with multiple subprocesses, so tasks can be executed in parallel, and thus it performs faster. Each subprocess executes one task, and subprocesses can run in parallel.

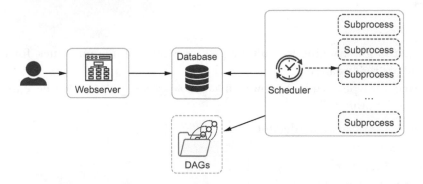

Figure 12.6   With the `LocalExecutor` all components can run on a separate machine. However, subprocesses created by the scheduler all run on one single machine.

Also, the `SequentialExecutor` is coupled to a SQLite database, while all other executors can work with more sophisticated databases such as MySQL and PostgreSQL, resulting in better performance.

To configure the `LocalExecutor`, set `AIRFLOW__CORE__EXECUTOR` to `LocalExecutor`. The scheduler can spawn a maximum number of subprocesses configured by `AIRFLOW__CORE__PARALLELISM` (default 32). Technically, these are not new processes but rather processes forked from the parent (scheduler) process.

There are other ways to limit the number of parallel tasks (e.g., by lowering the default pool size, `AIRFLOW__CORE__DAG_CONCURRENCY`, or `AIRFLOW__CORE__MAX_ACTIVE_RUNS_PER_DAG`).

Database-wise, install Airflow with the extra dependencies for the corresponding database system:

- MySQL: `pip install apache-airflow[mysql]`
- PostgreSQL: `pip install apache-airflow[postgres]`

The LocalExecutor is easy to set up and can get you decent performance. The system is limited by the resources of the scheduler's machine. Once the LocalExecutor no longer suffices (e.g., in terms of performance or redundancy), the CeleryExecutor and KubernetesExecutor, which we address in sections 12.2.3 and 12.2.4, respectively, are the logical next steps.

12.2.3 Setting up the CeleryExecutor

The CeleryExecutor is built on top of the Celery project. Celery provides a framework for distributing messages to workers via a queuing system (figure 12.7).

As you can see in figure 12.7, both the scheduler and Celery workers require access to both the DAGs and the database. For the database, this is not a problem since you can connect to it with a client. For the DAGs folder, this can be challenging to set up. You make the DAGs available to all machines either via a shared file system or by building a containerized setup where the DAGs are built into an image with Airflow. In the containerized setup, any change to the DAG code will result in a redeployment of the software.

To get started with Celery, first install Airflow with the Celery extra dependencies and configure the executor:

- pip install apache-airflow[celery]
- AIRFLOW__CORE__EXECUTOR=CeleryExecutor

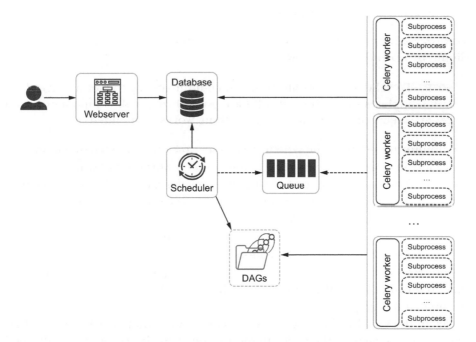

Figure 12.7 In the CeleryExecutor, tasks are divided among multiple machines running Celery workers. The workers wait for tasks to arrive on a queue.

The queueing system can be anything that Celery supports, which is Redis, RabbitMQ, and AWS SQS at the time of writing. In Celery, the queue is called *broker*. Installing a broker is not in the scope of this book, but after installation you must configure Airflow to the broker by setting `AIRFLOW__CELERY__BROKER_URL`:

- Redis: `AIRFLOW__CELERY__BROKER_URL=redis://localhost:6379/0`
- RabbitMQ: `AIRFLOW__CELERY__BROKER_URL=amqp://user:pass@localhost:5672//`

Check the documentation for your queueing system for the corresponding URI format. The `BROKER_URL` allows the scheduler to send messages to the queue. For the Celery workers to communicate with the Airflow metastore, we must also configure `AIRFLOW__CELERY__RESULT_BACKEND`. In Celery the prefix db+ is used to indicate a database connection:

- MySQL: `AIRFLOW__CELERY__RESULT_BACKEND=db+mysql://user:pass@localhost/airflow`
- PostgreSQL: `AIRFLOW__CELERY__RESULT_BACKEND=db+postgresql://user:pass@localhost/airflow`

Ensure the DAGs folder is also accessible on the worker machines on the same path, as configured by `AIRFLOW__CORE__DAGS_FOLDER`. After this, we should be good to go:

1 Start Airflow webserver.
2 Start Airflow scheduler.
3 Start Airflow Celery worker.

`airflow celery worker` is a small wrapper command starting a Celery worker. All should be up and running now.

> **NOTE** To validate the installation, you could manually trigger a DAG. If any task completes successfully, it will have gone through all components of the `CeleryExecutor` setup, meaning everything works as intended.

To monitor the status of the system, we can set up Flower, a web-based monitoring tool for Celery in which we can inspect (among others) workers, tasks, and the status of the whole Celery system. The Airflow CLI also provides a convenience command to start Flower: `airflow celery flower`. By default, Flower runs on port 5555. After starting, browse to http://localhost:5555 (figure 12.8).

In the first view of Flower, we see the number of registered Celery workers, their status, and some high-level information on the number of tasks each worker has processed. How can you tell if the system is performing well? The most useful graphic in the Flower interface is the Monitor page in figure 12.9, which shows the status of the system in a few graphs.

From the two distributed executor modes Airflow offers (Celery and Kubernetes), the `CeleryExecutor` is the easier to set up from scratch because you only need to set up one additional component: the queue. The Celery workers and Flower dashboard

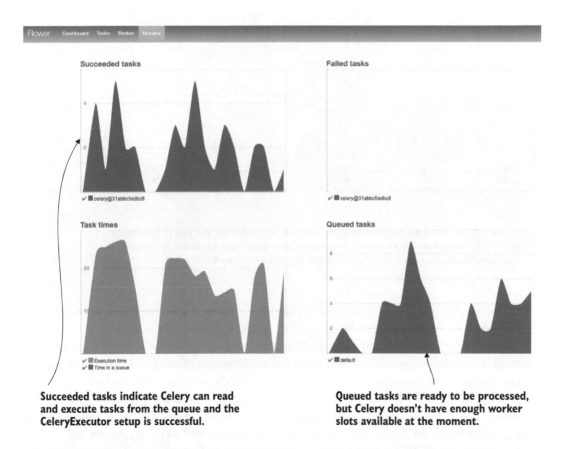

Figure 12.8   The Flower dashboard shows the status of all Celery workers.

Succeeded tasks indicate Celery can read and execute tasks from the queue and the CeleryExecutor setup is successful.

Queued tasks are ready to be processed, but Celery doesn't have enough worker slots available at the moment.

Figure 12.9   The monitoring tab of Flower shows graphs to understand the performance of the Celery system.

are integrated into Airflow, which makes it easy to set up and scale the execution of tasks over multiple machines.

12.2.4 *Setting up the KubernetesExecutor*

Last but not least is the `KubernetesExecutor`. Set `AIRFLOW__CORE__EXECUTOR=KubernetesExecutor` to use it. As the name implies, this executor type is coupled to Kubernetes, which is the most used system for running and managing software in containers. Many companies run their software on Kubernetes, since containers provide an isolated environment that ensures what you develop on your computer runs the same on the production system. Thus, the Airflow community expressed a strong desire to run Airflow on Kubernetes. Architecturally, the `KubernetesExecutor` looks like figure 12.10.

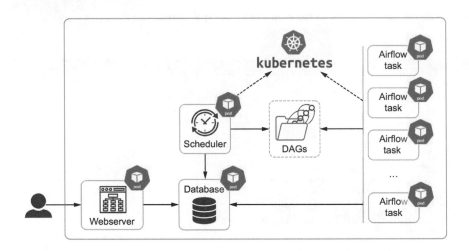

Figure 12.10   With the `KubernetesExecutor`, all tasks run in a pod in Kubernetes. While it is not necessary to run the webserver, scheduler, and database in Kubernetes, it is sensible to also run it there when using the `KubernetesExecutor`.

When working with the `KubernetesExecutor`, it helps to have prior knowledge of Kubernetes. Kubernetes can be large and complex. However, the Airflow `KubernetesExecutor` only uses a small part of all available components on the Kubernetes platform. For now, it's good to know a *pod* is the smallest unit of work in Kubernetes and can run one or more containers. In the context of Airflow, one task will run in one pod.

A pod is created every time a task is executed. When the scheduler decides to run a task, it sends a pod creation request to the Kubernetes API, which then creates a pod running an Airflow container, with the command `airflow tasks run ...`, as shown in listing 12.3 (disregarding several details). Kubernetes itself monitors the status of the pod.

With the other executor setups, there was a clear separation between physical machines. With Kubernetes, all processes run in pods, where they can be distributed over multiple machines, although they might also be running on the same machine. From a user's perspective, processes run in pods and the user does not know of underlying machines.

The most used way to deploy software on Kubernetes is with Helm, a package manager for Kubernetes. Various third-party Helm charts for Airflow are available on Helm Hub, the repository for Helm charts. At the time of writing, an official Airflow Helm chart is available on the master branch of the Airflow project. However, it is not yet available on public Helm repositories at the time of writing. The minimal installation instructions are therefore (assuming a functioning Kubernetes cluster and Helm 3+) as follows.

> **Listing 12.4   Airflow installation on Kubernetes with Helm chart**

Create an Airflow namespace in Kubernetes.

Download the Airflow source code containing the Helm chart.

Download specified versions of dependent Helm charts.

Install the Airflow Helm chart.

```
$ curl -OL https://github.com/apache/airflow/archive/master.zip
$ unzip master.zip
$ kubectl create namespace airflow
$ helm dep update ./airflow-master/chart
$ helm install airflow ./airflow-master/chart --namespace airflow

NAME: airflow
LAST DEPLOYED: Wed Jul 22 20:40:44 2020
NAMESPACE: airflow
STATUS: deployed
REVISION: 1
TEST SUITE: None
NOTES:
Thank you for installing Airflow!

Your release is named airflow.

You can now access your dashboard(s) by executing the following
command(s) and visiting the corresponding port at localhost in your browser:

Airflow dashboard:
kubectl port-forward svc/airflow-webserver 8080:8080 --namespace airflow
```

One of the trickier parts of setting up the KubernetesExecutor is determining how to distribute DAG files between Airflow processes. There are three methods for this:

1. Share DAGs between pods with a PersistentVolume.
2. Pull the latest DAG code from a repository with a Git-sync init container.
3. Build the DAGs into the Docker image.

First, let's establish how to deploy Airflow DAG code without using containers. All Airflow processes must have access to a directory containing DAG files. On a single machine, this isn't too hard: start all Airflow processes and point to the directory on the machine holding the DAG code.

However, it becomes difficult when running Airflow processes on different machines. In that case, you need some way to make DAG code accessible by both machines, such as a shared file system (figure 12.11).

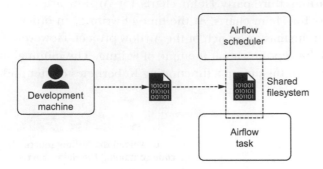

Figure 12.11   Without containers, a developer pushes code to a repository, after which the code should be made available to both Airflow processes.

However, getting code on a shared file system is not a trivial task. A file system is built for storing and retrieving files on a storage medium, not for providing an interface to the internet for easy file exchange. The exchange of files over the internet would be handled by an application running on the same machine as the file system is mounted to.

In more practical words, say you have a shared file system such as *NFS* (network file system) to share files between the Airflow scheduler and worker machines. You develop code on your development machine but cannot copy files directly to the NFS file system because it does not have an interface to the internet. To copy your files onto the NFS, it must be mounted to a machine, and files must be written onto it via an application running on the same machine, such as FTP (figure 12.12).

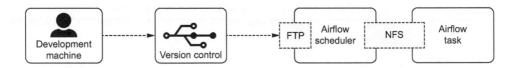

Figure 12.12   Files cannot be written directly to NFS because it provides no internet interface. For sending and receiving files over the internet, we could use FTP to store files on the same machine as the NFS is mounted to.

In figure 12.12, a developer or CI/CD system can push Airflow code to the Airflow system via an FTP server, which runs on one of the Airflow machines. Via the FTP server, the NFS volume should be made accessible for the CI/CD system to push DAG files to and make it accessible to all Airflow machines.

What if a pushing mechanism from the CI/CD system is not an option? This is a common challenge for various reasons, such as security or network limitations. In that case, an often seen solution is to pull the code in from an Airflow machine, via a DAG named "the DAG puller DAG."

Listing 12.5 Pulling in the latest code with a DAG puller DAG

```python
import datetime

from airflow.models import DAG
from airflow.operators.bash import BashOperator

dag = DAG(
    dag_id="dag_puller",
    default_args={"depends_on_past": False},
    start_date=datetime.datetime(2020, 1, 1),
    schedule_interval=datetime.timedelta(minutes=5),
    catchup=False,
)

fetch_code = BashOperator(
    task_id="fetch_code",
    bash_command=(
        "cd /airflow/dags && "
        "git reset --hard origin/master"
    ),
    dag=dag,
)
```

Ignore all dependencies; always run tasks. → (points to `default_args` / `catchup=False`)

Pull the latest code every five minutes. ← (points to `schedule_interval`)

Requires Git to be installed and configured ← (points to `git reset --hard origin/master`)

With the DAG puller DAG, the latest code from the master branch is pulled onto the Airflow machine every five minutes (figure 12.13). This obviously imposes a delay between the code on the master branch and the deployment of the code in Airflow, but it's sometimes the most practical solution.

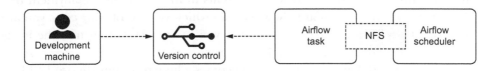

Figure 12.13   With a DAG puller DAG, code will be pulled from an Airflow machine.

Now that we know the challenges and potential solutions for deploying DAGs running Airflow in a distributed setup, let's see how to share DAGs between pods in Kubernetes.

SHARE DAGS BETWEEN PODS WITH A PERSISTENTVOLUME

PersistentVolumes are Kubernetes's abstraction over storage and allow mounting shared volumes to containers without having to know the underlying storage technology, such as NFS, Azure File Storage, or AWS EBS. One of the trickier parts is to set up a CI/CD pipeline where DAG code is pushed to the shared volume, which typically does not provide out-of-the-box functionality for pushing directly to the shared volume. To enable sharing DAGs with a PersistentVolume, set the configuration item `AIRFLOW__KUBERNETES__DAGS_VOLUME_CLAIM` to the name of the volume ("Volume-Claim" in Kubernetes) on the Airflow pod. DAG code must be copied to the volume, either with a pushing method, as shown in figure 12.12, or a pulling method, as shown in listing 12.5. The solution might depend on your chosen volume type, so refer to the Kubernetes documentation on volumes for more information.

PULL THE LATEST DAG CODE FROM A REPOSITORY WITH A GIT-SYNC INIT CONTAINER

The Airflow configuration holds a list of settings for pulling a Git repository via a sidecar container before running an Airflow task (not complete):

- `AIRFLOW__KUBERNETES__GIT_REPO` = https://mycompany.com/repository/airflow
- `AIRFLOW__KUBERNETES__GIT_BRANCH` = master
- `AIRFLOW__KUBERNETES__GIT_SUBPATH` = dags
- `AIRFLOW__KUBERNETES__GIT_USER` = username
- `AIRFLOW__KUBERNETES__GIT_PASSWORD` = password
- `AIRFLOW__KUBERNETES__GIT_SSH_KEY_SECRET_NAME` = airflow-secrets
- `AIRFLOW__KUBERNETES__GIT_DAGS_FOLDER_MOUNT_POINT` = /opt/airflow/dags
- `AIRFLOW__KUBERNETES__GIT_SYNC_CONTAINER_REPOSITORY` = k8s.gcr.io/git-sync
- `AIRFLOW__KUBERNETES__GIT_SYNC_CONTAINER_TAG` = v3.1.2
- `AIRFLOW__KUBERNETES__GIT_SYNC_INIT_CONTAINER_NAME` = git-sync-clone

While not all details are necessary to fill, setting the `GIT_REPO` and credentials (`USER` + `PASSWORD`, or `GIT_SSH_KEY_SECRET_NAME`) will enable the Git sync. Airflow will create a sync container that pulls the code from the configured repository before starting a task.

BUILD THE DAGS INTO THE DOCKER IMAGE

Lastly, building the DAG files into the Airflow image is also a popular option for its immutability; any change to DAG files results in the build and deployment of a new Docker image so that you are always certain which version of your code you are running on. To tell the `KubernetesExecutor` you've built DAG files into the image, set `AIRFLOW__KUBERNETES__DAGS_IN_IMAGE=True`.

The build and deployment process becomes a little different (figure 12.14).

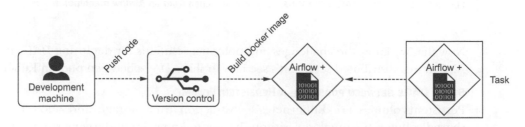

Figure 12.14   After a push to the version control system, a new Docker image is built.

Building an Airflow image together with DAG code provides several benefits:

- We are certain which version of the code is currently deployed.
- We can run the same Airflow environment locally as on production.
- Conflicts between new dependencies are found at build time, not at run time.

If we zoom in on the build, for performance it's preferable to install Airflow and add your DAG code in two separate steps:

1 Installation dependencies.
2 Add only DAG code.

The reason for this split is that Airflow contains lots of dependencies, which can take in the order of minutes to build. You probably will not change dependencies often during development but will mostly change DAG code. To avoid reinstalling dependencies with every small change, copy your DAG code into the image in a separate step. If your CI/CD system caches Docker layers, this could be in a separate Docker statement, because you can retrieve the base layers quickly. If your CI/CD system does not cache Docker layers, it's wise to build one base image for Airflow and dependencies and a second image for adding only the DAG code. Let's illustrate how the latter option works with two Dockerfiles.[2] First is the base Dockerfile.

Listing 12.6 Base Airflow Dockerfile example

```
FROM apache/airflow:2.0.0-python3.8        ◁────┐  Base on the official
                                                    Airflow image

USER root                       ◁───────────┐

RUN apt-get update && \                       Default user is a non-root
    apt-get install -y gcc && \               user Airflow, so switch to
    apt-get autoremove -y && \                root for installation.
    apt-get clean -y && \
    rm -rf /var/lib/apt/lists/*              Switch back to Airflow
                                             after installation.
USER airflow                    ◁───────────┘
COPY requirements.txt /opt/airflow/requirements.txt
RUN pip install --user -r /opt/airflow/requirements.txt && \
    rm /opt/airflow/requirements.txt
```

This base Dockerfile starts with the official Airflow 2.0.0 Docker image and installs additional dependencies listed in requirements.txt. Having a separate file for additional dependencies simplifies the CI/CD pipeline, since any change to requirements.txt should always trigger a rebuild of the base image. The command `docker build -f Dockerfile.base -t myrepo/airflow-base .` will build the base image.

---

[2] Both Dockerfiles are meant for demonstration purposes.

Listing 12.7   Final Airflow Dockerfile example

```
FROM myrepo/airflow-base:1.2.3

COPY dags/ /opt/airflow/dags/
```

Having a pre-built base image with all dependencies makes building the final image a very fast process since the only step required is copying the DAG files. Use the command `docker build -t myrepo/airflow .` to build it. However, this image will be built with every single change. Depending on the dependencies you're installing, the difference in time between building the base and final image can be very large.

Listing 12.8   Example requirements.txt

```
python-dotenv~=0.10.3
```

By splitting the build process of an Airflow Docker image into either separate statements or separate images, we can significantly speed up the build time because only the files changed most often (the DAG scripts) are copied into the Docker image. A more time-consuming full rebuild of the Docker image will be performed only when needed.

From the Kubernetes side, ensure your Airflow image tag is defined in the YAML by `AIRFLOW__KUBERNETES__POD_TEMPLATE_FILE`, or make sure `AIRFLOW__KUBERNETES__WORKER_CONTAINER_TAG` is set to the tag you want the worker pods to deploy. If using the Airflow Helm chart, you can update the deployed version with the Helm CLI by setting the tag of the newly built image.

Listing 12.9   Updating the deployed Airflow image with Helm

```
helm upgrade airflow ./airflow-master/chart --namespace airflow \
  --set images.airflow.repository=yourcompany/airflow \
  --set images.airflow.tag=1234abc
```

12.3   *Capturing logs of all Airflow processes*

What about logging? All systems produce some sort of output, and at times we want to know what's going on. In Airflow, there are three types of logs:

- *Webserver logs*—These hold information on web activity (i.e., which requests are sent to the webserver.
- *Scheduler logs*—These hold information on all scheduler activity, which includes DAG parsing, scheduling tasks, and more.
- *Task logs*—These hold the logs of one single task instance in each log file.

By default, logs are written in $AIRFLOW_HOME/logs on the local filesystem. Logging is configurable in various ways. In this section, we will demonstrate the default logging behavior, plus how to write logs to a remote storage system in section 12.3.4.

12.3.1 *Capturing the webserver output*

The webserver serves static files and every request to a file is displayed in the web-server output. See the following example:

- ➡ `127.0.0.1 - - [24/Mar/2020:16:50:45 +0100] "GET / HTTP/1.1" 302 221 "-" "Mozilla/5.0 (Macintosh; Intel Mac OS X 10_14_5) AppleWebKit/537.36 (KHTML, like Gecko) Chrome/80.0.3987.149 Safari/537.36"`
- ➡ `127.0.0.1 - - [24/Mar/2020:16:50:46 +0100] "GET /admin/ HTTP/1.1" 200 44414 "-" "Mozilla/5.0 (Macintosh; Intel Mac OS X 10_14_5) AppleWeb-Kit/537.36 (KHTML, like Gecko) Chrome/80.0.3987.149 Safari/537.36"`
- ➡ `127.0.0.1 - - [24/Mar/2020:16:50:46 +0100] "GET /static/bootstrap-theme.css HTTP/1.1" 200 0 "http://localhost:8080/admin/" "Mozilla/5.0 (Macintosh; Intel Mac OS X 10_14_5) AppleWebKit/537.36 (KHTML, like Gecko) Chrome/80.0.3987.149 Safari/537.36"`

When starting the webserver on the command line, you will see this output printed to stdout or stderr. What if you want to preserve logs after the webserver shuts down? Within the webserver, there are two types of logs: access logs, as shown, and error logs, which hold not only errors but also system information such as the following:

- [2020-04-13 12:22:51 +0200] [90649] [INFO] Listening at: http://0.0.0.0:8080 (90649)
- [2020-04-13 12:22:51 +0200] [90649] [INFO] Using worker: sync
- [2020-04-13 12:22:51 +0200] [90652] [INFO] Booting worker with pid: 90652

Both types of logs can be written to a file by providing a flag when starting Airflow webserver:

- airflow webserver –access_logfile [filename]
- airflow webserver –error_logfile [filename]

The filename will be relative to `AIRFLOW_HOME`, so setting "accesslogs.log" as the filename, for example, will create a file: /path/to/airflow/home/accesslogs.log.

12.3.2 *Capturing the scheduler output*

The scheduler does write logs to files by default, as opposed to the webserver. Looking at the `$AIRFLOW_HOME/logs` directory again, we see various files related to scheduler logs.

Listing 12.10 Log files generated by the scheduler

```
.
├── dag_processor_manager
│   └── dag_processor_manager.log
└── scheduler
    └── 2020-04-14
        ├── hello_world.py.log
        └── second_dag.py.log
```

This directory tree is the result of processing two DAGs: hello_world and second_dag. Every time the scheduler processes a DAG file, several lines are written to the respective file. These lines are key to understanding how the scheduler operates. Let's look at hello_world.py.log.

Listing 12.11   Scheduler reading DAG files and creating corresponding DAGs/tasks

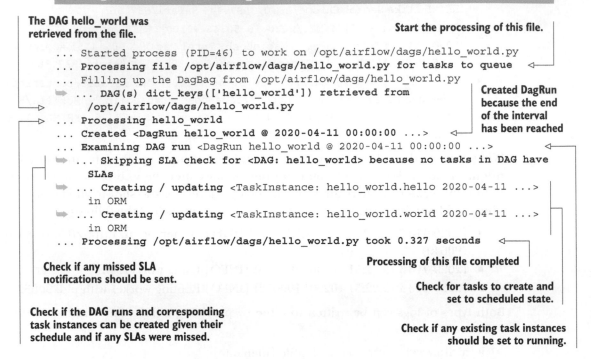

These steps of processing a DAG file, loading the DAG object from the file, and checking if many conditions are met, such as DAG schedules, are executed many times over and are part of the core functionality of the scheduler. From these logs, we can derive whether the scheduler is working as intended.

There is also a single file named dag_processor_manager.log (log rotation is performed once it reaches 100 MB), in which an aggregated view (default last 30 seconds) is displayed of which files the scheduler has processed (listing 12.2).

12.3.3 *Capturing task logs*

Lastly, we have task logs, where each file represents one attempt of one task.

Listing 12.12   Log files generated upon task execution

```
.
├── hello_world          ◁──── DAG name
│   ├── hello            ◁──── Task name
│   │   └── 2020-04-14T16:00:00+00:00    ◁──── Execution date
```

```
|   |           ├── 1.log          ◁──┐  Attempt number
|   |           └── 2.log
|   ├── world
|   |   └── 2020-04-14T16:00:00+00:00
|   |           ├── 1.log
|   |           └── 2.log
└── second_dag
    └── print_context
        ├── 2020-04-11T00:00:00+00:00
        |   └── 1.log
        └── 2020-04-12T00:00:00+00:00
            └── 1.log
```

The contents of these files reflect what we see when opening a task in the webserver UI.

12.3.4 *Sending logs to remote storage*

Depending on your Airflow setup, you might want to send logs elsewhere, for example, when running Airflow in ephemeral containers in which logs are gone when the container stops or for archival purposes. Airflow holds a feature named "remote logging," which allows us to ship logs to a remote system. At the time of writing, the following remote systems are supported:

- AWS S3 (requires `pip install apache-airflow[amazon]`)
- Azure Blob Storage (requires `pip install apache-airflow[microsoft.azure]`)
- Elasticsearch (requires `pip install apache-airflow[elasticsearch]`)
- Google Cloud Storage (requires `pip install apache-airflow[google]`)

To configure Airflow for remote logging, set the following configurations:

- `AIRFLOW__CORE__REMOTE_LOGGING=True`
- `AIRFLOW__CORE__REMOTE_LOG_CONN_ID=...`

The `REMOTE_LOG_CONN_ID` points to the id of the connection holding the credentials to your remote system. After this, each remote logging system can read configuration specific to that system. For example, the path to which logs should be written in Google Cloud Storage can be configured as `AIRFLOW__CORE__REMOTE_BASE_LOG_FOLDER=gs://my-bucket/path/to/logs`. Refer to the Airflow documentation for the details for each system.

12.4 *Visualizing and monitoring Airflow metrics*

At some point, you might want to know more about the performance of your Airflow setup. In this section, we focus on numerical data about the status of the system, called *metrics*, for example, the number of seconds delay between queueing a task and the actual execution of the task. In monitoring literature, observability and full understanding of a system are achieved by a combination of three items: logs, metrics, and traces. Logs (textual data) are covered in section 12.3, we cover metrics in this section, and tracing is not in the scope of this book.

Each Airflow setup has its own characteristics. Some installations are big; some are small. Some have few DAGs and many tasks; some have many DAGs with only a few tasks. It's impractical to cover every possible situation in a book, so we demonstrate the main ideas for monitoring Airflow, which should apply to any installation. The end goal is to get started with collecting metrics about your setup and actively using these to your advantage, such as with a dashboard (figure 12.15).

Figure 12.15   An example visualization of the number of running tasks. Here, the parallelism had the default value of 32, to which we sometimes see the number of tasks spike.

12.4.1 Collecting metrics from Airflow

Airflow is instrumented with StatsD (https://github.com/statsd/statsd). What does it mean to be instrumented? Instrumented in the context of StatsD and Airflow means certain events in Airflow result in information about the event being sent so it can be collected, aggregated, and visualized or reported. For example, whenever a task fails, an event named "ti_failures" is sent with a value of 1, meaning one task failure occurred.

PUSHING VS PULLING

When comparing metrics systems, a common discussion is about pushing versus pulling, or the *push versus pull model*. With the push model, metrics are sent, or pushed, to a metrics collection system. With the pull model, metrics are exposed by the system to monitor a certain endpoint, and a metrics collection system must fetch, or pull, metrics from the system to monitor from the given endpoint. Pushing might result in overflowing the metrics collection system when many systems start pushing many metrics simultaneously to the metrics collection system.

StatsD works with the push model. So, when starting with monitoring in Airflow, we must set up a metrics collection system to which StatsD can push its metrics before we can view the metrics.

WHICH METRICS COLLECTION SYSTEM?

StatsD is one of the many available metrics collection systems. Others include Prometheus and Graphite. A StatsD client is installed with Airflow. However, the server that will collect the metrics is something you have to set up yourself. The StatsD client communicates metrics to the server in a certain format, and many metrics collection systems can interchange components by reading each other's formats.

For example, Prometheus's server can be used for storing metrics from Airflow. However, the metrics are sent in StatsD format, so there must be a translation for Prometheus to understand the metrics. Also, Prometheus applies the pull model, whereas StatsD applies the push model, so some intermediary must be installed to which StatsD can push and Prometheus can pull, because Airflow does not expose Prometheus's metrics format, and thus Prometheus cannot pull metrics directly from Airflow.

Why the mixing and matching? Mainly because Prometheus is the tool of choice for metrics collection to many developers and sysadmins. It is used at many companies and prevails over StatsD on many points, such as its flexible data model, ease of operation, and integration with virtually any other system. Therefore, we also prefer Prometheus for dealing with metrics, and we demonstrate how to transform StatsD metrics into Prometheus metrics, after which we can visualize the collected metrics with Grafana. Grafana is a dashboarding tool for visualizing time series data for monitoring purposes.

The steps from Airflow to Grafana will look like figure 12.16.

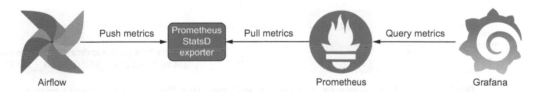

Figure 12.16　Software and steps required for collecting and visualizing metrics from Airflow. Prometheus collects metrics, and Grafana visualizes metrics in dashboards. The Prometheus StatsD exporter translates StatsD metrics to Prometheus's metrics format and exposes them for Prometheus to scrape.

Let's set up this system from left (Airflow) to right (Grafana) to create a dashboard visualizing metrics from Airflow.

12.4.2　*Configuring Airflow to send metrics*

To have Airflow push its StatsD metrics, we must install Airflow with the `statsd` extra dependency:

```
pip install apache-airflow[statsd]
```

Next, configure the location to which Airflow should push its metrics. Currently there is no system to collect the metrics, but we'll configure that next in section 12.4.3.

- `AIRFLOW__METRICS__STATSD_ON=True`
- `AIRFLOW__METRICS__STATSD_HOST=localhost` (default value)
- `AIRFLOW__METRICS__STATSD_PORT=9125`
- `AIRFLOW__METRICS__STATSD_PREFIX=airflow` (default value)

From the Airflow side, we are now done. With this configuration, Airflow will push events to port 9125 (over UDP).

12.4.3 *Configuring Prometheus to collect metrics*

Prometheus is software for systems monitoring. It features a wide array of features, but at its core, it's a time series database, which can be queried with a language named PromQL. You cannot manually insert data into the database like an `INSERT INTO ...` query with a relational database, but it works by pulling metrics into the database. Every X seconds, it pulls the latest metrics from targets you configure. If Prometheus gets too busy, it will automatically slow down on scraping the targets. However, this requires a large number of metrics to process, so it's not applicable right now.

First, we must install the Prometheus StatsD exporter, which translates Airflow's StatsD metrics into Prometheus metrics. The easiest way to do this is with Docker.

Listing 12.13   **Running a StatsD exporter with Docker**

Prometheus metrics will be shown on http://localhost:9102.

```
docker run -d -p 9102:9102 -p 9125:9125/udp prom/statsd-exporter
```

Ensure this port number aligns with the port set by AIRFLOW__SCHEDULER__STATSD_PORT.

Without Docker, you can download and run the Prometheus StatsD exporter from https://github.com/prometheus/statsd_exporter/releases.

To get started we can run the StatsD exporter without configuration. Go to http://localhost:9102/metrics, and you should see the first Airflow metrics.

Listing 12.14   **Sample Prometheus metrics, exposed using the StatsD exporter**

Each metric has a type such as a gauge.

Each metric comes with a default HELP message.

```
# HELP airflow_collect_dags Metric autogenerated by statsd_exporter.
# TYPE airflow_collect_dags gauge
airflow_collect_dags 1.019871
# HELP airflow_dag_processing_processes Metric autogenerated by statsd_exporter.
# TYPE airflow_dag_processing_processes counter
airflow_dag_processing_processes 35001
```

The metric airflow_collect_dags currently has a value of 1.019871. Prometheus registers the scrape timestamp together with this value.

```
# HELP airflow_dag_processing_total_parse_time Metric autogenerated by
    statsd_exporter.
# TYPE airflow_dag_processing_total_parse_time gauge
airflow_dag_processing_total_parse_time 1.019871
# HELP airflow_dagbag_import_errors Metric autogenerated by statsd_exporter.
# TYPE airflow_dagbag_import_errors gauge
airflow_dagbag_import_errors 0
# HELP airflow_dagbag_size Metric autogenerated by statsd_exporter.
# TYPE airflow_dagbag_size gauge
airflow_dagbag_size 4
```

Now that we've made the metrics available on http://localhost:9102, we can install and configure Prometheus to scrape this endpoint. The easiest way to do this is once again with Docker to run a Prometheus container. First, we must configure the StatsD exporter as a target in Prometheus so that Prometheus knows where to get the metrics from.

Listing 12.15   Minimal Prometheus configuration

```
scrape_configs:
  - job_name: 'airflow'            ⟵  Defines a Prometheus
    static_configs:                    metrics scraping job
    - targets: ['localhost:9102']  ⟵  The target URL of
                                       the scraping job
```

Save the content of listing 12.15 in a file, for example, /tmp/prometheus.yml. Then start Prometheus and mount the file.

Listing 12.16   Running Prometheus with Docker to collect metrics

```
docker run -d -p 9090:9090 -v /tmp/prometheus.yml:/etc/prometheus/
    prometheus.yml prom/prometheus
```

Prometheus is now up and running on http://localhost:9090. To verify, go to http://localhost:9090/targets and ensure the Airflow target is up (figure 12.17).

An up-and-running target means metrics are being scraped by Prometheus and we can start visualizing the metrics in Grafana.

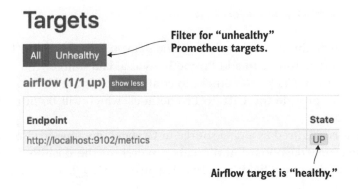

Figure 12.17   If all is configured correctly, the targets page in Prometheus should display the state of the Airflow target as UP. If the target cannot be reached, it is considered unhealthy.

Metrics data models

The data model of Prometheus identifies unique metrics by a name (for example, `task_duration`) and a set of key-value labels (for example, `dag_id=mydag` and `task_id=first_task`). This allows for great flexibility because you can select metrics with any desired combination of labels, for example, `task_duration{task_id="first_task"}`, for selecting only the `task_duration` of tasks named "first_task". An alternative data model seen in many other metrics systems such as StatsD is hierarchy-based, where labels are defined in dot separated metric names:

- task_duration.my_dag.first_task -> 123
- task_duration.my_other_dag.first_task -> 4

This is problematic when you want to select the metric `task_duration` of all tasks named first_task, which is one of the reasons why Prometheus gained popularity.

Prometheus's StatsD exporter applies generic rules to the supplied metrics to convert these from the hierarchical model used by StatsD to the label model used by Prometheus. Sometimes the default conversion rules work nicely, but sometimes they don't, and a StatsD metric results in a unique metric name in Prometheus. For example, in the metric `dag.<dag_id>.<task_id>.duration`, `dag_id` and `task_id` are not converted automatically to labels in Prometheus.

While technically still workable in Prometheus, this is not optimal. Therefore, the StatsD exporter can be configured to convert specific dot-separated metrics into Prometheus metrics. See Appendix C for such a configuration file. For more information, read the StatsD exporter documentation.

12.4.4 *Creating dashboards with Grafana*

After collecting metrics with Prometheus, the last piece of the puzzle is to visualize these metrics in a dashboard. This should provide us a quick understanding of the functioning of the system. Grafana is the main tool for visualizing metrics. The easiest way to get Grafana up and running is once again with Docker.

Listing 12.17   Running Grafana with Docker to visualize metrics

```
docker run -d -p 3000:3000 grafana/grafana
```

On http://localhost:3000, this is the first view of Grafana you will see (figure 12.18).

Click Add your first data source to add Prometheus as a data source. You will see a list of available data sources. Click Prometheus to configure it (figure 12.19).

On the next screen, provide the URL to Prometheus, which will be http://localhost:9090 (figure 12.20).

With Prometheus configured as a data source in Grafana, it's time to visualize the first metric. Create a new dashboard and create a panel on the dashboard. Insert the following metric in the query field: `airflow_dag_processing_total_parse_time`

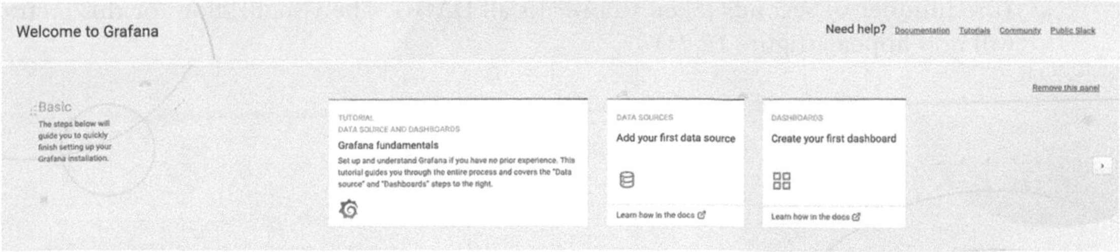

Figure 12.18   Grafana welcome screen

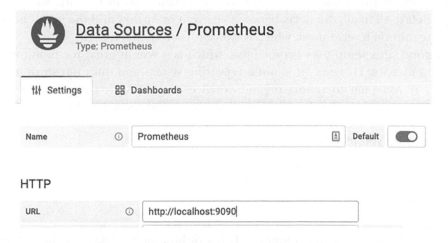

Figure 12.19   In the "Add data source" page, select Prometheus to configure it as a source to read metrics from.

Figure 12.20   Point Grafana to the Prometheus URL to read from it.

(the number of seconds taken to process all DAGs). The visualization for this metric will now appear (figure 12.21).

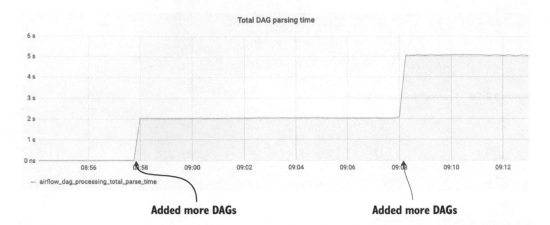

Figure 12.21   Plot of the number of seconds to process all DAG files. We see two change points at which more DAG files were added. A large spike in this graph could indicate a problem with the Airflow scheduler or a DAG file.

With Prometheus and Grafana in place, Airflow now pushes metrics to Prometheus's StatsD exporter, which are eventually plotted in Grafana. There are two things to note in this setup. First, the metrics in Grafana are close to real time, but not millisecond real time. Prometheus scrapes metrics in intervals (default: one minute, can be lowered), which causes a one-minute delay in the worst case. Also, Grafana periodically queries Prometheus (query refresh is off by default), so in Grafana we too have a slight delay. All in all, the delay between an event in Airflow and the graph in Grafana is at the minute level at most, which is typically more than enough.

Second, this setup uses Prometheus, which is a system great for monitoring and alerting metrics. However, it is not a reporting system and does not store individual events. If you plan to report on individual events in Airflow, you might consider InfluxDB as a time series database, as it is more geared toward event logging.

12.4.5   *What should you monitor?*

Now that we have a monitoring setup, what should we monitor to understand the functioning of Airflow? Starting in general terms, when monitoring anything there are four basic signals to monitor.

LATENCY
How long it takes to service requests? Think of how long it takes for the webserver to respond, or how long it takes the scheduler to move a task from queued to running

state. These metrics are expressed as a duration (e.g., "average milliseconds to return a webserver request" or "average seconds to move tasks from queued to running state").

TRAFFIC

How much demand is being asked of the system? Think of how many tasks your Airflow system has to process, or how many open pool slots Airflow has available. These metrics are typically expressed as an average per duration (e.g., "number of tasks running per minute" or "open pool slots per second").

ERRORS

Which errors were raised? In the context of Airflow, this can vary from "the number of zombie tasks" (running tasks where the underlying process has disappeared), "the number of non-HTTP 200 responses in the webserver" or "the number of timed out tasks."

SATURATION

What part of the capacity of your system is utilized? Measuring the machine metrics that Airflow is running on can be a good indicator, for example "the current CPU load" or "the number of currently running tasks." To determine how full a system is, you must know its upper boundary, which is sometimes not trivial to determine.

Prometheus features a wide range of exporters, exposing all sorts of metrics about a system. Thus, start by installing several Prometheus exporters to learn more about all systems involved running Airflow:

- *The node exporter*—For monitoring the machines Airflow is running on (CPU, memory, disk I/O, network traffic).
- *The PostgreSQL/MySQL server exporter*—For monitoring the database.
- *One of the several (unofficial) Celery exporters*—For monitoring Celery when using the `CeleryExecutor`.
- *The Blackbox exporter*—For polling a given endpoint to check if a predefined HTTP code is returned.
- *If using Kubernetes, one of the many Kubernetes exporters*—For monitoring Kubernetes resources. Refer to the Kubernetes monitoring documentation.

An overview of all available metrics is listed in the Airflow documentation; refer to that for your Airflow version. Some good metrics for getting to know the status of Airflow are as follows:

- For knowing the correct functioning of your DAGs, see the following:
  - `dag_processing.import_errors`—Gives the number of errors encountered while processing DAGs. Anything above zero is not good.
  - `dag_processing.total_parse_time`—Sudden large increases after adding/changing DAGs is not good.
  - `ti_failures`—The number of failed task instances.

- For understanding Airflow's performance, see the following:
  - `dag_processing.last_duration.[filename]`—Time taken to process a DAG file. High values indicate something bad.
  - `dag_processing.last_run.seconds_ago.[filename]`—The number of seconds since the scheduler last checked on the file containing DAGs. The higher the value, the worse it is; it means the scheduler is too busy. Values should be in the order of a few seconds at most.
  - `dagrun.[dag_id].first_task_scheduling_delay`—The delay between the scheduled execution date and actual execution date of a DAG run.
  - `executor.open_slots`—The number of free executor slots.
  - `executor.queued_tasks`—The number of tasks with queued state.
  - `executor.running_tasks`—The number of tasks with running state.

12.5   *How to get notified of a failing task*

When running any business-critical pipelines, we want to be notified of the incident the moment something goes wrong. Think of a failing task, or a task not finishing within an expected timeframe and delaying other processes. Let's look at various options Airflow provides for both detecting conditions that warrant alerts and sending the actual alerts.

12.5.1   *Alerting within DAGs and operators*

Within Airflow, there are several levels to configure alerts. First, within the definition of DAGs and operators, we can configure so-called *callbacks* (i.e., functions to call on certain events).

Listing 12.18   Defining a failure callback function to execute on DAG failure

```
def send_error():                    ◁──────────┐
    print("ERROR!")
                                         send_error is
                                         executed when
dag = DAG(                               a DAG run fails.
    dag_id="chapter12",
    on_failure_callback=send_error,   ◁──────────┘
    ...
)
```

The `on_failure_callback` is an argument on the DAG, which is executed whenever a DAG run fails. Think of sending a Slack message to an errors channel, a notification to an incident reporting system such as PagerDuty, or a plain old email. The function to execute is something you will need to implement yourself, though.

On a task level, there are more options to configure. You likely do not want to configure every task individually, so we can propagate configuration with the DAG's `default_args` down to all tasks.

Listing 12.19   Defining a failure callback function to execute on task failure

```
def send_error():
    print("ERROR!")



dag = DAG(
    dag_id="chapter12_task_failure_callback",
    default_args={"on_failure_callback": send_error},
    on_failure_callback=send_error,
    ...
)

failing_task = BashOperator(
    task_id="failing_task",
    bash_command="exit 1",
    dag=dag,
)
```

default_args
propagates arguments
down to tasks.

Note two notifications will be
sent here: one for task failure
and one for DAG failure.

This task will not return exit
code 0 and therefore fail.

The parent class of all operators (BaseOperator) holds an argument on_failure_
callback; therefore, all operators hold this argument. Setting on_failure_callback
in the default_args will set the configured arguments on all tasks in the DAG, so all
tasks will call send_error whenever an error occurs in listing 12.19. It is also possible
to set on_success_callback (in case of success) and on_retry_callback (in case a
task is retried).

While you could send an email yourself inside the function called by on_failure_
callback, Airflow provides a convenience argument, email_on_failure, which sends
an email without having to configure the message. However, you must configure
SMTP in the Airflow configuration; otherwise, no emails can be sent. This configuration is specific to Gmail.

Listing 12.20   Sample SMTP configuration for sending automated emails

```
AIRFLOW__SMTP__SMTP_HOST=smtp.gmail.com
AIRFLOW__SMTP__SMTP_MAIL_FROM=myname@gmail.com
AIRFLOW__SMTP__SMTP_PASSWORD=abcdefghijklmnop
AIRFLOW__SMTP__SMTP_PORT=587
AIRFLOW__SMTP__SMTP_SSL=False
AIRFLOW__SMTP__SMTP_STARTTLS=True
AIRFLOW__SMTP__SMTP_USER=myname@gmail.com
```

In fact, Airflow is configured to send emails by default, meaning there is an argument
email_on_failure on the BaseOperator which holds a default value of True. However, without the proper SMTP configuration, it will not email. Plus, a destination
email address must also be set on the email argument of an operator.

Listing 12.21   Configure email address to send alerts to

```
dag = DAG(
    dag_id="task_failure_email",
    default_args={"email": "bob@work.com"},
    ...
)
```

With the correct SMTP configuration and a destination email address configured, Airflow will now send an email notifying you of a failed task (figure 12.22).

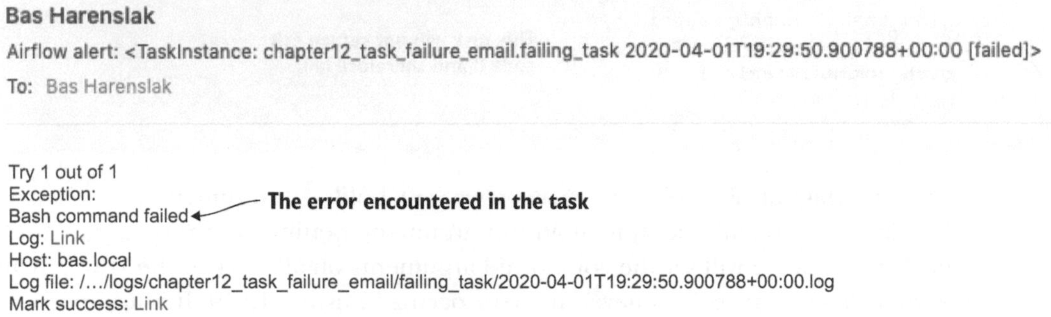

Bas Harenslak

Airflow alert: <TaskInstance: chapter12_task_failure_email.failing_task 2020-04-01T19:29:50.900788+00:00 [failed]>

To: Bas Harenslak

Try 1 out of 1
Exception:
Bash command failed ◄─────── **The error encountered in the task**
Log: Link
Host: bas.local
Log file: /…/logs/chapter12_task_failure_email/failing_task/2020-04-01T19:29:50.900788+00:00.log
Mark success: Link

Figure 12.22   Example email alert notification

The task logs will also tell us an email was sent:

```
INFO - Sent an alert email to ['bob@work.com']
```

12.5.2   *Defining service-level agreements*

Airflow also knows the concept of *SLAs* (service-level agreements). The general definition of an SLA is a certain standard to meet about a service or product. For example, your television provider may guarantee 99.999% uptime of television, meaning it's acceptable to have 5.26 minutes of downtime per year. In Airflow, we can configure SLAs on a task level to configure the latest acceptable date and time of a task's completion. If the SLA is not met, an email is sent or a self-defined callback function is called. To configure a date and time deadline to complete a task with an SLA, see the following.

Listing 12.22   Configuring an SLA

```
dag = DAG(
    dag_id="chapter12_task_sla",
    default_args={"email": "bob@work.com"},
    schedule_interval=datetime.timedelta(minutes=30),   ◄─┐  The DAG triggers
    start_date=datetime.datetime(2020, 1, 1, 12),          │  every 30 minutes,
                                                           └─ say 12:30.
```

```
        end_date=datetime.datetime(2020, 1, 1, 15),
)

sleeptask = BashOperator(
    task_id="sleeptask",
    bash_command="sleep 60",
    sla=datetime.timedelta(minutes=2),
    dag=dag,
)
```

This task sleeps
for 60 seconds.

The SLA defines the maximum delta
between scheduled DAG start and
task completion (e.g., 12:32).

SLAs function somewhat counter-intuitively. While you might expect them to function as maximum runtimes for given tasks, they function as the maximum time difference between the scheduled start of the DAG run and the completion of the task.

So, if your DAG starts at 12:30 and you want your task to finish no later than 14:30, you would configure a timedelta of two hours, even if you expect the task to run for just five minutes. An example argument to make for this seemingly obscure behavior is when you want a report to be sent no later than a certain time, say 14:30. If the data processing for the report takes longer than expected, the *send email with report* task would complete after the 14:30 deadline and an SLA would be triggered. The SLA condition itself is triggered around the time of the deadline instead of waiting for the completion of the task. If the task does not complete before the set deadline, an email is sent.

Listing 12.23   Sample missed SLA email report

```
Here's a list of tasks that missed their SLAs:
sleeptask on 2020-01-01T12:30:00+00:00

Blocking tasks:


        =,                    .=
      =.|         ,---.        |.=
      =.|      "-(:::::)-"     |.=
       \\__/`-.|.-'\__//
         `-| .::| .::|-'         Pillendreher
         _|`-._|_.-'|_           (Scarabaeus sacer)
        /.-|       | .::|-.\
       // ,|  .::|::::|. \\
       || //\:::::|::' /\\ ||
      /'\|| `._|__.' ||/'\
       ^    \\       //    ^
           /'\      /'\
            ^        ^
```

Yes, this ASCII art beetle is contained in the email! While the task in listing 12.22 serves as an example, setting an SLA can be desirable to detect a drift in your job. For example, if the input data of your job suddenly grows five times in size, causing the job to take considerably longer, you might consider re-evaluating certain parameters of your job. The drift in data size and resulting job duration can be detected with the help of an SLA.

The SLA email only notifies you of a missed SLA, so you might consider something other than email or your own format. This can be achieved with the `sla_miss_callback` argument. Confusingly, this is an argument on the DAG class, not on the `BaseOperator` class.

In case you're looking for a maximum runtime of a task, configure the `execution_timeout` argument on your operator. If the duration of the task exceeds the configured `execution_timeout`, it fails.

12.6   Scalability and performance

In sections 12.1 and 12.2, we covered the executor types Airflow offers:

- `SequentialExecutor` (default)
- `LocalExecutor`
- `CeleryExecutor`
- `KubernetesExecutor`

Let's take a closer look at how to configure Airflow and these executor types for adequate scalability and performance. By performance, we refer to the ability to respond quickly to events, without delays and as little waiting as possible. By scalability, we refer to the ability to handle a large (increase in) load without impact on the service.

We'd like to stress the importance of monitoring, as described in section 12.4. Without measuring and knowing the status of your system, optimizing anything is a guess in the dark. By measuring what you're doing, you know if a change has a positive effect on your system.

12.6.1   Controlling the maximum number of running tasks

Table 12.3 lists Airflow configurations that can control the number of tasks you may run in parallel. Note that the configuration items are somewhat oddly named, so read their description carefully.

Table 12.3   Overview of Airflow configurations related to running number of tasks

Configuration item	Default value	Description
`AIRFLOW__CORE__DAG_CONCURRENCY`	16	The maximum number of tasks to be in queued or running state, per DAG
`AIRFLOW__CORE__MAX_ACTIVE_RUNS_PER_DAG`	16	The maximum number of parallel DAG runs, per DAG
`AIRFLOW__CORE__PARALLELISM`	32	The maximum number of task instances to run in parallel, globally
`AIRFLOW__CELERY__WORKER_CONCURRENCY`	16	The maximum number of tasks per Celery worker (only for Celery)

If you're running a DAG with a large number of tasks, the default values limit your DAG to 16 parallel tasks due to `dag_concurrency` set to 16, even though `parallelism` is set to 32. A second DAG with a large number of tasks will also be limited at 16 parallel tasks, but together they will reach the global limit, 32, set by `parallelism`.

There is one more limiting factor to the global number of parallel tasks: by default, all tasks run in a pool named "default_pool," with 128 slots by default. `dag_concurrency` and `parallelism` will need to be increased before reaching the default_pool limit, though.

Specifically for the `CeleryExecutor`, the setting `AIRFLOW__CELERY__WORKER_CONCURRENCY` controls the number of processes per worker that Celery will handle. In our experience, Airflow can be quite resource consuming; therefore, account for at least 200 MB of RAM per process as a baseline for just having a worker with the configured concurrency number up and running. Also, estimate a worst-case scenario where your most resource-consuming tasks are running in parallel to estimate how many parallel tasks your Celery worker can handle. For specific DAGs, the default value `max_active_runs_per_dag` can be overridden with the `concurrency` argument on the DAG class.

On an individual task level, we can set the `pool` argument to run a specific task in a pool, which limits the number of tasks it can run. Pools can be applied for specific groups of tasks. For example, while it might be fine for your Airflow system to run 20 tasks querying a database and waiting for the result to return, it might be troublesome when 5 CPU-intensive tasks are started. To limit such high-resource tasks, you could assign these a dedicated `high_resource` pool with a low maximum number of tasks.

Also, on a task level, we can set the `task_concurrency` argument, which provides an additional limit of the specific task over multiple runs of the task. This can, again, be useful in case of a resource-intensive task, which can claim all resources of the machine when running with many instances in parallel (figure 12.23).

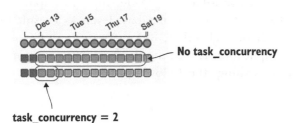

Figure 12.23 `task_concurrency` can limit the number of parallel executions of a task.

12.6.2 *System performance configurations*

When running any considerable number of tasks, you might notice the load on the metastore rising. Airflow relies heavily on the database for storing all state. Every new Airflow version generally includes several performance-related improvements, so it helps to update regularly. We can also tune the number of queries performed on the database.

Raising the value of `AIRFLOW__SCHEDULER__SCHEDULER_HEARTBEAT_SEC` (default: 5) can lower the number of check-ins Airflow performs on the scheduler job, resulting in fewer database queries. 60 seconds is a reasonable value. The Airflow UI will display a warning 30 seconds after the last scheduler heartbeat was received, but this number is configurable with `AIRFLOW__SCHEDULER__SCHEDULER_HEALTH_CHECK_THRESHOLD`.

The value of `AIRFLOW__SCHEDULER__PARSING_PROCESSES` (default: 2; fixed to 1 if using SQLite) controls how many processes the task scheduling part of the scheduler spins simultaneously to process a DAG's state; each process takes care of checking if new DAG runs should be created, new task instances should be scheduled or queued, and so on. The higher this number, the more DAGs will be checked simultaneously and the lower latency between tasks. Raising this value comes at the cost of more CPU usage, so increase and measure changes gently.

Lastly, from a user perspective, it might be interesting to configure `AIRFLOW__SCHEDULER__DAG_DIR_LIST_INTERVAL` (default: 300 seconds). This setting determines how often the scheduler scans the DAG directory for new, previously unseen files. If you happen to add new DAG files frequently, you will find yourself waiting for it to appear in the Airflow UI. Lowering this value will make Airflow scan the DAGs directory for new files more often but at the cost of more CPU usage, so also lower this value carefully.

12.6.3 *Running multiple schedulers*

A highly anticipated feature of Airflow 2 is the possibility to horizontally scale the scheduler (this feature does not exist in Airflow 1). Because the scheduler is the heart and brains of Airflow, being able to run multiple instances of the scheduler, both for scalability and redundancy, has long been a desire in the Airflow community.

Distributed systems are complex, and most systems require the addition of a consensus algorithm to determine which process is the leader. In Airflow, the aim was to make system operations as simple as possible, and leadership was implemented by row-level locking (`SELECT ... FOR UPDATE`) on the database level. As a result, multiple schedulers can run independently of each other, without requiring any additional tools for consensus. The only implication is that the database must support certain locking concepts. At the time of writing, the following databases and versions are tested and supported:

- PostgreSQL 9.6+
- MySQL 8+

To scale the scheduler, simply start another scheduler process:

```
airflow scheduler
```

Each scheduler instance will figure out which tasks (represented by rows in the database) are available for processing, based on a first-come, first-serve principle, and no additional configuration is required. Once running multiple instances, if one of the machines on which one of the schedulers is running fails, it will no longer take down your Airflow, since the other scheduler instances will remain running.

Summary

- The `SequentialExecutor` and `LocalExecutor` are limited to one single machine but are easy to set up.
- The `CeleryExecutor` and `KubernetesExecutor` take more work to set up but allow scaling tasks over multiple machines.
- Prometheus and Grafana can be used for storing and visualizing metrics from Airflow.
- Failure callbacks and SLAs can send emails or custom notifications in case of certain events.
- Deploying Airflow on multiple machines is not trivial because Airflow tasks and scheduler(s) all require access to the DAGs directory.

Securing Airflow

13

This chapter covers

- Examining and configuring the RBAC interface for controlling access
- Granting access to a central set of users by connecting with an LDAP service
- Configuring a Fernet key to encrypt secrets in the database
- Securing traffic between your browser and the webserver
- Fetching secrets from a central secret management system

Given the nature of Airflow, a spider in the web orchestrating a series of tasks, it must connect with many systems and is therefore a desirable target to gain access to. To avoid unwanted access, in this chapter we discuss the security of Airflow. We cover various security-related use cases and elaborate on these with practical examples. Security is often seen as a topic of black magic, where the understanding of a plethora of technologies, abbreviations, and intricate details is deemed necessary. While this is not untrue, we wrote this chapter for readers with little security knowledge in mind, and hence highlight various key points to avoid unwanted actions on your Airflow installation, which should serve as a starting point.

Airflow interfaces

Airflow 1.x comes with two interfaces:

- The original interface, developed on top of Flask-Admin
- The RBAC interface, developed on top of Flask-AppBuilder (FAB)

Airflow initially shipped with the original interface and first introduced the role-based access control (RBAC) interface in Airflow 1.10.0. The RBAC interface provides a mechanism that restricts access by defining roles with corresponding permissions and assigning users to these roles. The original interface is, by default, open to the world. The RBAC interface comes with more security features.

While writing this book, the original interface became deprecated and was removed in Airflow 2.0. The RBAC interface is now the one and only interface, so this chapter covers only the RBAC interface. To enable the RBAC interface running Airflow 1.x, set `AIRFLOW__WEBSERVER__RBAC=True`.

13.1 Securing the Airflow web interface

Start the Airflow webserver by running `airflow webserver` and go to http://localhost:8080, where you will see a login screen (figure 13.1).

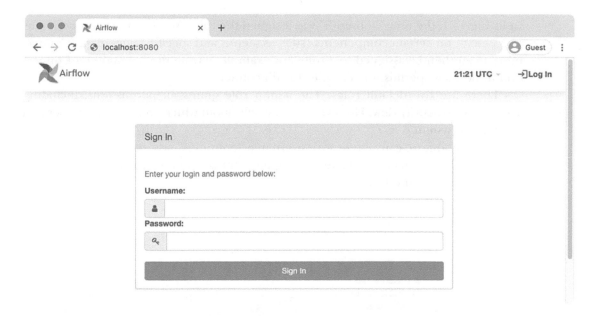

Figure 13.1 Home screen of the RBAC interface. Password authentication is enabled by default. No default user exists.

This is the first view of the RBAC interface. At this point, the webserver is asking for a username and password, but there are no users yet.

13.1.1   *Adding users to the RBAC interface*

We'll create an account for a user named Bob Smith.

Listing 13.1   Registering a user for the RBAC interface

```
airflow users create \
--role Admin \                       Admin role grants all
--username bobsmith \                permissions to this user.
--password topsecret \
--email bobsmith@company.com \       Leave out the --password
--firstname Bob \                    flag to prompt for a
--lastname Smith                     password.
```

This creates a user with a role named "Admin." The RBAC model consists of users, which are assigned to a (single) role with permissions (certain operations) assigned to those roles, which apply to certain components of the webserver interface (figure 13.2).

Figure 13.2   RBAC permissions model

In listing 13.1, the user "bobsmith" was assigned the role "Admin." Certain operations (e.g., edit) on certain components (such as menus and specific pages, e.g., "Connections") can then be assigned to a role. For example, having the "can edit on ConnectionModelView" permission allows us to edit connections.

There are five default roles. The admin role grants all permissions, including access to the security view. However, think wisely about which role to grant a user in a production system.

At this point, we can sign in with username "bobsmith" and password "topsecret." The main screen will look just like the original interface, but the top bar has a few new items, shown in figure 13.3.

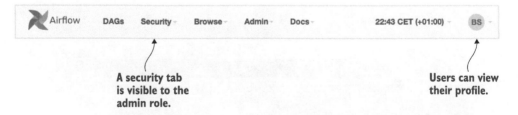

Figure 13.3   Top bar displaying menu items depending on the role and corresponding permissions your user has been granted

The security view is the most interesting feature of the RBAC interface. Opening the menu displays several options (figure 13.4).

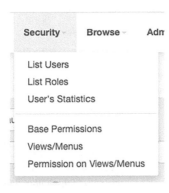

Figure 13.4   Options under the Security tab

Click List Roles to inspect all default roles (figure 13.5).

Figure 13.5   Default roles and corresponding permissions in Airflow. Several permissions are omitted for readability.

In the list roles view, we see the five roles available to use by default. The default permissions for these roles are given in table 13.1.

The just created "bobsmith" user was assigned the admin role, granting him all permissions (several permissions were omitted from figure 13.5 for readability). You might note the public role has no permissions. As the role name implies, all permissions attached to it are public (i.e., you do not have to be logged in). Say you want to allow people without an Airflow account to view the Docs menu (figure 13.6).

Table 13.1 Airflow RBAC interface default role permissions

Role name	Intended users/usage	Default permissions
Admin	Only necessary when managing security permissions	All permissions
Public	Unauthenticated users	No permissions
Viewer	Read-only view of Airflow	Read access to DAGs
User	Useful if you want strict separation in your team between developers who can and cannot edit secrets (connections, variables, etc.). This role only grants permissions to create DAGs, not secrets.	Same as viewer but with edit permissions (clear, trigger, pause, etc.) on DAGs
Op	All permissions required for developing Airflow DAGs	Same as user but with additional permissions to view and edit connections, pools, variables, XComs, and configuration

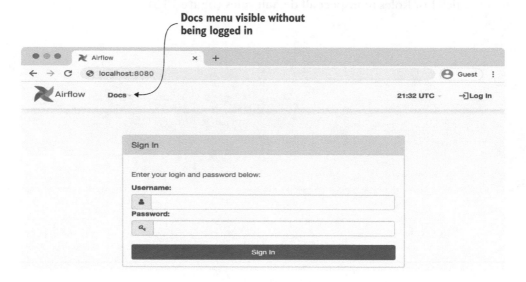

Docs menu visible without being logged in

Figure 13.6 Granting permissions to the public role makes components of the UI available to everybody.

To enable access to these components, we must edit the public role and add the correct permissions to it (figure 13.7).

The permissions are quite fine-grained; access to every menu and menu item is controlled by a permission. For example, to make the Docs menu visible, we must add the "menu access on Docs" permission. And to make the Documentation menu item within the Docs menu visible, we must add the "menu access on Documentation" permission. Finding the correct permissions can be cumbersome at times. It is easiest

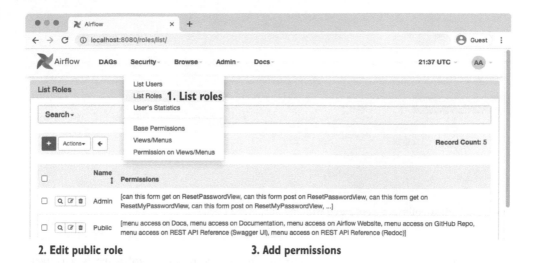

Figure 13.7 Adding permissions to the public role

to inspect the other roles to learn which permissions are available. Permissions are reflected by a string, which in most cases should be self-explanatory about the access it provides.

13.1.2 *Configuring the RBAC interface*

As noted, the RBAC interface is developed on top of the Flask-AppBuilder (FAB) framework. When you first run the RBAC webserver, you will find a file named web-server_config.py in $AIRFLOW_HOME. FAB can be configured with a file named config.py, but for clarity this same file was named webserver_config.py in Airflow. So, this file contains configuration to FAB, the underlying framework of Airflow's RBAC interface.

You can provide your own configuration to the RBAC interface by placing a web-server_config.py file in $AIRFLOW_HOME. If Airflow cannot find the file, it will generate a default one for you. For all details and available options in this file, refer to the FAB documentation. It holds all configurations for the RBAC interface (not just those that are security-related). For example, to configure a theme for your Airflow RBAC interface, set APP_THEME = "sandstone.css" in webserver_config.py. View the FAB documentation for all available themes (figure 13.8).

13.2 *Encrypting data at rest*

The RBAC interface requires users to exist in the database, with a username and password. This prevents random strangers "just looking around" from having access to Airflow, but is far from perfect. Before diving into encryption, let's look back at Airflow's basic architecture from figure 12.1.

Figure 13.8   RBAC interface configured with the sandstone theme

Airflow consists of several components. Every piece of software is a potential threat since it serves as a path through which uninvited guests can gain access to your systems (figure 13.9). Lowering the number of exposed entrance points (i.e., narrowing the *attack surface)* is therefore always a good idea. If you must expose a service for practical reasons, such as the Airflow webserver, always ensure it's not accessible publicly.[1]

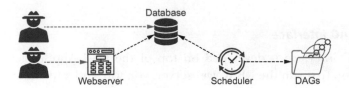

Figure 13.9   The webserver and database expose a service and can offer a potential access path for uninvited guests to Airflow. Protecting these will lower the attack surface.

13.2.1 *Creating a Fernet key*

You also want your data to be secure *after* an intruder has managed to gain access. Before creating any users and passwords, ensure encryption is enabled on your Airflow. Without encryption, passwords (and other secrets such as connections) are stored unencrypted in the database. Anybody with access to the database can then also read the passwords. When encrypted, they are stored as a sequence of seemingly random characters, which is essentially useless. Airflow can encrypt and decrypt secrets using a so-called Fernet key (figure 13.10).

---

[1] In any cloud, it's easy to expose a service to the internet. Simple measures you can take to avoid this include not using an external IP address and/or blocking all traffic and allowlisting your IP range only.

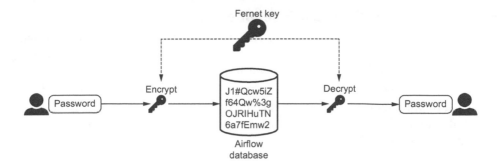

Figure 13.10 The Fernet key encrypts data before storing it in the database and decrypts data before reading it from the database. Without access to the Fernet key, passwords are useless to an intruder. One key for both encryption and decryption is called *symmetric encryption*.

The Fernet key is a secret string used for encryption and decryption. If this key is somehow lost, encrypted messages can no longer be decrypted. To provide Airflow with a Fernet key, we can generate one.

Listing 13.2 Creating a Fernet key

```python
from cryptography.fernet import Fernet

fernet_key = Fernet.generate_key()
print(fernet_key.decode())
# YlCImzjge_TeZc7jPJ7Jz2pgOtb4yTssA1pVyqIADWg=
```

Then we can provide it to Airflow by setting the AIRFLOW__CORE__FERNET_KEY configuration item:

```
AIRFLOW__CORE__FERNET_KEY=YlCImzjge_TeZc7jPJ7Jz2pgOtb4yTssA1pVyqIADWg=
```

Airflow will now use the given key to encrypt and decrypt secrets such as connections, variables, and user passwords. Now we can create our first user and safely store their password. Keep this key safe and secret, since anybody with access to it will be able to decrypt secrets; plus, you will not be able to decrypt secrets if you ever lose it!

To avoid storing the Fernet key in plain text in an environment variable, you can configure Airflow to read the value from a Bash command (e.g., cat /path/to/secret) instead. The command itself can be set in an environment variable: AIRFLOW__CORE __FERNET_KEY_CMD=cat /path/to/secret. The file holding the secret value can then be made read-only to only the Airflow user.

13.3   *Connecting with an LDAP service*

As demonstrated in section 13.1, we can create and store users in Airflow itself. In most companies, however, there are typically existing systems in place for user management. Wouldn't it be much more convenient to connect Airflow to such a user management system instead of managing your own set of users with yet another password?

A popular method for user management is via a service supporting the *LDAP protocol* (lightweight directory access protocol), such as Azure AD or OpenLDAP, which are called *directory services.*

> **NOTE**   Throughout this section, we will use the term *LDAP service* to indicate a directory service supporting queries via the LDAP protocol. A directory service is a storage system, typically used for storing information about resources such as users and services. LDAP is the protocol via which most of these directory services can be queried.

When Airflow is connected to an LDAP service, user information is fetched from the LDAP service in the background upon logging in (figure 13.11).

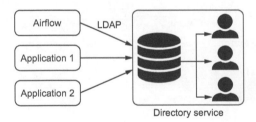

Figure 13.11   **Users are stored in a directory service such as Azure AD or OpenLDAP, which can be accessed with LDAP. This way, a user is created only once and connects to all applications.**

We first give a small introduction into LDAP and its corresponding technologies (section 13.3.1) and next demonstrate how to connect Airflow to an LDAP service (section 13.3.2).

13.3.1   *Understanding LDAP*

The relationship between SQL and a relational database (e.g., PostgreSQL or MySQL) is similar to the relationship between LDAP and a directory service (e.g., Azure AD or OpenLDAP). Just like a relational database stores data and SQL is used to query the data, a directory service also stores data (albeit in a different structure), and LDAP is used to query the directory service.

However, relational databases and directory services are built for different purposes: relational databases are designed for transactional use of any data you desire to store, while directory services are designed for high volumes of read operations, where the data follows a phonebook-like structure (e.g., employees in a company or devices within a building). For example, a relational database is more suitable for supporting a payment system since payments are made often and payment analysis involves different types of aggregation. A directory service, on the other hand, is more suitable for storing user accounts since these are requested often but usually do not change.

In a directory service, entities (e.g., users, printers, or network shares) are stored in a hierarchical structure named a *directory information tree* (DIT). Each entity is called an *entry*, where information is stored as key-value pairs named *attributes* and *values*. Also, each entry is uniquely identified by a *distinguished name* (DN). Visually, data in a directory service is represented like figure 13.12.

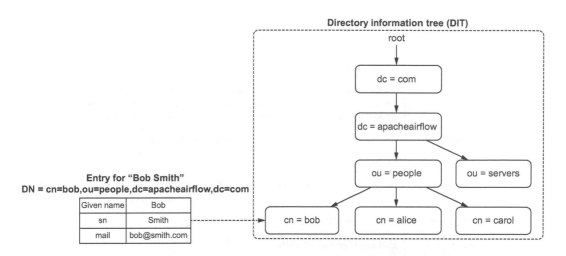

Figure 13.12 **Information in a directory service is stored in a hierarchical structure named DIT. Entries represent an entity such as a person and hold key-value attributes about the entity.**

You might wonder why we demonstrate this hierarchy and what the abbreviations *dc*, *ou*, and *cn* stand for. While a directory service is a database in which you can theoretically store any data, there are set LDAP requirements for how to store and structure data.[2] One of the conventions is to start the tree with a so-called *domain component* (dc), which we see in figure 13.12 represented as dc=com and dc=apacheairflow. As the name suggests, these are *components* of the domain, so your company domain is split by the dots, for example apacheairflow and com.

Next we have ou=people and cn=bob. *ou* is short for *organizational unit*, and *cn* is short for *common name*. While nothing is telling you how to structure your DIT, these are commonly used components.

The LDAP standard defines various *ObjectClasses*, which define a certain entity together with certain keys. For example, the ObjectClass *person* defines a human being with keys such as *sn* (surname, required) and *initials* (optional). Because the LDAP

---

[2] The standards are defined in RFC 4510-4519.

standard defined such ObjectClasses, applications reading the LDAP service are certain to always find the surname of a person in the field named sn, and thus any application that can query an LDAP service knows where to find the desired information.

Now that we know the main components of a directory service and how information is stored inside, what exactly is LDAP and how does it connect with a directory service? Just like SQL provides certain statements such as SELECT, INSERT, UPDATE, and DELETE, the LDAP provides a set of operations on a directory service (table 13.2).

Table 13.2   Overview of LDAP operations

LDAP operation	Description
Abandon	Abort a previously requested operation.
Add	Create a new entry.
Bind	Authenticate as a given user. Technically, the first connection to a directory service is anonymous. The bind operation then changes the identity to a given user, which allows you to perform certain operations on the directory service.
Compare	Check if a given entry contains a given attribute value.
Delete	Remove an entry.
Extended	Request an operation not defined by the LDAP standard but that is available on the directory service (depends on the type of directory service you're connecting to).
Modify DN	Change the DN of an entry.
Modify	Edit attributes of an entry.
Search	Search and return entries that match given criteria.
Unbind	Close the connection to a directory service.

For only fetching user information, we will require the operations bind (to authenticate as a user with permissions to read users in the directory service), search (to search for a given DN), and unbind to close the connection.

A search query contains a set of filters, typically a DN selecting part of the DIT, plus several conditions the entries must meet, such as uid=bsmith. This is what any application querying an LDAP service does under the hood.[3]

Listing 13.3   Example LDAP searches

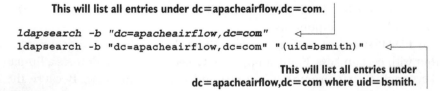

```
                This will list all entries under dc=apacheairflow,dc=com.

ldapsearch -b "dc=apacheairflow,dc=com"          ◁
ldapsearch -b "dc=apacheairflow,dc=com" "(uid=bsmith)"   ◁

                              This will list all entries under
                              dc=apacheairflow,dc=com where uid=bsmith.
```

---

[3] ldapsearch requires installation of the ldap-utils package.

Applications communicating with an LDAP service will perform such searches to fetch and validate user information for authentication to the application.

13.3.2 Fetching users from an LDAP service

LDAP authentication is supported via FAB; therefore, we must configure it in webserver_config.py (in $AIRFLOW_HOME). When configured correctly and upon logging in, FAB will search the LDAP service for the given username and password.

> **Listing 13.4 Configuring LDAP synchronization in webserver_config.py**

```
from flask_appbuilder.security.manager import AUTH_LDAP

AUTH_TYPE = AUTH_LDAP
AUTH_USER_REGISTRATION = True                    The default role assigned
AUTH_USER_REGISTRATION_ROLE = "User"      ◁──   to any user logging in

AUTH_LDAP_SERVER = "ldap://openldap:389"
AUTH_LDAP_USE_TLS = False                         Section of the DIT
AUTH_LDAP_SEARCH = "dc=apacheairflow,dc=com"  ◁─ to search for users
AUTH_LDAP_BIND_USER = "cn=admin,dc=apacheairflow,dc=com"   User on the LDAP
AUTH_LDAP_BIND_PASSWORD = "admin"                          service to connect
AUTH_LDAP_UID_FIELD = "uid"    ◁─                          (bind) with and
                                   Name of the field in    search
                                   LDAP service to search
                                   for username
```

If found, FAB will allow the found user access to the role configured by AUTH_USER _REGISTRATION_ROLE. At the time of writing, no feature exists to map LDAP groups to Airflow RBAC roles.[4]

With LDAP set up, you no longer have to manually create and maintain users in Airflow. All users are stored in the LDAP service, which is the only system in which user information will be stored, and all applications (including Airflow) will be able to verify user credentials in the LDAP service without having to maintain their own.

13.4 Encrypting traffic to the webserver

An intruder can obtain data at various places in your system. One of these places is during the transfer of data between two systems, also known as *data in transit.* A *man-in-the-middle attack* (MITM) is an attack where two systems or people communicate with each other, while a third person intercepts the communication, reading the message (potentially containing passwords and such), and forwarding it so that nobody notices the interception (figure 13.13).

Having secrets intercepted by an unknown person is undesirable, so how do we secure Airflow such that data in transit is safe? The details about how a man-in-the-middle

---

[4] It is possible to manually edit the table ab_user_role in the metastore to assign a different role (after the first login).

Figure 13.13 A man-in-the-middle attack intercepts traffic between a user and the Airflow webserver. Traffic is read and forwarded so that the user does not notice the interception, while the attacker reads all traffic.

attack is performed are not in the scope of this book, but we will discuss how to mitigate the impact of a man-in-the-middle attack.

13.4.1 *Understanding HTTPS*

We can work with the Airflow webserver via a browser, which communicates with Airflow through the HTTP protocol (figure 13.14). To communicate with the Airflow webserver securely, we must do so over HTTPS (HTTP Secure). Before securing traffic to the webserver, let's understand the difference between HTTP and HTTPS. If you already know this, you can skip to section 13.4.2.

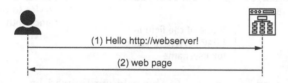

Figure 13.14 With HTTP, the validity of the caller is not checked, and data is transmitted in plain text.

What is different with HTTPS? To understand how HTTPS works and what the private key and certificate are for, let's first establish how HTTP works.

When browsing to an HTTP website, no checks are performed on either side (user's browser or webserver) to verify the identity of the request. All modern browsers display a warning of the insecure connection (figure 13.15).

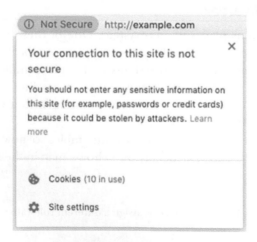

Figure 13.15 Navigating to http://example.com in Google Chrome will display "Not Secure" because HTTP traffic is unsecured.

Now that we know HTTP traffic is not secure, how does HTTPS traffic help us? First, from a user's perspective, modern browsers will display a lock or something green to indicate a valid certificate (figure 13.16).

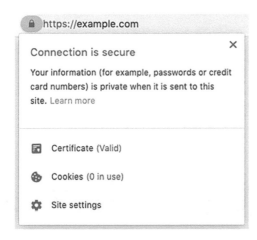

Figure 13.16 **Navigating to an HTTPS website in Google Chrome displays a lock (if the certificate is valid) to indicate a secure connection.**

When your browser and a webserver communicate over HTTPS, the initial handshake involves more steps to verify the validity of the remote side (figure 13.17).

Figure 13.17 **At the start of an HTTPS session, the browser and webserver agree on a mutual session key to encrypt and decrypt traffic between the two.**

The encryption used in HTTPS is TLS (transport layer security), which uses both *asymmetric encryption* and *symmetric encryption*. Whereas symmetric encryption applies a single key for both encryption and decryption, asymmetric encryption consists of two keys: public and private. The magic of asymmetric encryption is that data encrypted with the public key can only be decrypted with the private key (which only the webserver knows), and data encrypted with the private key can only be decrypted with the public key (figure 13.18).

At the start of an HTTPS session, the webserver first returns the certificate, which is a file with a publicly shareable key. The browser returns a randomly generated session key

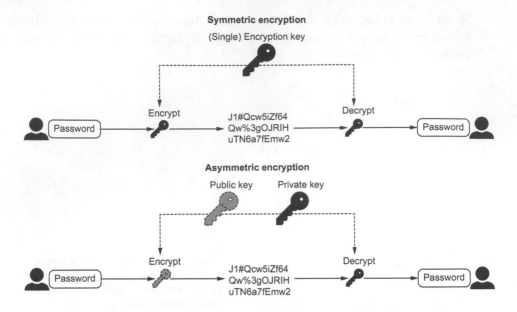

Figure 13.18   Using symmetric encryption, a loss of the encryption key allows others to both encrypt and decrypt messages. With asymmetric encryption, a public key is shared with others, but a loss of the public key does not compromise security.

to the webserver, encrypted with the public key. Only the private key can decrypt this message, which only the webserver should have access to. For this reason, it's important to never share the private key; anybody with this key is able to decrypt the traffic.

13.4.2   *Configuring a certificate for HTTPS*

Airflow consists of various components, and you want to avoid attacks on and between all of them, regardless if they're being used externally (e.g., exposed on a URL such as the webserver), or internally (e.g., traffic between the scheduler and database). Detecting and avoiding a man-in-the-middle attack can be difficult. However, it is straightforward to render the data useless to an attacker by encrypting the traffic.

By default, we communicate with Airflow over HTTP. When browsing to Airflow, we can tell if the traffic is encrypted by the URL: http(s)://localhost:8080. All HTTP traffic is transferred in plain text; a man-in-the-middle reading the traffic could intercept and read passwords as they're transmitted. HTTPS traffic means data is encrypted on one end and decrypted on the other. A man-in-the-middle reading HTTPS traffic will be unable to interpret the data because it's encrypted.

Let's view how to secure the one public endpoint in Airflow: the webserver. You will need two items:

- A private key (keep this secret)
- A certificate (safe to share)

We will elaborate on what these items entail later. For now, it's important to know the private key and certificate are both files provided by a *certificate authority* or a *self-signed certificate* (a certificate you generate yourself that is not signed by an official certificate authority).

Listing 13.5   Creating a self-signed certificate

```
openssl req \                                    Generate a key
-x509 \                                          valid for one year.
-newkey rsa:4096 \
-sha256 \                                        Filename of
-nodes \                                         private key
-days 365 \
-keyout privatekey.pem \                         Filename of
-out certificate.pem \                           certificate
-extensions san \
-config \
 <(echo "[req]";                                 Most browsers
    echo distinguished_name=req;                 require the SAN
    echo "[san]";                                extension for
    echo subjectAltName=DNS:localhost,IP:127.0.0.1   security reasons.
    ) \
-subj "/CN=localhost"
```

Both the private key and certificate must be stored on a path available to Airflow, and Airflow must be run with the following:

- AIRFLOW__WEBSERVER__WEB_SERVER_SSL_CERT=/path/to/certificate.pem
- AIRFLOW__WEBSERVER__WEB_SERVER_SSL_KEY=/path/to/privatekey.pem

Start the webserver and you will see that http://localhost:8080 does not serve the webserver anymore. Instead, it is served on https://localhost:8080 (figure 13.19).

At this point, traffic between your browser and the Airflow webserver is encrypted. While the traffic can be intercepted by an attacker, it will be useless to them since it's encrypted and thus unreadable. Only with the private key can the data be decrypted; that's why it's important to never share the private key and to keep it in a safe place.

When using the self-signed certificate, as generated in listing 13.5, you will initially receive a warning (Chrome displayed in figure 13.20).

Your computer holds a list of trusted certificates and their location, depending on your operating system. In most Linux systems, the trusted certificates are stored in /etc/ssl/certs. These certificates are provided with your operating system and agreed on by various authorities. These certificates enable you to go to https://www.google.com, receive Google's certificate, and verify it in your pre-trusted list of certificates because Google's certificate is shipped with your operating system.[5] Whenever your

---

[5] Various technical details are omitted for clarity. Storing billions of trusted certificates for all websites is impractical. Instead, few certificates high up in the chain are stored on your computer. Certificates are issued by certain trusted authorities. Reading a certificate should enable your browser to find the certificate's issuing authority, and their respective issuing authority, and again, until one of the certificates in the chain is found on your computer.

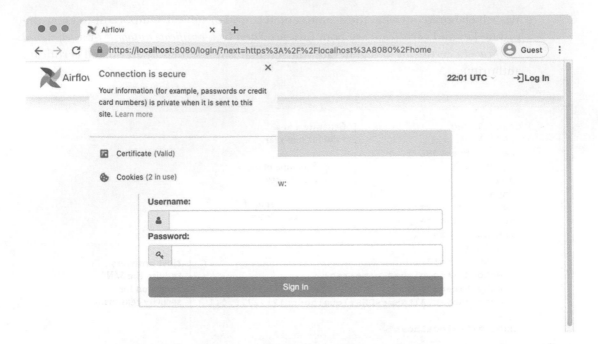

Figure 13.19   After providing a certificate and private key, the webserver is served on https://localhost:8080. Note that no official certificate can be issued for localhost; therefore, it must be self-signed. Self-signed certificates are by default untrusted, so you must add the certificate to your trusted certificates.

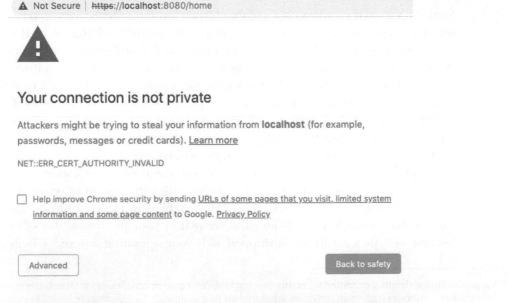

Figure 13.20   Most browsers display warnings when using self-signed certificates because their validity cannot be checked.

browser is directed to a website that returns a certificate not in this list, your browser will display a warning, as is the case when using our self-signed certificate. Therefore, we must tell our computer to trust our generated certificate, knowing we generated it ourselves and therefore trust it.

How to tell your computer to trust a certificate differs based on the operating system used. For macOS, it involves opening Keychain Access and importing your certificate in the system keychain (figure 13.21).

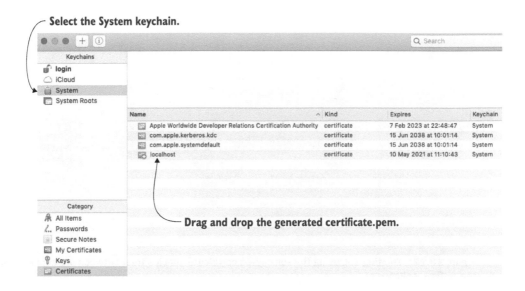

Figure 13.21 Adding a self-signed certificate to the system certificates on macOS

After this, the certificate is known to the system but still not trusted. To trust it, we must explicitly trust SSL when encountering the self-signed certificate (figure 13.22).

If you're hosting Airflow on an address accessible by others (i.e., not localhost), everybody will have to go through the hassle of trusting the self-signed certificate. This is obviously undesirable; therefore, you issue certificates by a trusted authority that can be validated. For further reading, search the internet for "TLS certificate" (for purchasing a certificate), or "Let's Encrypt" (for generating DNS-validated certificates, providing you with encryption).

13.5 *Fetching credentials from secret management systems*

Many companies apply a central secret storage system, enabling them to store secrets (passwords, certificates, keys, etc.) just once in one single system, and applications are able to request the secrets when needed without having to store their own. Examples include HashiCorp Vault, Azure Key Vault, AWS SSM, and GCP Secrets Manager. This avoids scattering secrets over various systems and instead keeps secrets all in a single

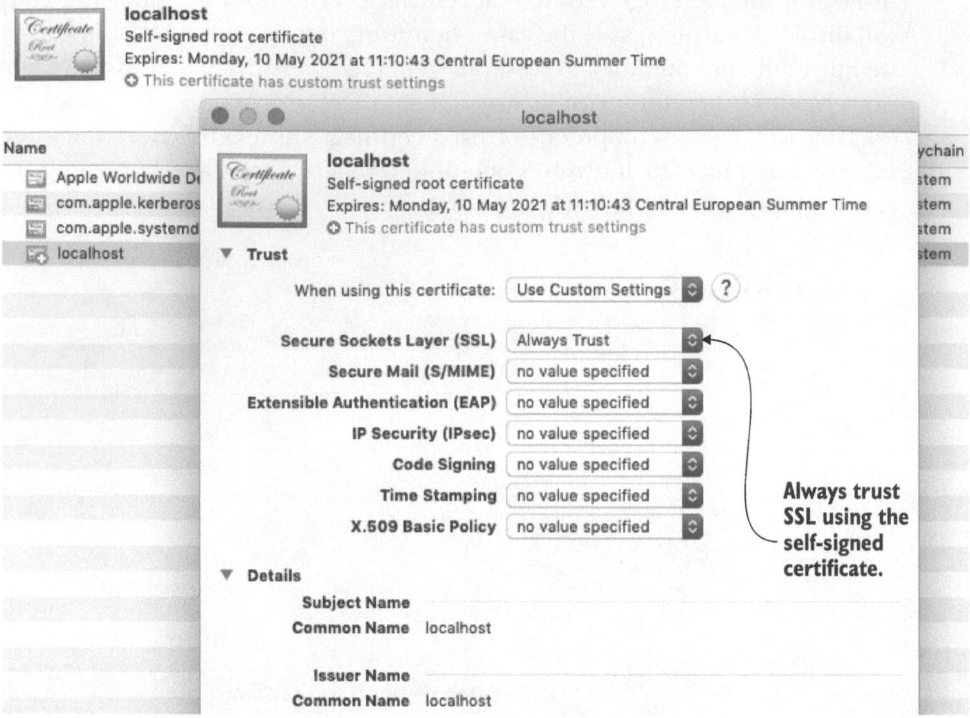

Figure 13.22   Trusting SSL using the self-signed certificate enables trust between our computer and the Airflow webserver.

system that is designed specifically for storing and managing secrets. Additionally, these systems provide features such as secret rotation and versioning, which you do not get in Airflow.

Secret values in Airflow can be stored in variables and connections. Wouldn't it be convenient and secure to connect with one of these secret storage systems instead of having to copy-paste secrets into Airflow? In Airflow 1.10.10, a new feature was introduced named the *Secrets Backend*, which provides a mechanism to fetch secrets from external secret storage systems while still using the existing variable and connection classes.

At the time of this writing, AWS SSM, GCP Secret Manager, and HashiCorp Vault are supported. The secrets backend provides a generic class that can be subclassed to implement and connect with your own desired secret storage system. Let's view an example using HashiCorp Vault.

Listing 13.6   Fetching connection details from a configured secrets backend

```
import airflow.utils.dates
from airflow.models import DAG
from airflow.providers.http.operators.http import SimpleHttpOperator
```

```
dag = DAG(
    dag_id="secretsbackend_with_vault",
    start_date=airflow.utils.dates.days_ago(1),
    schedule_interval=None,
)

call_api = SimpleHttpOperator(
    task_id="call_api",
    http_conn_id="secure_api",          Refers to the
    method="GET",                       secret id in Vault
    endpoint="",
    log_response=True,
    dag=dag,
)
```

As you can see in listing 13.6, there is no explicit reference to HashiCorp Vault in your DAG code. The SimpleHttpOperator makes an HTTP request, in this case to the URL set in the connection. Before the existence of secrets backends, you'd save the URL in an Airflow connection. Now we can save it in (among others) HashiCorp Vault. There are a couple of things to point out when doing this:

- Secrets backends must be configured with AIRFLOW__SECRETS__BACKEND and AIRFLOW__SECRETS__BACKEND_KWARGS.
- All secrets must have a common prefix.
- All connections must be stored in a key named "conn_uri."
- All variables must be stored in a key named "value."

The secret name is stored as a path (this applies to all secret managers), for example secret/connections/secure_api, where secret and connections can be seen as folders used for organization and secure_api is the name identifying the actual secret.

> **NOTE** The "secret" prefix is specific to the Vault backend. Refer to the Airflow documentation for all details of your secret backend of choice.

The hierarchical organization of secrets in all secret management systems allows Airflow to provide a generic secrets backend to interface with such systems. In the "Secrets Engines" section in HashiCorp Vault, the secret would be stored as displayed in figure 13.23.

Secrets Engines

:≡ **secret/**
v2 kv_cf711d62

Figure 13.23 Secrets in Vault are stored in "Secrets Engines," which can store secrets in various systems. By default, you get an engine named "secret" for storing key-value secrets.

Within a secret engine in Vault, we create a secret with the name connections/secure_api. While the prefix "connections/" is not necessary, Airflow's secrets backend takes a prefix under which it can search for secrets, which is convenient for searching within just one part of the secret hierarchy in Vault.

Storing an Airflow connection in any secret backend requires setting a key named conn_uri, which is the key Airflow will request (figure 13.24). The connection must be given in URI format. The URI will internally be passed to Airflow's connection class, where the proper details are extracted from the URI.

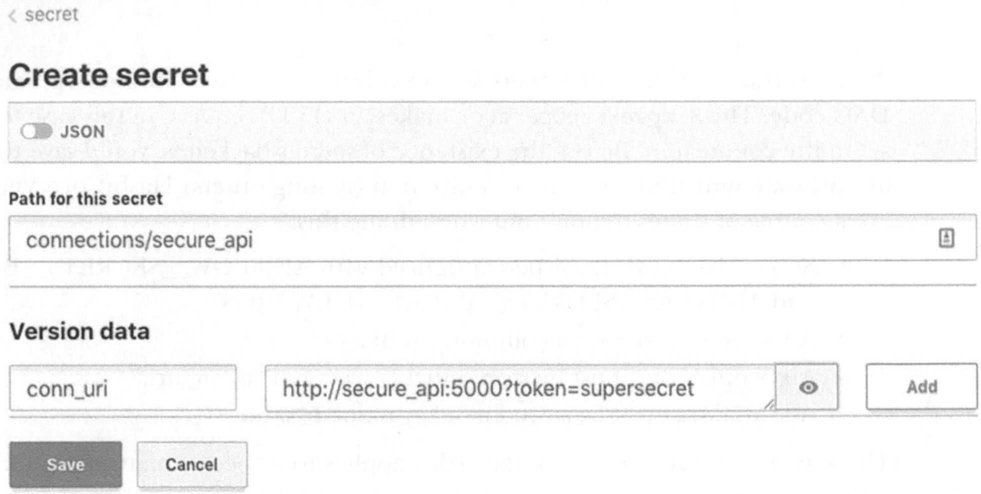

< secret

Create secret

◯ JSON

Path for this secret

```
connections/secure_api
```

Version data

| conn_uri | http://secure_api:5000?token=supersecret | ◉ | Add |

Save   Cancel

Figure 13.24   Saving Airflow connection details in Vault requires setting a key: conn_uri.

Say we have an API running on hostname secure_api, port 5000, and it requires a header with the name "token" and the value "supersecret" for authentication. To be parsed into an Airflow connection, the API details must be stored in URI format, as displayed in figure 13.24: `http://secure_api:5000?token=supersecret`

In Airflow, we must set two configuration options to fetch the credentials. First, AIRFLOW__SECRETS__BACKEND must be set to the class reading the secrets:

- HashiCorp Vault: airflow.providers.hashicorp.secrets.vault.VaultBackend
- AWS SSM: airflow.providers.amazon.aws.secrets.systems_manager.SystemsManagerParameterStoreBackend
- GCP Secret Manager: airflow.providers.google.cloud.secrets.secrets_manager.CloudSecretsManagerBackend

Next, various details specific to the chosen secrets backend must be configured in AIRFLOW__SECRETS__BACKEND_KWARGS. Refer to the Airflow documentation for all details of all secret backends. Take, for example, `BACKEND_KWARGS` for Vault: `{"url":"http://vault:8200","token":"airflow","connections_path":"connections"}`

Here, the `"url"` point to Vault's URL, `"token"` refers to a token for authenticating against Vault, and `"connections_path"` refers to the prefix to query for all connections. In the Vault backend, the default prefix for all secrets (both connections and variables) is set to `secret`. As a result, the full search query given a conn_id, "secure_api," becomes `secret/connections/secure_api`.

The secrets backend does not replace secrets stored in environment variables or the Airflow metastore. It's an alternative location to store secrets. The order of fetching secrets becomes the following:

1 Secret backend
2 Environment variables (`AIRFLOW_CONN_*` and `AIRFLOW_VAR_*`)
3 Airflow metastore

With a secret backend set up, we outsourced the storage and management of secret information into a system developed specifically for that purpose. Other systems can also connect to the secret management system so that you only store a secret value once, instead of distributing it over many systems, each with the potential for a breach. As a result, your attack surface becomes smaller.

Technically, the number of possibilities to breach into your systems are limitless. However, we've demonstrated various ways to secure data both inside and outside Airflow—all with the goal of limiting the number of options for an attacker and safeguarding against some of the most common ways attackers gain unwanted access. On a final note, ensure you keep up-to-date with Airflow releases, as these sometimes contain security fixes, closing bugs in older versions.

Summary

- In general, security does not focus on one item but involves securing various levels of your application to limit the potential attack surface.
- The RBAC interface features a role-based security mechanism to allow certain actions to the groups in which users are organized.
- Interception of traffic between the client and the Airflow webserver can be made useless by applying TLS encryption.
- Credentials in Airflow's database can be made unreadable to an attacker by encrypting the secrets with a Fernet key.
- A secret management system such as HashiCorp Vault can be used to store and manage secrets so that secrets are managed in one single location and shared only when needed with applications such as Airflow.

14

Project: Finding the fastest way to get around NYC

This chapter covers

- Setting up an Airflow pipeline from scratch
- Structuring intermediate output data
- Developing idempotent tasks
- Implementing one operator to handle multiple similar transformations

Transportation in New York City (NYC) can be hectic. It's always rush hour, but luckily there are more alternative ways of transportation than ever. In May 2013, Citi Bike started operating in New York City with 6,000 bikes. Over the years, Citi Bike has grown and expanded and has become a popular method of transportation in the city.

Another iconic method of transportation is the Yellow Cab taxi. Taxis were introduced in NYC in the late 1890s and have always been popular. However, in recent years the number of taxi drivers has plummeted, and many drivers started driving for ride-sharing services such as Uber and Lyft.

Regardless of what type of transportation you choose in NYC, typically the goal is to go from point A to point B as fast as possible. Luckily the city of New York is very active in publishing data, including rides from Citi Bikes and Yellow Taxis.

In this chapter, we try to answer this question: "If I were to go from A to B in NYC right now, which method of transportation is fastest?" We've created an Airflow mini project to extract and load data, transform it into a usable format, and ask the data which method of transportation is faster, depending on the neighborhoods you're traveling between and the time of the day.[1]

To make this mini project reproducible, a Docker Compose file was created running several services in Docker containers. This includes the following:

- One REST API serving Citi Bike data
- One file share serving Yellow Cab taxi data
- MinIO, an object store that supports the S3 protocol
- PostgreSQL database for querying and storing data
- A Flask application displaying results

This gives us the building blocks shown in figure 14.1.

Figure 14.1 Docker Compose file creates several services. Our task is to load data from the REST API and share and transform it to eventually view the fastest method of transportation on the resulting web page.

Our goal throughout this chapter is to use these building blocks to extract data from the REST API and share and develop a data pipeline connecting these dots. We choose MinIO since AWS S3 is often used for data storage and MinIO supports the S3 protocol. The results of the analysis will be written to the PostgreSQL database, and the web page will display the results. To get started, ensure your current directory holds the docker-compose.yml file and create all containers.

Listing 14.1 Running use case building blocks in Docker containers

```
$ docker-compose up -d
Creating network "airflow-use-case_default" with the default driver
Creating volume "airflow-use-case_logs" with default driver
Creating volume "airflow-use-case_s3" with default driver
Creating airflow-use-case_result_db_1       ... done
Creating airflow-use-case_citibike_db_1      ... done
Creating airflow-use-case_minio_1            ... done
Creating airflow-use-case_postgres_1         ... done
```

---

[1] Some of the ideas in this chapter are based on a blog post by Todd Schneider (https://toddwschneider .com/posts/taxi-vs-citi-bike-nyc), where he analyzes the fastest transportation method by applying a Monte Carlo simulation.

```
Creating airflow-use-case_nyc_transportation_api_1 ... done
Creating airflow-use-case_taxi_db_1                ... done
Creating airflow-use-case_webserver_1             ... done
Creating airflow-use-case_initdb_adduser_1        ... done
Creating airflow-use-case_scheduler_1             ... done
Creating airflow-use-case_minio_init_1            ... done
Creating airflow-use-case_citibike_api_1          ... done
Creating airflow-use-case_taxi_fileserver_1       ... done
```

This exposes the following services on localhost:[port], with [username]/[password] given between parentheses:

- 5432: Airflow PostgreSQL metastore (`airflow/airflow`)
- 5433: NYC Taxi Postgres DB (`taxi/ridetlc`)
- 5434: Citi Bike Postgres DB (`citi/cycling`)
- 5435: NYC Transportation results Postgres DB (`nyc/tr4N5p0RT4TI0N`)
- 8080: Airflow webserver (`airflow/airflow`)
- 8081: NYC Taxi static file server
- 8082: Citi Bike API (`citibike/cycling`)
- 8083: NYC Transportation web page
- 9000: MinIO (`AKIAIOSFODNN7EXAMPLE/wJalrXUtnFEMI/K7MDENG/bPxRfiCYEX-AMPLEKEY`)

Data for both the Yellow Cab and Citi Bikes rides has been made available in monthly batches:

- NYC Yellow Taxi: https://www1.nyc.gov/site/tlc/about/tlc-trip-record-data.page
- NYC Citi Bike: https://www.citibikenyc.com/system-data

The goal of this project is to demonstrate a real environment with several real challenges you might encounter and how to deal with them in Airflow. The data sets are released once a month. One-month intervals are quite long, and therefore we've created two APIs in the Docker Compose setup that provide the same data but on intervals configurable to a single minute. Also, the APIs mimic several characteristics of production systems such as authentication.

Let's look at a map of NYC to develop an idea for determining the fastest method of transportation (figure 14.2).

We can clearly see that Citi Bike stations are based only in the center of New York City. To give any meaningful advice about the fastest method of transportation, we are therefore limited to those zones where both Citi Bikes and Yellow Cab are present. In section 14.1, we will inspect the data and develop a plan of approach.

Figure 14.2   NYC Yellow Cab zones plotted with Citi Bike station locations

14.1 *Understanding the data*

The Docker Compose file provides two endpoints with the Yellow Cab and Citi Bike data:

- Yellow Cab data on http://localhost:8081
- Citi Bike data on http://localhost:8082

Let's examine how to query these endpoints and what data they return.

14.1.1 *Yellow Cab file share*

The Yellow Cab data is available on http://localhost:8081. Data is served as static CSV files, where each CSV file contains taxi rides finished in the last 15 minutes. It will keep only one full hour of data; data older than one hour is automatically removed. It does not require any authentication.

Listing 14.2   Sample request to the Yellow Cabfile share

```
$ curl http://localhost:8081
[
  ➥ { "name":"06-27-2020-16-15-00.csv", "type":"file", "mtime":"Sat, 27 Jun
    2020 16:15:02 GMT", "size":16193 },
  ➥ { "name":"06-27-2020-16-30-00.csv", "type":"file", "mtime":"Sat, 27 Jun
    2020 16:30:01 GMT", "size":16580 },
  ➥ { "name":"06-27-2020-16-45-00.csv", "type":"file", "mtime":"Sat, 27 Jun
    2020 16:45:01 GMT", "size":13728 },
  ➥ { "name":"06-27-2020-17-00-00.csv", "type":"file", "mtime":"Sat, 27 Jun
    2020 17:00:01 GMT", "size":15919 }
]
```

The index returns a list of available files. Each is a CSV file holding the Yellow Cab rides finished in the last 15 minutes, at the time given in the filename.

Listing 14.3   Sample snippet of Yellow Cab file

```
$ curl http://localhost:8081/06-27-2020-17-00-00.csv
➥ pickup_datetime,dropoff_datetime,pickup_locationid,dropoff_locationid,
    trip_distance
2020-06-27 14:57:32,2020-06-27 16:58:41,87,138,11.24
2020-06-27 14:47:40,2020-06-27 16:46:24,186,35,11.36
2020-06-27 14:47:01,2020-06-27 16:54:39,231,138,14.10
2020-06-27 15:39:34,2020-06-27 16:46:08,28,234,12.00
2020-06-27 15:26:09,2020-06-27 16:55:22,186,1,20.89
...
```

We can see each line represents one taxi ride, with a start and end time and start and end zone IDs.

14.1.2 *Citi Bike REST API*

The Citi Bike data is available on http://localhost:8082, which serves data via a REST API. This API enforces basic authentication, meaning we have to supply a username and password. The API returns Citi Bike rides finished within a configurable period of time.

Listing 14.4   Sample request to the Citi Bike REST API

```
$ date
Sat 27 Jun 2020 18:41:07 CEST                         Request data from
                                                         the last hour.
$ curl --user citibike:cycling http://localhost:8082/recent/hour/1   ⟵
```

```
[
 {
  "end_station_id": 3724,
  "end_station_latitude": 40.7667405590595,
  "end_station_longitude": -73.9790689945221,
  "end_station_name": "7 Ave & Central Park South",
  "start_station_id": 3159,
  "start_station_latitude": 40.77492513,
  "start_station_longitude": -73.98266566,
  "start_station_name": "W 67 St & Broadway",
  "starttime": "Sat, 27 Jun 2020 14:18:15 GMT",
  "stoptime": "Sat, 27 Jun 2020 15:32:59 GMT",
  "tripduration": 4483
 },
 {
  "end_station_id": 319,
  "end_station_latitude": 40.711066,
  "end_station_longitude": -74.009447,
  "end_station_name": "Fulton St & Broadway",
  "start_station_id": 3440,
  "start_station_latitude": 40.692418292578466,
  "start_station_longitude": -73.98949474096298,
  "start_station_name": "Fulton St & Adams St",
  "starttime": "Sat, 27 Jun 2020 10:47:18 GMT",
  "stoptime": "Sat, 27 Jun 2020 16:27:21 GMT",
  "tripduration": 20403
 },
 ...
]
```

Each JSON object represents one Citi Bike ride.

This query requests the Citi Bike rides finished in the last hour. Each record in the response represents one ride with Citi Bike and provides latitude/longitude coordinates of the start and end location as well as the start and end time. The endpoint can be configured to return rides at smaller or larger intervals:

```
http://localhost:8082/recent/<period>/<amount>
```

where <period> can be minute, hour, or day. The <amount> is an integer representing the number of given periods. For example, querying http://localhost:8082/recent/day/3 would return all Citi Bike rides finished in the last three days.

The API knows no limitations in terms of request size. In theory, we could request data for an infinite number of days. In practice, APIs often limit compute power and data transfer size. For example, an API could limit the number of results to 1,000. With such a limitation, you would have to know how many bike rides (approximately) are made within a certain time and make requests often enough to fetch all data while staying under the maximum 1,000 results.

14.1.3 Deciding on a plan of approach

Now that we've seen samples of the data in listings 14.3 and 14.4, let's lay out the facts and decide how to continue. To compare apples with apples, we must map locations in both data sets to something in common. The Yellow Cab ride data provides taxi zone IDs, and the Citi Bike data provides latitude/longitude coordinates of the bike stations. Let's simplify, enabling our use case but sacrificing a little on the accuracy, by mapping the latitude/longitude of Citi Bike stations to taxi zones (figure 14.3).

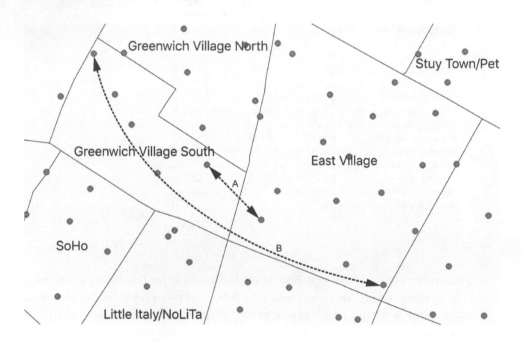

Figure 14.3   **Mapping Citi Bike stations (dots) to Yellow Cab zones enables accurate comparison but neglects the fact that rides within one zone can vary in distance. Ride A is obviously shorter than ride B. By averaging all ride times from Greenwich Village South to East Village, you lose such information.**

Since the Yellow Cab data is only provided for one hour on the file share, we must download and save it in our own systems. This way, we build a collection of historical taxi data over time and can always go back to the downloaded data if we change our processing. As mentioned, the Docker Compose file creates a MinIO service, which is an object storage service, so we'll use that to store the extracted data.

14.2   Extracting the data

When extracting multiple data sources, it is important to note the time intervals of the data. The Yellow Cab data is available at 15-minute intervals, and the Citi Bike data interval is configurable. To make it easy, let's also request Citi Bike data at 15-minute intervals. This allows you to make two requests at the same interval, in the same DAG, and process all data in parallel. If we choose a different interval, we have to align the processing of both data sets differently.

Listing 14.5 DAG running every 15 minutes

```
import airflow.utils.dates
from airflow.models import DAG

dag = DAG(
    dag_id="nyc_dag",
    schedule_interval="*/15 * * * *",          Run every
    start_date=airflow.utils.dates.days_ago(1), 15 minutes.
    catchup=False,
)
```

14.2.1 *Downloading Citi Bike data*

Within Airflow, we have the `SimpleHttpOperator` to make HTTP calls. However, this quickly turns out to not suit our use case: the `SimpleHttpOperator` simply makes an HTTP request but provides no functionality for storing the response anywhere.[2] In such a situation, you are quickly forced to implement your own functionality and call it with a `PythonOperator`.

Let's see how to query the Citi Bike API and store the output on the MinIO object storage.

Listing 14.6 Downloading data from the Citi Bike REST API onto MinIO

```
import json

import requests
from airflow.hooks.base import BaseHook
from airflow.models import DAG
from airflow.operators.python import PythonOperator
from airflow.providers.amazon.aws.hooks.s3 import S3Hook
from requests.auth import HTTPBasicAuth

                                                          Load Citi Bike
                                                          credentials from
def _download_citi_bike_data(ts_nodash, **_):            Airflow connection.
    citibike_conn = BaseHook.get_connection(conn_id="citibike")

    url = f"http://{citibike_conn.host}:{citibike_conn.port}/recent/minute/15"
    response = requests.get(url, auth=HTTPBasicAuth(citibike_conn.login,
        citibike_conn.password))
    data = response.json()
                                              Use S3Hook to
    s3_hook = S3Hook(aws_conn_id="s3")        communicate
    s3_hook.load_string(                      with MinIO.
        string_data=json.dumps(data),
        key=f"raw/citibike/{ts_nodash}.json",
```

Use the timestamp of the Airflow task in the resulting filename.

---

[2] By setting xcom_push=True, you can store the output in XCom.

```
        bucket_name="datalake"
    )


download_citi_bike_data = PythonOperator(
    task_id="download_citi_bike_data",
    python_callable=_download_citi_bike_data,
    dag=dag,
)
```

We have no Airflow operator to use for this specific HTTP-to-S3 operation, but we can apply Airflow hooks and connections. First, we must connect to the Citi Bike API (using the Python requests library) and MinIO storage (using the S3Hook). Since both require credentials to authenticate, we will store these in Airflow to be loaded at runtime.

Listing 14.7   Setting connection details via environment variables

```
➥ export AIRFLOW_CONN_CITIBIKE=http://citibike:cycling@citibike_api:5000
➥ export AIRFLOW_CONN_S3="s3://@?host=http://minio:9000&aws_access_key_id
    =AKIAIOSFODNN7EXAMPLE&aws_secret_access_key=wJalrXUtnFEMI/K7MDENG/bPxRfi
    CYEXAMPLEKEY"         ◁——  Custom S3 host must be given via extras.
```

By default, the S3 hook communicates with AWS S3 on http://s3.amazonaws.com. Since we're running MinIO on a different address, we must provide this address in the connection details. Unfortunately, this isn't a straightforward task, and sometimes such oddities result in having to read a hook's implementation to understand its inner workings. In the case of the S3Hook, the hostname can be provided via a key host in the extras (figure 14.4).

```
AIRFLOW_CONN_S3=s3://@?host=http://minio:9000&aws_access_key_id=...&aws_secret_access_key=...
```

Where you expect to   **Hostname provided**
set the hostname   **via extras**

Figure 14.4   A custom S3 hostname can be set, but not where you would expect it.

Now that we have the connections set up, let's transfer some data.

Listing 14.8   Uploading a piece of data to MinIO using the S3Hook

```
s3_hook = S3Hook(aws_conn_id="s3")
s3_hook.load_string(
    string_data=json.dumps(data),
    key=f"raw/citibike/{ts_nodash}.json",    ◁——  Write to object with the
    bucket_name="datalake"                         task timestamp templated
)                                                  in key name.
```

If all succeeds, we can log in on the MinIO interface at http://localhost:9000 and view the first downloaded file (figure 14.5).

Timestamp set by ts_nodash

Figure 14.5 Screenshot of the MinIO interface showing a file written to /datalake/raw/citibike, and the filename templated with ts_nodash.

If you were to perform this HTTP-to-S3 operation more often with different parameters, you'd probably want to write an operator for this task to avoid code duplication.

14.2.2 Downloading Yellow Cab data

We also want to download taxi data on the MinIO object storage. This is also an HTTP-to-S3 operation, but it has a few different characteristics:

- The file share serves files, whereas we had to create new files on MinIO for the Citi Bike data.
- These are CSV files, while the Citi Bike API returns data in JSON format.
- We don't know the filenames upfront; we have to list the index to receive a file list.

When you encounter such specific features, it usually results in having to implement your own behavior instead of applying an Airflow built-in operator. Some Airflow operators are highly configurable, and some are not, but for such specific features, you mostly have to resort to implementing your own functionality. With that said, let's see a possible implementation.

Listing 14.9 Downloading data from the Yellow Cab file share onto MinIO storage

```
def _download_taxi_data():
    taxi_conn = BaseHook.get_connection(conn_id="taxi")
    s3_hook = S3Hook(aws_conn_id="s3")

    url = f"http://{taxi_conn.host}"          Get a list
    response = requests.get(url)          ◄─┘ of files.
    files = response.json()
```

```
    for filename in [f["name"] for f in files]:
        response = requests.get(f"{url}/{filename}")        ◁──┐  Get one single file.
        s3_key = f"raw/taxi/{filename}"
      ⮡ s3_hook.load_string(string_data=response.text, key=s3_key,
   bucket_name="datalake")                                  ◁─┐
                                                              │  Upload the file
                                                              │  to MinIO.
download_taxi_data = PythonOperator(
    task_id="download_taxi_data",
    python_callable=_download_taxi_data,
    dag=dag,
)
```

This code will download data from the file server and upload it to MinIO, but there is
a problem. Can you spot it?

s3_hook.load_string() is not an idempotent operation. It does not override files
and will only upload one (or string in this case) if it doesn't exist yet. If a file with the
same name already exists, it fails:

```
⮡ [2020-06-28 15:24:03,053] {taskinstance.py:1145} ERROR - The key
    raw/taxi/06-28-2020-14-30-00.csv already exists.
...
    raise ValueError("The key {key} already exists.".format(key=key))
ValueError: The key raw/taxi/06-28-2020-14-30-00.csv already exists.
```

To avoid failing on existing objects we could apply Python's EAFP idiom (try first and
catch exceptions, instead of checking every possible condition) to simply skip when
encountering a ValueError.

> **Listing 14.10   Downloading data from the Yellow Cab file share onto MinIO storage**

```
def _download_taxi_data():
    taxi_conn = BaseHook.get_connection(conn_id="taxi")
    s3_hook = S3Hook(aws_conn_id="s3")

    url = f"http://{taxi_conn.host}"
    response = requests.get(url)
    files = response.json()

    for filename in [f["name"] for f in files]:
        response = requests.get(f"{url}/{filename}")
        s3_key = f"raw/taxi/{filename}"
        try:
            s3_hook.load_string(
                string_data=response.text,
                key=s3_key,
                bucket_name="datalake",
            )                                          ◁─┐  Catch ValueError
            print(f"Uploaded {s3_key} to MinIO.")        │  exceptions raised when
        except ValueError:                               │  file already exists.
            print(f"File {s3_key} already exists.")
```

Figure 14.6   First two tasks of the NYC transportation DAG downloading data

Adding this check for existing files won't make our pipeline fail anymore! We now have two download tasks, which both download data on the MinIO storage (figure 14.6).

Data for both the Citi Bike API and Yellow Cab file share are downloaded on the MinIO storage (figure 14.7).

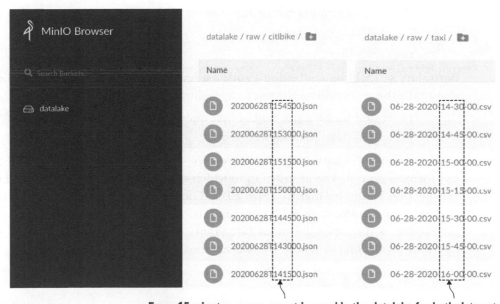

Figure 14.7   Data exported to the MinIO storage. We have MinIO under our own control and can always refer to these files later.

14.3   *Applying similar transformations to data*

After we've downloaded the Citi Bike and Yellow Cab data, we apply several transformations to map the Citi Bike station coordinates to Yellow Cab zones and to start accurately comparing them. There are various ways to do this, depending on the size of the data.

In a big-data scenario, you'd want to apply Apache Spark to process the data using a cluster of machines. A Spark job can be triggered with the SparkSubmitOperator or another operator that could trigger a Spark job such as the SSHOperator. The Spark job would then read from S3, apply transformations to the data, and write back to S3.

On a smaller scale (i.e., data processable on a single machine), we can apply Pandas for this task, but there is no PandasOperator at the time of writing, so Pandas code is typically executed using the PythonOperator. Note that Python code is run on the same machine as Airflow, whereas a Spark job is typically executed on other machines dedicated for that task, which will not impact the resources of the Airflow machine. In the latter case, Airflow is only responsible for starting and monitoring the Spark job. If a Pandas job is hitting the limits of the machine's resources, it could, in theory, take down the machine, and Airflow with it.

Another way to avoid claiming the Airflow machine's resources is to offload the job to Kubernetes using the KubernetesPodOperator or a similar containerized system, such as AWS ECS, using the ECSOperator.

Let's assume we apply Pandas for processing small data. Instead of demonstrating how to use yet another PythonOperator, let's look at how we can generalize some components for reusability and code deduplication. We have two data sets stored in /raw:

- /raw/citibike/{ts_nodash}.json
- /raw/taxi/*.csv

Both data sets will be read using Pandas, a few transformations will be applied, and eventually the result will be written to the following:

- /processed/citibike/{ts_nodash}.parquet
- /processed/taxi/{ts_nodash}.parquet

While the input formats differ, the object type into which they're loaded and the output formats do not. The abstraction to which operations are applied in Pandas is the Pandas DataFrame (similar to a Spark DataFrame). There are a few small differences between our transformations, input data sets, and output file locations, but the core abstraction is the same: a Pandas DataFrame. Hence, we could implement a single operator for dealing with both transformations.

Listing 14.11   A single operator for all Pandas DataFrame operations

```
import logging

from airflow.models import BaseOperator
from airflow.utils.decorators import apply_defaults
```

```
class PandasOperator(BaseOperator):
    template_fields = (
        "_input_callable_kwargs",          All kwargs arguments
        "_transform_callable_kwargs",      can hold templated
        "_output_callable_kwargs",         values.
    )

    @apply_defaults
    def __init__(
        self,
        input_callable,
        output_callable,
        transform_callable=None,
        input_callable_kwargs=None,
        transform_callable_kwargs=None,
        output_callable_kwargs=None,
        **kwargs,
    ):
        super().__init__(**kwargs)

        # Attributes for reading data
        self._input_callable = input_callable
        self._input_callable_kwargs = input_callable_kwargs or {}

        # Attributes for transformations
        self._transform_callable = transform_callable
        self._transform_callable_kwargs = transform_callable_kwargs or {}

        # Attributes for writing data
        self._output_callable = output_callable
        self._output_callable_kwargs = output_callable_kwargs or {}

    def execute(self, context):
        df = self._input_callable(**self._input_callable_kwargs)
        logging.info("Read DataFrame with shape: %s.", df.shape)

        if self._transform_callable:
            df = self._transform_callable(
                df,
                **self._transform_callable_kwargs,
            )
            logging.info("DataFrame shape after transform: %s.", df.shape)

        self._output_callable(df, **self._output_callable_kwargs)
```

Call the input callable to return a Pandas DataFrame. → `df = self._input_callable(**self._input_callable_kwargs)`

Apply transformations on the DataFrame. → `df = self._transform_callable(...)`

Write DataFrame. → `self._output_callable(df, **self._output_callable_kwargs)`

Let's break down how to use this `PandasOperator`. As mentioned, the commonality between various transformations is the Pandas DataFrame. We use this commonality to compose operations on the DataFrame given three functions:

- `input_callable`
- `transform_callable` (optional)
- `output_callable`

The `input_callable` reads data into a Pandas DataFrame, the `transform_callable` applies transformations to this DataFrame, and the `output_callable` writes the DataFrame. As long as the input/output of all three functions is a Pandas DataFrame, we can mix and match callables to process the data using this `PandasOperator`. Let's look at an example.

Listing 14.12 Applying the PandasOperator from listing 14.11

```
process_taxi_data = PandasOperator(
    task_id="process_taxi_data",
    input_callable=get_minio_object,                 ◁——  Read CSV from
    input_callable_kwargs={                                MinIO storage.
        "pandas_read_callable": pd.read_csv,
        "bucket": "datalake",
        "paths": "{{ ti.xcom_pull(task_ids='download_taxi_data') }}",
    },
    transform_callable=transform_taxi_data,          ◁——  Apply transformations
    output_callable=write_minio_object,                    on DataFrame.
    output_callable_kwargs={
        "bucket": "datalake",
        "path": "processed/taxi/{{ ts_nodash }}.parquet",
        "pandas_write_callable": pd.DataFrame.to_parquet,
        "pandas_write_callable_kwargs": {"engine": "auto"},
    },
    dag=dag,
)
```

Write Parquet to MinIO storage. (points to output_callable and pandas_write_callable lines)

The goal of the `PandasOperator` is to provide a single operator that allows mixing and matching various input, transformation, and output functions. As a result, defining an Airflow task glues these functions together by pointing to them and providing their arguments. We start with the input function, which returns a Pandas DataFrame, as follows.

Listing 14.13 Example function reading MinIO objects and returning Pandas DataFrames

```
def get_minio_object(
    pandas_read_callable,
    bucket,
    paths,
    pandas_read_callable_kwargs=None,
):
    s3_conn = BaseHook.get_connection(conn_id="s3")      Initialize a
    minio_client = Minio(                              ◁—— MinIO client.
        s3_conn.extra_dejson["host"].split("://")[1],
        access_key=s3_conn.extra_dejson["aws_access_key_id"],
        secret_key=s3_conn.extra_dejson["aws_secret_access_key"],
        secure=False,
    )

    if isinstance(paths, str):
        paths = [paths]
```

```
    if pandas_read_callable_kwargs is None:
        pandas_read_callable_kwargs = {}

    dfs = []
    for path in paths:
        minio_object = minio_client.get_object(
            bucket_name=bucket,
            object_name=path,
        )
        df = pandas_read_callable(              ⟵─┐ Read the file
            minio_object,                            from MinIO.
            **pandas_read_callable_kwargs,
        )
        dfs.append(df)                    ┌─ Return the Pandas
    return pd.concat(dfs)          ⟵─────┘  DataFrame.
```

The transformation function, which adheres to "DataFrame in, DataFrame out" is as follows.

Listing 14.14 Example function transforming taxi data

```
def transform_taxi_data(df):              ⟵─┐ DataFrame in
 ➥  df[["pickup_datetime", "dropoff_datetime"]] = df[["pickup_datetime",
    "dropoff_datetime"]].apply(
        pd.to_datetime
    )
 ➥  df["tripduration"] = (df["dropoff_datetime"] - df["pickup_datetime"])
    .dt.total_seconds().astype(int)
    df = df.rename(
        columns={
            "pickup_datetime": "starttime",
            "pickup_locationid": "start_location_id",
            "dropoff_datetime": "stoptime",
            "dropoff_locationid": "end_location_id",
        }
    ).drop(columns=["trip_distance"])
    return df                    ⟵─┐
                                    └─ DataFrame out
```

And last, the output function, which takes a Pandas DataFrame, is as follows.

Listing 14.15 Example function writing transformed DataFrame back to MinIO storage

```
def write_minio_object(
    df,
    pandas_write_callable,
    bucket,
    path,
    pandas_write_callable_kwargs=None
):
    s3_conn = BaseHook.get_connection(conn_id="s3")
    minio_client = Minio(
        s3_conn.extra_dejson["host"].split("://")[1],
        access_key=s3_conn.extra_dejson["aws_access_key_id"],
```

```
        secret_key=s3_conn.extra_dejson["aws_secret_access_key"],
        secure=False,
    )
bytes_buffer = io.BytesIO()
pandas_write_method = getattr(df, pandas_write_callable.__name__)
pandas_write_method(bytes_buffer, **pandas_write_callable_kwargs)
nbytes = bytes_buffer.tell()
bytes_buffer.seek(0)
minio_client.put_object(
        bucket_name=bucket,
        object_name=path,
        length=nbytes,
        data=bytes_buffer,
    )
```

Fetch the reference to the DataFrame writing method (e.g., pd.DataFrame.to_parquet).

Call the DataFrame writing method to write the DataFrame to a bytes buffer, which can be stored in MinIO.

Store the bytes buffer in MinIO.

Passing Pandas DataFrames between the input, transform, and output functions now provides the option to change the input format of a data set simply by changing the argument "pandas_read_callable": pd.read_csv to, for example, "pandas_read_callable": pd.read_parquet. As a result, we don't have to re-implement logic with every change or every new data set, resulting in no code duplication and more flexibility.

NOTE Whenever you find yourself repeating logic and wanting to develop a single piece of logic to cover multiple cases, think of something your operations have in common, for example a Pandas DataFrame or a Python file-like object.

14.4 Structuring a data pipeline

As you read in the previous section, we created the folders "Raw" and "Processed" in a bucket named "datalake." How did we get to those and why? In terms of efficiency, we could, in principle, write a single Python function that extracts data, transforms it, and writes the results to a database, all while keeping the data in memory and never touching the file system. This would be much faster, so why don't we?

First, data is often used by more than one person or data pipeline. In order to distribute and reuse it, it's stored in a location where other people and processes can read the data.

But more importantly, we want to make our pipeline reproducible. What does reproducibility imply in terms of a data pipeline? Data is never perfect, and software is always in progress; this means we want to be able to go back to previous DAG runs and rerun a pipeline with the data that was processed. If we're extracting data from a web service such as a REST API, which only returns a result for the state at that given point in time, we cannot go back to the API and ask for the same result from two months ago. In that situation, it's best to keep an unedited copy of the result. For privacy reasons, sometimes certain parts of the data are redacted, which is inevitable, but the starting point of a reproducible data pipeline should be to store a copy of the input data (that is edited as little as possible). This data is typically stored in a raw folder (figure 14.8).

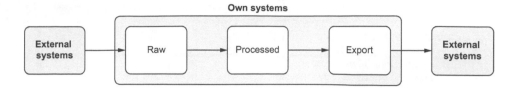

Figure 14.8   We cannot control the structure of data in external systems. In our own systems, it's logical to store data according to the life cycle of data. For example, unedited data is stored in Raw, derived and transformed data is stored in Processed, and data sets ready for transfer are stored in Export.

From this raw data, you (and others) can then alter, enrich, refine, transform, and mingle with it as much as you like, which is then written back to a processed folder. Transformations are often compute- and time-intensive, so we try to avoid rerunning a task and saving the results such that processed results can easily be read again.

In practice, many organizations apply more fine-grained separations between the stages of data, for example Raw > Preprocessed > Enriched > Processed > Export. No one structure suits all; your project and the project's requirements will determine how to best structure the movement of data.

14.5   Developing idempotent data pipelines

Now that we have data in the raw folder, we will process it and insert the results in a Postgres database. Since this chapter isn't about the best way to process data with Pandas or Spark, we will not discuss the details of this transformation job. Instead, let's reiterate an important aspect of data pipelines in general, namely ensuring a data pipeline can be executed multiple times without having to manually reset state or introduce a change in the results (idempotency).

There are two points in this data pipeline where we could introduce idempotency. The first is easy: when transforming the raw data into a processed state and storing it in a /processed folder, we should set a flag to overwrite destination files. This ensures rerunning a task will not fail due to an already existing output path.

The second stage, where we write results into the database, is less evident. Rerunning a task writing results to a database might not fail but could result in duplicate rows that might pollute the results. How can we ensure results are being written to a database in idempotent fashion so that we can rerun pipelines without duplicating results?

One way is to add a column to the table that can identify something unique about the job writing to the database, for example, the execution date of the Airflow job. Say we're using Pandas to write a DataFrame to a database, as shown in the following listing.

Listing 14.16 Writing a Pandas DataFrame to a SQL database

Pandas DataFrame and table structure must match.

```
--CREATE TABLE citi_bike_rides(
--    tripduration INTEGER,
--    starttime TIMESTAMP,
--    start_location_id INTEGER,
--    stoptime TIMESTAMP,
--    end_location_id INTEGER
--);

df = pd.read_csv(... citi bike data ...)
engine = sqlalchemy.create_engine(
    BaseHook.get_connection(self._postgres_conn_id).get_uri()
)
df.to_sql("citi_bike_rides", con=engine, index=False, if_exists="append")
```

There is no way to tell when executing df.to_sql() if we're going to insert already existing rows into the table. In this situation, we could alter the database table to add a column for Airflow's execution date.

Listing 14.17 Writing a Pandas DataFrame to a SQL database in one operation

```
--CREATE TABLE citi_bike_rides(
--    tripduration INTEGER,
--    starttime TIMESTAMP,
--    start_location_id INTEGER,
--    stoptime TIMESTAMP,
--    end_location_id INTEGER,
--    airflow_execution_date TIMESTAMP
--);

df = pd.read_csv(... citi bike data ...)
df["airflow_execution_date"] = pd.Timestamp(          Add execution_date
    context["execution_date"].timestamp(),            as a column to
    unit='s',                                         Pandas dataframe.
)
engine = sqlalchemy.create_engine(
    BaseHook.get_connection(self._postgres_conn_id).get_uri()
)
with engine.begin() as conn:          ◁─────  Begin a transaction.
    conn.execute(
        "DELETE FROM citi_bike_rides"
        f"WHERE airflow_execution_date='{context['execution_date']}';"
    )
    df.to_sql("citi_bike_rides", con=conn, index=False, if_exists="append")
```

First delete any existing records with the current execution_date.

In this example, we start a database transaction because the interaction with the database is twofold: first we delete any existing rows with a given execution date, and then we insert the new rows. If there are no existing rows with a given execution date, nothing is deleted. The two SQL statements (df.to_sql() executes SQL under the hood) are wrapped in a transaction, which is an atomic operation, meaning either both queries complete successfully or none do. This ensures no remainders are leftover in case of failure.

Once the data is processed and stored successfully in the database, we can start a web application on http://localhost:8083, which queries the results in the database (figure 14.9).

Start location	End location	Weekday	Time group	Avg time Citi Bike	Avg time Taxi
Alphabet City	East Village	Sunday	8 AM - 11 AM	1057.2	330.0
Alphabet City	Penn Station/Madison Sq West	Sunday	8 AM - 11 AM	1023.0	1318.0
Astoria	Long Island City/Hunters Point	Sunday	8 AM - 11 AM	700.0	358.0
Astoria	Old Astoria	Sunday	10 PM - 8 AM	206.0	1757.0
Astoria	Steinway	Sunday	8 AM - 11 AM	725.0	705.0
Battery Park City	Clinton East	Sunday	8 AM - 11 AM	1551.0	1788.0
Battery Park City	East Chelsea	Saturday	4 PM - 7 PM	715.0	913.0
Battery Park City	Financial District North	Sunday	8 AM - 11 AM	388.5	415.75

Figure 14.9 Web application displaying results stored in the PostgreSQL database, continuously updated by the Airflow DAG

The results display which method of transportation is faster between two neighborhoods at a given time. For example (row 1), on Sunday between 8:00 and 11:00, traveling from Alphabet City to East Village is (on average) faster by taxi: 330 seconds (5.5 minutes) by taxi versus 1057.2 (17.62 minutes) by Citi Bike.

Airflow now triggers jobs downloading, transforming, and storing data in the Postgres database at 15-minute intervals. For a real user-facing application, you probably want a better looking and more searchable frontend, but from the backend perspective, we now have an automated data pipeline, automatically running at 15-minute intervals and showing whether a taxi or Citi Bike is faster between given neighborhoods at given times, that is visualized in the table in figure 14.9.

Summary

- Developing idempotent tasks can be different based on case.
- Storing intermediate data ensures we can resume (partial) pipelines.
- When an operator's functionality does not fulfill, you must reside to calling a function with a `PythonOperator` or implement your own operator.

Part 4

In the clouds

At this point, you should be well on your way to mastering Airflow—being able to write complex pipelines and knowing how to deploy Airflow in a production-like setting.

So far, we've focused on running Airflow on a local system, either natively or using container technologies such as Docker. A common question is how to run and use Airflow in cloud settings, as many modern technological landscapes involve cloud platforms. Part 4 focuses entirely on running Airflow in the clouds, including topics such as designing architectures for Airflow deployments and leveraging the built-in functionality of Airflow to call various cloud services.

First, in chapter 15, we give a short introduction into the different components involved in designing cloud-based Airflow deployments. We'll also briefly discuss Airflow's built-in functionality for interacting with various cloud services and touch on vendor-managed Airflow deployments, which may save you from rolling your own deployment in the cloud.

After this introduction, we'll dive into specific Airflow implementations for several cloud platforms: Amazon AWS (chapter 16), Microsoft Azure (chapter 17), and Google Cloud Platform (chapter 18). In each of these chapters, we'll design architectures for deploying Airflow using services from the corresponding platform and discuss built-in Airflow functionality for interacting with platform-specific services. Finally, we'll close each chapter with an example use case.

After completing part 4, you should have a good idea of how to design an Airflow deployment for your cloud of interest. You should also be able to build pipelines that smoothly integrate with cloud services to leverage the scale of the clouds in your workflows.

Airflow in the clouds

This chapter covers

- Examining the components required to build Airflow cloud deployments
- Introduction to cloud-specific hooks/operators for integrating with cloud services
- Vendor-managed services as alternatives to rolling your own deployment

In this chapter, we'll start exploring how to deploy and integrate Airflow in cloud environments. First, we'll revisit the various components of Airflow and how these fit together in cloud deployments. We'll use this breakdown to map each of the components to their cloud-specific counterparts in Amazon AWS (chapter 16), Microsoft Azure (chapter 17), and Google Cloud Platform (chapter 18). Then we'll briefly introduce cloud-specific hooks/operators, which can be used to integrate with specific cloud services. We'll also provide some managed alternatives for deploying Airflow and discuss several criteria you should consider when weighing rolling your own deployment versus using a vendor-managed solution.

15.1 *Designing (cloud) deployment strategies*

Before we start designing deployment strategies for Airflow in the different clouds (AWS, Azure and GCP), let's start by reviewing the different components of Airflow (e.g., webserver, scheduler, workers) and what kind of (shared) resources these components will need access to (e.g., DAGs, log storage, etc.). This will help us later when mapping these components to the appropriate cloud services.

To keep things simple, we'll start with an Airflow deployment based on the Local-Executor. In this type of setup, the Airflow workers are running on the same machine as the scheduler, meaning we only need to set up two compute resources for Airflow: one for the webserver and one for the scheduler (figure 15.1).

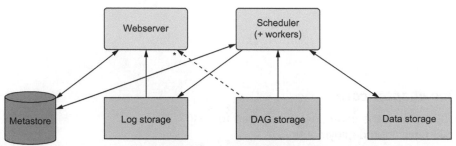

* In Airflow 1, the webserver needs access to the DAG directory unless DAG serialization is enabled. In Airflow 2, the webserver doesn't need access to the DAG directory.

Figure 15.1   Overview of the different compute and storage components involved in an Airflow deployment based on the LocalExecutor

Both the webserver and scheduler components will need access to a shared database (the Airflow metastore) and (depending on the version and configuration of Airflow[1]) shared storage for DAGs and logs. Depending on how you manage your data, you'll also want to have some external storage setup for storing any input and output data sets.

Besides these compute and storage resources, we also need to consider networking. Here we have two main concerns: how we will connect the different services together and how we organize our network setup to protect our internal services. As we will see, this typically involves setting up different network segments (public and private subnets) and connecting the different services to the appropriate subnets (figure 15.2). Additionally, a complete setup should also include services that protect any publicly exposed services from unauthorized access.

---

[1] In Airflow 1, both the Airflow webserver and scheduler require access to the DAG storage by default. In Airflow 1.10.10, an option was added for the webserver to store DAGs in the metastore so that it no longer requires access to the DAG storage if this option is enabled. In Airflow 2, this option is always enabled, so the webserver never needs access to the DAG storage.

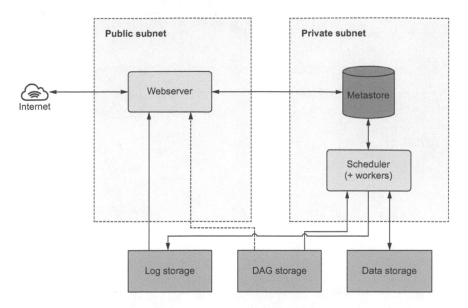

Figure 15.2   Networking overview for a deployment based on the `LocalExecutor`. Components are separated into two public/private subnets. Only publicly accessible services should be placed in the public subnet. Note that the storage services are drawn outside of both subnets, as many cloud storage services (e.g., AWS S3) are not necessarily bound to a given subnet. Nonetheless, these storage accounts should be protected from public access.

This gives us a fairly complete overview of the required components for a deployment based on the `LocalExecutor`.

Moving to the `CeleryExecutor` (which provides better scaling by running workers on separate machines) requires a little bit more effort, as Celery-based deployments require two extra resources: a pool of extra compute resources for the Airflow workers and a message broker that relays messages to the workers (figure 15.3).

These architecture sketches should hopefully give you some idea of the resources needed to implement the Airflow deployments in a cloud setting. In the following chapters, we'll dive into implementing these architectures on the different clouds.

15.2   Cloud-specific operators and hooks

Over the years, contributors to Airflow have developed a large number of operators and hooks that allow you to execute tasks involving different cloud services. For example, the `S3Hook` allows you to interact with the AWS S3 storage service (e.g., for uploading/downloading files), while the `BigQueryExecuteQueryOperator` allows you to execute queries on Google's BigQuery service.

In Airflow 2, these cloud-specific hooks and operators can be used by installing the corresponding provider packages. In earlier versions of Airflow, you can use the same functionality by installing the equivalent backport packages from PyPI.

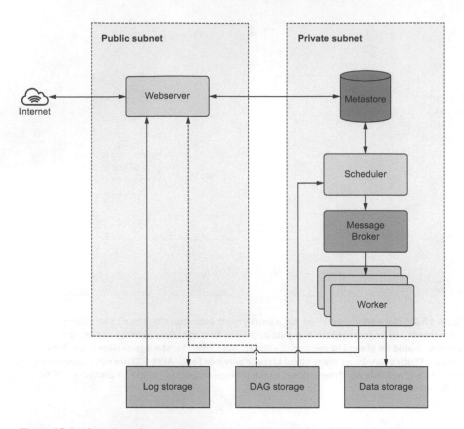

Figure 15.3   Overview of an architecture for an Airflow deployment based on the
`CeleryExecutor`. **Main additions include an extra pool of compute components for the**
Airflow workers and a message broker for relaying tasks. Note that the Celery-based setup
no longer requires the scheduler to have access to the data and log storages, as the worker
compute resources will be responsible for actually performing the work (and will therefore
actually be reading/writing data and generating log messages).

15.3 *Managed services*

Although rolling your own Airflow deployment can give you ultimate flexibility in how
you use it, setting up and maintaining such a deployment can be a lot of work. One
way to avoid this burden is to use a vendor-managed service, where you can offload
most of the work to an external provider. This provider will then typically give you
tools for easily creating and managing new Airflow deployments without all the hassle
of rolling your own. Usually the provider also promises to maintain the underlying
infrastructure so that you don't have to worry about keeping your operating system
and/or Airflow installation up-to-date with the latest security patches, monitoring the
systems, and so on.

Three prominent managed Airflow services are Astronomer.io, Google Cloud Composer, and Amazon MWAA. In the following sections, we'll provide a brief overview of
these services and their key features.

15.3.1 *Astronomer.io*

Astronomer.io is a Kubernetes-based solution for Airflow that can be used as a *SaaS* (software as a service) solution (Astronomer cloud), or can be deployed to your own Kubernetes cluster (Astronomer Enterprise). Compared to vanilla Airflow, Astronomer also provides extra tooling that helps you easily deploy Airflow instances from the UI or from their custom-built CLI. The CLI also allows you to run local instances of Airflow for development, which can ease DAG development (assuming you have Kubernetes available on your development machine).

Because it is built on Kubernetes, Astronomer.io should integrate well with any Kubernetes/Docker-based workflows you may be used to. This makes it easy to (for example) run your tasks in containers using the KubernetesExecutor and Kubernetes-PodOperator. Other deployment modes using the LocalExecutor or CeleryExecutor are also supported, giving you a lot of flexibility in how you run your jobs. Astronomer also allows you to customize your Airflow deployments by specifying extra OS or Python dependencies that should be installed into the cluster. Alternatively, you can build a custom Airflow base image should you need that extra flexibility.

Pricing for the SaaS solution is calculated using *Astronomer units* (AUs), with different configurations costing a different number of AUs. For an overview of these costs, see the Astronomer website (https://www.astronomer.io/).

It's also worth mentioning that Astronomer.io employs several key contributors to the Airflow project. As such, they contribute strongly to the Airflow project and regularly drive the development of important improvements to the open source version of Airflow, making sure everyone can benefit from these new features. Their helm charts for deploying Airflow on Kubernetes are also freely available online, should you want to try them outside of the Astronomer platform.

15.3.2 *Google Cloud Composer*

Google Cloud Composer is a managed version of Airflow that runs on top of the Google Cloud Platform (GCP). As such, Cloud Composer provides an easy, almost one-click solution for deploying Airflow into GCP that integrates well with its different services. GCP will also take care of managing the underlying resources, but you only pay for the resources they use. You can interact with Cloud Composer using the GCP CLI and/or monitor the state of your cluster(s) from within the GCP web interface.

Similar to Astronomer.io solution, Cloud Composer is also based on Kubernetes and runs on the Google Kubernetes Engine (GKE). A nice feature of Cloud Composer is that it integrates well with different services within GCP (such as Google Cloud Storage, BigQuery, etc.), making it easy to access these different services from within your DAGs. Cloud Composer also provides a lot of flexibility w.r.t. how you configure your Kubernetes cluster in terms of resources, and so on, so you can tune the deployment to your specific needs. Similar to Astronomer.io, you can install Python dependencies into your Airflow cluster(s) using the web interface or the GCP CLI.

Google Cloud composer includes a fee for the environment itself (number of nodes, database storage, network egress, etc.) in addition to costs for underlying services (GKE, Google Cloud Storage,[2] etc). For an up-to-date overview of these costs, see the GCP website (https://cloud.google.com/).

As a strong proponent of open source software, Google also regularly contributes to the Airflow open source project, and has helped develop an extensive suite of operators for its different services to enable their usage from within Airflow.[3]

15.3.3 *Amazon Managed Workflows for Apache Airflow*

Amazon Managed Workflows for Apache Airflow (MWAA) is an AWS service that allows you to easily create managed Airflow deployments in the AWS cloud, similar to Google's Cloud Composer. When using MWAA to run Airflow, the service will manage the underlying infrastructure and scale your deployment to meet the demands of your workflows. Additionally, Airflow deployments in MWAA are also promised to integrate well with AWS services such as S3, RedShift, Sagemaker, and with AWS CloudWatch for logging/alerting and AWS IAM for providing a single login for the web interface and securing access to your data.

Similar to the other managed solutions, MWAA uses the `CeleryExecutor` for scaling workers based on the current workload, with the underlying infrastructure managed for you. DAGs can be added or edited by uploading them to a predefined S3 bucket, where they will be deployed into your Airflow environment. Similar S3-based approaches can be used to install additional Airflow plug-ins or Python requirements into the cluster as needed.

Pricing includes a base fee for the Airflow environment itself and an additional fee for each of the Airflow worker instances. In both cases, you have the option to choose between small/medium/large machines to tailor the deployment to your specific use case. The dynamic scaling of workers means that worker use should be relatively cost-effective. There is also an extra (monthly) storage cost for the Airflow metastore, as well as any storage required for your DAGs or data. See the AWS website for an up-to-date overview and more details (https://aws.amazon.com/).

15.4   *Choosing a deployment strategy*

When picking a platform for running your Airflow workloads, we recommend examining the detailed features of the different offerings (and their pricing) to determine which service is best suited for your situation. In general, rolling your own deployment in one of the clouds will give you the most flexibility in choosing which components to use for running Airflow and how to integrate these into any existing cloud or on-site solution you already have. On the other hand, implementing your own cloud

---

[2] Used by Cloud Composer for storing DAGs and logs.

[3] Note that you don't necessarily need to use Google Composer to use these operators, as they also function perfectly fine from within Airflow (assuming permissions are set up correctly).

deployment requires some considerable work and expertise, especially if you want to keep a close eye on important factors such as security and cost management.

Using a managed solution allows you to push many of these responsibilities to a vendor, allowing you to focus on actually building your Airflow DAGs rather than on building and maintaining the required infrastructure. However, managed solutions may not always be flexible enough for your needs, if you have complicated requirements.

As an example, some important considerations may include the following:

- Do you want to use a Kubernetes-based workflow? If so, Astronomer.io or Google Cloud Platform provide an easy approach. Alternatively, you can roll your own Kubernetes cluster, for example using the Helm chart from Astronomer.io.
- Which services do you want to connect to from your DAGs? If you're heavily invested in GCP technologies, using Google Cloud Composer might be a no-brainer due to the easy integration between Composer and other GCP services. However, if you're looking to connect to on-site services or those in other clouds, running Airflow in GCP may make less sense.
- How do you want to deploy your DAGs? Both Astronomer.io and Google Cloud Composer provide an easy way to deploy DAGs using the CLI (Astronomer.io) or a cloud bucket (Cloud Composer). However, you might want to consider how you wish to tie this functionality into your CI/CD pipelines for automated deployments of new DAG versions, and so on.
- How much do you want to spend on your Airflow deployment? Kubernetes-based deployments can be expensive due to the costs of the underlying cluster. Other deployment strategies (using other compute solutions in the cloud) or SaaS solutions (like Astronomer.io) can be cheaper options. If you already have a Kubernetes cluster, you may also want to consider running Airflow on your own Kubernetes infrastructure.
- Do you need more fine-grained control or flexibility than provided by the managed services? In this case, you may want to roll your own deployment strategy (at the cost of more effort in setting up and maintaining the deployment, of course).

As this short list already demonstrates, there are many factors to consider when choosing a solution for deploying your Airflow cluster. While we cannot make this decision for you, we hope this provides you with some pointers to consider when choosing a solution.

Summary

- Airflow consists of several components (e.g., webserver, scheduler, metastore, storage) that need to be implemented using cloud services for cloud deployments.
- Airflow deployments with different executors (e.g., `Local`/`CeleryExecutors`) require different components that need to be accounted for in the deployment strategy.

- For integrating with cloud-specific services, Airflow provides cloud-specific hooks and operators that allow you to interact with the corresponding service.
- Vendor-managed services (e.g., Astronomer.io, Google Cloud Composer, Amazon MWAA) provide an easy alternative to rolling out your own deployment by managing many details for you.
- Choosing between vendor-managed services or creating your own cloud deployment will depend on many factors, with managed solutions providing greater ease in deployment and management at the expense of less flexibility and (possibly) higher running costs.

16

Airflow on AWS

> **This chapter covers**
>
> - Designing a deployment strategy for AWS using ECS, S3, EFS and RDS services
> - An overview of several AWS-specific hooks and operators
> - Demonstrating how to use AWS-specific hooks and operators with a use case

After our brief introduction in the previous chapter, this chapter will dive further into how to deploy and integrate Airflow with cloud services in Amazon AWS. First, we'll start by designing an Airflow deployment by mapping the different components of Airflow to AWS services. Then we'll explore some of the hooks and operators that Airflow provides for integrating with several key AWS services. Finally, we'll show how to use these AWS-specific operators and hooks to implement a use case for generating movie recommendations.

16.1 Deploying Airflow in AWS

In the previous chapter, we described the different components that comprise an Airflow deployment. In this section, we'll design a few deployment patterns for AWS by mapping them to specific AWS cloud services. This should give you a good idea of the process involved in designing an Airflow deployment for AWS and provide a good starting point for implementing one.

16.1.1 *Picking cloud services*

Starting with the Airflow webserver and scheduler components, one of the easiest approaches for running these components is probably Fargate, AWS's serverless compute engine for containers. One of the main advantages of Fargate (compared to other AWS services like ECS[1] or EKS[2]) is that it allows us to easily run containers in AWS without having to worry about provisioning and managing the underlying compute resources. This means we can simply provide Fargate with a definition of our webserver and scheduler container tasks and Fargate will take care of deploying, running, and monitoring the tasks for us.

For the Airflow metastore, we recommend looking toward AWS's hosted RDS solutions (e.g., Amazon RDS[3]), which helps with setting up relational databases in the cloud by taking care of time-consuming administration tasks such as hardware provisioning, database setup, patching, and backups. Amazon RDS provides several types of RDS engines you can choose from, including MySQL, Postgres, and Aurora (which is Amazon's proprietary database engine). In general, Airflow supports using all of these backends for its metastore, so your choice may depend on other requirements such as cost, or features such as high availability.

AWS provides several options for shared storage. The most prominent is S3, a scalable object storage system. S3 is generally great for storing large amounts of data with high durability and availability for a relatively low cost. As such, it is ideal for storing large data sets (which we may be processing in our DAGs) or storing temporary files such as the Airflow worker logs (which Airflow can write to S3 natively). A drawback of S3 is that it cannot be mounted as a local filesystem into the webserver or scheduler machines, making it less ideal for storing files such as DAGs, which Airflow requires local access to.

In contrast, AWS's EFS storage system is compatible with NFS and can therefore be mounted directly into the Airflow containers, making it suitable for storing DAGs. EFS is, however, quite a bit more expensive than S3, making it less ideal for storing data or our log files. Another drawback of EFS is that it is more difficult to upload files into EFS than S3, as AWS does not provide an easy web-based or CLI interface for copying files to EFS. For these reasons, it may still make sense to look to other storage options such as S3 (or alternatively Git) for storing DAGs and then use an automated process to sync the DAGs to EFS (as we will see later in this chapter).

Overall this gives us with the following setup (figure 16.1):

- Fargate for the compute components (Airflow webserver and scheduler)
- Amazon RDS (e.g., Aurora) for the Airflow metastore

---

[1] Elastic Compute Service, similar to Fargate but requires you to manage the underlying machines yourself.
[2] Elastic Kubernetes Service, AWS's managed solution for deploying and running Kubernetes.
[3] Amazon RDS includes several database types such as PostgreSQL, MySQL, and Aurora.

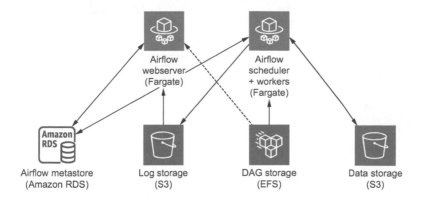

Figure 16.1 **Mapping the Airflow components from figure 15.1 to AWS services. Fargate is used for the compute components (webserver, scheduler, and workers), as it provides an easy and flexible container-based compute service. Amazon RDS is used as a managed database service for the metastore, while EFS and S3 are used for storage. Arrows indicate dependencies between the services.**

- S3 for storage of logs (and optionally also for data)
- EFS for storage of DAGs

16.1.2 *Designing the network*

We also need to consider how these services will be connected and how we can manage internet access to Airflow. A typical AWS networking setup is to create a VPC (virtual private cloud) containing both public and private subnets. In this type of setup, the private subnets inside the VPC can be used for services that should not be exposed directly to the internet, while the public subnets can be used to provide external access to services and outgoing connectivity to the internet.

We have a couple of services that need to be connected by network for our Airflow deployment. For example, both the webserver and scheduler containers need to have access to the Airflow metastore RDS and EFS for retrieving their DAGs. We can arrange this access by connecting both containers, the RDS and our EFS instance, to our private subnet, which will also ensure that these services are not directly accessible from the internet (figure 16.2). To provide access to S3 for our containers, we can also place a private S3 endpoint within the private subnet, which will ensure that any S3 bound traffic doesn't leave our VPC.

We also want to expose our Airflow webserver to the internet (with the proper access controls of course) so that we can access the webserver from our workspace. A typical approach is to place them behind an application load balancer (ALB), which is publicly accessible in the public subnet via an internet gateway. This ALB will handle any incoming connections and forward them to our webserver container if appropriate. To make sure that our webserver can also send back responses to our requests, we also need to place a NAT gateway in the public subnet.

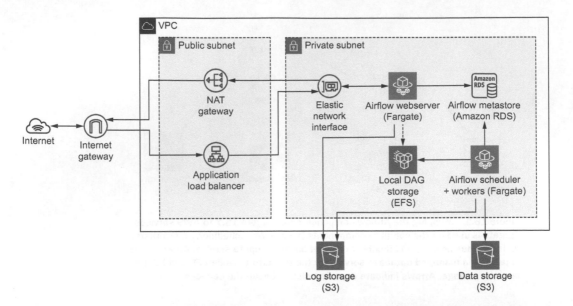

Figure 16.2 Projecting our components onto a network layout with public/private subnets. The public subnet provides access to the webserver over the internet via an application load balancer, coupled with an internet and NAT gateway for routing traffic from/to the internet. The private subnet ensures our compute/storage components can reach each other without being exposed online unintentionally. Arrows indicate the direction of information flowing between the services.

16.1.3 Adding DAG syncing

As mentioned before, a drawback of using EFS for storing DAGs is that EFS is not very easy to access using web-based interfaces or command line tools. As such, you may want to look toward setting up a process for automatically syncing DAGs from another storage backend, such as S3 or a Git repository.

One possible solution is to create a Lambda function that takes care of syncing DAGs from git or S3 to EFS (figure 16.3). This Lambda can be triggered (either by S3 events or a build pipeline in the case of Git) to sync any changed DAGs to EFS, making the changes available to Airflow.

16.1.4 Scaling with the CeleryExecutor

Although this setup should be robust enough to handle many workloads, we can improve the scalability of our Airflow deployment by switching to the `CeleryExecutor`. The main advantage of this switch is that the `CeleryExecutor` allows you to run each Airflow worker in its own container instance, thus substantially increasing the resources available to each worker.

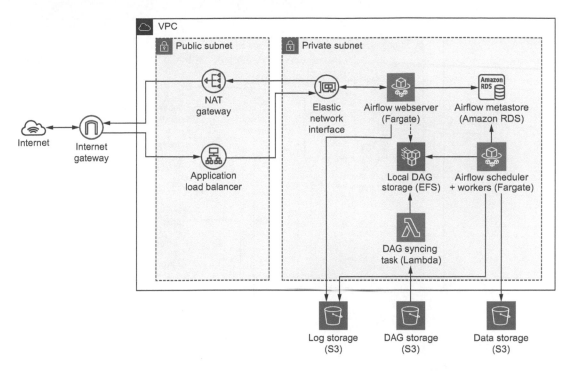

Figure 16.3 **Adding automated DAG syncing to our architecture. This allows us to store and edit DAGs in S3, which is generally easier to access and interact with than EFS. A Lambda service takes care of automatically syncing new DAGs from S3 to EFS.**

To use the `CeleryExecutor`, we have to make a number of changes to our design (figure 16.4). First, we need to set up a separate pool of Fargate tasks for the Airflow workers, which run in separate processes in the Celery-based setup. Note that these tasks also need to have access to the Airflow metastore and the logs bucket to be able to store their logs and results. Second, we need to add a message broker that relays jobs from the scheduler to the workers. Although we could choose to host our own message broker (e.g., RabbitMQ or possibly Redis) in Fargate or something similar, it is arguably easier to use AWS's SQS service, which provides a simple serverless message broker that requires little effort to maintain.

Of course, a drawback of using the `CeleryExecutor` is that the setup is a bit more complex than the `LocalExecutor` and therefore requires more effort. The added components (most notably the extra worker tasks) may also add some considerable costs for the extra compute resources required for each worker.

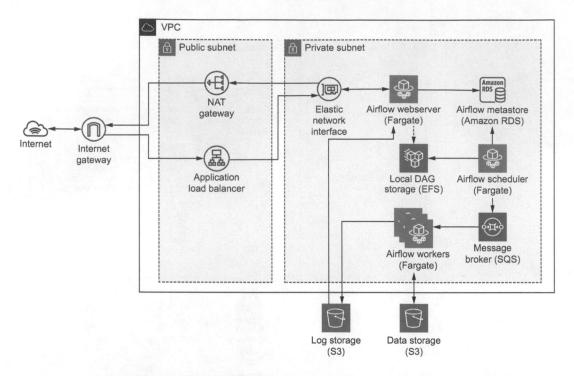

Figure 16.4   An alternative deployment based on the `CeleryExecutor`. The `CeleryExecutor` runs workers in separate compute processes, which are run as individual container instances on Fargate. Amazon's SQS service is used as a message broker to pass tasks to the workers after they have been scheduled.

16.1.5   *Further steps*

Although we have sketched some basic deployment strategies for Airflow in AWS, we should be careful to note that these setups should not be considered production-ready, as we still need to consider a number of factors.

First and foremost, security is an important consideration for production deployments. Although we have put some effort into shielding our different components from the public internet, we still need to consider further restricting access to components using security groups and network ACLs, limiting access to AWS resources using the appropriate IAM[4] roles and policies, and so on. At the Airflow level, you should also consider how you would like to secure Airflow (using Airflow's RBAC mechanism, etc.).

We would also expect production deployments to have a robust approach for logging, auditing, and tracking metrics and for raising alerts if issues are encountered with any of the deployed services. For this, we recommend looking at the corresponding services provided by AWS, including CloudTrail and CloudWatch.

---

[4] Identity and access management.

16.2 AWS-specific hooks and operators

Airflow provides a considerable number of built-in hooks/operators that allow you to interact with a great number of the AWS services. These allow you to (for example) coordinate processes involving moving and transforming data across the different services, as well as the deployment of any required resources. For an overview of all the available hooks and operators, see the Amazon/AWS provider package.[5]

Due to their large number, we won't go into any details of the AWS-specific hooks and operators but rather refer you to their documentation. However, tables 16.1 and 16.2 provide a brief overview of several hooks and operators with the AWS services they tie into and their respective applications. A demonstration of some of these hooks and operators is also provided in the next section.

Table 16.1 An excerpt of some of the AWS-specific hooks

Service	Description	Hook	Application(s)
Athena	Serverless big data queries	AWSAthenaHook	Execute queries, poll query status, retrieve results.
CloudFormation	Infrastructure resources (stacks) management	AWSCloudFormation Hook	Create and delete Cloud-Formation stacks.
EC2	VMs	EC2Hook	Retrieve details of VMs; wait for state changes.
Glue	Managed ETL service	AwsGlueJobHook	Create Glue jobs and check their status.
Lambda	Serverless functions	AwsLambdaHook	Invoke Lambda functions.
S3	Simple storage service	S3Hook	List and upload/download files.
SageMaker	Managed machine learning service	SageMakerHook	Create and manage machine learning jobs, endpoints, etc.

Table 16.2 An excerpt of some of the AWS-specific operators

Operator	Service	Description
AWSAthenaOperator	Athena	Execute a query on Athena.
CloudFormationCreateStackOperator	CloudFormation	Create a CloudFormation stack.
CloudFormationDeleteStackOperator	CloudFormation	Delete a CloudFormation stack.
S3CopyObjectOperator	S3	Copy objects in S3.
SageMakerTrainingOperator	SageMaker	Create a SageMaker training job.

---

[5] Can be installed in Airflow 2 using the `apache-airflow-providers-amazon` providers package, or in Airflow 1.10 using the backport package `apache-airflow-backport-providers-amazon`.

One hook that deserves special mention is the `AwsBaseHook`, which provides a generic interface to AWS services using AWS's boto3 library. To use the `AwsBaseHook`, instantiate it with a reference to an Airflow connection that contains the appropriate AWS credentials:

```
from airflow.providers.amazon.aws.hooks.base_aws import AwsBaseHook

hook = AwsBaseHook("my_aws_conn")
```

The required connection can be created in Airflow using the web UI (figure 16.5) or other configuration approaches (e.g., environment variables). The connection essentially requires two details: an access key and secret that point to an IAM user in AWS.[6]

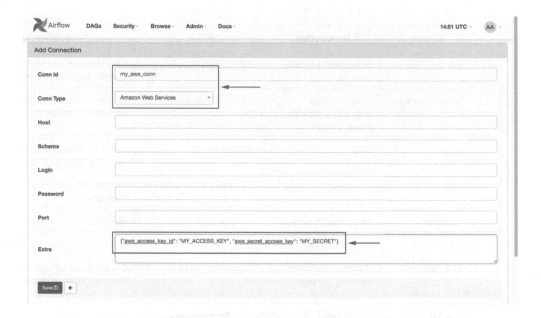

Figure 16.5   Creating a connection for the AWS hook in Airflow. Note that the access key and secret should be entered as a JSON construct in the extra field rather than in the login/password fields (contrary to what you might expect).

Once we have instantiated the hook, we can use it to create boto3 clients for different services using the `get_client_type` method. For example, you can create a client for the AWS Glue service as follows:

```
glue_client = hook.get_client_type("glue")
```

---

[6] We'll provide an example of how to obtain these details in the next section.

With this client, we can perform all kinds of operations on the Glue service in AWS. For more details on the different types of clients and the supported operations, you can reference the boto3 documentation (https://boto3.amazonaws.com/v1/documentation/api/latest/index.html). To be able to perform any of these operations, the hook's IAM user used should have the appropriate permissions in AWS. As such, make sure to assign the appropriate permissions to the respective user using IAM policies.

In the next section, we'll show an example of building a custom operator based on the AwsBaseHook, which demonstrates how this all ties together.

16.3 *Use case: Serverless movie ranking with AWS Athena*

To explore some of these AWS-specific features, let's turn to a small example.

16.3.1 *Overview*

In this example, we're interested in using some of the serverless services in AWS (S3, Glue, Athena) to analyze the movie data we encountered in previous chapters. Our goal is to find the most popular movies by ranking them by their average rating (using all the ratings up to that point in time). One of the advantages of using serverless services for this task is that we don't have to worry about running and maintaining any servers ourselves. This makes the overall setup relatively cheap (we only pay for things while they're running), and it requires relatively low maintenance.

To build this serverless movie ranking process, we need to implement a couple of steps:

- First, we fetch the movie ratings from our API and load them into S3 to make them available in AWS. We plan to load the data on a monthly basis so that we can calculate the ratings for each month as new data comes in.
- Second, we use AWS Glue (a serverless ETL service) to crawl the ratings data on S3. By doing so, Glue creates a table view of the data stored in S3, which we can subsequently query to calculate our rankings.
- Finally, we use AWS Athena (a serverless SQL query engine) to execute an SQL query on the ratings table to calculate our movie rankings. The output of this query is written to S3 so that we can use the rankings in any applications downstream.

This provides us with a relatively straightforward approach (figure 16.6) for ranking movies, which should scale easily to large data sets (as S3 and Glue/Athena are highly scalable technologies). Moreover, the serverless aspect means that we don't have to pay for any servers to run this one-in-a-month process, keeping down costs. Nice, right?

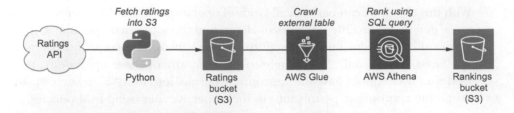

Figure 16.6   Overview of the data process involved in the serverless movie ranking use case. Arrows indicate data transformations performed in Airflow, marked by the corresponding AWS service used for performing the data transformation (where applicable).

16.3.2 *Setting up resources*

Before implementing the DAG, let's start by creating the required resources in AWS. Our DAG will require the following cloud resources:

- An S3 bucket that will contain our ratings data
- A second S3 bucket that will store the ranking results
- A Glue crawler that will create a table from our ratings data
- An IAM user that will allow us to access the S3 buckets and call services such as Glue and Athena

One way to configure these resources is to open the AWS Console (http://console .aws.amazon.com) and create the required resources manually in the respective sections of the console. However, for sake of reproducibility, we recommend defining and managing your resources using an infrastructure-as-code solution such as Cloud-Formation (AWS templating solution for defining cloud resources in code). For this example, we have provided a CloudFormation template that creates all of the required resources in your account. For brevity, we will not dive into the details of the template here, but happily refer you to its details online (https://github.com/BasPH/data-pipelines-with-apache-airflow/blob/master/chapter16/resources/stack.yml).

To create the required resources with our template, open the AWS console, go to the CloudFormation section, and click Create Stack (figure 16.7). On the following page, upload the provided template and click Next. On the Stack details page, enter a name for your stack (= this set of resources) and fill in a unique prefix for your S3 bucket names (which is required to make them globally unique). Now click Next a few more times (making sure to select "I acknowledge that AWS CloudFormation might create IAM resources with custom names" on the review page), and CloudFormation should start creating your resources.

Once complete, you should be able to see the status of the created stack in the CloudFormation stack overview page (figure 16.8). You can also see which resources CloudFormation created for you under the Resources tab (figure 16.9). This should include an IAM user and a bunch of access policies, the two S3 buckets, and our Glue crawler. Note that you can navigate to the different resources by clicking the physical

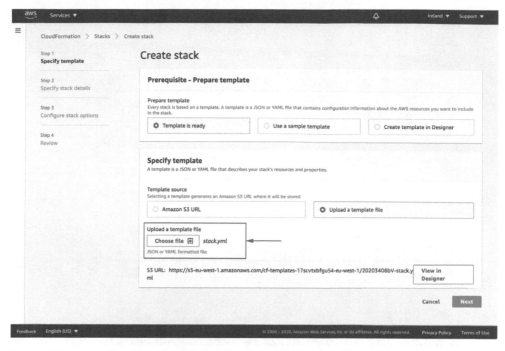

Figure 16.7 Creating a CloudFormation stack in the AWS console

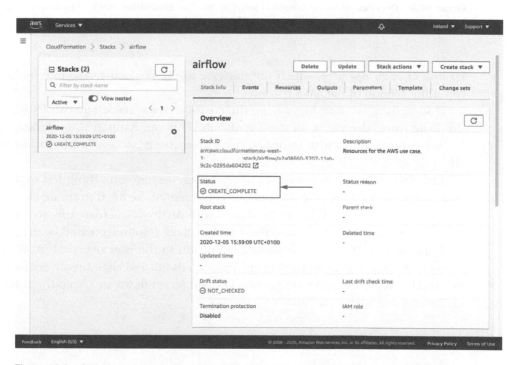

Figure 16.8 Overview of the created CloudFormation Stack in the AWS console. This page shows the overall status of the stack and provides you with controls for updating or deleting the stack, if needed.

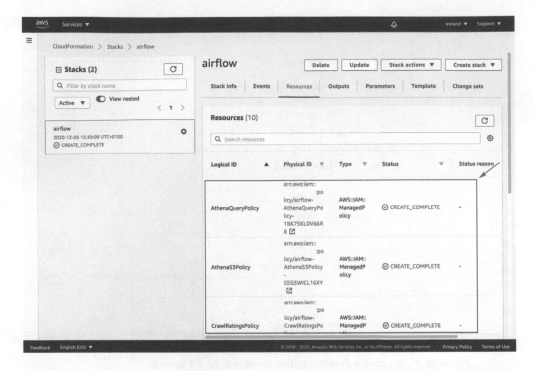

Figure 16.9   Overview of the resources created by the CloudFormation stack. You can use this view to navigate to the different resources created by the stack.

ID link of each resource, which will navigate to the respective resource in the corresponding section of the AWS console.

If something went wrong during the creation of the stack, you can try identifying the issue using the events in the Events tab. This can happen if, for example, your bucket names conflict with someone else's preexisting buckets (as they must be globally unique).

Once we have our required set of resources, we have one thing left to do. To be able to use the IAM user the stack in our DAG created, we need to create an access key and secret for the user that can be shared with Airflow. To create this access key and secret, scroll down until you find the AWS:IAM:USER resource created by the stack and click its physical ID link. This should bring you to the user overview in AWS's IAM console. Next, navigate to the Security credentials tab and click Create access key (figure 16.10). Write the generated access key and secret down and keep them secure, as we'll need this later in Airflow.

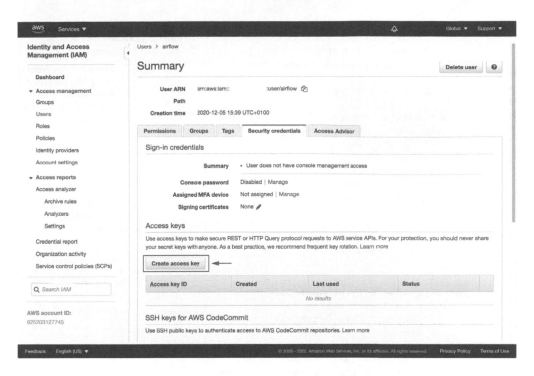

Figure 16.10 Creating an access key and secret for the generated user

16.3.3 Building the DAG

Now we have all the required resources, let's start implementing our DAG by looking for the appropriate hooks and operators. For the first step, we need an operator that fetches data from our movie ratings API and uploads them to S3. Although Airflow provides a number of built-in S3 operators, none of them allows us to fetch ratings from our API and upload them directly to S3. Fortunately, we can also implement this step by combining the PythonOperator and the S3Hook. Together, these classes allow us to fetch the ratings using our own Python function(s) and then upload the results to S3.

Listing 16.1 Uploading ratings using the S3Hook (dags/01_aws_usecase.py)

```
from airflow.operators.python import PythonOperator
from airflow.providers.amazon.aws.hooks.s3 import S3Hook

from custom.hooks import MovielensHook

def _fetch_ratings(api_conn_id, s3_conn_id, s3_bucket, **context):
    year = context["execution_date"].year
    month = context["execution_date"].month

    logging.info(f"Fetching ratings for {year}/{month:02d}")
    api_hook = MovielensHook(conn_id=api_conn_id)
```

```
        ratings = pd.DataFrame.from_records(
            api_hook.get_ratings_for_month(year=year, month=month),
            columns=["userId", "movieId", "rating", "timestamp"],
        )

        logging.info(f"Fetched {ratings.shape[0]} rows")

    with tempfile.TemporaryDirectory() as tmp_dir:
        tmp_path = path.join(tmp_dir, "ratings.csv")
        ratings.to_csv(tmp_path, index=False)

        logging.info(f"Writing results to ratings/{year}/{month:02d}.csv")
        s3_hook = S3Hook(s3_conn_id)
        s3_hook.load_file(
            tmp_path,
            key=f"ratings/{year}/{month:02d}.csv",
            bucket_name=s3_bucket,
            replace=True,
        )

fetch_ratings = PythonOperator(
    task_id="fetch_ratings",
    python_callable=_fetch_ratings,
    op_kwargs={
        "api_conn_id": "movielens",
        "s3_conn_id": "my_aws_conn",
        "s3_bucket": "my_ratings_bucket",
    },
)
```

Write ratings to a temporary directory.

Fetch ratings from the API using the MovielensHook from chapter 8 (code for the hook is available in dags/custom/hooks.py).

Upload the written ratings to S3 using the S3Hook.

Note that the S3Hook requires a connection ID that specifies which connection (i.e., which credentials) to use for connecting to S3. As such, we need to make sure that Airflow is configured with a connection that has an access key and secret for a user with sufficient permissions. Fortunately, we already created such a user in the previous section (using our CloudFormation stack) and can now use the credentials to create our Airflow connection (figure 16.5). After creating the connection, make sure to substitute its name and the name of your S3 bucket (under the op_kwargs argument to the PythonOperator).

For the second step, we need an operator that is able to connect to AWS to trigger our Glue crawler (which was also created by the CloudFormation stack). Unfortunately, Airflow does not provide an operator for this operation, meaning we have to build our own. However, we can use the built-in AwsBaseHook as a base for our operator, which provides us with easy access to the different AWS services using boto3.

Using this AwsBaseHook, we can create our own operator[7] (the GlueTrigger-CrawlerOperator) that essentially retrieves a Glue client using the AwsBaseHook and uses it to start our crawler using the Glue client's start_crawler method. After checking if the crawler started successfully, we can check the status of the crawler using the

---

[7] See chapter 8 for more details on creating custom operators.

client's `get_crawler` method, which (among other things) returns the status of the crawler. Once the crawler reaches the ready state, we can be fairly confident[8] that it has finished running, meaning we can continue with any downstream tasks. Altogether, an implementation of this operator could look something like the following.

Listing 16.2 Operator for triggering Glue crawlers (dags/custom/operators.py)

```
import time
from airflow.models import BaseOperator
from airflow.providers.amazon.aws.hooks.base_aws import AwsBaseHook
from airflow.utils.decorators import apply_defaults

class GlueTriggerCrawlerOperator(BaseOperator):
    """
    Operator that triggers a crawler run in AWS Glue.

    Parameters
    ----------
    aws_conn_id
        Connection to use for connecting to AWS. Should have the appropriate
        permissions (Glue:StartCrawler and Glue:GetCrawler) in AWS.
    crawler_name
        Name of the crawler to trigger.
    region_name
        Name of the AWS region in which the crawler is located.
    kwargs
        Any kwargs are passed to the BaseOperator.
    """
    @apply_defaults
    def __init__(
        self,
        aws_conn_id: str,
        crawler_name: str,
        region_name: str = None,
        **kwargs
    ):
        super().__init__(**kwargs)
        self._aws_conn_id = aws_conn_id
        self._crawler_name = crawler_name
        self._region_name = region_name

    def execute(self, context):
        hook = AwsBaseHook(
            self._aws_conn_id, client_type="glue",
            region_name=self._region_name
        )
        glue_client = hook.get_conn()

        self.log.info("Triggering crawler")
        response = glue_client.start_crawler(Name=self._crawler_name)
```

Create an AwsBaseHook instance and retrieve a client for AWS Glue.

Use the Glue client to start the crawler.

---

[8] This example could arguably be made more robust by adding more checks for unexpected responses, statuses, and so on.

Check if
starting the
crawler was
successful.

```
if response["ResponseMetadata"]["HTTPStatusCode"] != 200:
    raise RuntimeError(
        "An error occurred while triggering the crawler: %r" % response
    )

self.log.info("Waiting for crawler to finish")
while True:
    time.sleep(1)
    crawler = glue_client.get_crawler(Name=self._crawler_name)
    crawler_state = crawler["Crawler"]["State"]

    if crawler_state == "READY":
        self.log.info("Crawler finished running")
        break
```

Loop to
check the
crawler
state.

Stop once the crawler
has finished running
(indicated by the
READY state).

We can use GlueTriggerCrawlerOperator as follows.

Listing 16.3   Using the GlueTriggerCrawlerOperator (dags/01_aws_usecase.py).

```
from custom.operators import GlueTriggerCrawlerOperator

trigger_crawler = GlueTriggerCrawlerOperator(
    aws_conn_id="my_aws_conn",
    task_id="trigger_crawler",
    crawler_name="ratings-crawler",
)
```

Finally, for the third step, we need an operator that allows us to execute a query in Athena. This time we're in luck, as Airflow provides an operator for doing so: the AwsAthenaOperator. This operator requires a number of arguments: the connection to Athena, the database (which should have been created by the Glue crawler), the execution query, and an output location in S3 to write the results of the query to. Altogether, our usage of the operator would look something like this.

Listing 16.4   Ranking movies using the AWSAthenaOperator (dags/01_aws_usecase.py)

```
from airflow.providers.amazon.aws.operators.athena import AWSAthenaOperator

rank_movies = AWSAthenaOperator(
    task_id="rank_movies",
    aws_conn_id="my_aws_conn",
    database="airflow",
    query="""
        SELECT movieid, AVG(rating) as avg_rating, COUNT(*) as num_ratings
        FROM (
            SELECT movieid, rating,
                CAST(from_unixtime(timestamp) AS DATE) AS date
            FROM ratings
        )
        WHERE date <= DATE('{{ ds }}')
        GROUP BY movieid
        ORDER BY avg_rating DESC
```

Retrieve the
movie ID,
rating value
and date of
each rating.

Select all ratings up
to the execution date.

Group by movie ID to calculate
the average rating per movie.

```
    """,
    output_location=f"s3://my_rankings_bucket/{{ds}}",
)
```

Now that we have created all the required tasks, we can start tying everything together in the overall DAG.

```
import datetime as dt
import logging
import os
from os import path
import tempfile

import pandas as pd

from airflow import DAG
from airflow.providers.amazon.aws.hooks.s3 import S3Hook
from airflow.providers.amazon.aws.operators.athena import AWSAthenaOperator
from airflow.operators.dummy import DummyOperator
from airflow.operators.python import PythonOperator

from custom.operators import GlueTriggerCrawlerOperator
from custom.ratings import fetch_ratings

with DAG(
    dag_id="01_aws_usecase",
    description="DAG demonstrating some AWS-specific hooks and operators.",
    start_date=dt.datetime(year=2019, month=1, day=1),
    end_date=dt.datetime(year=2019, month=3, day=1),
    schedule_interval="@monthly",
    default_args={
        "depends_on_past": True
    }
) as dag:
    fetch_ratings = PythonOperator(...)
    trigger_crawler = GlueTriggerCrawlerOperator(...)
    rank_movies = AWSAthenaOperator(...)
    fetch_ratings >> trigger_crawler >> rank_movies
```

Set start/end dates to fit the ratings data set. → (annotation for `start_date`)

Use depends_on_past to avoid running queries before past data has been loaded (which would give incomplete results). ← (annotation for `"depends_on_past": True`)

With everything in place, we should now be able to run our DAG within Airflow (figure 16.11). Assuming everything is configured correctly, your DAG runs should be successful and you should see some CSV outputs from Athena appearing in your ratings output bucket (figure 16.12). If you run into issues, make sure that the AWS resources were set up correctly and that your access key and secret were configured correctly.

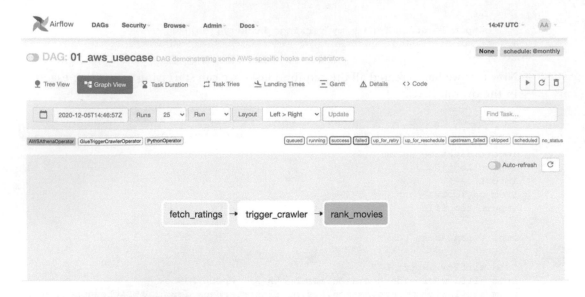

Figure 16.11 The resulting movie-ranking DAG in Airflow, illustrating the three different tasks and the corresponding operators involved in each task

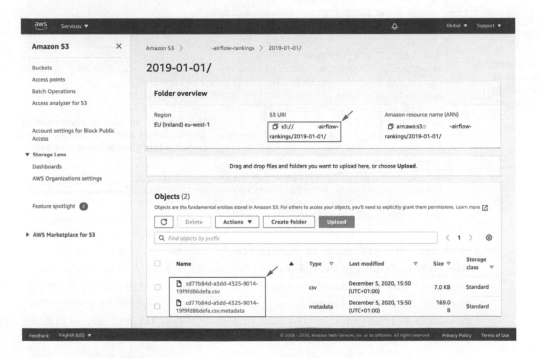

Figure 16.12 The results of the Athena query in the rankings bucket

16.3.4 *Cleaning up*

After finishing with this example, make sure to clean up any resources you created in AWS to avoid incurring any unnecessary costs. If you used our CloudFormation template for creating the resources, you can delete most by deleting the stack. Note that some resources, like the S3 buckets, will have to be removed manually even if you are using the template, as CloudFormation will not let you delete non-empty buckets automatically. Make sure to check if all created resources were deleted successfully, paying extra attention to check any resources you may have created manually.

Summary

- Airflow can be deployed in AWS using services such as ECS/Fargate for running the scheduler and webserver processes, EFS/S3 for storage, and Amazon RDS for the Airflow metastore.
- Airflow provides many AWS-specific hooks and operators that allow you to integrate with different services with the AWS cloud platform.
- The `AwsBaseHook` class provides low-level access to all services in AWS using the boto3 library, allowing you to implement your own high-level hooks and operators if these do not yet exist.
- Using AWS-specific hooks and operators generally requires you to configure the required resources and access permissions in AWS and Airflow so that Airflow is allowed to perform the required operations.

Airflow on Azure

17

This chapter covers

- Designing a deployment strategy for Azure
- An overview of several Azure-specific hooks and operators
- Demonstrating how to use Azure-specific hooks and operators with a use case

This chapter will dive further into how to deploy and integrate Airflow with cloud services in the Microsoft Azure cloud. First, we'll start designing an Airflow deployment by mapping the different components of Airflow to Azure services. Then we'll explore some of the hooks and operators that Airflow provides for integrating with several key Azure services. Finally, we'll show how to use these Azure-specific operators and hooks to implement a use case for generating movie recommendations.

17.1 Deploying Airflow in Azure

In chapter 15, we described the different components comprising an Airflow deployment. In this section, we'll design a few deployment patterns for Azure by mapping them to specific Azure cloud services. This should give you a good idea of the process involved in designing an Airflow deployment for Azure and provide a good starting point for implementing one.

17.1.1 Picking services

Let's start with the Airflow webserver and scheduler components. One of the easiest approaches for running these components is to use Azure's managed container services, such as Azure Container Instances (ACI) or Azure Kubernetes Service (AKS). However, for the webserver, we also have another option: the Azure App Service.

Azure App Service is, as Microsoft puts it, "a fully managed platform for building, deploying and scaling your web apps." In practice, it provides a convenient approach for deploying web services onto a managed platform that includes features such as authentication and monitoring. Importantly, App Service supports deploying applications in containers, which means that we can use it to deploy the Airflow webserver and allow it to take care of authentication for us. Of course, the scheduler doesn't need any of the web-related functionality provided by App Service. As such, it still makes sense to deploy the scheduler to ACI, which provides a more basic container runtime.

For the Airflow metastore, it makes a lot of sense to look toward Azure's managed database services, such as Azure SQL Database. This service effectively provides us with a convenient solution for a relational database on an SQL server without having to worry about the maintenance of the underlying system.

Azure provides a number of different storage solutions, including Azure File Storage, Azure Blob Storage, and Azure Data Lake Storage. Azure File Storage is the most convenient solution for hosting our DAGs, as File Storage volumes can be mounted directly into the containers running in App Service and ACI. Moreover, File Storage is easy to access using supporting user applications such as the Azure Storage Explorer, making it relatively straightforward to add or update any DAGs. For data storage, it makes more sense to look toward Azure Blob or Data Lake Storage, as these are better suited for data workloads than file storage.

This gives us the following setup (also shown in figure 17.1):

- App Service for the Airflow webserver
- ACI for the Airflow scheduler
- Azure SQL database for the Airflow metastore
- Azure File Storage for storing DAGs
- Azure Blob Storage for data and logs

17.1.2 Designing the network

Now we have picked services for each component, we can start designing the networking connectivity between them. In this case, we want to expose the Airflow webserver to the internet so that we can access it remotely. However, we want to keep other

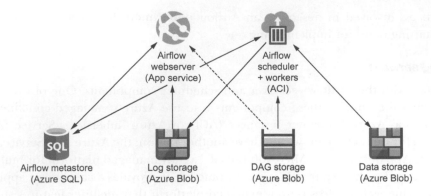

Figure 17.1   Mapping the Airflow components from figure 15.1 to Azure services. App Service and CI are used for the compute components (webserver, scheduler, and workers, respectively), as these provide convenient container-based compute services. App Service is used for the webserver instead of ACI, as it provides extra functionality for authenticating access to the webserver, and so on. Azure SQL Database is used as a managed database service for the metastore, while Azure File Storage and Azure Blob Storage services are used for storing DAGs, logs, and data. Arrows indicate dependencies between the services.

components, such as the Airflow metastore and the Airflow scheduler, in a private network to avoid exposing them online.

Fortunately, the Azure App Service makes it easy to expose the webserver as a web application; that is exactly what it is designed for. As such, we can let App Service take care of exposing the webserver and connecting it to the internet. We can also use the built-in functionally of App Service to add a firewall or an authentication layer (which can be integrated with Azure AD, etc.) in front of the webservice, preventing unauthorized users from accessing the webserver.

For the scheduler and metastore, we can create a virtual net (vnet) with a private subnet and place these more private components inside the private network (figure 17.2). This will provide us with connectivity between the metastore and the scheduler. To allow the webserver to access the metastore, we need to enable vnet integration for App Service.

Both Azure File Storage and Azure Blob Storage can be integrated with App Service and ACI. By default, both these storage services are accessible via the internet, meaning that they don't need to be integrated into our vnet. However, we also recommend looking into using private endpoints for connecting storage accounts to your private resources, which provides more security by ensuring that data traffic does not traverse the public internet.

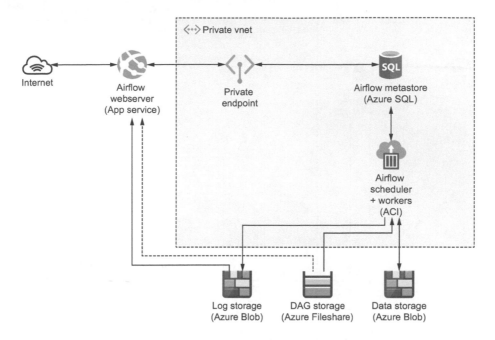

Figure 17.2 Projecting our components onto a network layout with a private virtual network (vnet). The private vnet sequesters our internal resources (e.g., the metastore and scheduler service) from the public internet, protecting them from external access. The webserver is exposed to the internet via Azure App Service so that it can be accessed remotely. Integration with the vnet is arranged using a private endpoint so that the webserver can reach the metastore. Arrows indicate the direction of information flowing between the services. The storage services are not sequestered to the vnet here but can be if desired.[1]

17.1.3 Scaling with the CeleryExecutor

Similar to the AWS solution, we can improve the scalability of our Azure deployment by switching from the `LocalExecutor` to the `CeleryExecutor`. In Azure, switching executors also requires us to create a pool of Airflow workers that the `CeleryExecutor` can use. As we are already running our scheduler in ACI, it makes sense to create the extra Airflow workers as additional container services running in ACI (figure 17.3).

Next, we also need to implement a message broker for relaying jobs between the scheduler and the workers. Unfortunately, there are (to our knowledge) no managed solutions in Azure that integrate well with Airflow for this purpose. As such, the easiest approach is to run an open source service in ACI that can function as a message broker for Airflow. Open source tools such as RabbitMQ and Redis can be used for this purpose.

---

[1] The availability of the storage services can be limited to the vnet using a combination of private endpoints and firewall rules to provide an extra layer of security.

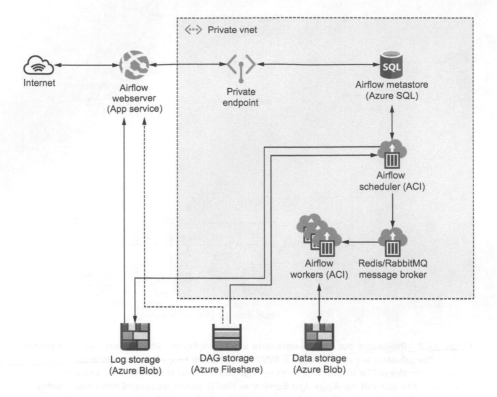

Figure 17.3   An alternative deployment based on the `CeleryExecutor`**. The** `Celery-`
`Executor` **runs workers in separate compute processes, which are run as individual container
instances on ACI. Additionally, a Redis or RabbitMQ instance is run in ACI to function as a
message broker for passing tasks to the workers after they have been scheduled.**

17.1.4 *Further steps*

Although this illustrates some basic deployment strategies for Airflow in Azure, we
should be careful to note that these are not production-ready. Similar to the AWS
designs, any production-ready setup will still need to take extra steps, such as setting
up proper firewalls and access controls. At the Airflow level, you should also consider
how you want to secure Airflow (e.g., using Airflow's RBAC mechanism, etc.).

   We also expect production deployments to have a robust approach for logging,
auditing, tracking metrics, and raising alerts if issues are encountered with any of the
deployed services. For this, we recommend looking at the corresponding services provided by Azure, including Azure Log Analytics, App Insights, and so on.

17.2   *Azure-specific hooks/operators*

At the time of writing this book, Airflow has relatively few built-in hooks and operators
specific for Azure cloud services. This probably reflects a bias of the Airflow community; however, it should be pretty straightforward to implement (and contribute) your

own using the Azure Python SDK. Additionally, several services can be accessed using more generic interfaces (e.g., ODBC, as we will see in the example use case), meaning that Airflow can still interact well with Azure cloud services.

Airflow's Azure-specific hooks and operators (tables 17.1 and 17.2) are provided by the Microsoft/Azure provider package.[2] Several of these hooks and operators can be used to interact with Azure's different storage services (e.g., Blob, File Share, and Data Lake Storage), with additional hooks providing access to specialized databases (e.g., CosmosDB) and container runtimes (e.g., Azure Container Service).

Table 17.1 An excerpt of some of the Azure-specific hooks

Service	Description	Hook	Applications
Azure Blob Storage	Blob storage service	`WasbHook`[a]	Uploading/downloading files
Azure Container Instances	Managed service for running containers	`AzureContainer-InstanceHook`	Running and monitoring containerized jobs
Azure Cosmos DB	Multi-modal database service	`AzureCosmosDBHook`	Inserting and retrieving database documents
Azure Data Lake Storage	Data lake storage for big-data analytics	`AzureDataLakeHook`	Uploading/downloading files to/from Azure Data Lake Storage
Azure File Storage	NFS-compatible file storage service	`AzureFileShareHook`	Uploading/downloading files

[a] Windows Azure Storage Blob.

Table 17.2 An excerpt of some of the Azure-specific operators

Operator	Service	Description
`AzureDataLakeStorageList-Operator`	Azure Data Lake Storage	Lists files under a specific file path
`AzureContainerInstances-Operator`	Azure Container Instances	Runs a containerized task
`AzureCosmosInsertDocument-Operator`	Azure Cosmos DB	Inserts a document into a database instance
`WasbDeleteBlobOperator`	Azure Blob Storage	Deletes a specific blob

---

[2] Can be installed in Airflow 2 using the `apache-airflow-providers-microsoft-azure` providers package or in Airflow 1.10 using the backport package `apache-airflow-backport-providers-microsoft-azure`.

17.3 *Example: Serverless movie ranking with Azure Synapse*

To get familiar with using some Azure services within Airflow, we'll implement a small movie recommender using several serverless services (similar to the AWS use case, but now applied to Azure). In this use case, we're interested in identifying popular movies by ranking them based on their user average rating. By using serverless technologies for this task, we hope to keep our setup relatively simple and cost-effective by not having to worry about running and maintaining any servers but letting Azure take care of this for us.

17.3.1 *Overview*

Although there are probably many different ways to perform this kind of analysis in Azure, we will focus on using Azure Synapse for performing our movie ranking, as it allows us to perform serverless SQL queries using its SQL on-demand capability. This means we only have to pay for the amount of data we process in Azure Synapse and don't have to worry about running the costs and maintenance of the compute resources it uses.

To implement our use case using Synapse, we need to perform the following steps:

1 Fetch ratings for a given month from our ratings API and upload the ratings into Azure Blob Storage for further analysis.
2 Use Azure Synapse to execute an SQL query that ranks our movies. The resulting list of ranked movies will be written back to Azure Blob Storage for further downstream consumption.

This gives us the data process shown in figure 17.4. The astute reader will notice we have one less step than we did for the AWS example using Glue and Athena. This is because our Azure example will directly reference files on the blob storage when performing the query (as we will see), instead of indexing them into a catalogue first (at the cost of having to manually specify a schema in the query).

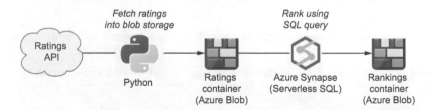

Figure 17.4   Overview of the data process involved in the serverless movie ranking use case. Arrows indicate data transformations performed in Airflow, marked by the corresponding Azure service used for performing the data transformation (where applicable).

17.3.2 Setting up resources

Before building our DAG, we first need to create the required resources. We'll do so from within the Azure Portal (https://portal.azure.com), which you should be able to access with a proper Azure subscription.

In the portal, we'll start by creating a resource group (figure 17.5), which represents the virtual container of our resources for this use case. Here we've named the resource group "airflow-azure," but in principle this can be anything you want.

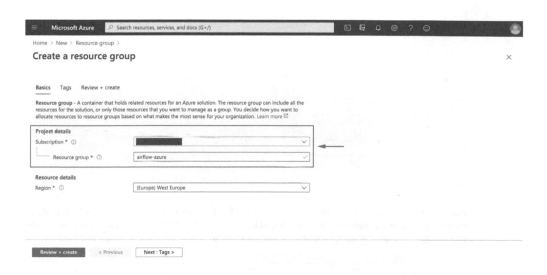

Figure 17.5 Creating an Azure resource group to hold our resources

After setting up the resource group, we can start creating an Azure Synapse workspace, which is currently named "Azure Synapse Analytics" (workspaces preview) in the Azure portal. To create a Synapse workspace, open the page of the service in the portal and click Create Synapse workspace. On the first page of the creation wizard (figure 17.6), select the previously created resource group and enter a name for your Synapse workspace. Under the storage options, make sure to create a new storage account and file system (choose any names you like).

On the next page of the wizard (figure 17.7), we have the option to specify a username and password for the SQL administrator account. Enter whatever you like, but remember what you filled in (we'll need these details when building our DAG).

On the third page (figure 17.8), you also have the option of restricting network access by deselecting "Allow connections from all IP addresses," but don't forget to add your personal IP address to the firewall exemptions if you deselect this option. Click Review + create to start creating the workspace.

Now that we have our Synapse workspace and corresponding storage account, we can start creating the containers (a kind of subfolder) that will hold our ratings and

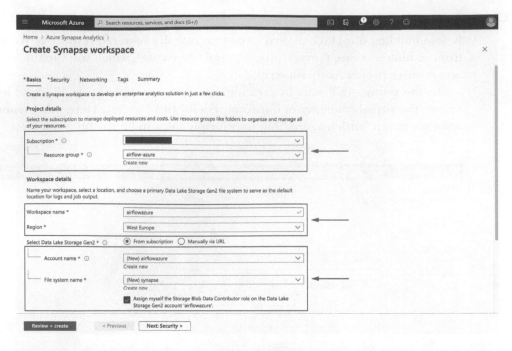

Figure 17.6   First page of the wizard for creating a Synapse workspace. Make sure to specify the correct resource group and a name for your workspace. To set up the storage, click Create new for both the account and file system options under storage and enter a name for the storage account and file system.

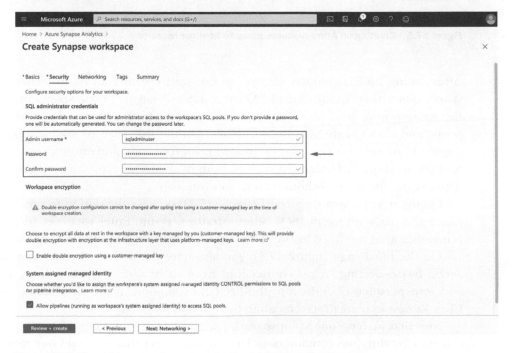

Figure 17.7   Specifying security options for the Synapse workspace

Figure 17.8   Specifying networking options for the Synapse workspace

rankings data in the blob storage. To do so, open the storage account (if you lost it, you should be able to find it back in your resource group), go to the Overview page and click Containers. On the Containers page (figure 17.9), create two new containers, ratings and rankings, by clicking + Container and entering the corresponding container name.

Finally, to ensure we can access our storage account from Airflow, we need to obtain an access key and secret. To get these credentials, click Access keys in the left

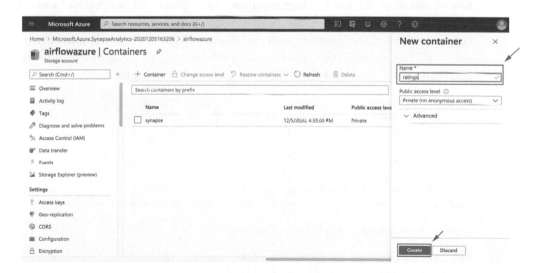

Figure 17.9   Creating blob containers for holding our ratings and rankings data in the storage account

panel of the (figure 17.10). Write down the storage account name and one of the two keys, which we'll pass as connection details to Airflow when implementing our DAG.

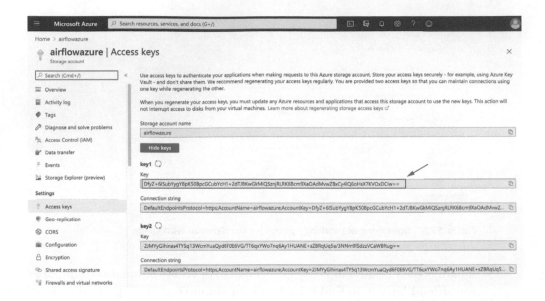

Figure 17.10   Obtaining the account name and key for accessing the blob storage account from Airflow

17.3.3 *Building the DAG*

Now that we have all of the required resources, we can start building our DAG. For the first of two steps, we need to implement an operation that fetches data from our ratings API and uploads them to Azure Blob Storage. The easiest way to implement this is to combine the `PythonOperator` with the `WasbHook` from the Microsoft/Azure provider package. This combination allows us to fetch the ratings using our own functions and then upload the results to Azure Blob Storage using the hook.

Listing 17.1   Uploading ratings using the WasbHook (dags/01_azure_usecase.py)

```
import logging
from os import path
import tempfile

from airflow.operators.python import PythonOperator
from airflow.providers.microsoft.azure.hooks.wasb import WasbHook

from custom.hooks import MovielensHook

def _fetch_ratings(api_conn_id, wasb_conn_id, container, **context):
    year = context["execution_date"].year
    month = context["execution_date"].month
```

Fetch ratings from the API using the Movielens-Hook from chapter 8 (code for the hook is available in dags/custom/hooks.py).

```
logging.info(f"Fetching ratings for {year}/{month:02d}")
api_hook = MovielensHook(conn_id=api_conn_id)
ratings = pd.DataFrame.from_records(
    api_hook.get_ratings_for_month(year=year, month=month),
    columns=["userId", "movieId", "rating", "timestamp"],
)
logging.info(f"Fetched {ratings.shape[0]} rows")

with tempfile.TemporaryDirectory() as tmp_dir:
    tmp_path = path.join(tmp_dir, "ratings.csv")
    ratings.to_csv(tmp_path, index=False)

    logging.info(f"Writing results to
    {container}/{year}/{month:02d}.csv")
    hook = WasbHook(wasb_conn_id)
    hook.load_file(
        tmp_path,
        container_name=container,
        blob_name=f"{year}/{month:02d}.csv",
    )

fetch_ratings = PythonOperator(
    task_id="upload_ratings",
    python_callable=_upload_ratings,
    op_kwargs={
        "wasb_conn_id": "my_wasb_conn",
        "container": "ratings"
    },
)
```

Write ratings to a temporary directory.

Upload the written ratings to Azure Blob using the WasbHook.

The WasbHook requires a connection ID that specifies which to use for connecting to the storage account. This connection can be created in Airflow using the credentials we obtained in the previous section, using the account name as the login and the account key as password (figure 17.11). The code is pretty straightforward: we fetch the ratings, write them to a temporary file, and upload the temporary file to the ratings container using the WasbHook.

For the second step, we need an operator that can connect to Azure Synapse, execute a query that generates our rankings, and write the results to the rankings container in our storage account. Although no Airflow hook or operator provides this kind of functionality, we can use the OdbcHook (from the ODBC provider package[3]) to connect to Synapse over an ODBC connection. This hook then allows us to perform the query and retrieve the results, which we can then write to Azure Blob Storage using the WasbHook.

The actual ranking will be performed by the Synapse SQL query in listing 17.2.

---

[3] Can be installed in Airflow 2 using the `apache-airflow-providers-odbc` provider package or in Airflow 1.10 using the backport package `apache-airflow-backport-providers-odbc`.

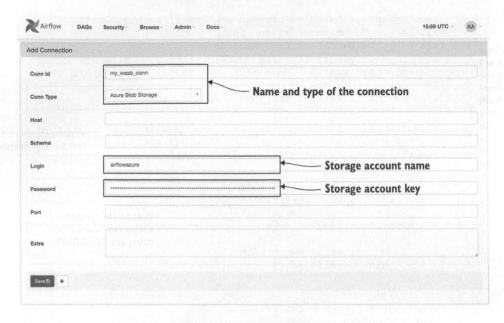

Figure 17.11   Creating an Airflow connection for the Azure Blob Storage account, using the storage account name and key obtained from the Azure Portal

---

Listing 17.2   Synapse SQL query for ranking movies (dags/01_azure_usecase.py)

```
RANK_QUERY = """
    SELECT movieId, AVG(rating) as avg_rating, COUNT(*) as num_ratings      ◁
    FROM OPENROWSET(
        BULK
            'https://{blob_account_name}.blob.core.windows.net/
            ➥ {blob_container}/*/*.csv',
        FORMAT = 'CSV',
        PARSER_VERSION = '2.0',
        HEADER_ROW = TRUE,
        FIELDTERMINATOR =',',
        ROWTERMINATOR = '\n',
    )
    WITH (
        [userId] bigint,
        [movieId] bigint,
        [rating] float,
        [timestamp] bigint
    ) AS [r]
    WHERE (
        (r.filepath(1) < '{year}') OR
        (r.filepath(1) = '{year}' AND r.filepath(2) <= '{month:02d}')
    )
    GROUP BY movieId
    ORDER BY avg_rating DESC
"""
```

Tell Synapse to look for our CSV data set in our blob storage account.

Retrieve the movie ID, rating value, and date of each rating.

Define the schema to use when reading the CSV data.

Select all ratings up to the execution date based on partition file names.

Group by movie ID to calculate the average rating per movie.

In this SQL query, the OPENROWSET statement tells Synapse to load the required data set from our storage account (referenced by the URL) and that the data files are in a CSV file format. Following OPENROWSET, the WITH statement tells Synapse what schema to use for data read from the external data set so that we can ensure the data columns have the correct types. Finally, the WHERE statement uses the different parts of the file paths to ensure we only read data up to the current month, while the rest of the statement performs our actual ranking (using the SELECT AVG, GROUP BY and ORDER BY statements).

> **NOTE**　In this case, Synapse has access to the storage account because we placed our files in the storage account coupled to the Synapse workspace. If you were to place the files in another storage account (not directly coupled to the workspace), you need to make sure to either grant your Synapse workspace's identity access to the corresponding account or register the it with the proper access credentials as an external data store in the workspace.

We can execute this query using the following function, which executes the query using the OdbcHook,[4] converts the rows in the result to a Pandas data frame and then uploads the contents of that data frame to the blob storage using the WasbHook.

Listing 17.3　Executing the Synapse query using ODBC (dags/01_azure_usecase.py)

```
def _rank_movies(
    odbc_conn_id, wasb_conn_id, ratings_container, rankings_container,
      **context
):
    year = context["execution_date"].year          ⎫ Retrieve the name of our blob storage
    month = context["execution_date"].month         ⎬ account (same as the login name for
                                                     ⎭ the storage account).

    blob_account_name = WasbHook.get_connection(wasb_conn_id).login    ◄──┘

    query = RANK_QUERY.format(      ◄──┐ Inject run parameters
        year=year,                      │ into the SQL query.
        month=month,
        blob_account_name=blob_account_name,
        blob_container=ratings_container,
    )
    logging.info(f"Executing query: {query}")

    odbc_hook = OdbcHook(
        odbc_conn_id,
        driver="ODBC Driver 17 for SQL Server",
    )
```

Connect to Synapse using the ODBC hook.

---

[4] Note that this requires the proper ODBC drivers to be installed. This driver should already be installed in our Docker image. If you're not using our image, more details on how to install the drivers yourself are available on the Microsoft website. Make sure to use the proper version for your operating system.

```
with odbc_hook.get_conn() as conn:
    with conn.cursor() as cursor:
        cursor.execute(query)               ◁——  Execute the query and
                                                  retrieve the resulting rows.
        rows = cursor.fetchall()            ◁——
        colnames = [field[0] for field in cursor.description]

    ranking = pd.DataFrame.from_records(rows, columns=colnames)   ◁——
    logging.info(f"Retrieved {ranking.shape[0]} rows")
                                                                  Convert the
                                                                  resulting rows
    logging.info(f"Writing results to                             into a pandas
        {rankings_container}/{year}/{month:02d}.csv")             data frame.
    with tempfile.TemporaryDirectory() as tmp_dir:
        tmp_path = path.join(tmp_dir, "ranking.csv")
        ranking.to_csv(tmp_path, index=False)      ◁——  Write the result to a
                                                         temporary CSV file.
        wasb_hook = WasbHook(wasb_conn_id)    ◁——
        wasb_hook.load_file(
            tmp_path,                             Upload the CSV file
            container_name=rankings_container,    containing rankings
            blob_name=f"{year}/{month:02d}.csv",  to Blob storage.
        )
```

Similar to the previous step, we can execute this function using the `PythonOperator`, passing in the required connection references and container paths as arguments to the operator.

Listing 17.4   Calling the movie ranking function (dags/01_azure_usecase.py)

```
rank_movies = PythonOperator(
    task_id="rank_movies",
    python_callable=_rank_movies,
    op_kwargs={
        "odbc_conn_id": "my_odbc_conn",
        "wasb_conn_id": "my_wasb_conn",
        "ratings_container": "ratings",
        "rankings_container": "rankings",
    },
)
```

Of course, we still need to provide the details for the ODBC connection to Airflow (figure 17.12). You can find the host URL for your Synapse instance in the overview page of the Synapse workspace in the Azure portal under "SQL on-demand endpoint" (on-demand = serverless SQL). For the database schema, we'll simply use the default database (master). Finally, for the user login/password, we can use the username and password we provided for our admin user when we created the workspace. Of course, we only use the admin account here for the purpose of this demonstration. In a more realistic setting, we recommend creating a separate SQL user with the required permissions and using that user to connect to Synapse.

All that remains it to combine these two operators into a DAG, which we'll run on a monthly interval to generate monthly movie rankings.

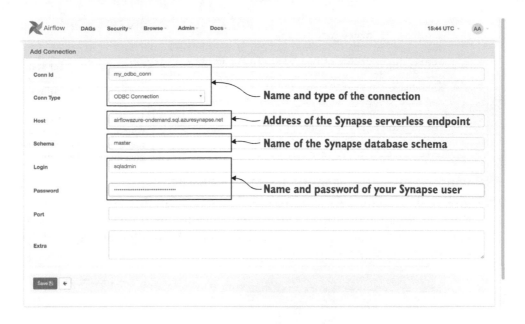

Figure 17.12   Creating an Airflow connection for the ODBC connection to Synapse. The corresponding user details should have been set when creating the Synapse workspace.

Listing 17.5   Building the overall recommender DAG (dags/01_azure_usecase.py)

```
import datetime as dt
import logging
from os import path
import tempfile

import pandas as pd

from airflow import DAG

from airflow.providers.microsoft.azure.hooks.wasb import WasbHook
from airflow.providers.odbc.hooks.odbc import OdbcHook
from airflow.operators.python import PythonOperator

from custom.hooks import MovielensHook

RANK_QUERY = ...

def _fetch_ratings(api_conn_id, wasb_conn_id, container, **context):
    ...

def _rank_movies(odbc_conn_id, wasb_conn_id, ratings_container,
        rankings_container, **context):
    ...
```

```
with DAG(
    dag_id="01_azure_usecase",
    description="DAG demonstrating some Azure hooks and operators.",
    start_date=dt.datetime(year=2019, month=1, day=1),
    end_date=dt.datetime(year=2019, month=3, day=1),
    schedule_interval="@monthly",
    default_args={"depends_on_past": True},
) as dag:
    fetch_ratings = PythonOperator(...)
    rank_movies = PythonOperator(...)
    upload_ratings >> rank_movies
```

Set start/end dates to fit the ratings data set.

Use depends_on_past to avoid running queries before past data has been loaded (which would give incomplete results).

With everything complete, we should finally be able to run our DAG in Airflow. If all goes well, we should see our tasks loading data from the ratings API and processing them in Synapse (figure 17.13). If you run into any problems, make sure that the paths to the data and the access credentials for Azure Blob Storage and Synapse are correct.

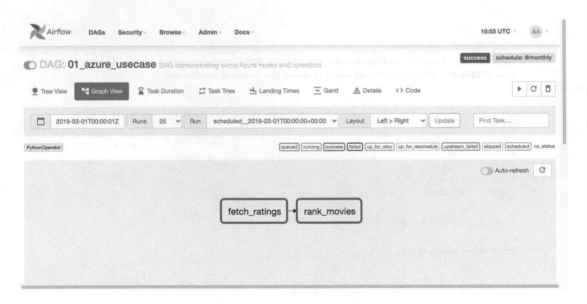

Figure 17.13 Successfully generating movie rankings using Azure Synapse in the movie ranking DAG

17.3.4 Cleaning up

After you're done with playing around with this example in Azure Synapse, you can remove all the created resources by deleting the resource group we created in the beginning of the use case (as this should contain all those resources). To do this, open the Overview page of the resource group in the Azure portal and click Delete resource group (figure 17.14). Confirm the deletion to start deleting all the underlying resources.

Figure 17.14 Cleaning up the created resources by deleting the corresponding resource group

Summary

- Airflow can be deployed in Azure using services such as ACI and App Service for running the scheduler and webserver processes, Azure File/Blob Storages for storing files, and Azure SQL Database for the Airflow metastore.

- Airflow provides several Azure-specific hooks and operators that allow you to integrate with different services with the Azure cloud platform.

- Some Azure services can be accessed using generalized hooks, such as the ODBC hook, if they conform to these standardized protocols.

- Using Azure-specific hooks and operators generally also requires you to configure the required resources and access permissions in Azure and Airflow so that Airflow is allowed to perform the required operations.

Airflow in GCP

This chapter covers

- Designing a deployment strategy for GCP
- An overview of several GCP-specific hooks and operators
- Demonstrating how to use GCP-specific hooks and operators

The last major cloud provider, Google Cloud Platform (GCP), is actually the best supported cloud platform in terms of the number of hooks and operators. Almost all Google services can be controlled with Airflow. In this chapter, we'll dive into setting up Airflow on GCP (section 18.1), operators and hooks for GCP services (section 18.2), and the same use case as demonstrated on AWS and Azure, applied to GCP (section 18.3).

We must also note that GCP features a managed Airflow service named "Cloud Composer," which is mentioned in more detail in section 15.3.2. This chapter covers a DIY Airflow setup on GCP, not Cloud Composer.

18.1 Deploying Airflow in GCP

GCP provides various services for running software. There is no one-size-fits-all approach, which is why Google (and all other cloud vendors) provide different services for running software.

18.1.1 Picking services

These services can be mapped on a scale, ranging from fully self-managed with the most flexibility, to managed completely by GCP with no maintenance required (figure 18.1).

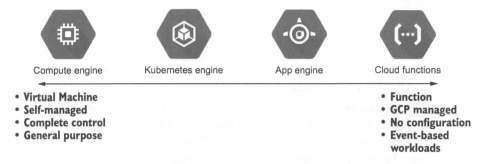

Figure 18.1 Overview of the different compute services available in the Google Cloud Platform

On the left-hand side, we have Compute Engine, which gives you a virtual machine to run any piece of software you desire. Compute Engine provides you complete freedom and control, which can be positive, but it also requires you to manage and configure the virtual machine yourself. For example, if traffic to a service you're running on Compute Engine increases, it is up to you to scale vertically by creating a new VM with a larger instance type or scale horizontally by configuring an autoscaling policy to create more of the same instances.

On the right-hand side, we have Cloud Functions, to which you can provide a function in one of the supported languages (Node.js, Python, Go, and Java at the time of writing), for example, a Python function that returns the current time in a given time zone. So, if you call the function with an argument, CEST, the function will return the time for the CEST time zone. Functions handle small workloads and operate event-based. Google manages your function (i.e., the underlying infrastructure) and will scale the number of deployed functions automatically. If a high load is requested from your function, Google will automatically scale up. Google handles all logging, monitoring, and the like; you only have to provide the function. If your use case fits the characteristics of a function, it can greatly improve your productivity.

It is not trivial to set up Airflow because of the shared storage it requires for storing and sharing DAG files (mostly applies when running `CeleryExecutor` or `Kubernetes-Executor`). This limits our options in GCP:

- Cloud functions serve stateless event-based functions, which Airflow is not, and therefore cannot be deployed on Cloud Functions.
- Running Airflow on App Engine might be technically possible but with a few caveats: App Engine expects a single Docker container, while the minimum Airflow installation is already split between a webserver and a scheduler process. This poses a challenge: typically, applications that expose something (e.g., a frontend or REST API) are run on App Engine, which scales automatically based on the load. Airflow does not fit this model, as it's a distributed application by default. The webserver could be a good candidate though to run on GAE.

  The Airflow scheduler does not fit the App Engine model, so this leaves us with two options: GCE and GKE. Kubernetes was already discussed in detail in chapter 10.
- The Kubernetes Engine is a good fit for Airflow. Helm charts for deploying Airflow on Kubernetes are available, plus it provides abstractions for mounting filesystems shared by multiple pods.
- The Compute Engine gives you complete freedom to run and configure your instance. We can distinguish two flavors of the Compute Engine: a Linux-based VM and a container-optimized OS (COS) VM. A COS system is ideal for running Docker containers, and therefore seems attractive from a deployment perspective but unfortunately poses an issue in combination with Airflow. Airflow requires a filesystem for DAG storage (potentially shared between multiple machines), for which storage accessible via NFS is a common solution. However, COS does not come with NFS libraries. While it might be technically possible to install these, this is not a simple task, so it's easier to switch to a Linux-based VM, which gives complete control.

For a shared file system, two (out of the many) options on GCP are as follows:

- Google Cloud Filestore (a GCP-managed NAS service)
- GCS mounted with FUSE

Shared file systems have long been a challenge, and each comes with pros and cons. If possible, we prefer avoiding FUSE filesystems as they apply a file system–like interface over something that was never intended to be a file system (e.g., GCS is an object store), which comes with poor performance and consistency challenges, especially when used by multiple clients.

For other Airflow components, the number of options is less and thus easier. For the metastore, GCP provides Cloud SQL, which can run both MySQL and PostgreSQL. For the storage of logs, we'll apply Google Cloud Storage (GCS), which is GCP's object storage service.

When running on GCP, deploying on Google Kubernetes Engine (GKE) is probably the easiest approach (figure 18.2). GKE is Google's managed Kubernetes service, which provides an easy way to deploy and manage containerized software. The other obvious option on GCP—running everything on Linux-based Compute Engine

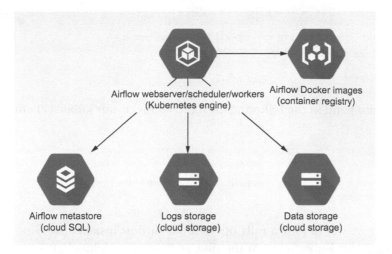

Figure 18.2 Mapping Airflow components to GCP in a Kubernetes-based deployment of Airflow

VMs—takes more work and time to get up and running as you have to configure everything yourself. Google already provides a managed Airflow service named Composer, but we will demonstrate how Airflow is deployed on GKE and can integrate with other GCP services.

18.1.2 Deploying on GKE with Helm

Let's start with getting GKE going. In this section, we aim to provide the basic commands for getting Airflow up and running, so we skip various details that are often required in a production setup, such as not exposing services on public IPs. The command in listing 18.1 will create a GKE cluster with a public endpoint.

Working with the gcloud cli

To tell Google to use a specific project, you can either configure a default with

```
gcloud config set project [my-project-id]
```

or add a flag to every command, like this one:

```
gcloud compute instances list --project [my-project-id]
```

For the gcloud commands shown, we do not display the `--project` flag and assume you set a default or add the `--project` flag to the command.

Listing 18.1   gcloud command to create a GKE cluster

```
gcloud container clusters create my-airflow-cluster \
--machine-type n1-standard-4 \
--num-nodes 1 \
--region "europe-west4"
```

Then use the command in the following listing to connect your kubectl client with the cluster.

Listing 18.2   gcloud command to configure a kubectl config entry

```
gcloud container clusters get-credentials my-airflow-cluster \
--region europe-west4
```

On this cluster, we will deploy a fully operational Airflow installation using Helm, a package manager for Kubernetes. At the time of writing, a Helm chart is included in the Airflow repository on GitHub but not released via an official channel. We must therefore download it to install. Check the Airflow documentation for the most recent details.

Listing 18.3   Downloading and installing the Airflow Helm chart

Download Airflow source code.

```
$ curl -OL https://github.com/apache/airflow/archive/master.zip    ◄
$ unzip master.zip
$ kubectl create namespace airflow
$ helm dep update ./airflow-master/chart                           ◄
$ helm install airflow ./airflow-master/chart –namespace airflow   ◄
```

Create a Kubernetes namespace for Airflow.

Download specified versions of dependent Helm charts.

Install the Airflow Helm chart, which will take some time.

```
NAME: airflow
LAST DEPLOYED: Wed Jul 22 20:40:44 2020
NAMESPACE: airflow
STATUS: deployed
REVISION: 1
TEST SUITE: None
NOTES:
Thank you for installing Airflow!

Your release is named airflow.

➥ You can now access your dashboard(s) by executing the following command(s)
      and visiting the corresponding port at localhost in your browser:

➥ Airflow dashboard:        kubectl port-forward svc/airflow-webserver
      8080:8080 --namespace airflow
```

The Helm chart in listing 18.3 installs a complete Airflow installation running in Kubernetes. That means everything runs inside Kubernetes. Many parts are configurable, but by default, it runs the KubernetesExecutor with a Postgres metastore, DAGs are baked into the Docker images, and the webserver username/password is "admin"/ "admin" (which you likely want to change). The webserver runs as a Kubernetes ClusterIP service, which gives you a service inside your cluster that other applications can access but is not accessible externally. To access it we can port forward to the pod.

Listing 18.4 Port forwarding to the Airflow webserver

```
kubectl port-forward svc/airflow-webserver 8080:8080 --namespace airflow
```

This makes the webserver accessible on http://localhost:8080.

DAGs can be added via two methods:

1 The default deployment method with the Helm chart is to build DAGs together with the Airflow Docker image. To build a new image and update the Docker image, run the following.

Listing 18.5 Updating the deployed Airflow image with Helm

```
helm upgrade airflow ./airtlow-master/chart \
  --set images.airflow.repository=yourcompany/airflow \
  --set images.airflow.tag=1234abc
```

2 Or you can point to a Git repository and configure a Git-sync (https://github .com/kubernetes/git-sync) sidecar container, which pulls in code from the Git repository every X (default 60) number of seconds.

Listing 18.6 Configuring a Git-sync sidecar with the Airflow Helm chart

```
helm upgrade airflow ./airflow-master/chart \
  --set dags.persistence.enabled=false \
  --set dags.gitSync.enabled=true
```

For all details and configuration options, refer to the Airflow documentation.

18.1.3 *Integrating with Google services*

After running Airflow on GKE, we can view how to make more use of Google's managed services so that we don't have to manage applications on Kubernetes ourselves. We will demonstrate how to create a GCP load balancer to expose the webserver externally. To do so, we must change the service type of the webserver, which is a ClusterIP service by default.

A ClusterIP-type service can route requests to the correct pod but provides no external endpoint to connect to, requiring a user to set up a proxy to connect to a service (figure 18.3, left). This is not user-friendly, so we want a different mechanism the user can connect to directly without any configuration. There are various options for doing this, and one of them is to create a Kubernetes service LoadBalancer (figure 18.3, right). The service type is applied in chart/values.yaml, in the section "webserver." Change the service type from ClusterIP to LoadBalancer and apply the changed Helm chart.

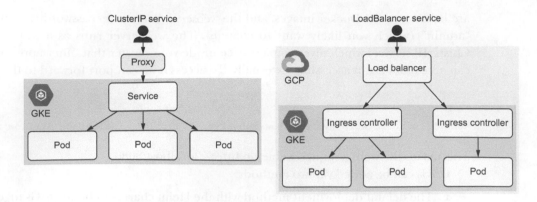

Figure 18.3   Different access patterns for services running in Kubernetes

---

Listing 18.7   Installing a new version of a Helm chart

```
helm upgrade --install airflow ./airflow-master/chart --namespace airflow
```

GKE receives the request to apply changes on the GKE cluster and notices the change from ClusterIP to LoadBalancer service. GKE integrates with various GCP services, and one of them is a load balancer. When creating a Kubernetes LoadBalancer in GKE, GCP will create a load balancer under the network services menu, serving traffic to your GKE cluster (figure 18.4).

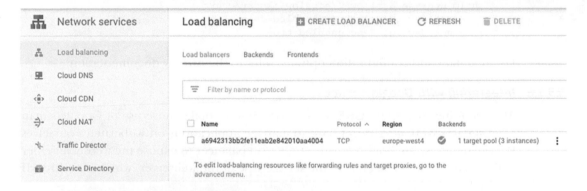

Figure 18.4   Creating a load balancer in the GCP console

Selecting the newly created load balancer will show the address, which is now accessible externally (figure 18.5).

In this screenshot, the Airflow webserver is now accessible on http://34.90.59 .14:8080.

Figure 18.5 Identifying the external address of the load balancer in the GCP console

Other components of the Airflow Helm installation can also be outsourced to GCP services; however, the required work is more involved:

- The Postgres database can run on Cloud SQL.
- We can run our own images from Google Cloud Repository (GCR).
- We can set up remote logging to GCS (described in section 12.3.4).

18.1.4 *Designing the network*

The network layout is a personal choice, and the number of options is limitless. For example, is it okay to have traffic going over the public internet and use external IPs, or does security require us to route all traffic internally within GCP and only use internal IPs? We aim to provide a network layout to help you get started, which does not (and cannot) fit everybody but can serve as a starting point. Using the components mentioned gives the result shown in figure 18.6.

As mentioned, Airflow is installed on GKE. The webserver can be exposed to the outside world via a load balancer. Cloud Storage is a globally available service that is not restricted to a VPC. However, GCP does provide a service named VPC Service Controls (VPC SC) to limit communications to selected services (including Cloud Storage) that can only be accessed from within your VPC. The Cloud SQL database serving the Airflow metastore cannot run in the same subnet as your own services. Google creates a fully managed database for you in its own perimeter. Thus, a connection to the database must be created either via the public internet or by peering your own VPC with Google's VPC.

18.1.5 *Scaling with the CeleryExecutor*

Celery relies on a message broker to distribute tasks to workers. GCP offers a messaging service named Pub/Sub; however, this is not supported by Celery. Thus, you are limited to using the open source tools Celery does support: RabbitMQ or Redis. From an architectural perspective, this won't change figure 18.6 since these services can run alongside the Airflow containers in GKE.

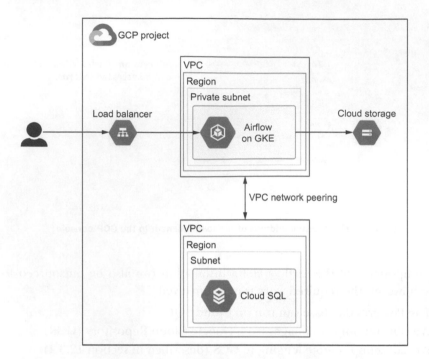

Figure 18.6   Example GCP network layout with Airflow running on GKE, Cloud SQL for the metastore, and the Airflow webserver exposed via a load balancer

By default, the Airflow Helm starts with the `KubernetesExecutor`. Luckily, it's very easy to configure the `CeleryExecutor`. Required components (e.g., Redis) are automatically installed with one command.

Listing 18.8   Configuring the CeleryExecutor

```
$ helm upgrade airflow ./airflow-master/chart --set executor=CeleryExecutor

Release "airflow" has been upgraded. Happy Helming!
...

You can now access your dashboard(s) by executing the following command(s)
    and visiting the corresponding port at localhost in your browser:

Airflow dashboard:       kubectl port-forward svc/airflow-webserver
    8080:8080 --namespace airflow
Flower dashboard:        kubectl port-forward svc/airflow-flower
    5555:5555 --namespace airflow
```

> The Celery Flower dashboard is installed for monitoring.

The number of Celery workers can be controlled manually with the Helm property `workers.replicas`, which is set to 1 by default. It does not scale automatically. However, there is a solution to do so, namely Kubernetes Event-Driven Autoscaling, better known as KEDA.[1] Based on a certain given condition, KEDA will automatically scale the number of containers up or down (known as HPA, or horizontal pod autoscaling, in Kubernetes), for example the workload on your Airflow setup. The Airflow Helm chart provides settings to enable KEDA autoscaling and defines the load on Airflow and corresponding workers as the following query on the Airflow metastore:

```
CEIL((RUNNING + QUEUED tasks) / 16)
```

For example, say we have 26 running tasks and 11 queued tasks: `CEIL((26 + 11)/16)` = 3 workers. By default, KEDA queries the database every 30 seconds and changes the number of workers if it differs from the current number of workers, enabling autoscaling of Celery workers, as shown in figure 18.7.

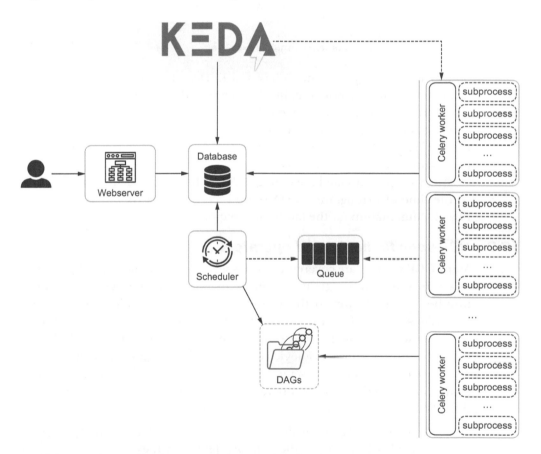

Figure 18.7 Airflow running the `CeleryExecutor` with KEDA automatically scaling the number of Celery workers up and down depending on the workload. This setup only works when installed on Kubernetes.

---

[1] The Celery and KEDA setup was first introduced by this blog post: https://www.astronomer.io/blog/the-keda-autoscaler.

Enable the KEDA autoscaling using the Airflow Helm chart.

Listing 18.9   Configuring the CeleryExecutor and autoscaling
---

```
helm repo add kedacore https://kedacore.github.io/charts

helm repo update

kubectl create namespace keda

helm install \
   --set image.keda=docker.io/kedacore/keda:1.2.0 \
➥  --set image.metricsAdapter=docker.io/kedacore/keda-metrics-adapter:1.2.0 \
   --namespace keda \
   keda kedacore/keda

helm upgrade airflow ./airflow-master/chart \
   --set executor=CeleryExecutor \
   --set workers.keda.enabled=true \
   --set workers.persistence.enabled=false
```

> **KEDA does not support Kubernetes StatefulSets, so it must be turned off.**

So why would you prefer the Celery and KEDA setup over the KubernetesExecutor? While both can scale horizontally, the Celery and KEDA setup is more desirable from a performance perspective since it keeps a certain number of Celery workers up and running, workers that immediately process new tasks arriving on the queue. However, the KubernetesExecutor must create a new Airflow pod to run a given task, resulting in startup overhead for every task.

All settings mentioned are configurable; refer to the documentation for all details. At the time of writing, the KEDA setup is considered experimental; refer to the Airflow documentation for the latest information.

18.2   *GCP-specific hooks and operators*

Many GCP services are covered by GCP-specific Airflow operators, hooks, sensors, and so on, providing much greater coverage than for AWS and Azure. Due to their sheer number, we refer you to the Google/Cloud provider package `apache-airflow-providers-google` for a full overview of the available hooks and operators.

The Google-related hooks don't inherit from the airflow.hooks.BaseHook, but from the airflow.providers.google.common.hooks.base_google.GoogleBaseHook class. This base class provides the same authentication mechanism to the Google REST API so that all derived hooks and operators using it don't have to implement authentication. Three methods of authentication are supported:

1. By configuring an environment variable GOOGLE_APPLICATION_CREDENTIALS (outside of Airflow) to the path of a JSON key file
2. By setting fields "Project id" and "Keyfile Path" in an Airflow connection of type Google Cloud Platform
3. By providing the contents of a JSON key file to an Airflow connection of type "Google Cloud Platform" in the field "Keyfile JSON"

Upon execution of any GCP-related operator, a request will be sent to GCP, which requires authentication. This authentication can be represented by a service account in GCP, an account that can be used by an application (such as Airflow) instead of a human. Airflow requires one of the three options to authenticate GCP with the given service account. For example, say we want to allow Airflow to run BigQuery jobs. Let's create a service account that grants these permissions.

First, in the GCP console, browse to Service Accounts (figure 18.8).

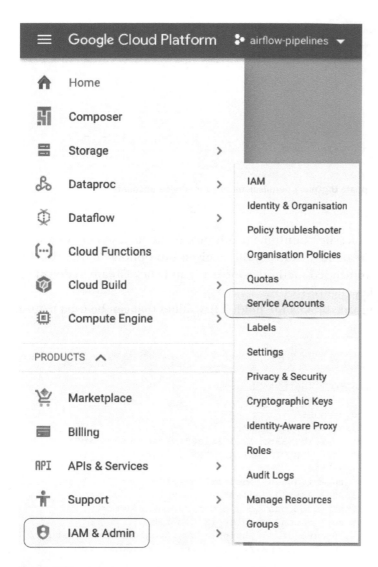

Figure 18.8 Creating a service account in the GCP console

Click Create Service Account and provide a name, for example, "run-bigquery-jobs." Next, provide the BigQuery Job User role, which holds permissions to run BigQuery jobs (figure 18.9).

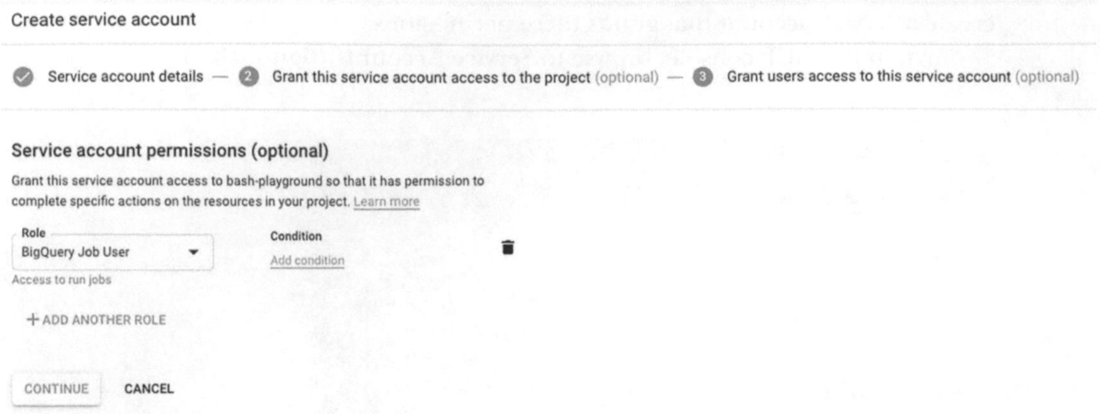

Create service account

✓ Service account details — ② Grant this service account access to the project (optional) — ③ Grant users access to this service account (optional)

Service account permissions (optional)

Grant this service account access to bash-playground so that it has permission to complete specific actions on the resources in your project. Learn more

Role
BigQuery Job User   ▼   Condition
                                  Add condition   🗑
Access to run jobs

╋ ADD ANOTHER ROLE

CONTINUE   CANCEL

Figure 18.9 Adding the appropriate BigQuery permissions to your service account

After adding the role, click Continue to advance to the next screen, where we can create a key. Click Create Key and you will be given two options to download a key file. JSON is the recommended method, so select it and click Create to download a JSON file holding the key (figure 18.10).

The just-downloaded JSON file holds a few values that can be used to authenticate with GCP.

Listing 18.10 Contents of a service account JSON key

```
$ cat airflow-pipelines-4aa1b2353bca.json
{
  "type": "service_account",
  "project_id": "airflow-pipelines",
  "private_key_id": "4aa1b2353bca412363bfa85f95de6ad488e6f4c7",
➥ "private_key": "-----BEGIN PRIVATE KEY-----\nMIIz...LaY=\n-----END
    PRIVATE KEY-----\n",
  "client_email": "run-bigquery-jobs@airflow-pipelines.iam...com",
  "client_id": "936502912366591303469",
  "auth_uri": "https://accounts.google.com/o/oauth2/auth",
  "token_uri": "https://oauth2.googleapis.com/token",
  "auth_provider_x509_cert_url": "https://www.googleapis.com/oauth2/...",
  "client_x509_cert_url": "https://...iam.gserviceaccount.com"
}
```

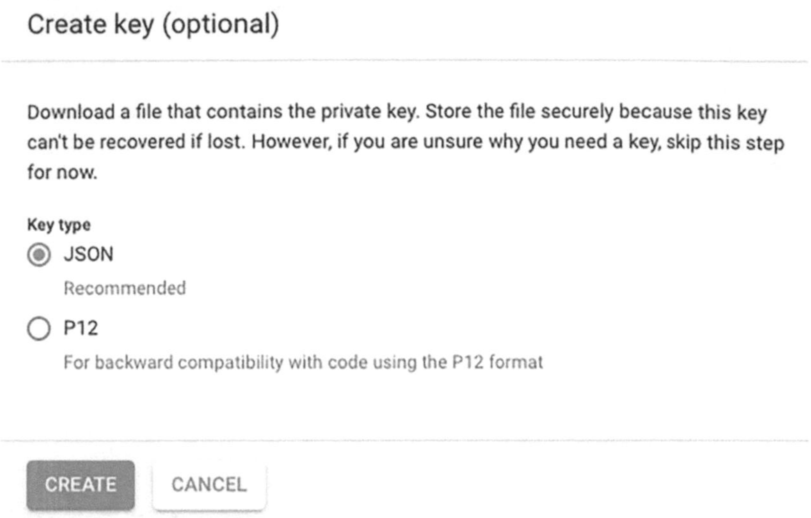

Create key (optional)

Download a file that contains the private key. Store the file securely because this key can't be recovered if lost. However, if you are unsure why you need a key, skip this step for now.

Key type

◉ JSON

    Recommended

○ P12

    For backward compatibility with code using the P12 format

CREATE   CANCEL

Figure 18.10   Creating and downloading the access key

Keep this file safe and secure. Anybody with access to it can authenticate to GCP and use the granted permissions. Let's provide it to Airflow so that we can run a BigQuery job. Given the three options, we can provide the key in three ways:

1 By setting an environment variable, GOOGLE_APPLICATION_CREDENTIALS.

Listing 18.11   Setting Google credentials using an environment variable

```
export GOOGLE_APPLICATION_CREDENTIALS=/path/to/key.json
```

Note this sets the credentials globally, and all applications authenticating with Google will read this JSON key.

2 By configuring an Airflow connection (figure 18.11).

3 By providing the contents of the JSON file to an Airflow connection (figure 18.12).

All three options will authenticate. Note that the JSON key is specific to a single project. Using option 1 will set the key globally on your system: all applications connecting with Google will authenticate using this key and use the same permissions. Option 2 also points to the file location of the JSON key but from an Airflow connection. This way you can provide different connection IDs to different tasks, using

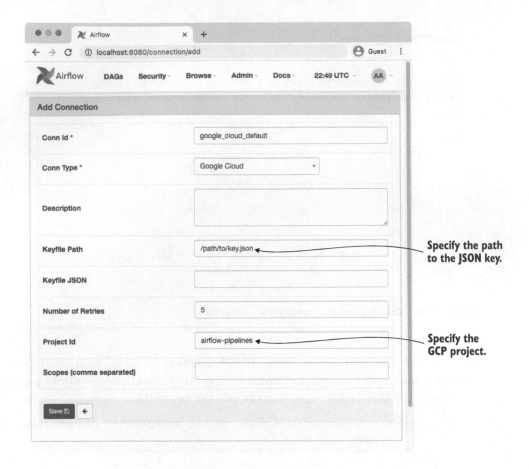

Figure 18.11   Creating an Airflow connection using the access key file

different sets of permissions between tasks, and possibly also connecting to different GCP projects. The difference between option 2 and 3 is that with option 3 your JSON key is stored *only* in Airflow and not as a file on your filesystem; this can be desirable, but if there are other applications on your system sharing the same key, go for option 2.

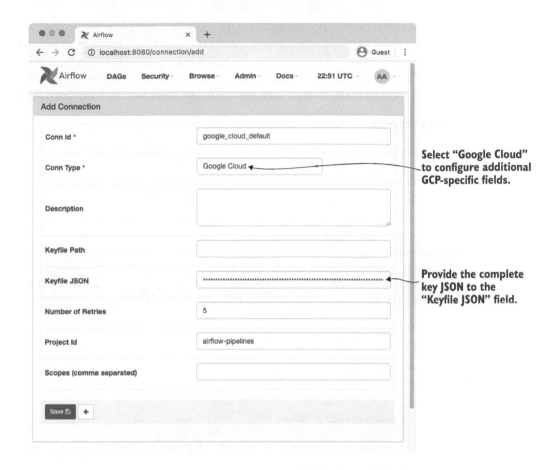

Figure 18.12   Creating an Airflow connection using the access key JSON

18.3   *Use case: Serverless movie ranking on GCP*

Let's look back at the use case previously applied to AWS and Azure. How would it work on GCP? Many of the cloud services can be mapped against each other (table 18.1).

Table 18.1   Comparing similar services on AWS, Azure, and GCP

AWS	Azure	GCP
S3	Blob Storage	GCS
Glue	Synapse	Dataflow
Athena	Synapse	BigQuery

The services mentioned here provide comparable functionality but are not identical. They can be used for similar purposes but differ in various features and details. For example, AWS Glue is a managed Apache Spark service plus the metadata store. GCP Dataflow is a managed Apache Beam service. Both Spark and Beam are aimed at processing big data but do so in different ways. For our use case, they will both do the job.

18.3.1 *Uploading to GCS*

Similar to chapters 16 and 17, the first part of the workflow fetches ratings from our ratings API and uploads these to GCS, Google's object storage service. Although most GCP services can be managed by an Airflow operator, there is obviously no operator for communicating with our custom API. While we could technically split up the work by first extracting ratings data, writing these to a local file, and then uploading the file to GCS in a second step using the LocalFilesystemToGCSOperator, for conciseness we will perform this action in one task. The only component from Airflow we can apply here is the GCSHook for performing actions on GCS.

> **Listing 18.12   DAG fetching ratings and uploading to GCS**

```
import datetime
import logging
import os
import tempfile
from os import path

import pandas as pd
from airflow.models import DAG
from airflow.operators.python import PythonOperator
from airflow.providers.google.cloud.hooks.gcs import GCSHook

from custom.hooks import MovielensHook

dag = DAG(
    "gcp_movie_ranking",
    start_date=datetime.datetime(year=2019, month=1, day=1),
    end_date=datetime.datetime(year=2019, month=3, day=1),
    schedule_interval="@monthly",
    default_args={"depends_on_past": True},
)


def _fetch_ratings(api_conn_id, gcp_conn_id, gcs_bucket, **context):
    year = context["execution_date"].year
    month = context["execution_date"].month

    logging.info(f"Fetching ratings for {year}/{month:02d}")

    api_hook = MovielensHook(conn_id=api_conn_id)
    ratings = pd.DataFrame.from_records(
        api_hook.get_ratings_for_month(year=year, month=month),
        columns=["userId", "movieId", "rating", "timestamp"],
    )
```

```
        logging.info(f"Fetched {ratings.shape[0]} rows")

        with tempfile.TemporaryDirectory() as tmp_dir:        First extract and write
            tmp_path = path.join(tmp_dir, "ratings.csv")      results to a local file.
            ratings.to_csv(tmp_path, index=False)

        # Upload file to GCS.
        logging.info(f"Writing results to ratings/{year}/{month:02d}.csv")
        gcs_hook = GCSHook(gcp_conn_id)
        gcs_hook.upload(                                The GCS bucket to which
            bucket_name=gcs_bucket,                     the file will be uploaded
            object_name=f"ratings/{year}/{month:02d}.csv",
            filename=tmp_path,                          The GCS key to
        )                                               which the data
                                                        will be written

fetch_ratings = PythonOperator(
    task_id="fetch_ratings",
    python_callable=_fetch_ratings,
    op_kwargs={
        "api_conn_id": "movielens",
        "gcp_conn_id": "gcp",
        "gcs_bucket": os.environ["RATINGS_BUCKET"],
    },
    dag=dag,
)
```

Initialize a connection to GCS.

Upload the local file to GCS.

If all succeeds, we now have data in a GCS bucket, shown in figure 18.13.

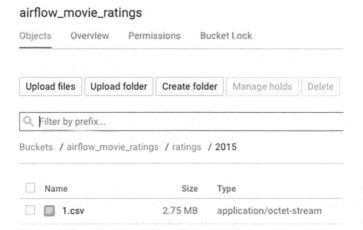

Figure 18.13   Results of a successful run of the initial DAG, with ratings being uploaded into the bucket, in Google Cloud Storage

18.3.2 *Getting data into BigQuery*

After uploading the data to GCS, we will load the data into BigQuery so that we can query it. While BigQuery can deal with external data, it is somewhat restricted in options when the data is partitioned, especially when creating external tables. It is best is to load the data into BigQuery internally. There are several Airflow operators related to operations on BigQuery; the GCSToBigQueryOperator is specifically for loading data stored on GCS into BigQuery.

Listing 18.13   Importing partitioned data from GCS into BigQuery

```
from airflow.providers.google.cloud.transfers.gcs_to_bigquery import
    GCSToBigQueryOperator

import_in_bigquery = GCSToBigQueryOperator(
    task_id="import_in_bigquery",
    bucket="airflow_movie_ratings",
    source_objects=[
        "ratings/{{ execution_date.year }}/{{ execution_date.month }}.csv"
    ],
    source_format="CSV",
    create_disposition="CREATE_IF_NEEDED",
    write_disposition="WRITE_TRUNCATE",
    bigquery_conn_id="gcp",
    autodetect=True,
    destination_project_dataset_table=(
        "airflow-pipelines:",
        "airflow.ratings${{ ds_nodash }}",
    ),
    dag=dag,
)

fetch_ratings >> import_in_bigquery
```

Create the table if it doesn't exist.

Overwrite partition data if it already exists.

Attempt to autodetect the schema.

Value after the $ symbol defines the partition to write to, called "partition decorator."

This produces the second part of this DAG (figure 18.14).

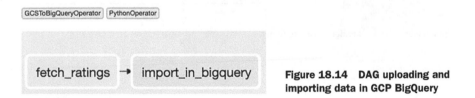

Figure 18.14   DAG uploading and importing data in GCP BigQuery

As you can see, we define a source (file in GCS bucket) and target (BigQuery table partition), but there are more configurations. For example, the create and write dispositions define the behavior in case no table exists or the partition already exists, respectively. Their values (CREATE_IF_NEEDED and WRITE_TRUNCATE) might seem to come out of the blue. The GCP-related Airflow operators, bluntly said, provide convenience wrappers around the underlying request to Google. They provide you, as a developer, an interface to call the underlying system while using Airflow's features such as variables that can be templated. But arguments such as create_disposition are specific to GCP and propagated directly to the request. As such, the only way to know their expected values is to carefully read the Airflow documentation or GCP documentation, or to inspect the source code as a last resort.

After running this workflow, we can inspect the data in BigQuery (figure 18.15).

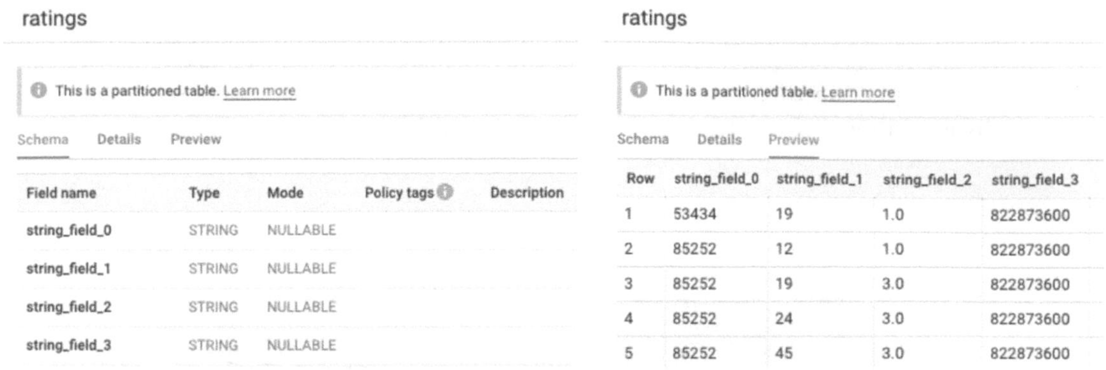

Figure 18.15 Inspecting imported data in BigQuery

As you can see on the right, the data was loaded successfully. However, as we can see on the left, the schema autodetection (which we set to `True`), did not manage to automatically infer the schema, which is evident from the column names "string_field_0," "string_field_1," and so on. While the schema autodetection does the job most of the time, there are no guarantees about the schema inference working correctly. In this situation, we know the structure of the data will not change. So, it is safe to provide the schema with the request.

Listing 18.14 Importing data from GCS into BigQuery with schema

```
from airflow.providers.google.cloud.transfers.gcs_to_bigquery import
    GCSToBigQueryOperator

import_in_bigquery = GCSToBigQueryOperator(
    task_id="import_in_bigquery",
    bucket="airflow_movie_ratings",
    source_objects=[
        "ratings/{{ execution_date.year }}/{{ execution_date.month }}.csv"
    ],
    source_format="CSV",
    create_disposition="CREATE_IF_NEEDED",
    write_disposition="WRITE_TRUNCATE",
    bigquery_conn_id="gcp",                    ⟵ Skip the header row.
    skip_leading_rows=1,
    schema_fields=[                            ⟵ Manually define
        {"name": "userId", "type": "INTEGER"},    the schema.
        {"name": "movieId", "type": "INTEGER"},
        {"name": "rating", "type": "FLOAT"},
```

```
        {"name": "timestamp", "type": "TIMESTAMP"},
    ],
    destination_project_dataset_table=(
        "airflow-pipelines:",
        "airflow.ratings${{ ds_nodash }}",
    ),
    dag=dag,
)
```

Now inspecting the BigQuery schema not only shows us the correct schema but also displays a nicely formatted timestamp (figure 18.16).

ratings

This is a partitioned table. Learn more

Schema   Details   Preview

Field name	Type	Mode	Policy tags	Description
userId	INTEGER	NULLABLE		
movieId	INTEGER	NULLABLE		
rating	FLOAT	NULLABLE		
timestamp	TIMESTAMP	NULLABLE		

ratings

This is a partitioned table. Learn more

Schema   Details   Preview

Row	userId	movieId	rating	timestamp
1	768	92257	2.0	2012-03-07 09:38:13 UTC
2	768	51937	2.0	2012-03-24 02:07:22 UTC
3	768	69481	3.0	2012-03-07 09:42:08 UTC
4	768	6484	3.0	2012-03-24 00:50:01 UTC
5	768	48833	3.5	2012-03-11 02:00:37 UTC

Figure 18.16   Inspecting imported data in BigQuery with a predefined schema

18.3.3 *Extracting top ratings*

Lastly, we want to compute the top ratings in BigQuery and store the results. Neither BigQuery nor Airflow provide an out-of-the-box solution for this. While we can run queries and export complete tables, we cannot export a query result directly. The workaround is to first store a query result in a new table, export the table, and then delete the intermediate table to clean up.

Listing 18.15   Exporting BigQuery query results via an intermediate table

```
from airflow.providers.google.cloud.operators.bigquery import
BigQueryExecuteQueryOperator, BigQueryDeleteTableOperator
⇒ from airflow.providers.google.cloud.transfers.bigquery_to_gcs import
    BigQueryToGCSOperator

query_top_ratings = BigQueryExecuteQueryOperator(
    task_id="query_top_ratings",
    destination_dataset_table=(
        "airflow-pipelines:",
        "airflow.ratings_{{ ds_nodash }}",        BigQuery query result
    ),                                             destination table
```

```
    sql="""SELECT
movieid,
AVG(rating) as avg_rating,
COUNT(*) as num_ratings
FROM airflow.ratings
WHERE DATE(timestamp) <= DATE("{{ ds }}")
GROUP BY movieid
ORDER BY avg_rating DESC
""",
    write_disposition="WRITE_TRUNCATE",
    create_disposition="CREATE_IF_NEEDED",
    bigquery_conn_id="gcp",
    dag=dag,
)

extract_top_ratings = BigQueryToGCSOperator(
    task_id="extract_top_ratings",
    source_project_dataset_table=(
        "airflow-pipelines:",
        "airflow.ratings_{{ ds_nodash }}",
    ),
    destination_cloud_storage_uris=(
        "gs://airflow_movie_results/{{ ds_nodash }}.csv"
    ),
    export_format="CSV",
    bigquery_conn_id="gcp",
    dag=dag,
)

delete_result_table = BigQueryTableDeleteOperator(
    task_id="delete_result_table",
    deletion_dataset_table=(
        "airflow-pipelines:",
        "airflow.ratings_{{ ds_nodash }}",
    ),
    bigquery_conn_id="gcp",
    dag=dag,
)

fetch_ratings >> import_in_bigquery >> query_top_ratings >>
    extract_top_ratings >> delete_result_table
```

- **SQL query to execute** → `"""..."""`
- **BigQuery table to extract** ← `"airflow.ratings_{{ ds_nodash }}",`
- **Extract destination path** ← `"gs://airflow_movie_results/{{ ds_nodash }}.csv"`
- **BigQuery table to delete** ← `"airflow.ratings_{{ ds_nodash }}",`

In the Airflow webserver, the result looks like figure 18.17.

Figure 18.17 The complete DAG for downloading ratings and uploading and processing using GCP BigQuery

Using the ds_nodash context variable, we managed to string together a series of tasks performing various actions on BigQuery. Within each DAG run, the value of ds_nodash remains the same and can thus be used to connect task results while avoiding overriding them by the same task at different intervals. The result is a bucket filled with CSVs (figure 18.18).

	Name	Size
☐	📄 20021201.csv	145.9 KB
☐	📄 20030101.csv	147.7 KB
☐	📄 20030201.csv	150.7 KB
☐	📄 20030301.csv	152.3 KB
☐	📄 20030401.csv	154.1 KB

Figure 18.18   Results are exported and stored as CSVs named with the corresponding datetime on GCS.

On the BigQuery side, if we run multiple DAG runs simultaneously, multiple intermediate tables will be created. These are conveniently grouped by BigQuery (figure 18.19).

Figure 18.19   BigQuery groups tables with equal suffixes. When running multiple DAG runs simultaneously, this could result in multiple intermediate tables.

The last task in this DAG cleans up the intermediate result table. Note the operation of querying BigQuery, extracting results, and deleting the intermediate table is now split over three tasks. No operation exists to perform this in one task, not in BigQuery and not in Airflow. Now, say extract_top_ratings fails for some reason—then we'd be left with a remainder in the form of a BigQuery table. BigQuery pricing is composed of multiple elements, including the storage of data, so beware when leaving remainders, as this could induce costs (as on any cloud). Once you've finished everything, remember to delete all resources. In Google Cloud, this is simply done by deleting the corresponding project (assuming all resources live under the same project). Under the menu IAM & Admin → Manage Resources, select your project and click Delete.

After clicking Shut Down, your project is removed. After approximately 30 days, Google removes all resources, although no guarantees are given and some resources might be deleted (much) sooner than others.

Summary

- The easiest way to install and run Airflow in GCP is on GKE, using the Airflow Helm chart as a starting point.
- Airflow provides many GCP-specific hooks and operators that allow you to integrate with different services in the Google Cloud Platform, installed with the `apache-airflow-providers-google` package.
- The `GoogleBaseHook` class provides authentication to GCP, allowing you to focus on the service details when implementing your own GCP hooks and operators.
- Using GCP-specific hooks and operators usually require you to configure the required resources and access permissions in GCP and Airflow so that Airflow is allowed to perform the required operations.

appendix A
Running code samples

This book comes with an accompanying code repository on GitHub (https://github.com/BasPH/data-pipelines-with-apache-airflow). The repository holds the same code as demonstrated in this book, together with easily executable Docker environments so that you can run all examples yourself. This appendix explains how the code is organized and how to run the examples.

A.1 Code structure

The code is organized per chapter, and each chapter is structured the same. The top level of the repository consists of several chapter directories (numbered 01–18), which contain self-contained code examples for the corresponding chapters. Each chapter directory contains at least the following files/directories:

- dags—Directory containing the DAG files demonstrated in the chapter
- docker-compose.yml—File describing the Airflow setup needed for running the DAGs
- README.md—Readme introducing the chapter examples and explaining any chapter-specific details on how to run the examples

Where possible, code listings in the book will refer to the corresponding file in the chapter directory. For some chapters, code listings shown in the chapters will correspond to individual DAGs. In other cases (particularly for more complex examples), several code listings will be combined into one single DAG, resulting in a single DAG file.

Other than DAG files and Python code, some examples later in the book (especially the cloud chapters 16, 17, and 18) require extra supporting resources or configuration to run the examples. The extra steps required to run these examples will be described in the corresponding chapter and the chapter's README file.

A.2 *Running the examples*

Each chapter comes with a Docker environment that can be used for running the corresponding code examples.

A.2.1 *Starting the Docker environment*

To get started with running the chapter examples, run inside the chapter directory:

```
$ docker-compose up --build
```

This command starts a Docker environment that contains several containers required for running Airflow, including the following containers:

- Airflow webserver
- Airflow scheduler
- Postgres database for the Airflow metastore

To avoid seeing the output of all three containers in your terminal, you can also start the Docker environment in the background by using

```
$ docker-compose up --build -d
```

Some chapters create additional containers, which provide other services or APIs needed for the examples. For example, chapter 12 demonstrates the following monitoring services, which are also created in Docker to make the examples to be as realistic as possible:

- Grafana
- Prometheus
- Flower
- Redis

Fortunately, running all these services will be taken care of for you by the details in the docker-compose file. Of course, don't hesitate to dive into the details of this file if you're interested.

A.2.2 *Inspecting running services*

Once an example is running, you can check out which containers are running using the docker ps command:

```
$ docker ps
CONTAINER ID         IMAGE                               ... NAMES
d7c68a1b9937         apache/airflow:2.0.0-python3.8      ... chapter02_scheduler_1
557e97741309         apache/airflow:2.0.0-python3.8      ... chapter02_webserver_1
742194dd2ef5         postgres:12-alpine                  ... chapter02_postgres_1
```

By default, docker-compose prefixes running containers with the name of the containing folder, meaning that containers belonging to each chapter should be recognizable by their container names.

You can also inspect the logs of the individual containers using `docker logs`:

```
$ docker logs -f chapter02_scheduler_1
➡ [2020-11-30 20:17:36,532] {scheduler_job.py:1249} INFO - Starting the
    scheduler
➡ [2020-11-30 20:17:36,533] {scheduler_job.py:1254} INFO - Processing each
    file at most -1 times
➡ [2020-11-30 20:17:36,984] {dag_processing.py:250} INFO - Launched
    DagFileProcessorManager with pid: 131
```

These logs should hopefully be able to provide you with valuable feedback if things go awry.

A.2.3   *Tearing down the environment*

Once you're done running an example, you can exit docker-compose using CTRL+C. (Note that this isn't needed if you're running docker-compose in the background.) To fully teardown the Docker environment, you can run the following command from the chapter directory:

```
$ docker-compose down -v
```

In addition to stopping the various containers, this should also take care of removing any Docker networks and volumes used in the example.

To check if all containers have indeed been fully removed, you can use the following command to see any containers that have been stopped but not yet deleted:

```
$ docker ps -a
```

If you're anything like us, this might still show a list of containers that you'll want to remove. You can remove containers one by one using the following command:

```
$ docker rm <container_id>
```

where the `container_id` is obtained from the list of containers shown by the `ps` command. Alternatively, you can use the following shorthand to remove all containers:

```
$ docker rm $(docker ps -aq)
```

Finally, you can also remove any unused volumes previously used by these containers using

```
$ docker volume prune
```

However, we urge you to use caution when using this command, as it may result in inadvertent data loss if you end up discarding the wrong Docker volumes.

appendix B
Package structures
Airflow 1 and 2

Most of this book was based on Airflow 1. Just before the release of this book, Airflow 2 was released, and we decided to update all code for Airflow 2.

One of the most involved changes are the new providers packages in Airflow 2. Many modules were removed from the core Airflow and are now installed via a separate "providers" package in order to shrink the core Airflow package. In this appendix, we list all Airflow imports used in the book and their paths in both Airflow 1 and Airflow 2.

B.1   Airflow 1 package structure

In Airflow 1, a split was made between "core" components (operators/hooks/ sensors/etc.) and "contrib" components, for example `airflow.operators.python _operator.PythonOperator` and `airflow.contrib.sensors.python_sensor.Python Sensor`.

This was a historic artifact from the time Airflow was developed at Airbnb, where the organization of components in "core" and "contrib" made sense within Airbnb. When the Airflow project gained traction as an open source project, the split between core and contrib became a gray area and a frequent point of discussion in the community. Throughout the development of Airflow 1, modules that originated in the contrib package were kept in contrib to avoid breaking changes.

B.2   Airflow 2 package structure

With Airflow 2, the community finally reached a point where it could allow breaking changes and thus decided to restructure the Airflow package to create a structure that suited the global scale of the project it now operates in. One other common source of annoyance was the large number of dependencies Airflow requires to be installed.

Therefore, the community decided to strip the Airflow project into separate projects:

- A "core" project, containing only a few generic operators, hooks, and such.
- Other components that can be installed via separate packages, allowing developers to choose which components are installed while maintaining a manageable set of dependencies. These additional packages are named "providers." Each providers package is named `apache-airflow-providers-[name]`, for example `apache-airflow-providers-postgres`.

All components now contained in a providers package are removed from the core of Airflow. For example, the Airflow 1 class `airflow.hooks.postgres_hook.Postgres-Hook` is not contained anymore in Airflow 2. To add it, install

```
pip install apache-airflow-providers-postgres
```

and import `airflow.providers.postgres.operators.postgres.PostgresOperator`.

> **NOTE**   If you wish to prepare your DAGs for a smooth transition from Airflow 1 to Airflow 2, each providers package also exists in a "backports" form. These packages hold the Airflow 2 structure, but all components are compatible with Airflow 1. For example, to use the new postgres providers structure in Airflow 1, use
>
> ```
> pip install apache-airflow-backport-providers-postgres
> ```

Table B.1 lists all Airflow imports made throughout code examples in this book, showing the paths in both Airflow 1 and 2, and if applicable, the additional providers package to install in Airflow 2.

Table B.1   Airflow imports

Airflow 2 import path	Airflow 2 additional package	Airflow 1 import path
`airflow.providers.amazon.aws` `.hooks.base_aws.AwsBaseHook`	`apache-airflow-` `providers-amazon`	`airflow.contrib.hooks.aws_hook` `.AwsHook`
`airflow.providers.microsoft` `.azure.hooks.wasb.WasbHook`	`apache-airflow-` `providers-` `microsoft-azure`	`airflow.contrib.hooks.wasb_hook` `.WasbHook`
`kubernetes.client.models` `.V1Volume`	`kubernetes`	`airflow.contrib.kubernetes` `.volume.Volume`
`kubernetes.client.models` `.V1VolumeMount`	`kubernetes`	`airflow.contrib.kubernetes` `.volume_mount.VolumeMount`

Table B.1 Airflow imports *(continued)*

Airflow 2 import path	Airflow 2 additional package	Airflow 1 import path
airflow.providers.amazon .aws.operators.athena.AWS- AthenaOperator	apache-airflow- providers-amazon	airflow.contrib.operators.aws_ athena_operator.AWSAthena- Operator
airflow.providers.google .cloud.operators.bigquery .BigQueryExecuteQueryOperator	apache-airflow- providers-google	airflow.contrib.operators .bigquery_operator.BigQuery- Operator
airflow.providers.google .cloud.operators.bigquery .BigQueryDeleteTableOperator	apache-airflow- providers-google	airflow.contrib.operators .bigquery_table_delete_operator .BigQueryTableDeleteOperator
airflow.providers.google .cloud.transfers.bigquery_ to_gcs.BigQueryToGCSOperator	apache-airflow- providers-google	airflow.contrib.operators .bigquery_to_gcs.BigQueryTo- CloudStorageOperator
airflow.providers.google .cloud.transfers.local_to_gcs .LocalFilesystemToGCSOperator	apache-airflow- providers-google	airflow.contrib.operators.file_ to_gcs.FileToGoogleCloudStorage Operator
airflow.providers.google .cloud.transfers.gcs_to_ bigquery.GCSToBigQueryOperator	apache-airflow- providers-google	airflow.contrib.operators.gcs_ to_bq.GoogleCloudStorageToBig- QueryOperator
airflow.providers.cncf .kubernetes.operators.kuberne tes_pod.KubernetesPodOperator	apache-airflow- providers-cncf- kubernetes	airflow.contrib.operators.kuber netes_pod_operator.Kubernetes- PodOperator
airflow.providers.amazon.aws .operators.s3_copy_object .S3CopyObjectOperator	apache-airflow- providers-amazon	airflow.contrib.operators.s3_ copy_object_operator.S3Copy- ObjectOperator
airflow.providers.amazon.aws .operators.sagemaker_endpoint .SageMakerEndpointOperator	apache-airflow- providers-amazon	airflow.contrib.operators .sagemaker_endpoint_operator .SageMakerEndpointOperator
airflow.providers.amazon.aws .operators.sagemaker_training .SageMakerTrainingOperator	apache-airflow- providers-amazon	airflow.contrib.operators .sagemaker_training_operator .SageMakerTrainingOperator
airflow.sensors.filesystem .FileSensor		airflow.contrib.sensors.file sensor.FileSensor
airflow.sensors.python .PythonSensor		airflow.contrib.sensors.python _sensor.PythonSensor
airflow.DAG		airflow.DAG
airflow.exceptions.Airflow- SkipException		airflow.exceptions.AirflowSkip- Exception
airflow.hooks.base_hook.Base- Hook		airflow.hooks.base_hook.Base- Hook

Table B.1 Airflow imports *(continued)*

Airflow 2 import path	Airflow 2 additional package	Airflow 1 import path
`airflow.providers.postgres .hooks.postgres.PostgresHook`	`apache-airflow- providers-postgres`	`airflow.hooks.postgres_hook .PostgresHook`
`airflow.providers.amazon.aws .hooks.s3.S3Hook`	`apache-airflow- providers-amazon`	`airflow.hooks.S3_hook.S3Hook`
`airflow.models.BaseOperator`		`airflow.models.BaseOperator`
`airflow.models.Connection`		`airflow.models.Connection`
`airflow.models.DAG`		`airflow.models.DAG`
`airflow.models.Variable`		`airflow.models.Variable`
`airflow.operators.bash.BashOp erator`		`airflow.operators.bash_operator .BashOperator`
`airflow.operators.dagrun_ operator.TriggerDagRun- Operator`		`airflow.operators.dagrun_ operator.TriggerDagRunOperator`
`airflow.providers.docker .operators.docker.Docker- Operator`	`apache-airflow- providers-docker`	`airflow.operators.docker_ operator.DockerOperator`
`airflow.operators.dummy_ operator.DummyOperator`		`airflow.operators.dummy_ operator.DummyOperator`
`airflow.providers.http .operators.http.SimpleHttp- Operator`	`apache-airflow- providers-http`	`airflow.operators.http_ operator.SimpleHttpOperator`
`airflow.operators.latest_ only.LatestOnlyOperator`		`airflow.operators.latest_only_ operator.LatestOnlyOperator`
`airflow.providers.postgres .operators.postgres.Postgres- Operator`	`apache-airflow- providers-postgres`	`airflow.operators.postgres_ operator.PostgresOperator`
`airflow.operators.python .PythonOperator`		`airflow.operators.python_ operator.PythonOperator`
`airflow.utils`		`airflow.utils`
`airflow.utils.decorators .apply_defaults`		`airflow.utils.apply_defaults`
`airflow.utils.dates`		`airflow.utils.dates`
`airflow.utils.decorators .apply_defaults`		`airflow.utils.decorators.apply_ defaults`

appendix C
Prometheus
metric mapping

This appendix holds a mapping for metrics from StatsD format to Prometheus format, as explained in chapter 12. It is also contained in the accompanying GitHub repository (https://github.com/BasPH/data-pipelines-with-apache-airflow), where it is demonstrated using the Prometheus StatsD exporter. The StatsD exporter takes StatsD metrics (provided by Airflow) and exposes these in a format that Prometheus can read. However, some conversions are not efficient or in line with Prometheus's naming conventions. Therefore, this mapping explicitly maps Airflow's StatsD metrics to Prometheus metrics. Due to the nature of Airflow being an open source project, this mapping can be subject to change.

Listing C.1 Prometheus StatsD exporter mapping for Airflow metrics

```
mappings:

- match: "airflow.dag_processing.total_parse_time"
 help: Number of seconds taken to process all DAG files
 name: "airflow_dag_processing_time"

- match: "airflow.dag.*.*.duration"
 name: "airflow_task_duration"
 labels:
   dag_id: "$1"
   task_id: "$2"

- match: "airflow.dagbag_size"
 help: Number of DAGs
 name: "airflow_dag_count"
```

```
- match: "airflow.dag_processing.import_errors"
  help: The number of errors encountered when processing DAGs
  name: "airflow_dag_errors"

- match: "airflow.dag.loading-duration.*"
  help: Loading duration of DAGs grouped by file. If multiple DAGs are found
      in one file, DAG ids are concatenated by an underscore in the label.
  name: "airflow_dag_loading_duration"
  labels:
    dag_ids: "$1"

- match: "airflow.dag_processing.last_duration.*"
  name: "airflow_dag_processing_last_duration"
  labels:
    filename: "$1"

- match: "airflow.dag_processing.last_run.seconds_ago.*"
  name: "airflow_dag_processing_last_run_seconds_ago"
  labels:
    filename: "$1"

- match: "airflow.dag_processing.last_runtime.*"
  name: "airflow_dag_processing_last_runtime"
  labels:
    filename: "$1"

- match: "airflow.dagrun.dependency-check.*"
  name: "airflow_dag_processing_last_runtime"
  labels:
    dag_id: "$1"

- match: "airflow.dagrun.duration.success.*"
  name: "airflow_dagrun_success_duration"
  labels:
    dag_id: "$1"

- match: "airflow.dagrun.schedule_delay.*"
  name: "airflow_dagrun_schedule_delay"
  labels:
    dag_id: "$1"

- match: "airflow.executor.open_slots"
  help: The number of open executor slots
  name: "airflow_executor_open_slots"

- match: "airflow.executor.queued_tasks"
  help: The number of queued tasks
  name: "airflow_executor_queued_tasks"

- match: "airflow.executor.running_tasks"
  help: The number of running tasks
  name: "airflow_executor_running_tasks"
```

index